The Ideology of the Aesthetic

For Toril

The Ideology of the Aesthetic

Terry Eagleton

Basil Blackwell

Copyright © Terry Eagleton 1990

First published 1990

Basil Blackwell Ltd
108 Cowley Road, Oxford, OX4 1JF, UK

Basil Blackwell Inc.
3 Cambridge Center
Cambridge, MA 02142, USA

British Library Cataloguing in Publication Data

A CIP catalogue record for this book is available from the British Library.

Library of Congress Cataloging in Publication Data
Eagleton, Terry, 1943–
    The ideology of the aesthetic / Terry Eagleton.
        p. cm.
    Includes index.
    ISBN 0–631–16301–8 – ISBN 0–631–16302–6 (pbk.)
    1. Aesthetics, Modern.   I. Title.
BH151.E2   1990   89–35824
111'.85'0903–dc20   CIP

Typeset in Ehrhardt on 11/13 pt.
by Hope Services (Abingdon) Ltd.
Printed in Great Britain by
T. J. Press Ltd, Padstow, Cornwall

Contents

Introduction		1
1	Free Particulars	13
2	The Law of the Heart: Shaftesbury, Hume, Burke	31
3	The Kantian Imaginary	70
4	Schiller and Hegemony	102
5	The World as Artefact: Fichte, Schelling, Hegel	120
6	The Death of Desire: Arthur Schopenhauer	153
7	Absolute Ironies: Søren Kierkegaard	173
8	The Marxist Sublime	196
9	True Illusions: Friedrich Nietzsche	234
10	The Name of the Father: Sigmund Freud	262
11	The Politics of Being: Martin Heidegger	288
12	The Marxist Rabbi: Walter Benjamin	316
13	Art after Auschwitz: Theodor Adorno	341
14	From the *Polis* to Postmodernism	366
Index		419

Introduction

This is not a history of aesthetics. There are many important aestheticians whom I pass over in silence in this book, and even in the case of the thinkers I do consider it is not always their most obviously aesthetic texts which attract my attention. The book is rather an attempt to find in the category of the aesthetic a way of gaining access to certain central questions of modern European thought – to light up, from that particular angle, a range of wider social, political and ethical issues.

Anyone who inspects the history of European philosophy since the Enlightenment must be struck by the curiously high priority assigned by it to aesthetic questions. For Kant, the aesthetic holds out a promise of reconciliation between Nature and humanity. Hegel grants art a lowly status within his theoretical system, but nevertheless produces an elephantine treatise on it. The aesthetic for Kierkegaard must yield ground to the higher truths of ethics and religious faith, but remains a recurrent preoccupation of his thought. For Schopenhauer and Nietzsche, in sharply contrasting ways, aesthetic experience represents a supreme form of value. Marx's impressively erudite allusions to world literature are matched by Freud's modest confession that the poets had said it all before him. In our own century, Heidegger's esoteric meditations culminate in a kind of aestheticized ontology, while the legacy of Western Marxism from Lukács to Adorno allots to art a theoretical privilege surprising at first glance for a materialist current of thought.[1] In the contemporary debates on modernity, modernism and postmodernism, 'culture' would seem a key category for the analysis and understanding of late capitalist society.

To claim such a lofty status for aesthetics in modern European thought in general might seem too unqualified a gesture. Almost all of the thinkers I discuss in this book are in fact German, even if some of the concepts I bring to bear upon their work stem from the intellectual milieu of modern France. It would seem plausible to argue that the characteristically idealist cast of German thought has proved a more hospitable medium for aesthetic enquiry than the rationalism of France or the empiricism of Britain. Even so, the influence of this largely German legacy has spread far beyond its own national frontiers, as the so-called English 'Culture and Society' tradition would attest; and the question of the strange tenacity of aesthetic matters in modern Europe as a whole thus insists upon posing itself. Why, more particularly, should this *theoretical* persistence of the aesthetic typify an historical period when cultural *practice* might be claimed to have lost much of its traditional social relevance, debased as it is to a branch of general commodity production?

One simple but persuasive answer to this question springs from the progressively abstract, technical nature of modern European thought. In this rarefied context, art would still appear to speak of the human and the concrete, providing us with a welcome respite from the alienating rigours of other more specialized discourses, and offering, at the very heart of this great explosion and division of knowledges, a residually common world. As far as scientific or sociological questions are concerned, only the expert seems licensed to speak; when it comes to art, each of us can hope to contribute our two ha'pence worth. Yet the peculiarity of aesthetic discourse, as opposed to the languages of art themselves, is that, while preserving a root in this realm of everyday experience, it also raises and elaborates such supposedly natural, spontaneous expression to the status of an intricate intellectual discipline. With the birth of the aesthetic, then, the sphere of art itself begins to suffer something of the abstraction and formalization characteristic of modern theory in general; yet the aesthetic is nevertheless thought to retain a charge of irreducible particularity, providing us with a kind of paradigm of what a non-alienated mode of cognition might look like. Aesthetics is thus always a contradictory, self-undoing sort of project, which in promoting the theoretical value of its object risks emptying it of exactly that specificity or ineffability which was thought to rank among its most precious features. The very language which elevates art offers perpetually to undermine it.

If the aesthetic has played such a dominant role in modern thought, it is no doubt in part because of the versatility of the concept. For a notion which is supposed to signify a kind of functionlessness, few ideas can have served so many disparate functions. Some readers will doubtless find my use of the category inadmissibly loose and broad, not least when it comes at times to merge into the idea of bodily experience as such. But if the aesthetic returns with such persistence, it is partly because of a certain indeterminacy of definition which allows it to figure in a varied span of preoccupations: freedom and legality, spontaneity and necessity, self-determination, autonomy, particularity and universality, along with several others. My argument, broadly speaking, is that the category of the aesthetic assumes the importance it does in modern Europe because in speaking of art it speaks of these other matters too, which are at the heart of the middle class's struggle for political hegemony. The construction of the modern notion of the aesthetic artefact is thus inseparable from the construction of the dominant ideological forms of modern class-society, and indeed from a whole new form of human subjectivity appropriate to that social order. It is on this account, rather than because men and women have suddenly awoken to the supreme value of painting or poetry, that aesthetics plays so obtrusive a role in the intellectual heritage of the present. But my argument is also that the aesthetic, understood in a certain sense, provides an unusually powerful challenge and alternative to these dominant ideological forms, and is in this sense an eminently contradictory phenomenon.

In charting any intellectual current, it is always difficult to know how far back to go. I do not claim that, as far as discourses of art are concerned, something entirely novel sprang into being in the mid-eighteenth century. Several of the aesthetic motifs I trace could be pursued back to the Renaissance or even to classical antiquity; and little of what is said of self-realization as a goal in itself would have been unfamiliar to Aristotle. There is no theoretical cataclysm at the centre of the Enlightenment which throws up a manner of talking about art utterly devoid of intellectual antecedents. Whether as rhetoric or poetics, such debates extend back far beyond the earliest historical moment of this study, which is the writing of that devoted disciple of Renaissance neo-Platonism, the Earl of Shaftesbury. At

3

the same time, it belongs to my argument that something new is indeed afoot in the period which this work takes as its starting-point. If ideas of absolute breaks are 'metaphysical', so also are notions of wholly unruptured continuity. One of the aspects of that novelty has, indeed, already been alluded to – the fact that in this particular epoch of class-society, with the emergence of the early bourgeoisie, aesthetic concepts (some of them of distinguished historical pedigree) begin to play, however tacitly, an unusually central, intensive part in the constitution of a dominant ideology. Conceptions of the unity and integrity of the work of art, for example, are commonplaces of an 'aesthetic' discourse which stretches back to classical antiquity; but what emerges from such familiar notions in the late eighteenth century is the curious idea of the work of art as a kind of *subject*. It is, to be sure, a peculiar kind of subject, this newly defined artefact, but it is a subject nonetheless. And the historical pressures which give rise to such a strange style of thought, unlike concepts of aesthetic unity or autonomy in general, by no means extend back to the epoch of Aristotle.

This is a Marxist study – at once, it might be claimed, too much and too little so. Too much so, because the book could be accused at times of straying into a species of 'left-functionalism' which reduces the internal complexity of the aesthetic to a direct set of ideological functions. It is true that for a certain kind of contemporary critic, any historical or ideological contextualization of art whatsoever is *ipso facto* reductionist; the only difference between such critics and old-style formalists is that while the latter candidly acknowledged this prejudice, elevated it indeed to a whole elaborate theory of art in itself, the former tend to be a little more elusive. It is not, they feel, that the relation between art and history need be in principle a reductive one; it is just that somehow, in all actual manifestations of it, it always is. I do not really intend to suggest that the eighteenth-century bourgeoisie assembled around a table over their claret to dream up the concept of the aesthetic as a solution to their political dilemmas, and the political contradictoriness of the category is itself testimony to the mistakenness of such a viewpoint. The political left always needs to be on guard against reductionism and conspiracy theories – though as far as the latter are concerned it would be unwise for radicals to wax so subtle and sophisticated, become so coy of

4

appearing crude, as to forget that certain theoretical concepts are indeed from time to time put to the uses of political power, and sometimes in quite direct ways. If it may seem forcing the issue somewhat to discern relations between the turn to the aesthetic in the Enlightenment and certain problems of absolutist political power, one has only to read Friedrich Schiller to find such relations explicitly formulated, no doubt to the embarrassment of those 'anti-reductionists' who might have wished him to be somewhat more discreet about the matter. If the study is, on the other hand, too little Marxist, it is because a satisfactory historical materialist account of the work of any one of the writers with which it deals, placing their thought in the context of the material development, forms of state power and balance of class forces of their historical moments, would have required a volume to itself.

In the current left triptych of concerns with class, race and gender, it is sometimes felt that an excessive emphasis on the first of these categories is in danger of dominating and distorting enquiry into the other two, which are at present somewhat less securely established in the left theoretical canon and thus vulnerable to appropriation by a narrowly conceived class politics. It would be foolish for those primarily concerned with political emancipation in the spheres of race and gender to relax their vigilance in this respect – to accept the mere good intentions or bleeding-heart liberalism of those white male radicals who, products as they are of a political history which has often violently marginalized these issues, cannot now be trusted to have miraculously voided such bad habits from their systems overnight. At the same time, it is difficult not to feel, in surveying certain quarters of the left political scene in Europe and above all in the USA, that the complaint that socialist discourse now universally overshadows these alternative political projects is not only increasingly implausible but, in some contexts at least, darkly ironic. The truth is that a combination of factors has contributed in many areas of contemporary left-wing thought to the open or surreptitious denigration of such questions as social class, historical modes of production and forms of state power, in the name of a commitment to more 'topical' modes of political struggle. Paramount among these factors has been the newly aggressive turn to the political right of several Western bourgeois regimes, under pressure of global capitalist crisis – a dramatic shift in the political spectrum and ideological climate which has succeeded in muting and demoralizing many of those who earlier spoke up more combatively and confidently for a revolutionary politics. There has been in this respect what one can only characterize as a pervasive failure of political nerve, and in some cases an accelerating, sometimes squalid process of accommodation by sectors of the left to the priorities of a capitalist politics. In such a context, where certain long-term forms of emancipatory politics appear either intractable or implausible, it is understandable that some on the political left should turn more readily and hopefully to alternative kinds of issues where more immediate gains might seem possible – issues which a narrowly class-based politics has too often demeaned, travestied and excluded.

To claim that this attention to non-class styles of politics is in part a response, consciously or not, to the current difficulties of more traditional political aspirations is in no sense to undervalue the intrinsic importance of these alternative movements. Any project of socialist transformation which hoped to succeed without an alliance with such currents which fully respected their autonomy would deliver no more than a hollow mockery of human emancipation. It is rather to remind ourselves that, just as a socialist strategy which left unaffected those oppressed in their race or gender would be resoundingly empty, so these particular forms of oppression can themselves only be finally undone in the context of an end to capitalist social relations. The former point is nowadays often enough emphasized; the latter is in some danger of being obscured. The paucity of socialist thought in the USA in particular – in the society, that is to say, where much emancipatory cultural theory has been elaborated – has gravely intensified this more general difficulty. Of the left triptych of preoccupations, it has undoubtedly been social class which has been in such quarters the subject of the most polite, perfunctory hat-tipping, as the feeble American concept of 'classism' bears witness. But the problem is a pressing one in Europe too. We have now produced a generation of left-inclined theorists and students who, for reasons for which they are in no sense culpable, have often little political memory or socialist education. Little political memory, in the sense that a post-Vietnam generation of radicals has often not much of radical political substance to remember within the confines of the West; little socialist education, in that the last thing that can now be taken for granted is a close familiarity with the complex history of international socialism and its attendant theoretical debates. We live within societies whose aim is not simply to combat radical ideas – that one would readily expect – but to wipe them from living memory: to bring about an amnesiac condition in which it would be as though such notions had never existed, placing them beyond our very powers of conception. In such a situation, it is vital that the more recently prominent forms of political engagement should not be allowed to erase, distort or overshadow the rich legacies of the international socialist movement. I write as one born into and brought up within a working-class socialist tradition, one who has been reasonably active in such politics since adolescence, and who believes that any form of political radicalism today which attempts to by-pass that lineage is bound to be impoverished. There are now, predominantly in the USA but also in many areas of Europe, those whose undoubted radicalism on particular political issues co-exists with an insouciance and ignorance of socialist struggle typical of any middle-class suburbanite; and I do not believe that socialist men and women should acquiesce in this indifference for fear of being thought sectarian or unfashionable.

There is a relation between these issues and the fact that one constant theme of this book concerns the body. Indeed I am half inclined to apologize for the modishness of this topic: few literary texts are likely to make it nowadays into the new historicist canon unless they contain at least one mutilated body. A recovery of the importance of the body has been one of the most precious achievements of recent radical thought, and I hope that this book may be seen as extending that fertile line of enquiry in a new direction. At the same time, it is difficult to read the later Roland Barthes, or even the later Michel Foucault, without feeling that a certain style of meditation on the body, on pleasures and surfaces, zones and techniques, has acted among other things as a convenient displacement of a less immediately corporeal politics, and acted also as an *ersatz* kind of ethics. There is a privileged, privatized hedonism about such discourse, emerging as it does at just the historical point where certain less exotic forms of politics found themselves suffering a setback. I try in this book, then, to reunite the idea of the body with more traditional political topics of the state, class conflict and modes of production, through the mediatory category of the aesthetic; and to this extent the study distances itself equally from a class politics which has little of significance to say of the body, and from a post-class politics which takes refuge from such rebarbatively 'global' matters in the body's intensities.

In writing this book, I am clearly concerned to argue against those critics for whom any linkage of aesthetics and political ideologies must appear scandalous or merely bemusing. But I must confess that I also have in my sights those on the political left for whom the aesthetic is simply 'bourgeois ideology', to be worsted and ousted by alternative forms of cultural politics. The aesthetic is indeed, as I hope to show, a bourgeois concept in the most literal historical sense, hatched and nurtured in the Enlightenment; but only for the drastically undialectical thought of a vulgar Marxist or 'post-Marxist' trend of thought could this fact cue an automatic condemnation. It is left moralism, not historical materialism, which having established the bourgeois provenance of a particular concept, practice or institution, then disowns it in an access of ideological purity. From the *Communist Manifesto* onwards, Marxism has never ceased to sing the praises of the bourgeoisie – to cherish and recollect that in its great revolutionary heritage from which radicals must either enduringly learn, or face the prospect of a closed, illiberal socialist order in the future. Those who have now been correctly programmed to reach for their decentred subjectivities at the very mention of the dread phrase 'liberal humanist' repressively disavow the very history which constitutes them, which is by no means uniformly negative or oppressive. We forget at our political peril the heroic struggles of earlier 'liberal humanists' against the brutal autocracies of feudalist absolutism. If we can and must be severe critics of Enlightenment, it is Enlightenment which has empowered us to be so. Here, as always, the most intractable process of emancipation is that which involves freeing ourselves from ourselves. One of the tasks of radical critique, as Marx, Brecht and Walter Benjamin understood, is to salvage and redeem for left political uses whatever is still viable and valuable in the class legacies to which we are heirs. 'Use what you can' is a sound enough Brechtian slogan – with, of course, the implicit corollary that what turns out to be unusable in such traditions should be jettisoned without nostalgia.

It is the contradictoriness of the aesthetic which, I would claim, only a dialectical thought of this kind can adequately encompass. The emergence of the aesthetic as a theoretical category is closely bound up with the material process by which cultural production, at an early stage of bourgeois society, becomes 'autonomous' – autonomous, that is, of the various social functions which it has traditionally served. Once artefacts become commodities in the market place, they exist for nothing and nobody in particular, and can consequently be rationalized, ideologically speaking, as existing entirely and gloriously for themselves. It is this notion of autonomy or self-referentiality which the new discourse of aesthetics is centrally concerned to elaborate; and it is clear enough, from a radical political viewpoint, just how disabling any such idea of aesthetic autonomy must be. It is not only, as radical thought has familiarly insisted, that art is thereby conveniently sequestered from all other social practices, to become an isolated enclave within which the dominant social order can find an idealized refuge from its own actual values of competitiveness, exploitation and material possessiveness. It is also, rather more subtly, that the idea of autonomy – of a mode of being which is entirely self-regulating and self-determining – provides the middle class with just the ideological model of subjectivity it requires for its material operations. Yet this concept of autonomy is radically double-edged: if on the one hand it provides a central constituent of bourgeois ideology, it also marks an emphasis on the self-determining nature of human powers and capacities which becomes, in the work of Karl Marx and others, the anthropological foundation of a revolutionary opposition to bourgeois utility. The aesthetic is at once, as I try to show, the very secret prototype of human subjectivity in early capitalist society, and a vision of human energies as radical ends in themselves which is the implacable enemy of all dominative or instrumentalist thought. It signifies a creative turn to the sensuous body, as well as an inscribing of that body with a subtly oppressive law; it represents on the one hand a liberatory concern with concrete particularity, and on the other hand a specious form of universalism. If it offers a generous utopian image of reconciliation between men and women at present divided from one another, it also blocks and mystifies the real political movement towards such historical community. Any account of this amphibious concept which either uncritically celebrates or un-equivocally denounces it is thus likely to overlook its real historical complexity.

An example of such one-sidedness can be found, among other places, in the later work of Paul de Man, between which and my own enquiries I am glad to observe a certain unexpected convergence.[2] De Man's later writing represents a bracing, deeply intricate demystification of the idea of the aesthetic which, it could be claimed, was present in his thought throughout; and there is much that he has to say on this score with which I find myself in entire agreement. For de Man, aesthetic ideology involves a phenomenalist reduction of the linguistic to the sensuously empirical, a confusing of mind and world, sign and thing, cognition and percept, which is consecrated in the Hegelian symbol and resisted by Kant's rigorous demarcation of aesthetic judgement from the cognitive, ethical and political realms. Such aesthetic ideology, by repressing the contingent, aporetic relation which holds between the spheres of language and the real, naturalizes or phenomenalizes the former, and is thus in danger of converting the accidents of meaning to organic natural process in the characteristic manner of ideological thought. A valuable, resourceful politics is undoubtedly at work here, *pace* those left-wing critics for whom de Man is merely an unregenerate 'formalist'. But it is a politics bought at an enormous cost. In what one might see as an excessive reaction to his own earlier involvements with organicist ideologies of an extreme right-wing kind, de Man is led to suppress the potentially positive dimensions of the aesthetic in a way which perpetuates, if now in a wholly new style, his earlier hostility to an emancipatory politics. Few critics have been more bleakly unenthused by bodiliness – by the whole prospect of a creative development of the sensuous, creaturely aspects of human existence, by pleasure, Nature and self-delighting powers, all of which now figure as insidious aesthetic seductions to be manfully resisted. The last critic by whom one can imagine de Man being in the least enchanted is Mikhail Bakhtin. One might question some of the assumptions of de Man's later politics – not least the unwarranted belief that all ideology, without exception, is crucially concerned to 'naturalize' or organicize social practice. But there is no doubt that de Man is indeed a thoroughly political critic from the outset. It is simply that the consistency of that politics, the figure in the carpet of his work, lies in an unremitting hostility to the practice of political emancipation. In this sense Antonio Gramsci was right when, in a remarkable flash of prescience, he wrote in his *Prison Notebooks* that 'It could be asserted that Freud is the last of the Ideologues, and that de Man is also an "ideologue".'[3]

There are two major omissions in this work which I should perhaps clarify. The first is of any extensive reference to the British traditions of aesthetic thought. Readers will no doubt find a number of echoes of that history, of Coleridge and Matthew Arnold and William Morris, in the mainly German writing I examine; but this particular terrain has been well enough ploughed already, and since much in the Anglophone tradition is in fact derivative of German philosophy, I have thought it best to have recourse here, so to speak, to the horse's mouth. The other omission, perhaps a more irritating one for some readers, is of any examination of actual works of art. Those trained in literary critical habits of thought are usually enamoured of 'concrete illustration'; but since I reject the idea that 'theory' is acceptable if and only if it performs the role of humble handmaiden to the aesthetic work, I have tried to frustrate this expectation as far as possible by remaining for the most part resolutely silent about particular artefacts. I must admit, however, that I did originally conceive of the book as a kind of doubled text, in which an account of European aesthetic theory would be coupled at every point to a consideration of the literary culture of Ireland. Taking my cue from a passing reference of Kant to the revolutionary United Irishmen, I would have looked at Wolfe Tone and his political colleagues in the context of the European Enlightenment, and reviewed Irish cultural nationalism from Thomas Davis to Padraic Pearse in the light of European idealist thought. I also intended to harness somewhat loosely such figures as Marx, James Connolly and Sean O'Casey, and to link Nietzsche with Wilde and Yeats, Freud with Joyce, Schopenhauer and Adorno with Samuel Beckett, and (wilder flights, these) Heidegger with certain aspects of John Synge and Seamus Heaney. The result of this ambitious project would have been a volume which only readers in regular weight-training would have been able to lift; and I will therefore reserve this work either for a patented board game, in which players would be awarded points for producing the most fanciful possible connections between European philosophers and Irish writers, or for some future study.

I hope it will not be thought that I consider the kind of research embodied in this book somehow prototypical of what radical critics should now most importantly be doing. An analysis of Kant's third *Critique* or an inspection of Kierkegaard's religious meditations are hardly the most urgent tasks facing the political left. There are many forms of radical cultural enquiry of considerably greater political significance than such high theoretical labour; but a deeper understanding of the mechanisms by which political hegemony is currently maintained is a necessary prerequisite of effective political action, and this is one kind of insight which I believe an enquiry into the aesthetic can yield. While such a project is by no means everything, it is not, perhaps, to be sniffed at either.

I am not a professional philosopher, as the reader is no doubt just about to discover; and I am therefore deeply grateful to various friends and colleagues more expert in this area than myself, who have read this book in whole or part and offered many valuable criticisms and suggestions. I must thank in particular John Barrell, Jay Bernstein, Andrew Bowie, Howard Caygill, Jerry Cohen, Peter Dews, Joseph Fell, Patrick Gardiner, Paul Hamilton, Ken Hirschkop, Toril Moi, Alexander Nehamas, Peter Osborne, Stephen Priest, Jacqueline Rose and Vigdis Songe Møller. Since these individuals charitably or carelessly overlooked my mistakes, they are to that extent partly responsible for them. I am grateful as always to my editors Philip Carpenter and Susan Vice, whose acumen and efficiency remain undiminished since the days of their student essays. Finally, since I am now taking my leave of it, I would like to record my gratitude to Wadham College, Oxford, which for almost twenty years has supported and encouraged me in the building of an English school there true to its own long traditions of nonconformity and critical dissent.

T.E.

Notes

1 See Perry Anderson, *Considerations on Western Marxism* (London, 1979), chapter 4.
2 See in particular Paul de Man, 'Phenomenality and Materiality in Kant', in G. Shapiro and A. Sica (eds), *Hermeneutics: Questions and Prospects* (Amherst, Mass., 1984).
3 Antonio Gramsci, *Selections from the Prison Notebooks*, edited and translated by Quintin Hoare and Geoffrey Nowell-Smith (London, 1971), p. 376.

1

Free Particulars

Aesthetics is born as a discourse of the body. In its original formulation by the German philosopher Alexander Baumgarten, the term refers not in the first place to art, but, as the Greek *aisthesis* would suggest, to the whole region of human perception and sensation, in contrast to the more rarefied domain of conceptual thought. The distinction which the term 'aesthetic' initially enforces in the mid-eighteenth century is not one between 'art' and 'life', but between the material and the immaterial: between things and thoughts, sensations and ideas, that which is bound up with our creaturely life as opposed to that which conducts some shadowy existence in the recesses of the mind. It is as though philosophy suddenly wakes up to the fact that there is a dense, swarming territory beyond its own mental enclave which threatens to fall utterly outside its sway. That territory is nothing less than the whole of our sensate life together – the business of affections and aversions, of how the world strikes the body on its sensory surfaces, of that which takes root in the gaze and the guts and all that arises from our most banal, biological insertion into the world. The aesthetic concerns this most gross and palpable dimension of the human, which post-Cartesian philosophy, in some curious lapse of attention, has somehow managed to overlook. It is thus the first stirrings of a primitive materialism – of the body's long inarticulate rebellion against the tyranny of the theoretical.

The oversight of classical philosophy was not without its political cost. For how can any political order flourish which does not address itself to this most tangible area of the 'lived', of everything that belongs to a society's somatic, sensational life? How can 'experience' be allowed to fall outside a society's ruling concepts? Could it be that this realm is impenetrably opaque to reason, eluding its categories as surely as the smell of thyme or the taste of potatoes? Must the life of the body be given up on, as the sheer unthinkable other of thought, or are its mysterious ways somehow mappable by intellection in what would then prove a wholly novel science, the science of sensibility itself? If the phrase is nothing more than an oxymoron, then the political consequences are surely dire. Nothing could be more disabled than a ruling rationality which can know nothing beyond its own concepts, forbidden from enquiring into the very stuff of passion and perception. How can the absolute monarch of Reason retain its legitimacy if what Kant called the 'rabble' of the senses remains forever beyond its ken? Does not power require some ability to anatomize the feelings of what it subordinates, some science or concrete logic at its disposal which would map from the inside the very structures of breathing, sentient life?

The call for an aesthetics in eighteenth-century Germany is among other things a response to the problem of political absolutism. Germany in that period was a parcellized territory of feudal-absolutist states, marked by a particularism and idiosyncrasy consequent on its lack of a general culture. Its princes imposed their imperious diktats through elaborate bureaucracies, while a wretchedly exploited peasantry languished in conditions often little better than bestial. Beneath this autocratic sway, an ineffectual bourgeoisie remained cramped by the nobility's mercantilist policies of state-controlled industry and tariff-protected trade, overwhelmed by the conspicuous power of the courts, alienated from the degraded masses and bereft of any corporate influence in national life. The Junkerdom, rudely confiscating from the middle class their historic role, themselves sponsored much of what industrial development there was for their own fiscal or military purposes, leaving a largely quiescent middle class to do business with the state, rather than force the state to shape its policies to their own interests. A pervasive lack of capital and enterprise, poor communications and locally based trade, guild-dominated towns marooned in a backward countryside: such were the unpropitious conditions of the German bourgeoisie in this parochial, benighted social order. Its professional and intellectual strata, however, were steadily growing, to produce for the first time in the later eighteenth century a professional literary caste; and this group showed all the signs of exerting a cultural and spiritual leadership beyond the reach of the self-serving aristocracy. Unrooted in political or economic power, however, this bourgeois enlightenment remained in many respects enmortgaged to feudalist absolutism, marked by that profound respect for authority of which Immanuel Kant, courageous *Aufklärer* and docile subject of the king of Prussia, may be taken as exemplary.

What germinates in the eighteenth century as the strange new discourse of aesthetics is not a challenge to that political authority; but it can be read as symptomatic of an ideological dilemma inherent in absolutist power. Such power needs for its own purposes to take account of 'sensible' life, for without an understanding of this no dominion can be secure. The world of feelings and sensations can surely not just be surrendered to the 'subjective', to what Kant scornfully termed the 'egoism of taste'; instead, it must be brought within the majestic scope of reason itself. If the *Lebenswelt* is not rationally formalizable, have not all the most vital ideological issues been consigned to some limbo beyond one's control? Yet how can reason, that most immaterial of faculties, grasp the grossly sensuous? Perhaps what makes things available to empirical knowledge in the first place, their palpable materiality, is also in a devastating irony what banishes them beyond cognition. Reason must find some way of penetrating the world of perception, but in doing so must not put at risk its own absolute power.

It is just this delicate balance which Baumgarten's aesthetics seek to achieve. If his *Aesthetica* (1750) opens up in an innovative gesture the whole terrain of sensation, what it opens it up to is in effect the colonization of reason. For Baumgarten, aesthetic cognition mediates between the generalities of reason and the particulars of sense: the aesthetic is that realm of existence which partakes of the perfection of reason, but in a 'confused' mode. 'Confusion' here means not 'muddle' but 'fusion': in their organic interpenetration, the elements of aesthetic representation resist that discrimination into discrete units which is characteristic of conceptual thought. But this does not mean that such representations are obscure: on the contrary, the more 'confused' they are – the more unity-in-variety they attain – the more clear, perfect and determinate they become. A poem is in this sense a perfected form of sensate discourse. Aesthetic unities are thus open to rational analysis, though they demand a specialized form or idiom of reason, and this is aesthetics. Aesthetics, Baumgarten writes, is the 'sister' of logic, a kind of *ratio inferior* or feminine analogue of reason at the lower level of sensational life. Its task is to order this domain into clear or perfectly determinate representations, in a manner akin to (if relatively autonomous of) the operations of reason proper. Aesthetics is born of the recognition that the world of perception and experience cannot simply be derived from abstract universal laws, but demands its own appropriate discourse and displays its own inner, if inferior, logic. As a kind of concrete thought or sensuous analogue of the concept, the aesthetic partakes at once of the rational and the real, suspended between the two somewhat in the manner of the Lévi-Straussian myth. It is born as a woman, subordinate to man but with her own humble, necessary tasks to perform.

Such a mode of cognition is of vital importance if the ruling order is to understand its own history. For if sensation is characterized by a complex individuation which defeats the general concept, so is history itself. Both phenomena are marked by an irreducible particularity or concrete determinateness which threatens to put them beyond the bounds of abstract thought. 'Individuals', writes Baumgarten, 'are determined in every respect . . . particular representations are in the highest degree poetic.'[1] Since history is a question of 'individuals', it is 'poetic' in precisely this sense, a matter of determinate specificities; and it would therefore seem alarmingly to fall outside the compass of reason. What if the history of the ruling class were itself opaque to its knowledge, an unknowable exteriority beyond the pale of the concept? Aesthetics emerges as a theoretical discourse in response to such dilemmas; it is a kind of prosthesis to reason, extending a reified Enlightenment rationality into vital regions which are otherwise beyond its reach. It can cope, for example, with questions of desire and rhetorical effectivity: Baumgarten describes desire as 'a sensate representation because a confused representation of the good',[2] and examines the ways in which poetic sense-impressions can arouse particular emotive effects. The aesthetic, then, is simply the name given to that hybrid form of cognition which can clarify the raw stuff of perception and historical practice, disclosing the inner structure of the concrete. Reason as such pursues its lofty ends far removed from such lowly particulars; but a working replica of itself known as the aesthetic springs into being as a kind of cognitive underlabourer, to know in its uniqueness all that to which the higher reason is necessarily blind. Because the aesthetic exists, the dense particulars of perception can be made luminous to thought, and determinate concretions assembled into historical narrative. 'Science', writes Baumgarten, 'is not to be dragged down to the region of sensibility, but the sensible is to be lifted to the dignity of knowledge.'[3] Dominion over all inferior powers, he warns, belongs to reason alone; but this dominion must never degenerate into tyranny. It must rather assume the form of what we might now, after Gramsci, term 'hegemony', ruling and informing the senses from within while allowing them to thrive in all of their relative autonomy.

Once in possession of such a 'science of the concrete' – 'a contradiction in terms', Schopenhauer was later to call it – there is no need to fear that history and the body will slip through the net of conceptual discourse to leave one grasping at empty space. Within the dense welter of our material life, with all its amorphous flux, certain objects stand out in a sort of perfection dimly akin to reason, and these are known as the beautiful. A kind of ideality seems to inform their sensuous existence from within, rather than floating above it in some Platonic space; so that a rigorous logic is here revealed to us in matter itself, felt instantly on the pulses. Because these are objects which we can agree to be beautiful, not by arguing or analysing but just by looking and seeing, a spontaneous consensus is brought to birth within our creaturely life, bringing with it the promise that such a life, for all its apparent arbitrariness and obscurity, might indeed work in some sense very like a rational law. Such, as we shall see, is something of the meaning of the aesthetic for Kant, who will look to it for an elusive third way between the vagaries of subjective feeling and the bloodless rigour of the understanding.

For a modern parallel to this meaning of the aesthetic, we might look less to Benedetto Croce than to the later Edmund Husserl. For Husserl's purpose in *The Crisis of European Sciences* is precisely to rescue the life-world from its troubling opacity to reason, thereby renewing an Occidental rationality which has cut alarmingly adrift from its somatic, perceptual roots. Philosophy cannot fulfil its role as the universal, ultimately grounding science if it abandons the life-world to its anonymity; it must remember that the body, even before it has come to think, is always a sensibly experiencing organism positioned in its world in a way quite distinct from the placing of an object in a

17

box. Scientific knowledge of an objective reality is always already grounded in this intuitive pre-givenness of things to the vulnerably perceptive body, in the primordial physicality of our being-in-the-world. We scientists, Husserl remarks with faint surprise, are after all human beings; and it is because a misguided rationalism has overlooked this fact that European culture is in the crisis it is. (Husserl, victim of fascism, is writing in the 1930s.) Thought must thus round upon itself, retrieving the *Lebenswelt* from whose murky depths it springs, in a new 'universal science of subjectivity'. Such a science, however, is not in fact new in the least: when Husserl admonishes us that we must 'consider the surrounding life-world concretely, in its neglected relativity . . . the world in which we live intuitively, together with its real entities',[4] he is speaking, in the original sense of the term, as an aesthetician. It is not, of course, a question of surrendering ourselves to 'this whole merely subjective and apparently incomprehensible "Heraclitean flux" '[5] which is our daily experience, but rather of rigorously formalizing it. For the life-world exhibits a general structure, and this structure, to which everything that exists relatively is bound, is not itself relative. 'We can attend to it in its generality and, with sufficient care, fix it once and for all in a way equally accessible to all.'[6] Indeed it turns out conveniently enough that the life-world discloses just the same structures that scientific thought presupposes in its construction of an objective reality. Higher and lower styles of reasoning, in Baumgartenian terms, manifest a common form. Even so, the project of formalizing the life-world is not a simple one, and Husserl is frank enough to confess that 'one is soon beset by extraordinary difficulties . . . every "ground" that is reached points to further grounds, every horizon opened up awakens new horizons'.[7] Pausing to console us with the thought that this 'endless whole, in its infinity of flowing movement, is oriented toward the unity of one meaning', Husserl brutally undoes this solace in the next breath by denying that this is true 'in such a way that we could ever simply grasp and understand the whole'.[8] Like Kafka's hope, it would appear that there is plenty of totality, but not for us. The project of formalizing the life-world would seem to scupper itself before getting off the ground, and with it the proper grounding of reason. It will be left to Maurice Merleau-Ponty to develop this 'return to living history and the spoken word' – but in doing so to question the assumption that this is simply 'a preparatory

18

step which should be followed by the properly philosophical task of universal constitution'.[9] From Baumgarten to phenomenology, it is a question of reason deviating, doubling back on itself, taking a *detour* through sensation, experience, 'naivety' as Husserl calls it in the Vienna lecture, so that it will not have to suffer the embarrassment of arriving at its *telos* empty-handed, big with wisdom but deaf, dumb and blind into the bargain.

We shall see a little later, especially in the work of Friedrich Schiller, how such a detour through sensation is politically necessary. If absolutism does not wish to trigger rebellion, it must make generous accommodation for sensual inclination. Yet this turn to the affective subject is not without its perils for an absolutist law. If it may succeed in inscribing that law all the more effectively on the hearts and bodies of those it subjugates, it may also, by a self-deconstructive logic, come to subjectivize such authority out of existence, clearing the ground for a new concept of legality and political power altogether. In a striking historical irony recorded by Karl Marx, the very idealist cast into which conditions of social backwardness had forced the thinking of the late eighteenth-century German middle class led to the prefiguration in the mind of a bold new model of social life as yet quite unachievable in reality. From the depths of a benighted late feudal autocracy, a vision could be projected of a universal order of free, equal, autonomous human subjects, obeying no laws but those which they gave to themselves. This bourgeois public sphere breaks decisively with the privilege and particularism of the *ancien régime*, installing the middle class, in image if not in reality, as a truly universal subject, and compensating with the grandeur of this dream for its politically supine status. What is at stake here is nothing less than the production of an entirely new kind of human subject – one which, like the work of art itself, discovers the law in the depths of its own free identity, rather than in some oppressive external power. The liberated subject is the one who has appropriated the law as the very principle of its own autonomy, broken the forbidding tablets of stone on which that law was originally inscribed in order to rewrite it on the heart of flesh. To consent to the law is thus to consent to one's own inward being. 'The heart', writes Rousseau in *Émile*, 'only receives laws from itself; by wanting to enchain it one releases it; one only enchains it by leaving it free.'[10] Antonio Gramsci will write later in the *Prison Notebooks* of a form of civil society 'in which the individual can govern himself without his self-government thereby entering into conflict with political society – but rather becoming its normal continuation, its organic complement'.[11] In a classic moment in *The Social Contract*, Rousseau speaks of the most important form of law as one 'which is not graven on tablets of marble or brass, but on the hearts of the citizens. This forms the real constitution of the State, takes on every day new powers, when other laws decay or die out, restores them or takes their place, keeps a people in the ways it was meant to go, and insensibly replaces authority by the force of habit. I am speaking of morality, of custom, above all of public opinion; a power unknown to political thinkers, on which nonetheless success in everything else depends.'[12]

The ultimate binding force of the bourgeois social order, in contrast to the coercive apparatus of absolutism, will be habits, pieties, sentiments and affections. And this is equivalent to saying that power in such an order has become *aestheticized*. It is at one with the body's spontaneous impulses, entwined with sensibility and the affections, lived out in unreflective custom. Power is now inscribed in the minutiae of subjective experience, and the fissure between abstract duty and pleasurable inclination is accordingly healed. To dissolve the law to custom, to sheer unthinking habit, is to identify it with the human subject's own pleasurable well-being, so that to transgress that law would signify a deep self-violation. The new subject, which bestows on itself self-referentially a law at one with its immediate experience, finding its freedom in its necessity, is modelled on the aesthetic artefact.

This centrality of custom, as opposed to some naked reason, lies at the root of Hegel's critique of Kantian morality. Kant's practical reason, with its uncompromising appeal to abstract duty as an end in itself, smacks rather too much of the absolutism of feudalist power. The aesthetic theory of the *Critique of Judgement* suggests, by contrast, a resolute turn to the subject: Kant retains the idea of a universal law, but now discovers this law at work in the very structure of our subjective capacities. This 'lawfulness without a law' signifies a deft compromise between mere subjectivism on the one hand, and an excessively abstract reason on the other. There is indeed for Kant a kind of 'law' at work in aesthetic judgement, but one which seems inseparable from the very particularity of the artefact. As such, Kant's 'lawfulness without a law' offers a parallel to that 'authority which is

20

not an authority' (*The Social Contract*) which Rousseau finds in the structure of the ideal political state. In both cases, a universal law of a kind lives wholly in its free, individual incarnations, whether these are political subjects or the elements of the aesthetic artefact. The law simply *is* an assembly of autonomous, self-governing particulars working in spontaneous reciprocal harmony. Yet Kant's turn to the subject is hardly a turn to the *body*, whose needs and desires fall outside the disinterestedness of aesthetic taste. The body cannot be figured or represented within the frame of Kantian aesthetics; and Kant ends up accordingly with a formalistic ethics, an abstract theory of political rights, and a 'subjective' but non-sensuous aesthetics.

It is all of these which Hegel's more capacious notion of reason seeks to sweep up and transform. Hegel rejects Kant's stern opposition between morality and sensuality, defining instead an idea of reason which will encompass the cognitive, practical and affective together.[13] Hegelian Reason does not only apprehend the good, but so engages and transforms our bodily inclinations as to bring them into spontaneous accord with universal rational precepts. And what mediates between reason and experience here is the self-realizing *praxis* of human subjects in political life. Reason, in short, is not simply a contemplative faculty, but a whole project for the hegemonic reconstruction of subjects – what Seyla Benhabib has called 'the successive transformation and reeducation of inner nature'.[14] Reason works out its own mysterious ends through human beings' sensuous, self-actualizing activity in the realm of *Sittlichkeit* (concrete ethical life) or Objective Spirit. Rational moral behaviour is thus inseparable from questions of human happiness and self-fulfilment; and if this is so then Hegel has in some sense 'aestheticized' reason by anchoring it in the body's affections and desires. It is not of course aestheticized *away*, dissolved to some mere hedonism or intuitionism; but it has lapsed from the lofty Kantian domain of Duty to become an active, transfigurative force in material life.

The 'aesthetic' dimension of this programme can best be disclosed by suggesting that what Hegel confronts in emergent bourgeois society is a conflict between a 'bad' particularism on the one hand, and a 'bad' universalism on the other. The former is a matter of civil society: it stems from the private economic interest of the solitary citizen, who as Hegel comments in the *Philosophy of Right* is each his own end and has no regard for others. The latter is a question of the political state, where these unequal, antagonistic monads are deceptively constituted as abstractly free and equivalent. In this sense, bourgeois society is a grotesque travesty of the aesthetic artefact, which harmoniously interrelates general and particular, universal and individual, form and content, spirit and sense. In the dialectical medium of *Sittlichkeit*, however, the subject's participation in universal reason takes the shape at each moment of a unified, concretely particular form of life. It is through '*Bildung*', the rational education of desire through *praxis*, or as we might say a programme of spiritual hegemony, that the bond between individual and universal is ceaselessly constituted. Knowledge, moral practice and pleasurable self-fulfilment are thus coupled together in the complex interior unity of Hegelian Reason. The ethical, Hegel remarks in the *Philosophy of Right*, appears not as law but as custom, an habitual form of action which becomes a 'second nature'. Custom is the law of the spirit of freedom; the project of education is to show individuals the way to a new birth, converting their 'first' nature of appetites and desires to a second, spiritual one which will then become customary to them. No longer torn asunder between blind individualism and abstract universalism, the reborn subject lives its existence, we might claim, aesthetically, in accordance with a law which is now entirely at one with its spontaneous being. What finally secures social order is that realm of customary practice and instinctual piety, more supple and resilient than abstract rights, where the living energies and affections of subjects are invested.

That this should be so follows necessarily from the social conditions of the bourgeoisie. Possessive individualism abandons each subject to its own private space, dissolves all positive bonds between them and thrusts them into mutual antagonism. 'By "antagonism"', writes Kant in his 'Idea for a Universal History', 'I mean the unsociable sociability of men, i.e. their propensity to enter into society bound together with a mutual opposition which constantly threatens to break up the society.'[15] In a striking irony, the very practices which reproduce bourgeois society also threaten to undermine it. If no positive social bonds are possible at the level of material production or 'civil society', one might perhaps look to the political arena of the state to bear the burden of such interrelationship. What one finds here, however, is a merely notional community of abstractly symmetrical subjects, too rarefied and theoretic to provide a rich *experience* of consensuality. Once the bourgeoisie has dismantled the centralizing political apparatus of absolutism, either in fantasy or reality, it finds itself bereft of some of the institutions which had previously organized social life as a whole. The question therefore arises as to where it is to locate a sense of unity powerful enough to reproduce itself by. In economic life, individuals are structurally isolated and antagonistic; at the political level there would seem nothing but abstract rights to link one subject to the other. This is one reason why the 'aesthetic' realm of sentiments, affections and spontaneous bodily habits comes to assume the significance it does. Custom, piety, intuition and opinion must now cohere an otherwise abstract, atomized social order. Moreover, once absolutist power has been overturned, each subject must function as its own seat of self-government. An erstwhile centralized authority must be parcellized and localized: absolved from continuous political supervision, the bourgeois subject must assume the burden of its own internalized governance. This is not to suggest that absolutist power itself requires no such internalization: like any successful political authority, it demands complicity and collusion from those it subordinates. It is not a question of some stark contrast between a purely heteronomous law on the one hand, and an insidiously consensual one on the other. But with the growth of early bourgeois society, the ratio between coercion and consent is undergoing gradual transformation: only a rule weighted towards the latter can effectively regulate individuals whose economic activity necessitates a high degree of autonomy. It is in this sense, too, that the aesthetic moves into the foreground in such conditions. Like the work of art as defined by the discourse of aesthetics, the bourgeois subject is autonomous and self-determining, acknowledges no merely extrinsic law but instead, in some mysterious fashion, gives the law to itself. In doing so, the law becomes the form which shapes into harmonious unity the turbulent content of the subject's appetites and inclinations. The compulsion of autocratic power is replaced by the more gratifying compulsion of the subject's self-identity.

To rely on sentiment as a source of one's social cohesion is not as precarious a matter as it looks. The bourgeois state, after all, still has its coercive instruments at the ready should this project falter; and what bonds could in any case be stronger, more unimpeachable, than those of the senses, of 'natural' compassion and instinctive allegiance?

Such organic liaisons are surely a more trustworthy form of political rule than the inorganic, oppressive structures of absolutism. Only when governing imperatives have been dissolved into spontaneous reflex, when human subjects are linked to each other in their very flesh, can a truly corporate existence be fashioned. It is for this reason that the early bourgeoisie is so preoccupied with *virtue* – with the lived habit of moral propriety, rather than a laborious adherence to some external norm. Such a belief naturally demands an ambitious programme of moral education and reconstruction, for there is no assurance that the human subjects who emerge from the *ancien régime* will prove refined and enlightened enough for power to found itself on their sensibilities. It is thus that Rousseau writes the *Émile* and the *Nouvelle Heloïse*, intervening in the realms of pedagogy and sexual morality to construct new forms of subjectivity. Similarly, the law in *The Social Contract* has behind it a Legislator, whose role is the hegemonic one of educating the people to receive the law's decrees. 'The (Rousseauan) state', comments Ernst Cassirer, 'does not simply address itself to already existing and given subjects of the will; rather its first aim is to *create* the sort of subjects to whom it can address its call.'[16] Not just any subject can be 'interpellated', in Althusserian phrase;[17] the task of political hegemony is to produce the very forms of subjecthood which will form the basis of political unity.

The virtue of Rousseau's ideal citizen lies in his passionate affection for his fellow citizens and for the shared conditions of their common life. The root of this civic virtue is the pity we experience for each other in the state of nature; and this pity rests on a kind of empathetic imagination, 'transporting ourselves outside ourselves, and identifying ourselves with the suffering animal, leaving our being, so to speak, in order to take his . . . Thus no one becomes sensitive except when his imagination is animated and begins to transport himself outside of himself.'[18] At the very root of social relations lies the aesthetic, source of all human bonding. If bourgeois society releases its individuals into lonely autonomy, then only by such an imaginative exchange or appropriation of each other's identities can they be deeply enough united. Feeling, Rousseau claims in *Émile*, precedes knowledge; and the law of conscience is such that what I *feel* to be right is right. Even so, social harmony cannot be grounded in such sentiments alone, which suffice only for the state of nature. In the state of civilization, such sympathies must find their formal articulation in law, which involves a similar 'exchange' of subjects: 'Each of us puts his person and all his power in common under the supreme direction of the general will, and, in our corporate capacity, we receive each member as an indivisible part of the whole.'[19] In Rousseau's view, for the subject to obey any law other than one it has personally fashioned is slavery; no individual is entitled to command another, and the only legitimate law is thus of a self-conferred kind. If all citizens alienate their rights entirely to the community, 'each man, in giving himself to all, gives himself to nobody', and so receives himself back again as a free, autonomous being. The citizen surrenders his 'bad' particularism – his narrowly selfish interests – and through the 'general will' identifies instead with the good of the whole; he retains his unique individuality, but now in the form of a disinterested commitment to a common well-being. This fusion of general and particular, in which one shares in the whole at no risk to one's unique specificity, resembles the very form of the aesthetic artefact – though since Rousseau is not an organicist thinker, the analogy is only approximate. For the mystery of the aesthetic object is that each of its sensuous parts, while appearing wholly autonomous, incarnates the 'law' of the totality. Each aesthetic particular, in the very act of determining itself, regulates and is regulated by all other self-determining particulars. The enheartening expression of this doctrine, politically speaking, would be: 'what appears as my subordination to others is in fact self-determination'; the more cynical view would run: 'my subordination to others is so effective that it appears to me in the mystified guise of governing myself.'

The emergent middle class, in an historic development, is newly defining itself as a universal subject. But the abstraction this process entails is a source of anxiety for a class wedded in its robust individualism to the concrete and the particular. If the aesthetic intervenes here, it is as a dream of reconciliation – of individuals woven into intimate unity with no detriment to their specificity, of an abstract totality suffused with all the flesh-and-blood reality of the individual being. As Hegel writes of classical art in his *Philosophy of Fine Art*: 'Though no violence is done . . . to any feature of expression, any part of the whole, and every member appears in its independence, and rejoices in its own existence, yet each and all is content at the same time to be only an aspect in the total evolved presentation.'[20] Rousseau's general will, as a kind of mighty totalizing

25

artefact, might be seen as imaginative empathy assuming a rational, objective form.

Rousseau does not think that feeling can simply replace rational law; but he does hold that reason in itself is insufficient for social unity, and that to become a regulative force in society it must be animated by love and affection. It is thus that he quarrelled with the Encyclopaedists, whose dream of reconstructing society from pure reason seemed to him simply to erase the problem of the subject. And to overlook the subject is to ignore the vital question of political hegemony, which the ultra-rationalism of the Enlightenment is powerless in itself to address. 'Sensibility', then, would seem unequivocally on the side of the progressive middle class, as the aesthetic foundation of a new form of polity. Yet if the conservative Edmund Burke found Rousseau's sentimentalism offensive, he was also revolted by what he saw as his impious rationalism. Such rationalism seemed to Burke just that effort to reconstruct the social order from metaphysical first principles which was most calculated to undermine an organic cultural tradition of spontaneous pieties and affections.[21] Rationalism and sentimentalism do indeed in this sense go together: if a new social order is to be constructed on the basis of virtue, custom and opinion, then a radical rationalism must first of all dismantle the political structures of the present, submitting their mindless prejudices and traditionalist privileges to disinterested critique. Conversely, both rationalism and an appeal to feeling can be found on the political right. If the given social order defends itself in Burkeian fashion through 'culture' – through a plea for the values and affections richly implicit in national tradition – it will tend to provoke an abrasive rationalism from the political left. The left will round scathingly on the 'aesthetic' as the very locus of mystification and irrational prejudice; it will denounce the insidiously naturalizing power which Burke has in mind when he comments that customs operate better than laws, 'because they become a sort of Nature both to the governors and the governed'.[22] If, however, the existing order ratifies itself by an appeal to absolute law, then the 'subjective' instincts and passions which such law seems unable to encompass can become the basis of a radical critique.

The form which these conflicts take is partly determined by the nature of the political power in question. In late eighteenth-century Britain, an evolved tradition of bourgeois democracy had produced a social order which sought on the whole to work 'hegemonically', however savagely coercive it could also show itself. Authority, as Burke recommends, has regard to the senses and sentiments of at least some of its subjects; and in this situation two alternative counter-strategies become available. One is to explore the realm of affective life which authority seeks to colonize and turn it against the insolence of power itself, as in some eighteenth-century cults of sensibility. A new kind of human subject – sensitive, passionate, individualist – poses an ideological challenge to the ruling order, elaborating new dimensions of feeling beyond its narrow scope. Alternatively, the fact that power utilizes feelings for its own ends may give rise to a radical rationalist revolt against feeling itself, in which sensibility is assailed as the insidious force which binds subjects to the law. If, however, political dominance assumes in German fashion more openly coercive forms, then an 'aesthetic' counter-strategy – a cultivation of the instincts and pieties over which such power rides roughshod – can always gather force.

Any such project, however, is likely to be deeply ambivalent. For it is never easy to distinguish an appeal to taste and sentiment which offers an alternative to autocracy from one which allows such power to ground itself all the more securely in the living sensibilities of its subjects. There is a world of political difference between a law which the subject really does give to itself, in radical democratic style, and a decree which still descends from on high but which the subject now 'authenticates'. Free consent may thus be the antithesis of oppressive power, or a seductive form of collusion with it. To view the emergent middle-class order from either standpoint alone is surely too undialectical an approach. In one sense, the bourgeois subject is indeed mystified into mistaking necessity for freedom and oppression for autonomy. For power to be individually authenticated, there must be constructed within the subject a new form of inwardness which will do the unpalatable work of the law for it, and all the more effectively since that law has now apparently evaporated. In another sense, this policing belongs with the historic victory of bourgeois liberty and democracy over a barbarously repressive state. As such, it contains within itself a genuinely utopian glimpse of a free, equal community of independent subjects. Power is shifting its location from centralized institutions to the silent, invisible depths of the subject itself; but this shift is also part of a profound political

27

emancipation in which freedom and compassion, the imagination and the bodily affections, strive to make themselves heard within the discourse of a repressive rationalism.

The aesthetic, then, is from the beginning a contradictory, double-edged concept. On the one hand, it figures as a genuinely emancipatory force – as a community of subjects now linked by sensuous impulse and fellow-feeling rather than by heteronomous law, each safeguarded in its unique particularity while bound at the same time into social harmony. The aesthetic offers the middle class a superbly versatile model of their political aspirations, exemplifying new forms of autonomy and self-determination, transforming the relations between law and desire, morality and knowledge, recasting the links between individual and totality, and revising social relations on the basis of custom, affection and sympathy. On the other hand, the aesthetic signifies what Max Horkheimer has called a kind of 'internalised repression', inserting social power more deeply into the very bodies of those it subjugates, and so operating as a supremely effective mode of political hegemony. To lend fresh significance to bodily pleasures and drives, however, if only for the purpose of colonizing them more efficiently, is always to risk foregrounding and intensifying them beyond one's control. The aesthetic as custom, sentiment, spontaneous impulse may consort well enough with political domination; but these phenomena border embarrassingly on passion, imagination, sensuality, which are not always so easily incorporable. As Burke put it in his *Appeal from the New to the Old Whigs*: 'There is a boundary to men's passions when they act from feeling; none when they are under the influence of imagination.'[23] 'Deep' subjectivity is just what the ruling social order desires, and exactly what it has most cause to fear. If the aesthetic is a dangerous, ambiguous affair, it is because, as we shall see in this study, there is something in the body which can revolt against the power which inscribes it; and that impulse could only be eradicated by extirpating along with it the capacity to authenticate power itself.

Notes

1 Alexander Baumgarten, *Reflections on Poetry*, translated by K. Aschenbrenner and W. B. Holther (Berkeley, 1954), p. 43. For a useful recent

essay on Baumgarten, see Rodolphe Gasché, 'Of aesthetic and historical determination', in D. Attridge, G. Bennington and R. Young (eds), *Post-Structuralism and the Question of History* (Cambridge, 1987). See also David E. Wellbery, *Lessing's Laocoön: Semiotics and Aesthetics in the Age of Reason* (Cambridge, 1984), chapter 2, and K.E. Gilbert and H. Kuhn, *A History of Esthetics* (New York, 1939), chapter 10. For a splendid survey of English and German aesthetics from which I have benefited a good deal in chapters 1 and 2, see Howard Caygill, 'Aesthetics and Civil Society: Theories of Art and Society 1640–1790', unpublished Ph.D thesis, University of Sussex, 1982; and see Caygill, *Art of Judgement* (Oxford, 1989).

2 Baumgarten, *Reflections on Poetry*, p. 38.

3 Quoted by Ernst Cassirer, *The Philosophy of the Enlightenment* (Boston, 1951), p. 340.

4 Edmund Husserl, *The Crisis of European Sciences and Transcendental Phenomenology* (Evanston, 1970), p. 156.

5 Ibid.

6 Ibid., p. 139.

7 Ibid., p. 170.

8 Ibid.

9 Maurice Merleau-Ponty, *Signs* (Evanston, 1964), p. 110.

10 Jean-Jacques Rousseau, *Émile ou de l'éducation* (Paris, 1961), vol. IV, p. 388.

11 Antonio Gramsci, *Selections from the Prison Notebooks*, ed. Q. Hoare and G. Nowell Smith (London, 1971), p. 268.

12 Jean-Jacques Rousseau, *The Social Contract and Discourses*, ed. G.D.H. Cole (London, 1938), p. 48.

13 See Seyla Benhabib, *Critique, Norm, and Utopia* (New York, 1986), pp. 80–4. For the relation between custom and law in the Enlightenment, see I.O. Wade, *The Structure and Form of the French Enlightenment* (Princeton, 1977), vol. 1, Part 11.

14 Benhabib, *Critique, Norm, and Utopia*, p. 82.

15 Immanuel Kant, 'Idea for a Universal History', in I. Kant, *On History*, ed. Lewis White Beck (Indianapolis, 1963), p. 15.

16 Ernst Cassirer, *The Question of Jean-Jacques Rousseau* (Bloomington, 1954), pp. 62–3.

17 See Louis Althusser, 'Ideology and Ideological State Apparatuses', in *Lenin and Philosophy* (London, 1971).

18 Rousseau, *Émile*, vol. IV, p. 261.

19 Rousseau, *The Social Contract*, p. 15.

20 G. W. F. Hegel, *The Philosophy of Fine Art* (London, 1920), vol. 11, p. 10 (translation slightly amended).

21 See Annie Marie Osborn, *Rousseau and Burke* (London, 1940), a work which at one point strangely speaks of Burke as an Englishman. See also, for Rousseau's political thought, J. H. Broome, *Rousseau: A Study of his Thought* (London, 1963); Stephen Ellenburg, *Rousseau's Political Philosophy* (Ithaca, 1976); Roger D. Master, *The Political Philosophy of Rousseau* (Princeton, 1968); Lucio Colletti, *From Rousseau to Lenin* (London, 1972), Part 3.

22 Edmund Burke, *An Abridgement of English History*, quoted in W. J. T. Mitchell, *Iconology* (Chicago, 1986), p. 140.

23 *The Works of Edmund Burke*, ed. George Nichols (Boston, 1865–7), vol. 4, p. 192.

2

The Law of the Heart: Shaftesbury, Hume, Burke

While the German middle class languished beneath the yoke of nobility, their English counterparts had been energetically at work transforming a social order still heavily aristocratic in nature to their own advantage. Uniquely among European nations, the English landowning elite had itself long been a capitalist class proper, already accustomed to wage labour and commodity production as early as the sixteenth century. They thus anticipated by a considerable period that conversion from feudal to capitalist agriculture which the Prussian Junkerdom would accomplish, more partially and precariously, only in the wake of its defeat in the Napoleonic wars. At once the most stable and wealthy estate-owners in Europe, the English patriciate succeeded superbly in combining high capitalist productivity on the land with an enviable degree of cultural solidarity and unbroken continuity. It was within this unusually favourable matrix, offering at once the general preconditions for further capitalist development and a resilient political framework to safeguard it, that the English mercantile class was able to inaugurate its own key institutions (the stock exchange, the Bank of England), and secure the predominance of its own form of political state (parliament), in the aftermath of the 1688 revolution. Under these propitious conditions, Britain was able to emerge in the eighteenth century as the world's leading commercial power, vanquishing its foreign rivals and extending its imperial sway across the globe. By the mid-eighteenth century, London had become the largest centre of international trade, the premier port and warehouse of the world, and witnessed the forging of some spectacular fortunes. The Hanoverian state, staffed and controlled by the aristocracy, protected and promoted mercantile interests with impressive zeal, securing for Britain a rapidly expanding economy and an immensely profitable empire.

In eighteenth-century Britain, then, we encounter a robust, well-founded unity of agrarian and mercantile interests, accompanied by a marked ideological *rapprochement* between new and traditional social elites. The idealized self-image of this ruling social bloc is less of itself as a 'state' class than as a 'public sphere' – a political formation rooted in civil society itself, whose members are at once stoutly individualist and linked to their fellows by enlightened social intercourse and a shared set of cultural manners. Assured enough of its political and economic stability, this governing bloc is able to disseminate some of its power in the forms of a general culture and 'civility', founded less on the potentially divisive realities of social rank and economic interest than on common styles of sensibility and a homogeneous reason. 'Civilized' conduct takes its cue from traditional aristocratism: its index is the fluent, spontaneous, taken-for-granted virtue of the gentleman, rather than the earnest conformity to some external law of the petty bourgeois. Moral standards, while still implacably absolute in themselves, may thus be to some extent diffused into the textures of personal sensibility; taste, affect and opinion testify more eloquently to one's participation in a universal common sense than either moral strenuousness or ideological doctrine. Both of these now carry with them ominous reminiscences of a disruptive puritanism. Yet if the prototype of this public sphere is drawn from the realm of gentility, the predominance it grants to individual sensibility, the free circulation of enlightened opinion, and the abstractly equalized status of its socially diverse participants, mark it also as a peculiarly bourgeois social formation. A community of sensibility consorts as well with the bourgeois's stout empiricist disregard for metaphysical abstraction, and also with his deepening domestic sentimentalism, as it does with that carelessness of theoretical justification which is the badge of aristocracy. For both strata, an abstract rationalism now sinisterly recalls the metaphysical excesses of the Commonwealth. If social power is to be effectively naturalized, it must somehow take root in the sensuous immediacies of empirical life, beginning with the affective, appetitive individual of civil society, and tracing from there the affiliations which might bind him to a greater whole.

The project of early German aesthetics, as we have seen, is to

32

mediate between general and particular, elaborating a kind of concrete logic which will clarify the sensory world without abstracting it away. Reason must grant experience its peculiar density, without allowing it for a moment to escape; and this is hardly an easy tension to maintain. The proto-materialist impulse of this project soon surrenders to a full-blown formalism; indeed no sooner has sensation been ushered into the court of reason then it is subjected to a rigorous discrimination. Only certain sensations are fit subject for aesthetic enquiry; and this means for the Hegel of the *Philosophy of Fine Art* only sight and hearing, senses which are, as he says, 'ideal'. Vision for Hegel is 'appetiteless'; all true looking is without desire. There can be no aesthetics of odour, texture or flavour, which are mere debased modes of access to the world. 'Botticher's mere feeling with the hand of the effeminately smooth portions of statues of goddesses', Hegel remarks frostily, 'is not a part of artistic contemplation or enjoyment at all.'[1] Reason, then, in some sense selects those perceptions which already appear to collude with it. The aesthetic representation of a Kant is quite as unsensual as the concept, expelling the materiality of its object. But if German rationalism has a problem in descending from the universal to the particular, the dilemma of British empiricism is quite the reverse: how to move from the particular to the general without the latter merely collapsing back into the former. If rationalism is politically vulnerable, it is because it risks a mere empty totalization which expels the experiential; if empiricism is politically problematic, it is because it has difficulty in totalizing at all, mired as it is in a web of particulars. It is the impossible conundrum of a 'science of the concrete': how is a ruling order to root itself in the sensuously immediate, yet elaborate this into something more compelling than a heap of fragments? Empiricism risks ending up trapped here in some intolerable impasse, either undoing its own totalizations at every step, or subverting immediacy in the very effort to ground it more securely. If rationalism feels the need to supplement itself with the logic of the aesthetic, then it would seem that empiricism was all along too aesthetic for its own good. How is a thought already so thoroughly sensationalized to break the hold of the body over it, drag itself free of the clammy embrace of the senses and rise to something a little more conceptually dignified?

The answer, perhaps, is that there is no need. Could we not stay with the senses themselves, and find there our deepest relation to an overall rational design? What if we could discover the trace of such a providential order on the body itself, in its most spontaneous, prereflexive instincts? Perhaps there is somewhere within our immediate experience a sense with all the unerring intuition of aesthetic taste, which discloses the moral order to us. Such is the celebrated 'moral sense' of the British eighteenth-century moralists, which allows us to experience right and wrong with all the swiftness of the senses, and so lays the groundwork for a social cohesion more deeply felt than any mere rational totality. If the moral values which govern social life are as self-evident as the taste of peaches, a good deal of disruptive wrangling can be dispensed with. Society as a whole, given its fragmented condition, is increasingly opaque to totalizing reason; it is difficult to discern any rational design in the workings of the market place. But we might turn nevertheless to what seems the opposite of all that, to the stirrings of individual sensibility, and find there instead our surest incorporation into a common body. In our natural instincts of benevolence and compassion we are brought by some providential law, itself inscrutable to reason, into harmony with one another. The body's affections are no mere subjective whims, but the key to a well-ordered state.

Morality, then, is becoming steadily aestheticized, and this in two related senses. It has been moved closer to the springs of sensibility; and it concerns a virtue which like the artefact is an end in itself. We live well in society neither from duty nor utility, but as a delightful fulfilment of our nature. The body has its reasons, of which the mind may know little: a benign providence has so exquisitely adapted our faculties to its own ends as to make it keenly pleasurable to realize them. To follow out our self-delighting impulses, provided they are shaped by reason, its unwittingly to promote the common good. Our sense of morality, the Earl of Shaftesbury argues, consists in 'a real antipathy or aversion to injustice or wrong, and in a real affection or love towards equity and right, for its own sake, and on account of its natural beauty and worth'.[2] The objects of moral judgement are for Shaftesbury as immediately attractive or repulsive as those of aesthetic taste, which is not to convict him of moral subjectivism. On the contrary, he believes strongly in an absolute, objective moral law, rejects the suggestion that immediate feeling is a sufficient condition of the good, and holds like Hegel that the moral sense must be educated and disciplined by reason. He also rejects the hedonist creed that the good is simply what pleases us. Even so, all moral action for Shaftesbury must be mediated through the affections, and what is not done through affection is simply non-moral. Beauty, truth and goodness are ultimately at one: what is beautiful is harmonious, what is harmonious is true, and what is at once true and beautiful is agreeable and good. The morally virtuous individual lives with the grace and symmetry of an artefact, so that virtue may be known by its irresistible aesthetic appeal: 'For what is there on earth a fairer matter of speculation, a goodlier view or contemplation, than that of a beautiful, proportion'd, and becoming action?'[3] Politics and aesthetics are deeply intertwined: to love and admire beauty is 'advantageous to social affection, and highly assistant to virtue, which is itself no other than the love of order and beauty in society'.[4] Truth for this passed-over Platonist is an artistic apprehension of the world's inner design: to understand something is to grasp its proportioned place in the whole, and so is at once cognitive and aesthetic. Knowledge is a creative intuition which discloses the dynamic forms of Nature, and has about it a brio and exuberance inseparable from pleasure. Indeed Nature for Shaftesbury is itself the supreme artefact, brimful with all possibilities of being; and to know it is to share in both the creativity and the sublime disinterestedness of its Maker. The root of the idea of the aesthetic is thus theological: like the work of art, God and his world are autonomous, autotelic and utterly self-determining. The aesthetic is a suitably secularized version of the Almighty himself, not least in its blending of freedom and necessity. Mere libertinism must be rejected for a freedom based on law, restraint seen as the very basis of emancipation: in the work of art, as in the world in general, 'the truly austere, severe, and regular, restraintive character . . . corresponds (not fights or thwarts) with the free, the easy, the secure, the bold.'[5]

As the grandson of the founder of the Whig party, Shaftesbury is a firm upholder of civic liberties, and in this sense an eloquent spokesman for the bourgeois public sphere of eighteenth-century England. Yet he is also a notable traditionalist, an aristocratic neo-Platonist fiercely antagonistic to bourgeois utility and self-interest.[6] Horrified by a nation of Hobbesian shopkeepers, Shaftesbury speaks up for the 'aesthetic' as its alternative: for an ethics entwined with the sensuous affections, and for a human nature which is a self-pleasuring end in itself. In this sense, he is able to furnish bourgeois society, from his traditional aristocratic resources, with some rather more edifying, experiential principle of unity than its political or economic practice can provide. His philosophy unites the absolute law of the old school with the subjective freedom of the new, sensualizing the one while spiritualizing the other. His genially aristocratic trust that sociality is rooted in the very structure of the human animal runs counter to the whole of bourgeois practice; yet it can supply just the felt, intuitive links between individuals that the middle class urgently needs, unable as it is to derive any such positive corporate existence from either market place or political state. Shaftesbury is in this sense a central architect of the new political hegemony, of justified European renown. Cusped conveniently between traditionalism and progress, he introduces the bourgeois public sphere to a rich humanist heritage, aestheticising its social relations. But he also clings firmly to that absolute rational law which will prevent such relations from lapsing into mere libertinism or sentimentalism.

To live 'aesthetically' for Shaftesbury is to flourish in the well-proportioned exercise of one's powers, conforming to the law of one's free personality in the casual, affable, taken-for-granted style of the stereotypical aristocrat. What the middle class can learn from this doctrine is its stress on autonomy and self-determination – its deconstruction of any too rigid opposition between freedom and necessity, impulse and law. If the aristocrat gives the law to himself individually, the bourgeoisie aspires to do so collectively. To this extent, the middle class inherits the aesthetic as a legacy from its superiors; but some aspects of it are more usable than others. The aesthetic as the rich, all-round development of human capacities is bound to prove something of an embarrassment for a class whose economic activity leaves it spiritually impoverished and one-sided. The bourgeoisie can appreciate the aesthetic as self-autonomy, but much less as wealth of being, realized purely for its own sake. By the time it has embarked upon its industrial career, its leaden, repressive Hebraism will seem light years removed from Schiller's 'grace', Burke's 'enjoyment' or Shaftesbury's delight in wit and ridicule. 'Wealth of being', indeed, will become in the hands of Arnold, Ruskin and William Morris a powerful critique of middle-class individualism. If the aesthetic is in part a bequest from nobility to middle class, then, it is a divided, ambivalent one – a set of key concepts for the new social order, but also for the critical tradition which opposes it.

In the 'moral sense' philosophers, then, ethics, aesthetics and politics are drawn harmoniously together. To do good is deeply enjoyable, a self-justifying function of our nature beyond all crass utility. The moral sense, as Francis Hutcheson argues, is 'antecedent to advantage and interest and is the foundation of them'.[7] Like Shaftesbury, Hutcheson speaks of virtuous actions as beautiful and vicious ones as ugly or deformed; for him too, moral intuition is as swift in its judgements as aesthetic taste. 'Human society', writes Adam Smith in his *Theory of Moral Sentiments*,

> when we contemplate it in a certain abstract and philo-sophical light, appears like a great, an immense machine, whose regular and harmonious movements produce a thousand agreeable effects. As in any other beautiful and noble machine that was the production of human art, whatever tended to render its movements more smooth and easy, would derive a beauty from this effect, and, on the contrary, whatever tended to obstruct them would displease on that account: so virtue, which is, as it were, the fine polish to the wheels of society, necessarily pleases; while vice, like the vile rust, which makes them jar and grate upon one another, is as necessarily offensive.[8]

The whole of social life is aestheticized; and what this signifies is a social order so spontaneously cohesive that its members no longer need to think about it. Virtue, the easy habit of goodness, is like art beyond all mere calculation. A sound political regime is one in which subjects conduct themselves gracefully – where, as we have seen, the law is no longer external to individuals but is lived out, with fine cavalier insouciance, as the very principle of their free identities. Such an internal appropriation of the law is at once central to the work of art and to the process of political hegemony. The aesthetic is in this sense no more than a name for the political unconscious: it is simply the way social harmony registers itself on our senses, imprints itself on our sensibilities. The beautiful is just political order lived out on the body, the way it strikes the eye and stirs the heart. If it is inexplicable, beyond all rational debate, it is because our fellowship with others is likewise beyond all reason, as gloriously pointless as a poem. The socially disruptive, by contrast, is as instantly offensive as a foul smell. The unity of social life sustains itself, requiring no further legitimation, anchored as it is in our most primordial instincts. Like the work of art, it is immune from all rational analysis, and so from all rational criticism.

To aestheticize morality and society in this way is in one sense the mark of a serene confidence. If moral responses are as self-evident as the taste of sherry, then ideological consensus must run deep indeed. What more flattering compliment could there be to the rationality of the social whole than that we apprehend it in the least reflective aspects of our lives, in the most apparently private, wayward of sensations? Is there even any need for some cumbersome apparatus of law and the state, yoking us inorganically together, when in the genial glow of benevolence we can experience our kinship with others as immediately as a delectable taste? In another sense, one might argue, moral sense theory testifies to a bankrupt tendency of bourgeois ideology, forced to sacrifice the prospect of a *rational* totality to an intuitive logic. Unable to found ideological consensus in its actual social relations, to derive the unity of humankind from the anarchy of the market place, the ruling order must ground that consensus instead in the stubborn self-evidence of the gut. We know there is more to social existence than self-interest, because we feel it. What cannot be socially demonstrated has to be taken on faith. The appeal is at once empty and potent: feelings, unlike propositions, cannot be controverted, and if a social order *needs* to be rationally justified then, one might claim, the Fall has already happened. Yet to found society on intuition is not without its problems, as the critics of these theorists were quick to see.[9]

If the moral sense philosophers help to oil the wheels of political hegemony, they also provide, contradictorily, what can be read as a discourse of utopian critique. Speaking up from the Gaelic margins (Hutcheson, Hume, Smith, Ferguson and others), or from a threatened traditional culture (Shaftesbury), these thinkers denounce possessive individualism and bourgeois utility, insisting like Smith that the maladroit workings of reason can never render an object agreeable or disagreeable to the mind for its own sake. Before we have even begun to reason, there is already that faculty within us which makes us feel the sufferings of others as keenly as a wound, spurs us to luxuriate in another's joy with no sense of self-advantage, stirs us to detest cruelty and oppression like a hideous wound. The disgust we feel at the sight of tyranny or injustice is as previous to all rational calculation as the retching occasioned by some noxious food. The body is anterior to self-interested rationality, and will force its instinctual approbations and aversions upon our social practice. The vicious, Shaftesbury considers, must certainly be wretched; for how could someone violate the very core of his or her compassionate being and still be happy? The Hobbesian ideology is fatally flawed, and bound to come to grief: how can any vision survive which flattens all that makes men and women what they are – their tender delight in each other's well-being, their relish for human company as an end in itself – to this base caricature? If there is no developed language of political protest against such a travesty, then at least there is the aesthetic, the very sign and model of disinterestedness. Disinterestedness here means indifference not to others' interests, but to one's own. The aesthetic is the enemy of bourgeois egoism: to judge aesthetically means to bracket as far as possible one's own petty prejudices in the name of a common general humanity. It is in the act of taste above all, David Hume argues in his essay 'Of the Standard of Taste', that 'considering myself as a man in general, [I must] forget, if possible, my individual being, and my peculiar circumstances'.[10] Aesthetic disinterestedness involves a radical decentring of the subject, subduing its self-regard to a community of sensibility with others. It is thus in its vacuously idealist way the image of a generous new conception of social relations, the enemy of all sinister interests. Only the imagination, Adam Smith considers, can furnish an authentic bond between individuals, carrying us beyond the selfish compass of the senses into mutual solidarity: '[our senses] never did, and never can, carry us beyond our own person, and it is by the imagination only that we can form any conception of what are (the other's) sensations'.[11] The imagination is frailer than sense but stronger than reason: it is the precious key releasing the empiricist subject from the prison-house of its perceptions. If the access it allows us to others is poorer than direct bodily experience, it is at least more immediate than reason, for which the very reality of others is bound to remain a speculative fiction. To imagine is to have a kind of image, suspended somewhere between percept and concept, of what it feels like to be somebody else; and the moral sense philosophers are convinced that nothing less than this will ever be ideologically effective. Shaftesbury, Hutcheson and Hume are deeply sceptical of the power of mere rational comprehension to move men and women to politically virtuous action. From this viewpoint, the British rationalist thinkers emerge as dangerously deluded: purveyors of an abstract ethics, they wantonly elide the entire medium of senses and sentiments through which alone such imperatives could take on flesh in human lives. The aesthetic is in this sense the relay or transmission mechanism by which theory is converted to practice, the detour taken by ethical ideology through the feelings and senses so as to reappear as spontaneous social practice.

If to aestheticize morality is to make it ideologically effective, it is also to risk leaving it theoretically disarmed. 'Our ideas of morality, if this account is right', complains the rationalist Richard Price, 'have the same origin with our ideas of the sensible qualities of bodies, the harmony of sounds, or the beauties of painting and sculpture . . . Virtue (as those who embrace this scheme say) is an affair of taste. Moral right and wrong signify nothing *in the objects themselves* to which they are applied, any more than agreeable and harsh; sweet and bitter; pleasant and painful; but only *certain effects in us* . . . All our discoveries and boasted knowledge vanish, and the whole universe is reduced into a creature of fancy. Every sentiment of every being is equally just.'[12] Price is a militant anti-aesthetician, scandalized by this rampant subjectivizing of values. The senses and the imagination can take us nowhere in moral enquiry, but must yield to the understanding. Is torture wrong merely because we find it distasteful? If the moral, like the aesthetic, is a quality of our responses to the object, are actions mere blank texts coloured simply by our sentiments? And what if those sentiments disagree?

Unable to derive values from facts – which is to say, to ground moral ideology in bourgeois social practice – the moral sense theorists turn instead to the notion of value as autotelic. But they do this, so their opponents claim, at the cost of aestheticizing it away, dissolving it into the vagaries of subjectivism. In seeking to lodge an objective ethics more securely in the subject, they end up dissevering the two, leaving a delicate sensibility confronting a commodified object stripped of its inherent properties. To be sentimental is to consume less the object itself than one's own fine feelings about it. If ideology

40

is to work efficiently, it must be pleasurable, intuitive, self-ratifying: in a word, aesthetic. But this, in a striking paradox, is exactly what threatens to undermine its objective force. The very move of inserting ideology more deeply in the subject ends up by subverting itself. To aestheticize moral value is in one sense to display an enviable confidence: virtue consists fundamentally in being oneself. Yet it also betrays a considerable anxiety: virtue had better be its own reward, since in this sort of society it is unlikely to receive any other. We have something finer and subtler than the concept to bind us into mutuality, namely a sentiment which appears every bit as metaphysically founded as one's taste in stockings. To appeal to rational foundations, on the other hand, would seem little more of a solution in a society where a rational grasp of the whole, granted that it is even possible, seems to have little influence on actual behaviour. The ruling order is accordingly caught between a rational ethics which seems ideologically ineffectual, and an affectively persuasive theory which appears to rest on nothing more intellectually reputable than what Richard Price scornfully terms 'a species of mental taste'.

Shaftesbury's unity of ethics and aesthetics, virtue and beauty, is most evident in the concept of manners. Manners for the eighteenth century signify that meticulous disciplining of the body which converts morality to style, deconstructing the opposition between the proper and the pleasurable. In these regulated forms of civilized conduct, a pervasive aestheticizing of social practices gets under way: moral imperatives no longer impose themselves with the leaden weight of some Kantian duty, but infiltrate the very textures of lived experience as tact or know-how, intuitive good sense or inbred decorum. If the process of hegemony is to be successful, ethical ideology must lose its coercive force and reappear as a principle of spontaneous consensus within social life. The subject itself is accordingly aestheticized, living with all the instinctual rightness of the artefact. Like the work of art, the human subject introjects the codes which govern it as the very source of its free autonomy, and so comes in Althusserian phrase to work 'all by itself', without need of political constraint.[13] That 'lawfulness without a law' which Kant will find in the aesthetic representation is first of all a matter of the social *Lebenswelt*, which seems to work with all the rigorous encodement of a rational law, but where such a law is never quite abstractable from the concretely particular conduct which instantiates it.

41

The middle class has won certain historic victories within political society, by dint of long struggle; but the problem with such struggles is that, in rendering the Law perceptible as a discourse, they threaten to denaturalize it. Once the law of authority is objectified through political conflict, it becomes itself a possible object of contestation. Legal, political and economic transformations must therefore be translated into new forms of unthinking social practice, which in a kind of creative repression or amnesia can come to forget the very conventions they obey. It is thus that Hegel writes in the *Phenomenology of Spirit*, with a sardonic eye on subjectivism, of 'the blessed unity of the law with the heart'.[14] Structures of power must become structures of feeling; and the aesthetic is a vital mediation in this shift from property to propriety. Shaftesbury, comments Ernst Cassirer, requires a theory of beauty 'in order to answer the question of the true fashioning of character, of the law governing the structure of the inward personal world'.[15] 'Manners', writes Edmund Burke,

> are more important than laws. Upon them, in a great measure, the laws depend. The law touches us but here and there, and now and then. Manners are what vex and soothe, corrupt or purify, exalt or debase, barbarise or refine us . . . They give their whole form and colour to our lives. According to their quality, they add morals, they supply them, or they totally destroy them.[16]

We encounter the law, if we are lucky, only sporadically, as an unpleasantly coercive power; but in the aesthetics of social conduct, or 'culture' as it would later be called, the law is always with us, as the very unconscious structure of our life. If politics and aesthetics, virtue and beauty, are deeply at one, it is because pleasurable conduct is the true index of successful hegemony. A graceless virtue is thus something of a contradiction in terms, since virtue is that cultivation of the instinctive habit of goodness of which social fluency is the outward expression. The maladroit or aesthetically disproportioned thus signals in its modest way a certain crisis of political power.

If the aesthetic comes in the eighteenth century to assume the significance it does, it is because the word is shorthand for a whole project of hegemony, the massive introjection of abstract reason by the life of the senses. What matters is not in the first place art, but this

42

process of refashioning the human subject from the inside, informing its subtlest affections and bodily responses with this law which is not a law. It would thus ideally be as inconceivable for the subject to violate the injunctions of power as it would be to find a putrid odour enchanting. The understanding knows well enough that we live in conformity to impersonal laws; but in the aesthetic it is as though we can forget about all that – as though it is *we* who freely fashion the laws to which we subject ourselves. Human nature, writes Spinoza in his *Tractatus Theologico-Politicus*, 'will not submit to unlimited coercion', and the law must be accordingly framed to accommodate the interests and desires of those over whom it holds sway.[17]

The moment when moral actions can be classified chiefly as 'agreeable' or 'disagreeable', when these aesthetic terms will do service for more complex distinctions, marks a certain mature point of evolution in the history of a social class. Once the dust and heat of its struggles for political power have subsided, moral questions which were at that time necessarily cast in stridently absolutist terms may now be allowed to crystallize into routine response. Once new ethical habits have been installed and naturalized, the sheer quick feel or impression of an object will be enough for sure judgement, short-circuiting discursive contention and thus mystifying the rules which regulate it. If aesthetic judgement is every bit as coercive as the most barbarous law – for there is a right and a wrong to taste quite as absolute as the death sentence – this is not at all the way it feels. The social order has grown beyond the point where it was at every moment the subject of apocalyptic debate, and its rulers can now settle down to enjoying the fruits of their labour, shifting from polemic to pleasure. 'It has been the misfortune . . . of this age', Burke writes in *The French Revolution*, 'that everything is to be discussed, as if the constitution of our country were to be always a subject rather of altercation, than enjoyment.'[18] The most glorious work of art is the English Constitution itself, unformalizable yet ineluctable. Puritan utility will yield ground to an aestheticism of power only when society is redefined as an artefact, having no instrumental purpose beyond our self-delight. It is then that the strenuous habits of philosophy will give place to wit, that genteel act of *jouissance* in which a thought lives and dies in a single ludic moment. If one wished to name the most important cultural instrument of this hegemony in the nineteenth century, one which never ceases to grasp universal reason in

43

concretely particular style, uniting within itself an economy of abstract form with the effect of lived experience, one might do worse than name the realist novel. As Franco Moretti has written:

It is not enough that the social order is 'legal'; it must also appear *symbolically legitimate* . . . It is also necessary that, as a 'free individual', not as a fearful subject but as a convinced citizen, one perceives the social norms as *one's own*. One must internalise them and fuse external compulsion and internal impulse into a new unit until the former is no longer distinguishable from the latter. This fusion is what we usually call 'consent' or 'legitimation'. If the *Bildungsroman* appears to us still today as an essential, pivotal point of our history, this is because it has succeeded in representing this fusion with a force of conviction and optimistic clarity that will never be equalled again.[19]

The growing aestheticization of social life, then, represents a major hegemonic advance on the part of the governing bloc. But it is not, as we have seen, without its attendant dangers. Richard Price once more, in his *Review of Morals*: 'But what can be more evident, than that *right* and *pleasure*, *wrong* and *pain*, are as different as a cause and its effect; what is *understood*, and what is *felt*; absolute truth, and its *agreeableness* to the mind?'[20] Price is well aware of the perils of this subjectivizing current, as is his more celebrated namesake Fanny Price, heroine of *Mansfield Park*. To uphold moral standards in a dissolute social order, Fanny must to some degree sacrifice the aesthetically agreeable in her Kantian devotion to duty, which then renders the moral law visible in all its unlovely imperiousness. That this gesture is at once admirable and, from an ideal standpoint, something of a regrettable necessity is the sign of an ideological dilemma. In one sense, nothing could strengthen power more than its diffusion through the unconscious textures of everyday life. Yet in another sense this diffusion threatens fatally to undermine it, debasing its diktats to the level of enjoying an apple. 'Sensibility' seems at once the surest foundation, and no foundation at all.

But there is another danger too, which is quite as potentially harmful. German aesthetics was born as a kind of supplement to pure reason; but we have learned from Jacques Derrida that it is in the manner of such lowly supplements to end up supplanting what they are meant to subserve.[21] What if it were the case that not only morality, but cognition itself, was 'aesthetic'? That sensation and intuition, far from figuring as its opposites, were in fact its very basis? The name for this alarming claim in Britain is David Hume, who not content with reducing morality to mere sentiment, threatens also to reduce knowledge to fictional hypothesis, belief to an intense feeling, the continuity of the self to a fiction, causality to an imaginative construct and history to a kind of text.[22] Indeed Norman Kemp Smith holds that Hume's originality lies precisely in his inverting of the traditional priorities of reason and feeling, seeing Francis Hutcheson as the primary influence on his thought.[23] Hume brackets 'morals and criticism' together in the Introduction to his *Treatise of Human Nature*, and holds that morality 'consists not in any *matter of fact*, which can be discovered by the understanding . . . when you pronounce any action or character to be vicious, you mean nothing, but that from the constitution of your nature you have a feeling or sentiment of blame from the contemplation of it'.[24] Like other moral sense theorists, Hume argues in his *Enquiry Concerning the Principles of Morals* that 'virtue is an end, and is desirable on its own account, without fee and reward, merely for the immediate satisfaction which it conveys'.[25]

If Hume lends his support to the aestheticization of ethics, he also extends the gesture to the understanding. Probable reason, he claims in the *Treatise*, is nothing but a species of sentiment' (103), and belief is no more than 'a more vivid and intense conception of any idea' (120), 'more properly an act of the sensitive, than of the cogitative part of our natures' (183). All reasonings, he maintains, 'are nothing but the effect of custom; and custom has no influence, but by inlivening the imagination, and giving us a strong conception of any object' (149). It follows for the *Enquiry* that 'Custom, then, is the great guide of human life' (44), a case whose implications for political hegemony Edmund Burke will not be slow to seize on. Causality, in perhaps the most notorious of all Hume's doctrines, is radically subjectivized: it resides less in objects themselves than 'in the determination of the mind to pass from one to the other' (166), an impulse entirely conditioned by imaginative expectation. Continuous identity, somewhat similarly, is a quality which we attribute to things, a bond we feel rather than perceive. Hume speaks in a revealing aesthetic image of the mind as 'a kind of theatre, where several perceptions successively make their appearance; pass, re-pass, glide away, and mingle in an infinite variety of postures and situations' (253).

The imagination, indeed, is for Hume 'the ultimate judge of all systems of philosophy' (255). Lest this appear too fragile a basis on which to erect a theory, he instantly distinguishes between those imaginative principles which are 'permanent, irresistable [sic], and universal', and those which are 'changeable, weak, and irregular' (225). In the extraordinary Conclusion to the first book of the *Treatise*, however, we observe the poignant spectacle of this distinction crumbling away to nothing in his hands. Having laid out his system with aplomb, Hume breaks down before our eyes, turning helplessly to the reader in an access of anxiety. He feels himself to be 'some strange uncouth monster', expelled from all human society and 'left utterly abandon'd and disconsolate' (264). What possible foundation, he asks himself, does he have for these scandalous assertions, which would seem to shake rational enquiry to its very roots? If belief is no more than a vivacious sort of feeling, must not his belief that this is the case be no more than this too, boomeranging pointlessly on itself? 'After the most accurate and exact of my reasonings', he confesses, 'I can give no reason why I should assent to [this view]; and feel nothing but a *strong* propensity to consider objects *strongly* in that view, under which they appear to me' (265). There can be no appeal beyond experience and habit, which stimulate the imagination; and it is on these slender supports that all assent, and hence all social consensus, is based. 'The memory, senses, and understanding, are, therefore, all of them founded on the imagination, or the vivacity of our ideas' (265). In an intended addition to the *Treatise*, Hume acknowledges how completely this 'vivacity' slips through the conceptual net in the effort to distinguish between beliefs and fictions: 'when I would explain this *manner*, I scarce find any word that fully answers the case, but am oblig'd to have recourse to every one's feeling, in order to give him a perfect notion of this operation of the mind. An idea assented to *feels* different from a fictitious idea, that the fancy alone presents to us . . .' (629). The imagination, source of all knowledge, is, so Hume tells us, an 'inconsistent and fallacious' principle (265), which is why philosophy tends to come unstuck; two pages later, having just reduced reason to imagination, he protests that 'Nothing is more

46

dangerous to reason than the flights of the imagination, and nothing has been the occasion of more mistakes among philosophers' (267). The very principle of reason, in short, would seem the subversion of it. The clue to this apparent inconsistency lies in a distinction between wilder and more reliable forms of imagining: we must reject 'all the trivial suggestions of the fancy, and adhere to the understanding, that is, to the more general and more established properties of the imagination' (267). What will rescue us from the imagination is reason, which is just another version of it; the imagination must be rejected for – the imagination.

This deconstruction is then in turn deconstructed. The understanding, when it acts alone, 'entirely subverts itself': it consists in nothing more than a dizzying infinite regress, in which we check the probability of our assertions, then check our checking and then check that, at each stage moving further away from the original evidence and introducing fresh uncertainties. What can arrest this abysmal plunge into scepticism is, of all things, the imagination, which in the form of customary sentiment induces us to view 'certain objects in a stronger and fuller light, upon account of their customary connexion with a present impression' (183). What we feel of the certainty of the near, in other words, countervails the infinite regress of understanding; it is beneficial that our beliefs are based on feeling, on some 'sensation or peculiar manner of conception' (184), for if they were not there would be nothing to stop reason spiralling ceaselessly down its own indeterminacies, one doubt doubting another to infinity. However, in so far as this clinging to the near which arrests reason's self-destruction is itself a 'singular and seemingly trivial property of the fancy' (268), it belongs to exactly the kind of inferior imagination which Hume has just told us constitutes the chief threat to reason.

Either, then, we may dismiss all elaborate processes of reasoning out of hand, adhering to what feels closest and surest; or we may cling, whatever its perils, to a sophisticated rationality. The former option is not only unpleasantly drastic, cutting us off at a stroke from all science and philosophy, but self-contradictory, since it is only by an elaborate process of reasoning that we arrive at it. If we stay faithful to reason, however, we land up with the self-undoing cognitions of the sceptic, and so might as well not have bothered. 'We have, therefore,' Hume remarks gloomily, 'no choice left but betwixt a false reason and none at all' (268). His solution to the dilemma is, in effect, to forget about it, since the problem is itself an instance of highly refined reasoning, and 'Very refined reflections have little or no influence upon us' (268). Practical people do well not to become engrossed by such metaphysical questions – though we can hardly formulate this as a universal imperative, since this is precisely part of what is in doubt. Hume's solution, in brief, is a carefully cultivated false consciousness, which consigns the whole vexed affair to comfortable oblivion: he goes off to play backgammon and make merry with his friends, and will later find his own speculations so ridiculous that he has no heart to pursue them further. Rather like some contemporary sceptics in the field of literary theory, one continues to catch trains and rear one's children, cook food and lace one's boots, in cavalier disregard of one's theoretical doubts about the ontological solidity of all this. Theory and practice, far from being mutually supportive, are entirely at odds, so that for Hume only some form of Nietzschean amnesia would seem to hold society together. It is a sobering thought, however, that society survives only by dint of intellectual suicide, and Hume is understandably rattled by his own defensive strategy. Customary practice no longer mediates absolute norms, but actually substitutes itself for them. Practices must provide their own rationales, and theory, far from securing them, now actively disables them. If intuition persuades you that there is truth, theory informs you that there is just intuition. In an ironic reversal, society itself, which works by custom and blind sentiment in the manner of Nietzsche's healing Apollonian illusions, assumes that there is somewhere some solid ground for its conduct, which philosophy can supply; philosophy, supposed to demonstrate such grounds, brutally whittles them away to custom and sentiment. Paradoxically, the philosopher is an anti-social monstrosity precisely because he reduces ideas to social practices – because his thought imitates how society actually is. Society itself, by contrast, is remorselessly metaphysical, gullibly convinced that its opinions have some unimpeachable basis. The layperson in fact lives by habit but trusts that there is more to the world than this; the philosopher faithfully reflects the pragmatic truth of this condition, and so becomes an outcast from it. He is a monster not because he comes bearing some outlandish message from beyond the social pale, but because he arrives hotfoot with the rather more disturbing news that the habits of human nature are all there is. The hairy prophet howling in the wilderness is the one who discloses the dreadful secret that backgammon is more or less what it comes down to. The sole lame justification Hume can then find for philosophy is that it is relatively toothless – less socially disruptive, for example, than religious superstition. If the metaphysical is a natural possibility of the mind, if humanity cannot rest content with its narrow circuit of sense impressions, then better for it to fantasize in the 'mild and moderate' style we term philosophy, than to cook up dangerously fanatical schemes. Philosophy may be somewhat absurd, but at least it is unlikely to topple the state.

We seem, then, to have traced a kind of circle. Reason, having spun off with Baumgarten the subaltern discourse of aesthetics, now appears to have been swallowed up by it. The rational and the sensuous, far from reproducing one another's inner structure, have ended up wholly at odds. 'Thus there is', Hume comments in the *Treatise*, 'a direct and total opposition betwixt our reason and our senses' (231). Striving to incarnate themselves in daily practice, rational ordinances are now at risk of being reduced to it. Reason seeks in the aesthetic to encompass the experiential; but what, to paraphrase Nietzsche, if experience were a woman? What if it were that elusive thing that plays fast and loose with the concept? At once intimate and unreliable, precious and precarious, experience would seem to have all the duplicity of the eternal female. It is this treacherous terrain that Baumgarten must subject to reason. The British moral sense thinkers follow a more liberal path: the feminine, in the form of pure intuition, is a surer guide to moral truth than the masculine cult of calculative reason. But such intuitions do not hang in the air: they are the inscription within us of a providential logic too sublime for rational decipherment. The feminine is thus no more than a passage or mode of access to the masculine regime of Reason, whose sway, whatever the alarmed protests of rationalists like Price, remains largely unchallenged in most moral sense philosophy. It will not prove very hard, however, to kick away this providential platform altogether; and this in effect is what happens in Hume, who has little patience with the metaphysical baggage tied to the moral sense by some of his colleagues. Hume takes over something of Francis Hutcheson's ethics but strips that case of its strongly providential cast, substituting for this the harder-headed idea of social utility. The experience of beauty for Hume is a kind of sympathy arising from reflected utility: the aesthetically appealing object pleases by virtue of its uses to the species as a whole. His essay 'Of the Standard of Taste' suggests just how unstable such aesthetic criteria are: 'the sentiments of men', he writes, 'often differ with regard to beauty and deformity',[26] and though he is insistent that there are indeed universal standards of taste, it is not easy for him to say where they are to be found. Some aesthetic conflicts, the essay ends by acknowledging, are simply irresolvable, 'and we seek in vain for a standard, by which we can reconcile the contrary sentiments'.[27] Indeed Hume seeks in vain for a sure standard in anything. Knowledge, belief, ethics: all these have now been remorselessly 'feminized', converted one by one to feeling, imagination, intuition.

Not only these, indeed, but the whole material foundation of the bourgeois social order. Hume finds no metaphysical sanction underpinning private property, which depends like everything else on the imagination. Our relentlessly metonymic minds simply find it natural to make a permanent state of affairs out of somebody's possessing something at a particular time. We also tend to make a natural imaginative connection between objects we own and others contiguous to them, like the work of our slaves or the fruits of our garden, which we therefore feel we can claim as well. (Since the imagination passes more easily from small to great rather than *vice versa*, it might seem more logical for a small proprietor to annex a larger contiguous object rather than the other way round; so Hume has to engage in a deft piece of philosophical footwork to justify, for example, the British possession of Ireland.) If all of this naturalizes possessive individualism, it also scandalously demystifies all talk of metaphysical rights. There is no inherent reason why my property should not be yours tomorrow, were it not for that imaginative inertia which makes it easier to associate it with me. Since the idea of my constant possession of a thing is imaginatively closer to my actual possession of it than than is the notion of your ownership of it, the indolence of the imagination tends conveniently to confirm my possession in perpetuity. Hume, in other words, is fully conscious of the fictional nature of the bourgeois economy, blandly proclaiming that property 'is not any thing real in the objects, but is the offspring of the sentiments . . .' (509). The whole of bourgeois society is based on metaphor, metonymy, imaginary correspondence:

The same love of order and uniformity, which arranges the books in a library, and the chairs in a parlour, contributes to the formation of society, and to the well-being of mankind, by modifying the general rule concerning the stability of possession. As property forms a relation betwixt a person and an object, 'tis natural to found it on some preceding relation; and as property is nothing but a constant possession, secur'd by the laws of society, 'tis natural to add it to the present possession which is a relation that resembles it. (504–5n)

What guarantees the property rights of the middle class is less the law of economics than the instinctual economizing of the mind.

If imagination is in this way the unstable foundation of civil society, it is, curiously enough, a lack of imagination which forms the basis of the political state. Since individuals are governed largely by self-interest, their imaginative sympathy with what lies beyond this narrow circuit tends to be feeble; so that though they all share an interest in maintaining social justice, it is one they are likely to feel only dimly. Objects close to us strike us with more imaginative force than those more distant; and the state is a regulative mechanism which compensates for this parochial deficiency, composed as it is of individuals who have a direct interest in ensuring the observance of justice. Politics springs from a failure of imagination; civil society is anchored in it; and so also is the realm of moral or interpersonal relations. Pity and compassion, the very ground of our social solidarity, involve an imaginative empathy with others, for Hume as much as for Adam Smith. 'All human creatures are related to us by resemblance. Their persons, therefore, their interests, their passions, their pains and pleasures must strike upon us in a lively manner, and produce an emotion similar to the original one; since a lively idea is easily converted into an impression' (369). Relations with others involve a kind of inner artistic miming of their inward condition, a set of imaginary correspondences; and Hume illustrates his point with an aesthetic image, that of the sympathy for suffering we experience when watching tragic drama.

Society, then, is based on a faculty which in its 'proper' functioning ensures stability and continuity, but which as Hume recognizes carries within it the permanent structural possibility of prejudice and extravagant fantasy. The principle of social cohesion is thus at the same time a source of potential anarchy. If this 'feminine' aestheticizing is alarming, however, it has a 'masculine' counterpart which is equally problematic. Like Joseph Butler or Immanuel Kant, one can appeal away from sentiment to a moral duty which has no direct relation to human pleasure or happiness. But this is to replace one kind of 'aesthetic' morality with a different kind: it leaves morality, like the artefact, self-grounding and self-determining, a lofty end in itself beyond all utility. Womanly feeling is thus ousted by the phallic absolutism of conscience and the inner light. In neither case can moral values be derived from concrete social relations: either they must be validated by instinct, or they must validate themselves.

It is not surprising, given what is at stake in these debates, that Edmund Burke should begin his work on the sublime and the beautiful by seeking to defend the possibility of a science of taste. If beauty is merely relative, then the bonds which leash society together are in danger of loosening. Beauty for Burke is not just a question of art:

> I call beauty a social quality; for when men and women, and not only they, but when other animals give us a sense of joy and pleasure in beholding them (and there are many that do so), they inspire us with sentiments of tenderness and affection towards their persons; we like to have them near us, and we enter willingly into a kind of relation with them, unless we should have strong reasons to the contrary.[28]

Burke is quite confident that such taste is uniform and universal: 'I never remember that anything beautiful, whether a man, a beast, a bird, or a plant, was ever shown, though it were to a hundred people, that they did not all immediately agree that it was beautiful . . .' (70). If aesthetic judgement is unstable, then so must be the social sympathies founded on it, and with them the whole fabric of political life. Uniformity of taste for Burke must be dependent on a uniformity of the senses themselves; but he is realistic enough to recognize that the senses are actually variable, and aesthetic responses accordingly divergent. Burke's political conservatism is thus to some degree at odds with his empiricist psychology. These discrepancies of response, however, can be laid at the door of individuals themselves, rather than of taste itself, which remains self-identical throughout its manifold irregular expressions. 'Whilst we consider taste merely according to its nature and species, we shall find its principles entirely uniform; but the degree in which these principles prevail, in the several individuals of mankind, is altogether as different as the principles themselves are similar' (78). It is as though human size is absolutely unalterable, even though individuals happen to be of different heights.

What knits society together for Burke, as with Hume, is the aesthetic phenomenon of mimesis, which is a matter more of custom than of law: 'It is by imitation, far more than by precept, that we learn everything; and what we learn thus, we acquire not only more effectually, but more pleasantly. This forms our manners, our opinions, our lives. It is one of the strongest links of society; it is a species of mutual compliance, which all men yield to each other without constraint to themselves, and which is extremely flattering to all' (101). Laws or precepts are simply derivatives of what is first nurtured through customary practice, and coercion is thus secondary to consent. We become human subjects by pleasurably imitating practical forms of social life, and in the enjoyment of this lies the relation which binds us hegemonically to the whole. To mime is to submit to a law, but one so gratifying that freedom lies in such servitude. Such consensuality is less an artificial social contract, laboriously wrought and maintained, than a kind of spontaneous metaphor or perpetual forging of resemblances. The only problem is where all this imitating ends: social life for Burke would appear a kind of infinite chain of representations of representations, without ground or origin. If we do as others do, who do the same, then all of these copies would seem to lack a transcendental original, and society is shattered to a wilderness of mirrors.

This ceaseless mutual mirroring has about it something of the stasis of the imaginary, and if taken too literally would spell the death of difference and history. 'Although imitation is one of the great instruments used by Providence in bringing our nature towards its perfection, yet if men gave themselves up to imitation entirely, and each followed the other, and so on in an eternal circle, it is easy to see that there could never be any improvement amongst them' (102). The very conditions which guarantee social order also paralyse it: sunk in this narcissistic closure, men of affairs grow effete and enervated, sympathy becomes cloying and incestuous, and beauty sinks to a by-word for stagnation. Some countervailing energy is therefore necessary, which Burke discovers in the virile strenuousness of the sublime. 'To prevent this [complacency], God has planted in man a sense of ambition, and a satisfaction arising from the contemplation of his excelling his fellows in something deemed valuable amongst them' (102). The sublime is on the side of enterprise, rivalry and individuation: it is a phallic 'swelling' arising from our confrontation of danger, although a danger we encounter figuratively, vicariously, in the pleasurable knowledge that we cannot actually be harmed. In this sense, the sublime is a suitably defused, aestheticized version of the values of the *ancien régime*. It is as though those traditionalist patrician virtues of daring, reverence and free-booting ambition must be at once cancelled and preserved within middle-class life. As actual qualities, they must be outlawed by a state devoted to domestic peace; but to avoid spiritual emasculation they must still be fostered within it in the displaced form of aesthetic experience. The sublime is an imaginary compensation for all the uproarious old upper-class violence, tragedy repeated as comedy. It is beauty's point of inner fracture, a negation of settled order without which any order would grow inert and wither. The sublime is the anti-social condition of all sociality, the infinitely unrepresentable which spurs us on to yet finer representations, the lawless masculine force which violates yet perpetually renews the feminine enclosure of beauty. Its social connotations are interestingly contradictory: in one sense the memory trace of an historically surpassed barbarism, it also has something of the challenge of mercantile enterprise to a too-clubbable aristocratic indolence. Within the figure of the sublime, warring barons and busy speculators merge to prod society out of its specular smugness. These, it may be noted, are the political thoughts of a man who as a child attended a hedge school in County Cork.

As a kind of terror, the sublime crushes us into admiring submission; it thus resembles a coercive rather than a consensual power, engaging our respect but not, as with beauty, our love: 'we submit to what we admire, but we love what submits to us; in one case we are forced, in the other flattered, into compliance' (161). The distinction between the beautiful and the sublime, then, is that between woman and man; but it is also the difference between what Louis Althusser had called the ideological and the repressive state apparatuses.[29] For Althusser, the repressive institutions of society would seem to be purely negative; it is in ideology alone that we are constructed as subjects. For Burke, a more subtle political theorist in this respect, this opposition can be to some extent deconstructed. The sublime may terrorize us into cowed submission, but since we are all constitutional masochists who delight in being humiliated, this coerciveness contains the pleasures of the consensual as well as the pains of constraint. 'Sensations of a pleasurable nature have nothing inherently impelling about them', writes Sigmund Freud in *The Ego and the Id*, 'whereas unpleasurable ones have it in the highest degree. The latter impel towards change, towards discharge, and that is why we interpret unpleasure as implying a heightening and pleasure as a lowering of energetic cathexis.'[30] Conversely, the beauty which wins our free consent, and beguiles us like a woman, is based nevertheless on a kind of cunningly dissimulated law.

Burke confesses that he can see no way of uniting these two registers, which clearly poses a political problem. The dilemma is that the authority we love we do not respect, and the one we respect we do not love. 'The authority of a father, so useful to our well-being, and so justly venerable upon all accounts, hinders us from having that entire love for him that we have for our mothers, where the parental authority is almost melted down into the mother's fondness and indulgence' (159). The political paradox is plain: only love will truly win us to the law, but this love will erode the law to nothing. A law attractive enough to engage our intimate affections, and so hegemonically effective, will tend to inspire in us a benign contempt. On the other hand, a power which rouses our filial fear, and hence our submissive obedience, is likely to alienate our affections and so spur us to Oedipal resentment. Casting around desperately for a reconciling image, Burke offers us, of all things, the figure of the grandfather, whose male authority is enfeebled by age into a 'feminine partiality'. Mary Wollstonecraft is quick to assail the sexism of Burke's argument in her *Vindication of the Rights of Men*. His distinction between love and respect, she points out, aestheticizes women in ways which remove them from the sphere of morality. 'The affection [women] excite, to be uniform and perfect, should not be tinctured with the respect which the moral virtues inspire, lest pain should be blended with pleasure, and admiration disturb the soft intimacy of love.'[31] 'This laxity of morals in the female', Wollstonecraft continues, 'is certainly more captivating to a libertine imagination than the cold arguments of reason, that give no sex to virtue. But should experience prove that there is a beauty in virtue, a charm in order, which necessarily implies exertion, a depraved sensual taste may give way to a more manly one – and *melting* feelings to rational satisfactions.'[32] For Wollstonecraft, Burke is a kind of aesthete who divorces beauty (woman) from moral truth (man); against this, she argues at once that virtue is sexless and that it involves a manly taste. We shall see, however, that Burke is not so much an aesthete as an aestheticizer, which makes a significant difference.

Authority, then, lives in a kind of ceaseless self-undoing, as coercion and consent reinforce yet undermine one another. An enervate beauty must be regularly shattered by a sublime whose terrors must in turn be quickly defused, in a constant rhythm of erection and detumescence. At the heart of power lies the oxymoron 'free bondage', of which the aesthetic is a vital symbol. The greater the freedom the deeper the bondage; but the more, by the same token, spontaneity can get out of hand. The more the human subject works 'all by itself', the better – and the worse – for authority. If freedom transgresses the submission which is its very condition, the repressiveness of the sublime can be invoked; but this ultimate efficacy of power is also its potential downfall, breeding as well as subduing rebellion. Power is thus a kind of riddle, of which the mystery of the aesthetic, with its impossibly lawless lawfulness, is an apt sign.

The aesthetic experience of the sublime is confined to the cultivated few; and there would thus seem the need for a kind of poor person's version of it. Religion is of course one obvious such candidate; but Burke also proposes another, which is, surprisingly enough, the lowly activity of labour. Like the sublime, labour is a masochistic affair, since we find work at once painful in its exertion yet pleasurable in its arousal of energy. 'As common labour, which is a mode of pain, is the exercise of the grosser, a model of terror is the exercise of the finer parts of the system' (181). The sublime, with its 'delightful horror', is the rich man's labour, invigorating an otherwise dangerously complacent ruling class. If that class cannot know the uncertain pleasures of loading a ship, it can gaze instead at one tossed on the turbulent ocean. Providence has so arranged matters that a state of rest becomes soon obnoxious, breeding melancholy and despair; we are thus naturally driven to work, reaping enjoyment from its surmounting of difficulties. Labour involves a gratifying coerciveness, and is thus an aesthetic experience all in itself, at least for those who theorize about it. Both material production and political life, base and superstructure, display a unity of force and fulfilment. Hegemony is not only a matter of the political state, but is installed within the labour process itself. Our wrestling with Nature's recalcitrance is itself a kind of socialized sublime; and this agreeableness of labour is even more gratifying to those who profit from it.

What the aesthetic in Burke sets its face most firmly against is the notion of natural rights. It is precisely that drily theoretic discource, a revolutionary one in his day, that the appeal to the intimate habits of the body is out to worst. The essay on the beautiful and the sublime is a subtle phenomenology of the senses, a mapping of the body's delicacies and disgusts: Burke is fascinated by what happens when we hear low vibrations or stroke smooth surfaces, by the dilation of the eye's pupil in darkness or the feel of a slight tap on the shoulder. He is much preoccupied with sweet smells and violent startings from sleep, with the vibratory power of salt and the question of whether proportion is the source of beauty in vegetables. All of this strange homespun psycho-physiology is a kind of politics, willing to credit no theoretical notion which cannot somehow be traced to the muscular structure of the eye or the texture of the fingerpads. If there are indeed metaphysical rights, then they enter this dense somatic space as dispersed and non-identical: like 'rays of light which pierce into a dense medium', Burke argues in *Reflections on the French Revolution*, such rights are 'by the laws of nature, refracted from their straight line', enduring 'such a variety of refractions and reflections, that it becomes absurd to talk of them as if they continued in the simplicity of their original direction'.[33] What is natural about such rights is their deviance or aberrancy; their self-disseminatory power is part of their very essence. When Burke adds that 'the nature of man is intricate; the objects of society are of the greatest possible complexity', he speaks, in the original sense of the term, as an aesthetician.

It is not that Burke rejects all concept of the rights of man. It is less that such rights do not exist than that they are incapable of definition.

57

'The rights of man are in a sort of *middle*, incapable of definition, but not impossible to be discerned.'[34] They are, in short, just like the laws of the artefact, indubitably present yet impossible to abstract from their particular incarnations. Tradition, for Burke, is equally a kind of lawfulness without law. The true danger of the revolutionaries is that as fanatical anti-aestheticians they offer to reduce hegemony to naked power. They are Protestant extremists who would believe insanely that men and women could look on this terrible law in all its nakedness and still live, who would strip from it every decent mediation and consoling illusion, break every representational icon and extirpate every pious practice, thus leaving the wretched citizen helpless and vulnerable before the full sadistic blast of authority. Angered by this iconoclasm, Burke speaks up instead for what Gramsci will later term 'hegemony':

> But now all is to be changed. All the pleasing illusions, which made power gentle and obedience liberal, which harmonised assimilation, incorporated into politics the sentiments which beautify and soften private society, are to be dissolved by this new conquering empire of light and reason. All the decent drapery of life is to be rudely torn off. All the superadded ideas, furnished from the wardrobe of a moral imagination, which the heart owns, and the understanding ratifies, as necessary to cover the defect of our naked, shivering nature, and to raise it to dignity in our own estimation, are to be exploded as a ridiculous, absurd, and antiquated fashion.[35]

With the executed Marie Antoinette in mind, Burke goes on to denounce revolutionary discourtesy to women: 'All homage paid to the sex in general as such, and without distinct views, is to be regarded as romance and folly.' The law is male, but hegemony is a woman; this transvestite law, which decks itself out in female drapery, is in danger of having its phallus exposed. Power is ceasing to be aestheticized: what grapples individuals to it on this radical view is less their affections than the gallows. The whole crucial middle region of social life between state and economy, the rich tapestry of customs which transmute laws to feelings, is being disastrously abandoned.

These public sentiments, combined with manners, are required sometimes as supplements, sometimes as correctives, always as aids to law. The precept given by a wise man, as well as a great critic, for the construction of poems, is equally true as to states: *Non satis est pulchra esse poemata, dulcia sunto*. There ought to be a system of manners in every nation, which a well-formed mind would be disposed to relish. To make us love our country, our country ought to be lovely.[36]

Woman, the aesthetic and political hegemony are now in effect synonymous.

We can return in the light of this to the quarrel between Burke and Mary Wollstonecraft. It is not quite true, as Wollstonecraft suggests, that Burke is an aesthete concerned to divorce beauty from moral truth. On the contrary, he wishes to *aestheticize* such truth, in order to render it securely hegemonic. Woman, or beauty, thus becomes a kind of mediation of man; but what Wollstonecraft rightly sees is that this process does not operate in reverse. Beauty must be included within the sublimity of the masculine law, in order to soften its rigours, but moral sublimity is not to be included within the beautiful. Women are indeed in this sense excluded from the domain of truth and morality. Burke deconstructs the opposition between beauty and truth, but only partially and unilaterally. Beauty is necessary for power, but does not itself contain it; authority has need of the very femininity it places beyond its bounds.

Burke's plea for the aesthetic is not to be mistaken for some errant subjectivism. Though he believes strongly in an intuitive response antecedent to reason, he is stern on what he takes to be a pernicious aestheticizing of moral value, and fulminates in his essay on aesthetics against 'an infinite deal of whimsical theory' which has 'misled us both in the theory of taste and of morals' (159). We must not be induced by these fanciful flights to 'remove the science of our duties from their proper basis (our reason, our relations, and our necessities) to rest it upon foundations altogether visionary and unsubstantial' (159). When it comes to moral ideology, Burke is quite as absolute and objectivist as any rationalist: it is just that, like the moral sense theorists, he cannot believe that any power not appropriated by experience, lived on the body, will move men and women to their proper civic duties. But Shaftesbury, as we have seen, was a strong moral realist too, holding that virtue resides in the nature of things rather than in custom, fancy or will. The moral relativism which others feared in him was exactly what he himself denounced in the work of his tutor John Locke, who 'struck at all fundamentals, threw all order and virtue out of the world and made the very ideas of these . . . *unnatural* and without foundation in our minds'.[37] Francis Hutcheson, equally, distinguishes between rather than simply conflates the moral and aesthetic senses: to assert that we possess a moral sense as intuitive as the aesthetic is not to identify the one with the other. And David Hume, like Shaftesbury, believes that taste involves a firm commitment to the rational. For both men, false taste can be corrected by argument and reflection, as the understanding comes to intervene in the process of feeling. There is no question with any of these thinkers of some wholesale abandonment of head for heart.

Even so, the general tendency of this current of thought can be seen as a steady undermining of the mind in the name of the body; and the political consequences of this are ambivalent. On the one hand, there is surely no doubt that to affirm the claims of affective experience against a ruthlessly exclusivist reason is in principle progressive. The very emergence of the aesthetic marks in this sense a certain crisis of traditional reason, and a potentially liberating or utopian trend of thought. By the end of the eighteenth century, such appeals to feeling will have become identified as dangerously radical. There is in the aesthetic an ideal of compassionate community, of altruism and natural affection, which along with a faith in the self-delighting individual represents an affront to ruling-class rationalism. On the other hand, it might be claimed that such a movement comes eventually to represent a devastating loss for the political left. From Burke and Coleridge to Matthew Arnold and T. S. Eliot, the aesthetic in Britain is effectively captured by the political right. The autonomy of culture, society as expressive or organic totality, the intuitive dogmatism of the imagination, the priority of local affections and unarguable allegiances, the intimidatory majesty of the sublime, the incontrovertible character of 'immediate' experience, history as a spontaneous growth impervious to rational analysis: these are some of the forms in which the aesthetic becomes a weapon in the hands of political reaction. Lived experience, which can offer a powerful critique of Enlightenment rationality, can also be the very homeland of conservative ideology. The clear bold light of republican rationalism, and the intimate affective depths of the poetic, come to figure throughout the nineteenth century as effective antinomies. Tom Paine's plain-minded scoffing at Burke's extravagantly metaphorical diction is an earlier case in point: 'Mr. Burke', he comments in *The Rights of Man*, 'should recollect that he is writing history and not *plays*, and that his readers will expect truth, and not the spouting rant of high-toned exclamation.'[38] Mary Wollstonecraft writes scathingly of Burke's 'pampered sensibility', viewing his reason as 'the weather-cock of unrestrained feelings' and his cast of mind as lamentably effeminate. 'Even the ladies, Sir,' she mocks, 'may repeat your sprightly sallies, and retail in theatrical attitudes many of your sentimental exclamations.'[39] Her own definition of the rights of man, so she proclaims, will be by contrast a 'manly' one.

After the work of Blake and Shelley, myth and symbol in English literature becomes increasingly a preserve of the political right, and 'political poetry' an effective oxymoron. The discourse of radical rationalism would seem peculiarly resistant to the aesthetic – resistant, that is to say, to what are now the hegemonic definitions of art. There can be little truck between an analytic language of political dissent and those subtly sensuous intensities which are now coming to monopolize the meaning of poetry. At the same time, the aesthetic clearly cannot serve as a dominant ideology for the middle class, which in the turmoil of industrial capitalist accumulation will need something a good deal more solid than sentiment and intuition to secure its rule. Sentimentalism, from the standpoint of Victorian England, will appear increasingly as the badge of an earlier, somewhat more serenely self-possessed bourgeoisie, which had yet to endure the cataclysms of political revolution abroad and industrial trans-formation at home. It is, of course, still intensively cultivated on the side; but the ruling ideology of Victorian England is a virulently anti-aesthetic Utilitarianism, belated offspring of Enlightenment rationalism. Self-interest wins out over moral sense, as custom, tradition and sensibility are subjected to the cold light of rational critique. Yet it is not easy to see how this bloodlessly analytic ideology can actually be lived: if the Benthamite subject must laboriously calculate the probable consequences of each of its actions, how can social practices ever be effectively naturalized? What has become of habit and virtue, spontaneous impulse and the political unconscious? And how, shorn of these features, can this upstart doctrine ever achieve moral hegemony? Alarmed by these lacunae, John Stuart Mill turns to a synthesis of the rationalist and aesthetic traditions, reviving the language of Burkeian hegemony: '[Benthamism] will do nothing . . . for the spiritual interests of society; nor does it suffice of itself even for the material interests. That which alone causes any material interests to exist, which alone enables any body of human beings to exist as a society, is national character . . . A philosophy of laws and institutions, not founded on a philosophy of national character, is an absurdity . . .'[40] Bentham, Mill claims, errs in considering only the moral aspect of human conduct, whereas one must also have regard to its aesthetic (beautiful) and sympathetic (lovable) qualities. If the error of sentimentalism is to set the last two over against the first, the disaster of an unreconstructed Utilitarianism is to ditch them entirely. All that remains to be done, then, is to dovetail Bentham and Coleridge together, viewing each as the other's 'completing counterpart'. It is as though a structural contradiction in ruling-class ideology can be resolved by holding a different book in either hand.

Yet Mill's gesture is not as idly academicist as it seems. It is true that the industrial middle class, with its aridly instrumentalist doctrines, is incapable of generating under its own steam a persuasive aesthetics – unable, that is, to develop the styles and forms which would weave its unlovely power into the fabric of everyday life. To do this it must look elsewhere, to what Antonio Gramsci termed the 'traditional' intellectuals; and this, in the evolution from the later Coleridge to John Ruskin and Matthew Arnold, is exactly what takes place. The uneasy nineteenth-century alliance of patrician and philistine, culture and society, is among other things the tale of an ideology in search of hegemony – of a spiritually disabled bourgeoisie constrained to go to school with an aestheticizing right which speaks of organic unity, intuitive certainty and the free play of the mind. That this aesthetic lineage also produces a powerful idealist critique of bourgeois utility is the other side of the story; if philistine and patrician are allied in some ways, they are at loggerheads in others. Indeed the relations between them are an exemplary case of the fraught connection between facts and values. The only truly compelling moral ideology is one which succeeds in grounding itself to some degree in real material conditions; if it fails to do so, its idealism will prove a constant source of political embarrassment. Discourses of ideal value too palpably dissevered from the way men and women actually experience their social conditions merely mark their own redundancy, and are thus politically vulnerable. This is a progressive problem for the nineteenth-century middle class, which is still deeply dependent upon certain metaphysical values for its ideological legitimation, but which is in danger of subverting some of those very values by the nature of its material activities. Its secularizing, rationalizing practices are bringing many traditional pieties, not least religious ones, into increasing discredit; and in this sense the nature of the 'base' is perilously at odds with the requirements of the 'superstructure'. The Kantian critique of metaphysics marks the point at which it has become theoretically difficult to justify many of the doctrines on which, in its routine ideological practices, the ruling order still relies. Industrial capitalism can by no means brusquely discount 'spiritual' values; but such values will come to have about them an increasingly hollow, implausible ring. As far as the Victorian bourgeoisie is concerned, the nostalgic neo-feudalism of a Carlyle or a Ruskin can be neither credited nor entirely disowned: eccentric and risibly unreal though such visions may be, they are nevertheless a source of ideological stimulus and moral edification which the market place, at least for the lower orders, is distressingly unable to provide.

The aesthetic is one answer to this vexed question of how values are to be derived, in a condition where neither civil society nor the political state would seem to provide such values with a particularly plausible foundation. We have seen already some of the difficulties involved for the middle class in founding its spiritual solidarity on the degraded basis of civil society; and an alternative strategy is therefore to turn in Arnoldian style to the state, as the ideal locus of 'culture'. Throughout the nineteenth century, many a thinker had recourse to this apparently promising solution. It has, however, one signal drawback: the fact that the state is ultimately a coercive apparatus, and so at odds with the ideal of a community which would be gratifyingly unconstrained. The whole point of aesthetic taste, as a model of spiritual community, is that it cannot be forced. If, then, value is increasingly hard to derive either from the way the world is or from the way it might feasibly become; if civil society is too lowly a habitation for it and the metaphysical too lofty a one, then there would seem no alternative but to acknowledge such value's profound mysteriousness. 'Moral sense' is equivalent to confessing that there is no longer any rationally demonstrable basis for value, even if we nevertheless continue to experience it. Morality, like aesthetic taste, becomes a *je ne sais quoi*: we just know what is right and wrong, as we know that Homer is superb or that someone is standing on our foot. Such a viewpoint combines the dogmatism of all appeals to intuition or 'felt experience' with a serenely pre-Freudian trust in the subject's immediate presence to itself.

One aestheticizing response to the problematic origins of value is thus to root value in the delicacies of the affective body. Another, sharply different aestheticizing strategy is to found value not in sensibility, but in itself. In this perspective, value is not anything one could ever get *behind*, reduce to a more fundamental order or principle; it is radically self-derivative, a law unto itself which bows to no external determination. This, in effect, is the standpoint of Kant's second *Critique*, for which the moral law is wholly autonomous. One should be good not because it is pleasant or practical, but because it is moral to be so, in the sense that reason has an interest in its own practical function. Such a case draws not upon the aesthetic as affective – indeed it sets its face sternly against all mere sensibility – but upon the aesthetic as autotelic: as that which in divine fashion bears its ends entirely within itself, generates itself up miraculously out of its own substance. This move, to be sure, secures value absolutely; but it does so at the dire cost of threatening to remove it from the material world in which it is supposed to be active. As with the early Wittgenstein, value is in a certain sense no longer *in* the world at all. If value is thus inviolable, it is partly because it is invisible. The governing order would consequently seem left with little choice but to subjectivize value, thus drawing it rather too close for comfort to the relativistic flux of daily life, or to seal it off from that sphere in a splendid autonomy not easily distinguishable from sheer impotence. Once more, it is the dilemma of either entrusting value to the mercies of everyday civil society, or alienating it to an Olympian height where it will merely succeed in measuring the disabling distance between itself and the actual world.

In a notable historical irony, the birth of aesthetics as an intellectual discourse coincides with the period when cultural production is beginning to suffer the miseries and indignities of commodification.

The peculiarity of the aesthetic is in part spiritual compensation for this degradation: it is just when the artist is becoming debased to a petty commodity producer that he or she will lay claim to transcendent genius. But there is another reason for the foregrounding of the artefact which aesthetics achieves. What art is now able to offer, in that ideological reading of it known as the aesthetic, is a paradigm of more general social significance – an image of self-referentiality which in an audacious move seizes upon the very functionlessness of artistic practice and transforms it to a vision of the highest good. As a form of value grounded entirely in itself, without practical rhyme or reason, the aesthetic is at once eloquent testimony to the obscure origins and enigmatic nature of value in a society which would seem everywhere to deny it, and a utopian glimpse of an alternative to this sorry condition. For what the work of art imitates in its very pointlessness, in the constant movement by which it conjures itself up from its own inscrutable depths, is nothing less than human existence itself, which (scandalously for the rationalists and Utilitarians) requires no rationale beyond its own self-delight. For this Romantic doctrine, the art work is most rich in political implications where it is most gloriously futile.

It may also be, however, that the aesthetic does more than figure a new concept of value. If it is on the one hand autonomous of the real, it might also hold out a promise of reconciling the sundered realms of fact and value. For Baumgarten, as we have seen, the aesthetic is a region adjacent to but distinct from the cognitive; with Hume, the cognitive is steadily reduced to a form of sensibility not far removed from the aesthetic. One can, however, look at the relation between these two spheres in a quite different way. When science contemplates the world, what it knows is an impersonal space of causes and processes quite independent of the subject, and so alarmingly indifferent to value. But the fact that we can know the world at all, however grim the news which this knowledge might have to deliver, must surely entail some fundamental harmony between ourselves and it. For there to be knowledge in the first place, our faculties must be somehow marvellously adjusted to material reality; and for Immanuel Kant it is the contemplation of this pure form of our cognition, of its very enabling conditions, which is the aesthetic. The aesthetic is no longer on this view a mere supplement to reason, or a sentiment to which that reason can be reduced; it is simply the state in which common knowledge, in the act of reaching out to its object, suddenly arrests and rounds upon itself, forgetting its referent for a moment and attending instead, in a wondering flash of self-estrangement, to the miraculously convenient way in which its inmost structure seems geared to the comprehension of the real. It is cognition viewed in a different light, caught in the act, so that in this little crisis or revelatory breakdown of our cognitive routines, not *what* we know but *that* we know becomes the deepest, most delightful mystery. The aesthetic and the cognitive are thus neither divisible spheres nor reducible to one another. Indeed the aesthetic is not a 'sphere' at all: it is just the moment of letting go of the world and clinging instead to the formal act of knowing it. If, then, society has cleaved human experience down the middle, confronting an object drained of intrinsic value with a subject now forced to generate all value from itself, the aesthetic will become in Kant's hands a way of healing that rift, reuniting humanity with a world which seems to have turned its back on it.

Notes

1 G. W. F. Hegel, *The Philosophy of Fine Art* (London, 1920), vol. 111, p. 14.
2 Shaftesbury, 'An Enquiry Concerning Virtue or Merit', in L.A. Selby-Bigge (ed.), *British Moralists* ((Oxford, 1897), p. 15. For the 'moral sense' school in general, see Stanley Grean, *Shaftesbury's Philosophy of Religion and Ethics* (Ohio, 1967); Henning Jensen, *Motivation and the Moral Sense in Hutcheson's Ethical Theory* (The Hague, 1971); Gladys Bryson, *Man and Society: The Scottish Enquiry of the 18th Century* (Princeton, 1945); Peter Kivy, *The Seventh Sense: A Study of Francis Hutcheson's Aesthetics* (New York, 1976); R.L. Brett, *The Third Earl of Shaftesbury* (London, 1951); and E. Tuveson, 'Shaftesbury and the Age of Sensibility', in H. Anderson and J. Shea (eds), *Studies in Aesthetics and Criticism* (Minneapolis, 1967). For an account of John Locke's influence on Hutcheson, see J. Stolnitz, 'Locke, value and aesthetics', *Philosophy*, vol. 38 (1963).
3 Selby-Bigge, *British Moralists* p. 37.
4 Shaftesbury, *Characteristics* (Gloucester, Mass, 1963), vol. 1, p. 79.
5 Shaftesbury, *Second Characters*, quoted in Grean, *Shaftesbury's Philosophy*, p. 91.
6 For a suitably acerbic review of Shaftesbury's regressive ideological tendencies, see Robert Markley, 'Sentimentality as Performance:

Shaftesbury, Sterne, and the Theatrics of Virtue', in F. Nussbaum and L. Brown (eds), *The New Eighteenth Century* (New York, 1987).

7 Hutcheson, 'An Inquiry concerning the Original of our Ideas of Virtue or Moral Good', in Selby-Bigge, *British Moralists* p. 70.

8 Adam Smith, 'The Theory of Moral Sentiments', in Selby-Bigge, *British Moralists* p. 321. For a useful account of problems of social cohesion in the eighteenth century, see John Barrell, *English Literature in History 1730–80: An Equal, Wide Survey* (London, 1983), Introduction.

9 It is worth pointing out that if the moral sense theorists are correct in what they affirm, then they are the last moralists. For if right conduct is grounded in intuition, then it is hard to see why there is a need for ethical discourse at all. The moral sense philosophers do of course see the need for such discourse as a way of elaborating, clarifying and if necessary transforming our intuitions; but the tendency of their case at its most euphoric is to argue themselves steadily out of business. Ethical discourse is necessary precisely because what *counts* as being, say, compassionate in particular circumstances is far from clear. The very existence of 'moral language' thus testifies to our moral self-opaqueness. It is precisely because of this self-opaqueness, and because we are sometimes confronted with choices between incompatible goods, that the language of ethics is necessary.

10 David Hume, 'Of the Standard of Taste', in *Essays* (London, n.d.), p. 175. See also Jerome Stolnitz, 'On the Origins of 'Aesthetic Disinterestedness', *Journal of Aesthetics and Art Criticism*, vol. XX, no. 2 (1961).

11 Selby-Bigge, *British Moralists* p. 258.

12 Richard Price, 'A Review of the Principal Questions in Morals', in Selby-Bigge, *British Moralists* pp. 106–7, 133.

13 Louis Althusser, 'Ideology and Ideological State Apparatuses', in *Lenin and Philosophy* (London, 1971).

14 Hegel, *Pheneomenology of Spirit* (Oxford, 1977), p. 222.

15 Ernst Cassirer, *Philosophy of the Enlightenment* (Boston, 1951), p. 313.

16 Edmund Burke, 'First Letter on a Regicide Peace', quoted by Tony Tanner, *Jane Austen* (London, 1986), p. 27.

17 Baruch Spinoza, *The Political Works*, ed. A. G. Wernham (Oxford, 1958), p. 93.

18 Edmund Burke, *Reflections on the French Revolution* (London, 1955), p. 88.

19 Franco Moretti, *The Way of the World* (London, 1987), p. 16.

20 Selby-Bigge, *British Moralists* p. 107.

21 See Jacques Derrida, *Of Grammatology* (Baltimore, 1974), Part 2, chapter 2.

22 As far as the 'textuality' of history goes, Hume comments in his *Treatise* on the multiple copies by which any particular historical fact is transmitted: 'Before the knowledge of the fact could come to the first historian, it must be convey'd thro' many mouths; and after it is committed to writing, each new copy is a new object, of which the connextion with the foregoing is known only by experience and observation' (*Treatise of Human Nature*, p. 145). Hume well grasped, *avant la lettre*, the modern principle of 'intertextuality' and the scepticism with which it is sometimes coupled; he concludes this piece of argument with the claim that the evidence of all ancient history is now lost to us.

23 See Norman Kemp Smith, *The Philosophy of David Hume* (London, 1941). See also, for useful accounts of Hume, Peter Jones, 'Cause, Reason and Objectivity in Hume's Aesthetics', in D. W. Livingston and J. T. King (eds), *Hume: A Revaluation* (New York, 1976); Barry Stroud, *Hume* (London, 1977); Robert J. Fogelin, *Hume's Skepticism in the 'Treatise of Human Nature'* (London, 1985), and Alasdair MacIntyre, *Whose Justice? Which Rationality?* (London, 1988), chapters 15 and 16.

24 David Hume, *Treatise of Human Nature*, ed. L. A. Selby-Bigge (Oxford, 1978), p. 469. All subsequent references to this work will be given parenthetically after quotations in the text.

25 David Hume, *Enquiries concerning the Human Understanding and the Principles of Morals*, ed. L. A. Selby-Bigge (Oxford, 1961), p. 293. All subsequent references to this work will be given parenthetically after quotations in the text.

26 Hume, *Essays*, p. 165.

27 Ibid., p. 178.

28 Edmund Burke, *Philosophical Inquiry into the Origin of our Ideas of the Sublime and the Beautiful*, in *The Works of Edmund Burke* (London, 1906), vol. 1, p. 95. All subsequent references to this work will be given parenthetically after quotations in the text. See also, for studies of the relations between Burke's politics and aesthetics, Neal Wood, 'The Aesthetic Dimension of Burke's Political Thought', *Journal of British Studies* no. 4 (1964); Ronald Paulson, 'The Sublime and the Beautiful', in *Representations of Revolution* (New Haven, 1983), and W. J. T. Mitchell, 'Eye and Ear: Edmund Burke and the Politics of Sensibility', in *Iconology* (Chicago, 1986).

29 Althusser, 'Ideology and Ideological State Apparatuses'.

30 Sigmund Freud, *The Ego and the Id*, in *Sigmund Freud: On Metapsychology* (Harmondsworth, 1984), p. 360.

31 Mary Wollstonecraft, *Vindication of the Rights of Men* (Gainesville, Florida, 1960), p. 114.

32 Ibid., p. 116.

33 Burke, *Reflections on the French Revolution*, p. 59.
34 Ibid., p. 59.
35 Ibid., p. 74.
36 Ibid., p. 75.
37 Quoted in Kivy, *The Seventh Sense* p. 9.
38 Thomas Paine, *The Rights of Man* (London, 1958), p. 22.
39 Wollstonecraft, *Vindication*, p. 5.
40 John Stuart Mill, *Essays on Bentham and Coleridge*, ed. F. R. Leavis (London, 1962), p. 73.

3

The Kantian Imaginary

Why is it that modern philosophy has returned so often to the
question of epistemology? Why should the drama of subject and
object, the fraught narrative of their couplings and splittings,
matchings and misalliances, have so consistently dominated the
modern philosophical stage, like the tale of two incompatible partners
continually warring to gain an edge over each other, who nevertheless
cannot relinquish their fatal fascination for one another and resolve
yet again, after another painful separation, to make a go of it?

That the individual subject should come to occupy centre stage,
reinterpreting the world with reference to itself, follows logically
enough from bourgeois economic and political practice. But the more
the world is thus subjectivized, the more this all-priviledged subject
begins to undermine the very objective conditions of its own pre-
eminence. The wider the subject extends its imperial sway over
reality, the more it relativizes that terrain to its own needs and desires,
dissolving the world's substance into the stuff of its own senses. Yet
the more it thereby erodes any objective criteria by which to measure
the significance or even reality of its own experience. The subject
needs to know that it is supremely valuable; but it cannot know this if
its own solipsism has cancelled out any scale by which such value
might be assessed. What is this subject privileged *over*, if the world
has been steadily dwindled to no more than an obedient mirror image
of itself? The bourgeois subject would seem in this sense a tragically
self-defeating creature, one whose very self-affirmation turns inexorably back upon itself to eat away at its own enabling conditions.
'We must ponder the anomaly', writes Fredric Jameson,

that it is only in the most completely humanised environment, the one the most fully and obviously the end product of human labour, production, and transformation, that life becomes meaningless, and that existential despair first appears as such in direct proportion to the elimination of nature, the non- or anti-human, to the increasing rollback of everything that threatens human life and the prospect of a well-nigh limitless control over the external universe.[1]

A certain objectivity is the very condition of subjecthood, which must have all the solidity of a material fact, and yet which cannot be by definition any such thing. It is vital that the world confirms my subjectivity, yet I am a subject only in so far as I bring this world to be in the first place. In appropriating the whole of external nature, the bourgeois subject discovers to its consternation that it has appropriated its own objectivity along with it.

'Objectivity' could here be roughly translated as the imperative: 'You respect my property and I'll respect yours.' The other establishes my objectivity by leaving me alone, and confers freedom and objectivity on himself in the same act. Property, the very mark and seal of subjectivity, is nothing if not backed by a complex system of legal safeguards and political guarantees; but the very subjectivism of a property-owning order will tend to turn treacherously against all such objective sanctions, which can never have the same existential force or ontological reality as the subject itself. The non-subjective can be authenticated only through the medium of the subject's experience, where it is always in peril of being converted into selfhood and so abolished. Alternatively, that which remains beyond the self is equally derealized in a world where subjectivity is the measure of all things. The bourgeois subject requires some Other to assure itself that its powers and properties are more than hallucinatory, that its activities have meaning because they take place in a shared objective world; yet such otherness is also intolerable to the subject, and must be either expelled or introjected. There can be no sovereignty without someone to reign over, yet his very presence threatens to throw one's lordship into jeopardy. That which confirms the subject's identity cannot help exposing it as constrained; to mark *your* limit ('keep off my property!') is to sketch, impossibly, my own.

Without some standard of objectivity, the subject is reduced to conferring value upon itself, in what is at once the defiant boast of the modern ('I take value from myself alone!') and its hollow cry of anguish ('I am so lonely in this universe!'). It is the double nature of humanism, which appears to know no middle ground between the mania of exerting its powers and the depressive knowledge that it does so in empty space. So it is that Kant will strive to repair the subjectivist damage wrought by Hume's sceptical empiricism by restoring the objective order of things, but restoring it – since there can now be no lapsing back into a subjectless rationalism – from within the standpoint of the subject itself. In an heroic labour, the objective world must be salvaged from the ravages of subjectivism and patiently reconstructed, but in a space where the subject, however constituted by the celebrated categories, is still sovereign. Not only sovereign, indeed, but (in contrast to the sluggish subject of empiricism) buoyantly active, with all the productive energy of an epistemological entrepreneur. The point will be to preserve that shaping energy without subverting the objective realm which guarantees its significance; and Kant will thus trace within the very texture of the subject's experience that which points beyond it to the reality of the material world. The productive activity of *this* subject will secure objectivity rather than undermine it; there will be no more sawing away at the branch on which one sits.

If the essence of subjecthood is freedom, then bourgeois man seems condemned to self-blindness at the very peak of his powers, since freedom is by definition unknowable. What can be known is the determinate; and all we can say of subjectivity is that whatever it is it is certainly not that. The subject, the founding principle of the whole enterprise, slips through the net of representation and figures in its very uniqueness as no more than a mute epiphany or pregnant silence. If the world is the system of cognizable objects, then the subject which knows these objects cannot itself be in the world, any more than (as the early Wittgenstein remarks) the eye can be an object within its own visual field. The subject is not a phenomenal entity to be reckoned up along with the objects it moves among; it is that which brings such objects to presence in the first place, and so moves in a different sphere entirely. The subject is not a phenomenon in the world but a transcendental viewpoint upon it. We can, so to speak, squint at it sideways as it gives itself along with the things it represents, but like the spectral other who walks beside you in *The*

Waste Land it vanishes if you try to look at it straight. Getting a fix on the subject opens up the dizzying prospect of an infinite regress of meta-subjects. Perhaps, then, the subject can figure only negatively, as empty excess or transcendence of any particular. We cannot comprehend the subject, but as with the Kantian sublime we can, as it were, comprehend its incomprehensibility, which appears as the negation of all determinacy. The subject seems somehow squeezed out of the very system of which it is the lynchpin, at once source and supplement, creator and leftover. It is that which brings the world to presence, but is banished from its own creation and can by no means be deduced from it, other than in the phenomenological sense that there must be something which appearance is an appearance *to*. It governs and manipulates Nature, yet since it contains no particle of materiality in its own make-up it is a mystery how it comes to have truck with anything as lowly as mere objects. This prodigal structuring power or unfathomable capacity seems at the same time sheer paucity and negation, lying as it does at the very limit of what can be known. Freedom is the very lifebreath of the bourgeois order, yet it cannot be imaged in itself. The moment we try to encircle it with a concept, seize upon our own shadows, it slips over the horizon of our knowledge, leaving nothing in our grasp but the grim laws of necessity of external Nature. The 'I' denotes not a substance but a formal perspective upon reality, and there is no clear way of descending from this transcendental unity of apperception to one's humdrum material existence in the world. The enterprise of science is possible, but must fall outside the domain it investigates. Knower and known do not occupy a shared field, even if that intimate traffic between them which is knowledge might suggest that they do.

If freedom is to flourish, if the subject is to extend its colonizing sway over things and stamp them with its indelible presence, then systematic knowledge of the world is essential, and this must include knowledge of other subjects. You cannot hope to operate as an efficient capitalist in blithe ignorance of the laws of human psychology; and this is one reason why the ruling order needs at its disposal a body of detailed knowledge of the subject, which goes by the name of the 'human sciences'. Without knowledge you cannot hope to be free; yet knowledge and freedom are also in a curious sense antithetical. If it is essential to my freedom that I should know others, then it follows that they can know me too, in which case my freedom may be curtailed. I can always console myself with the thought that whatever can be known of me is by definition not me, is heteronomous to my authentic being, since the subject cannot be captured in an objective representation. But in this case, one might argue, I merely purchase my freedom at its own expense, gain it and lose it at a stroke; for I have now also deprived myself of the possibility of knowing others in their very essence, and it might be thought that such knowledge is essential to my self-development.

Knowledge, in other words, is to some degree in contradiction with the power it exists to promote. For the 'human sciences', subjects must be intelligible and predictable; but the transparency which this entails is at odds with the doctrine of the inscrutability of the human with which capitalism strives to mystify its social relations. All knowledge, as Romanticism is aware, contains a secret irony or incipient contradiction: it must at once master its object and confront it as other, acknowledge in it an autonomy it simultaneously subverts. The fantasy of total technological omnipotence conceals a nightmare: in appropriating Nature you risk eradicating it, appropriating nothing but your own acts of consciousness. There is a similar problem with predictability, which in surrendering phenomena into the hands of the sociological priests threatens to abolish history. Predictive science founds the great progressive narratives of middle-class history, but by the same stroke offers to undermine them, converting all diachrony to a secret synchrony. History as risk, enterprise and adventure is in deadlock with the most privileged form of bourgeois cognition, the *Eros* of history at odds with the *Thanatos* of science. To be free means to calculate the moves of your competitors while remaining securely impervious to such calculability oneself; but such calculations may themselves modify one's competitors' behaviour in ways that impose limits on one's own free project. There would be no way for the mind to master this volatile situation as a whole; such knowledge, in Kant's terms, would be the metaphysical fantasy of a non-perspectival understanding. A certain blindness is the very condition of bourgeois history, which thrives on its ignorance of an assured outcome. Knowledge is power, but the more you have of it the more it threatens to rob you of your desire and render you impotent.

For Kant, all cognition of others is doomed to be purely phenomenal, forever remote from the secret springs of subjectivity. Someone can tabulate my interests and desires, but if I am not to be a mere empirical object I must be transcendent of these things, of all that can be mapped by empirical knowledge. No such research can resolve the delicate issue of how such interests and desires come to be *mine* – of what it is for me, rather than you, to experience this particular yearning. Knowledge of human subjects is impossible not because they are so devious, multiple and decentred as to be impenetrably opaque, but because it is simply a mistake to think that the subject is the kind of thing that could ever possibly be known. It is just not a feasible object of cognition, any more than 'Being' is something we could know in the same manner as a slab of marzipan. Whatever we think we are knowing will always turn out to be some suitably spiritualized entity, thought along the lines of a material object, the mere parody or ghostly after-image of a thing. Indeed Jacques Derrida has shown how, when Kant comes to imagine human freedom, he slips into conceiving this most immaterial of realities in terms of an organic natural object.[2] The subject is absolutely nothing whatsoever of an object – which is to say that it is a kind of nothing, that this vaunted liberty is also a vacancy.

Of course, to have a phenomenal knowledge of others may in fact be enough for using them to our own advantage. But it may not be felt sufficient for constructing the kind of universal subjectivity which a ruling class requires for its ideological solidarity. For this purpose, it might be possible to attain to something which, while not strictly knowledge, is nonetheless very like it. This pseudo-knowledge is what is known as the aesthetic. When, for Kant, we find ourselves concurring spontaneously in an aesthetic judgement, able to agree that a certain phenomenon is sublime or beautiful, we exercise a precious form of intersubjectivity, establishing ourselves as a community of feeling subjects linked by a quick sense of our shared capacities. The aesthetic is in no way cognitive, but it has about it something of the form and structure of the rational; it thus unites us with all the authority of a law, but at a more affective, intuitive level. What brings us together as subjects is not knowledge but an ineffable reciprocity of feeling. And this is certainly one major reason why the aesthetic has figured so centrally in bourgeois thought. For the alarming truth is that in a social order marked by class division and market competition, it may finally be here, and only here, that human beings belong together in some intimate *Gemeinschaft*. At the level of theoretical discourse, we know one another only as objects; at the level of morality, we know and respect each other as autonomous subjects, but can have no concept of what this means, and a sensuous feeling for others is no essential element of such knowledge. In the sphere of aesthetic culture, however, we can experience our shared humanity with all the immediacy of our response to a fine painting or magnificent symphony. Paradoxically, it is in the apparently most private, frail and intangible aspects of our lives that we blend most harmoniously with one another. This is at once an astonishingly optimistic and bitterly pessimistic doctrine. On the one hand: 'How marvellous that human unity can be found installed in the very inwardness of the subject, and in that most seemingly wayward and capricious of responses, aesthetic taste!' On the other hand: 'How sickeningly precarious human solidarity must be, if it can finally be rooted in nothing more resilient than the vagaries of aesthetic judgement!' If the aesthetic must bear the burden of human community, then political society, one might suspect, must leave a good deal to be desired.

Kant's own political society was not, of course, by any means of a fully-developed bourgeois kind; and to speak of him as a bourgeois philosopher may therefore seem to some merely anachronistic. There are many ways, however, in which his thought adumbrates the ideals of middle-class liberalism – in which his thinking is utopian in that positive, enrichening sense. From the heart of autocracy, Kant speaks up bravely for values which will prove ultimately subversive of that regime; but it is curiously one-sided to claim Kant in this style as a liberal champion, and to overlook the ways in which his thought is already disclosing some of the problems and contradictions of the emergent middle-class order.

If we cannot, strictly speaking, know the subject, then at least – so we can console ourselves – we can know the object. In a notable irony, however, this latter operation turns out in bourgeois society to be quite as unthinkable as the former. If it is well known that Kant views the human subject as noumenal, quite beyond the pale of conceptual enquiry, then it is even better known that he believes just the same of the object, the infamous, inscrutable *Ding-an-sich* which slides over one horizon of our knowledge as the phantasmal subject vanishes over the other. Georg Lukács has argued that this opaqueness of the object in Kant is an effect of reification, whereby material products remain heterogeneous in their rich particularity to the formal, commodified categories which seek to encompass them.[3] They must accordingly be consigned to the 'irrational' outer darkness of the unknowable, leaving thought to confront the mere shadow of itself. The *Ding-an-sich* is in this sense less some suprasensible entity than the material limit of all such reificatory thought, a faint echo of the real's mute resistance to it. To recover the so-called thing in itself as use-value and social product would then be simultaneously to reveal it as suppressed social totality, restoring those social relations which the commodified categories bleach out. Preoccupied with materiality though Kant undoubtedly is, it is as though matter cannot appear in all its irreducibility *within* the Kantian system; but it is precisely this matter, in the form of certain contradictory social relations, which generates the structure of the entire system in the first place.

The thing in itself is thus a kind of empty signifier of that total knowledge which the bourgeoisie never ceases to dream of, but which its own fragmenting, dissevering activities continually frustrate. In the act of knowing, the subject cannot help but project from its inevitably partial perspective the phantasmal possibility of a knowledge beyond all categories, which then risks striking what it *can* know meagrely relative. The subject languishes in the grip of a rabid epistemophilia which is at once logical to its project – to hold the whole world in a single thought! – and potentially subversive of it. For such metaphysical delusions simply distract it from the proper business of actual knowledge, which must always be knowledge from one perspective or another. 'On the one hand', writes Lukács, '[the bourgeoisie] acquires increasing control over the details of its social existence, subjecting them to its needs. On the other hand, it loses – likewise progressively – the possibility of gaining intellectual control of society as a whole and with that it loses its own qualifications for leadership.'[4] At the height of its dominance, then, the bourgeois class finds itself curiously dispossessed by the order it has created, wedged as it is between an unknowable subjectivity on the one side and an unmasterable object on the other. The real world is irrational, beyond the mastery of the subject, a sheer invisible trace of resistance to the categories of the understanding, which confront it in the manner of empty, abstract forms expelling some brute facticity. The categories themselves are in this sense modelled on the commodity form. In this situation, one can settle stoically for the irreducibility of the real to thought, thus recognizing the limits of one's own subjectivity; or one can follow the path of a Hegel and seek to recuperate the material object itself within the mind. The former, Kantian strategy secures for the subject a real environment, but at the cost of a curtailment of its powers. Objects indubitably exist, but they can never be fully appropriated. The latter, Hegelian manoeuvre allows you fully to appropriate the object; but in what sense it is then truly an *object* is troublingly obscure. Expansive powers are secured for the subject, but at the risk of dissolving away the objective realm which might guarantee them.

Once again, however, the aesthetic is able to come to philosophy's aid. For in the sphere of aesthetic judgement, objects are uncovered which seem at once real yet wholly given for the subject, veritable bits of material Nature which are nevertheless delightfully pliant to the mind. However contingent their existence, these objects display a form which is somehow mysteriously necessary, which hails and engages us with a grace quite unknown to the things in themselves, which merely turn their backs upon us. In the aesthetic representation, that is to say, we glimpse for an exhilarated moment the possibility of a non-alienated object, one quite the reverse of a commodity, which like the 'auratic' phenomenon of a Walter Benjamin returns our tender gaze and whispers that it was created for us alone.[5] In another sense, however, this formal, desensualized aesthetic object, which acts as a point of exchange between subjects, can be read as a kind of spiritualized version of the very commodity it resists.

Displaced from the understanding, from the domains of Nature and history, totality in Kant comes to take up its home instead in the realm of practical reason. To act morally for Kant is to set aside all desire, interest and inclination, identifying one's rational will instead with a rule which one can propose to oneself as a universal law. What makes an action moral is something it manifests over and above any particular quality or effect, namely its willed conformity to universal law. What is important is the act of rationally willing the action as an end in itself. What we will when we act morally is the only thing of absolute, unconditional worth: rational agency itself. We should be moral because it is moral to be so.[6]

To be free and rational – in short, to be a subject – means to be entirely self-determining, obeying only such laws as I propose to myself, and treating myself and my action as an end rather than a means. Free subjectivity is thus a noumenal affair, quite absent from the phenomenal world. Freedom cannot be directly captured in a concept or image, and must be known practically rather than theoretically. I know I am free because I catch myself acting that way out of the corner of my eye. The moral subject inhabits the intelligible rather than material sphere, though it must constantly strive in mysterious fashion to materialize its values in the actual world. Human beings live simultaneously as free subjects and determined objects, slaves in Nature to laws which have no bearing on them in the spirit. Like the Freudian subject, the Kantian individual is radically 'split', though with a certain inversion: the world beyond appearances – the unconscious – is where for Freud we are most thoroughly determined, and the 'phenomenal' sphere of the ego the place where we can exert a frail degree of will. The material world for Kant is nothing like a subject, apparently inhospitable to freedom; but it is the locus of free subjects even so, who belong to it completely at one level and not at all at another.

The subject for Kant, then, is everywhere free and everywhere in chains; and it is not difficult to decipher the social logic of this contradiction. In class society, the subject's exercise of freedom is not only characteristically at the expense of others' oppression, but is gathered up into an anonymous, subjectless process of cause and effect which will finally come to confront the subject itself with all the dead weight of a fatality or 'second nature'. In an eloquent passage, Karl Marx sketches as social contradiction what remains for Kant an unsurpassable conundrum in thought:

> In our days, everything seems pregnant with its contrary. Machinery gifted with the wonderful power of shortening and fructifying human labour, we behold starving and overworking it. The new-fangled sources of wealth, by some strange, weird spell, are turned into sources of want. The victories of art seem bought by the loss of character. At the same pace that mankind masters nature, man seems to have become enslaved to other men and to his own infamy. Even the pure light of science seems unable to shine but on the dark background of ignorance. All our invention and progress seem to result in endowing material forces with intellectual life, and in stultifying human life

into a material force. This antagonism between modern industry and science on the one hand, between misery and dissolution on the other; this antagonism between the productive forces and the social relations of our epoch is a fact, palpable, overwhelming, and not to be controverted.[7]

In such conditions, freedom is bound to appear at once as the essence of subjectivity and as utterly unfathomable, the dynamic of history which is nowhere locatable in the material world, the condition of all action which nevertheless cannot be represented within it. Freedom in such circumstances is strangely undecidable: that we *must* be free if all this has come about, yet that what comes about is the negation of liberty, is the social correlative of Kant's philosophical double-think. My freedom involves being treated by others as an end in myself; yet once I am established in that autonomy, I can then proceed in the real social world to strip those others of their own equivalent independence. Noumenal and phenomenal realms thus constantly undo each other, as the subject is tossed to and fro between them. Just as the *Ding-an-sich* is the dark shadow thrown by the light of phenomenal knowledge, so iron necessity is the secret underside of liberty. It is not, as Kant believes, that we move in two simultaneous but incompatible worlds, but that our movement in the ghostly arena of 'noumenal' freedom is precisely the perpetual reproduction of phenomenal enslavement. The subject lives not in divided and distinguished worlds but at the aporetic intersection of the two, where blindness and insight, emancipation and subjection, are mutually constitutive.

Alasdair MacIntyre has argued that the purely formal nature of moral judgement in such thinkers as Kant is the consequence of a history in which moral questions have ceased to be intelligible against a settled background of social roles and relations.[8] In certain forms of pre-bourgeois society, the question of how a subject ought to behave is closely bound up with its location within the social structure, so that a sociological description of the complex relations in which an individual stands would inescapably involve a normative discourse too. Certain rights, duties and obligations are internal to social functions, so that no firm distinction is possible between a sociological idiom of fact and an ethical discourse of value. Once the bourgeois social order begins to reify fact, and to construct a kind of human subject transcendentally prior to its social relations, this historically grounded ethics is bound to enter into crisis. What one ought to do can no longer be deduced from what, socially and politically speaking, one actually is; a new distribution of discourses accordingly comes about, in which a positivist language of sociological description breaks loose from ethical evaluation. Ethical norms thus float free, breeding one or another form of intuitionism, decisionism or finalism. If one can return no social answer to the question of how one ought to behave, then virtuous behaviour, for some theorists at least, must become an end in itself. *Sollen* is removed from the sphere of historical action and analysis; one must behave in a particular way simply because one must.

The moral, that is to say, is tending towards the autotelic nature of the aesthetic – or, what amounts to the same thing, the work of art is now becoming ideologically modelled on a certain self-referential conception of ethical value. Kant has no truck with the heady Romantic impulse to aestheticize morality: the moral law is a supreme court of appeal elevated above all mere beauty, even if that beauty is in some sense a symbol of it. What is right is by no means necessarily agreeable; indeed for the severely puritanical sage of Königsberg there is a clear implication that the more we act against affective impulse, the more morally admirable we become. But if the moral law is radically anti-aesthetic in content, dismissing all considerations of happiness, spontaneity, benevolence and creative fulfilment for the single stark imperative of duty, it nonetheless mimes the aesthetic in its form. Practical reason is wholly autonomous and self-grounding, bears its ends within itself, spurns all vulgar utility and brooks no argument. As with the work of art, law and freedom are here at one: our submission to the moral law, Kant remarks, is at once free, yet bound up with an unavoidable compulsion.

It is in this sense, among others, that the moral and the aesthetic are for Kant somewhat analogous. While in the phenomenal realm we live subject to mechanical causality, our noumenal selves are simultaneously weaving behind or across this region some awesome artefact or magnificent poem, as the free subject shapes its actions not in terms of mechanical cause and effect but in relation to that teleological totality which is Reason. A truly free will is one determined only by its resolute orientation to this organic totality of ends and to the requirement of their harmonious unity, moving in a sphere where all instrumental adaptation of means to ends has been transmuted into purposive or expressive activity. Any human act can be viewed simultaneously as conditioned by a causal chain of events received from the past, and as directed towards future ends and their systematic coherence – viewed, that is to say, as phenomenal fact from the former perspective and as value from the latter.[9] And this reconcilation of ends and means in the kingdom of Reason is also the construction of a noumenal community of free subjects, a realm of norms and persons rather than of objects and desires, each of whom is an end in herself yet by that very fact integrally inserted into a total intelligible design. If we live our lives at one level in material history, we live them at another level as part of an organic artefact.

Nothing is more reprehensible, Kant protests in the *Critique of Pure Reason*, than to seek to derive the laws prescribing what ought to be done from what actually is done. Facts are one thing, and values another – which is to say that there is a gap, at once troubling and essential, between bourgeois social practice and the ideology of that practice. The distinction between fact and value is here one between actual bourgeois social relations, and the ideal of a community of free rational subjects who treat one another as ends in themselves. You must not derive values from facts, from routine market-place practice, because if you did you would end up with all the most undesirable kinds of value: egoism, aggressiveness, mutual antagonism. Values do not flow from facts, in the sense that ideologies are intended not simply to reflect existing social behaviour, but to mystify and legitimate it. As such, values are indeed related to that behaviour, but in a disjunctive, contradictory way: the highly oblique affinities between bourgeois idealism and capitalist production are exactly their most significant interrelation, as the former comes to ratify and dissemble the latter. But if this hiatus is essential, it is also embarrassing. An ideology too feebly rooted in the actual will, as we have argued, always be politically vulnerable, and Kant's noumenal sphere is in danger of just this implausibility. If it safeguards moral dignity from the market place, it does so only by removing it to a place so remote as to be effectively out of sight. Freedom is so deeply the essence of everything that it is nowhere to be empirically found. It is not so much a *praxis* in the world as a transcendental viewpoint upon it, a way of describing one's condition which at once makes all the difference and seems to leave everything exactly as it was. It cannot directly show itself forth as it is, and ideology is precisely a matter of sensuous representation. Kant is therefore in need of a mediatory zone which will bring this order of pure intelligibility home to felt experience; and this, as we shall see, is one of the meanings of the aesthetic.

The qualities of the Kantian moral law are those of the commodity form. Abstract, universal and rigorously self-identical, the law of Reason is a mechanism which, like the commodity, effects formally equal exchanges between isolated individual subjects, erasing the difference of their needs and desires in its homogenizing injunctions. The Kantian community of moral subjects is at one level a powerful critique of actual market-place ethics: in this world, nobody is to be debased from a person to a thing. In its general form, however, that community appears as an idealized version of the abstract, serialized individuals of bourgeois society, whose concrete distinctions are of no account to the law which governs them. The equivalent of this law in the discourse of psychoanalysis is the transcendental signifier of the phallus. Like the phallic signifier, the moral law subjects individuals to its rule, but brings them through that subjection to mature subjecthood. In Kant's version of affairs, it is a peculiarly censorious Law or Name-of-the-Father, the pure distilled essence of authority: rather than telling us what to do, it merely intones 'You must'.[10] Its august aim is to persuade us to repress our sensual inclinations in the name of its own higher imperatives; the law is what severs us from Nature and relocates us in the symbolic order of a suprasensible world, one of pure intelligibilities rather than of sensuous objects. The Kantian subject is accordingly split, one part of it remaining forever entangled in the phenomenal order of instinct and desire, the 'id' of the unregenerate ego, while the other climbs upward and inward to higher things. Like the Freudian subject, the Kantian individual inhabits simultaneously two contradictory spheres, in which everything which is true of the one is negated in the other. Everyone may possess the phallus, have access to rational freedom; yet in another sense nobody does, since this phallic law of reason does not *exist*. It is a fiction, this moral law, a hypothesis which we must construct in order to act as rational creatures at all, yet an entity of which the world yields no trace of evidence. The Kantian moral law is a fetish; and as such it is a poor basis for human solidarity, which is precisely its ideological paucity. In order to universalize my actions I must have regard to others, but only at the abstract level of the understanding, not with any spontaneous sense of their complex particular needs. Kant values the role of culture in helping to develop the conditions for men and women to follow the moral law; but that law has too little regard in itself for men and women's concrete cultural existence. There is a need, then, which neither politics nor morality can fulfil, to 'promote a unity between individuals on the basis of their subjectivity';[11] and it is this which the aesthetic can provide. If the aesthetic is a vital register of being, it is in part because of the reified, abstract, individualist nature of the moral and political spheres.

Practical reason assures us that freedom is real; pure reason can never tell us what it is. To explain how pure reason can be practical is, as Kant dolefully comments, beyond the power of human reason. All, however, is not lost. For there is after all a way in which Nature and reason may be harmonized, since there is a type of contemplation which participates equally in the principle of empirical explanation of Nature and in the principle of moral judgement. There is a way of viewing Nature such that the apparent lawfulness of its forms might at least suggest the possibility of ends in Nature which act in accordance with the ends of human freedom. It is possible to look at the world as though it were itself a mysterious sort of subject or artefact, governed like human subjects by a self-determining rational will. In the aesthetic and teleological modes of judgement, as presented in the *Critique of Judgement*, the empirical world appears in its freedom, purposiveness, significant totality and self-regulating autonomy to conform to the ends of practical reason.

The pleasure of the aesthetic is in part the *surprise* that this is the case. It is a delightful lucky chance that certain phenomena should seem to display a purposive unity, where such unity is not in fact deducible as necessary from logical premises. The occurrence seems fortuitous, contingent and so not subsumable under a concept of the understanding; but it nevertheless appears as if it *could* somehow be brought under such a concept, *as if* it conforms spontaneously to some law, even though we are quite unable to say what that law might be. If there is no actual law to which we might subsume this phenomenon, then the law in question seems one inscribed in its very material form, inseparable from its unique particularity, a kind of contingent or fortuitous lawfulness intuitively present to us in the thing but quite untheorizable. In the operations of pure reason, we bring a particular under a concept of universal law, thus sliding its specificity beneath the general; in matters of practical reason we subordinate the particular to a universal maxim. In aesthetic judgement, however, we have the curious sense of a lawful totality indissociable from our intuition of the immediate form of the thing. Nature appears animated by an indwelling finality which defeats the understanding; and this finality, in a pleasurable ambiguity, seems at once a law to which the object conforms and nothing less than the irreducible structure of the object itself.

Since aesthetic judgement does not engage any determinate concept, we are quite indifferent to the nature of the object in question, or whether it even exists. But if the object does not in this sense involve our cognition, it addresses itself to what we might call our capacity for cognition in general, revealing to us in a kind of Heideggerian 'pre-understanding' that the world is the kind of place we can in principle comprehend, that it is adapted to our minds even before any determinate act of knowing has yet taken place. Some of the pleasure of the aesthetic, then, arises from a quick sense of the world's delightful conformity to our capacities: instead of pressing ahead to subsume to some concept the sensuous manifold we confront, we just reap enjoyment from the general formal possibility of doing so. The imagination creates a purposive synthesis, but without feeling the need for a theoretical detour. If the aesthetic yields us no knowledge, then, it proffers us something arguably deeper: the consciousness, beyond all theoretical demonstration, that we are at home in the world because the world is somehow mysteriously designed to suit our capacities. Whether this is actually true or not we cannot say, since we can know nothing of what reality is like in itself. That things are conveniently fashioned for our purposes must remain a hypothesis; but it is the kind of heuristic fiction which permits us a sense of purposiveness, centredness and significance, and thus one which is of the very essence of the ideological.

Aesthetic judgement is then a kind of pleasurable free-wheeling of our faculties, a kind of parody of conceptual understanding, a non-referential pseudo-cognition which does not nail down the object to an identifiable thing, and so is agreeably free of a certain material constraint. It is an undecidable half-way house between the uniform laws of the understanding and some utter chaotic indeterminacy – a kind of dream or fantasy which displays its own curious lawfulness, but one of the image rather than the concept. Since the aesthetic representation is not passed through a determinate thought, we are able to savour its form free of all humdrum material content – as in reading symbolist poetry, for example, we seem to be in the presence of the pure eidetic forms of language itself, purged of any very determinate semantic substance. It is as though in aesthetic judgement we are grasping with out hands some object we cannot see, not because we need to use it but simply to revel in its general graspability, in the way its convexity seems to insinuate itself so pliantly into our palms, delectably well designed as it appears for our prehensile powers.

What we have in the aesthetic and teleological standpoints, then, is the consoling fantasy of a material world which is perhaps not after all indifferent to us, which has a regard for our cognitive capacities. As one of Kant's commentators writes:

> It is a great stimulus to moral effort and a strong support to the human spirit if men can believe that the moral life is something more than a mortal enterprise in which he can join with his fellow men against a background of a blind and indifferent universe until he and the human race are blotted out forever. Man cannot be indifferent to the possibility that his puny efforts towards moral perfection may, in spite of appearances, be in accord with the purpose of the universe . . .[12]

Part of the trauma of modernity is exactly this mind-shaking suspicion that the world is not enlistable on humanity's side – that human values must resign themselves to being grounded in nothing more solid than themselves, and perhaps suffer a panic-stricken internal collapse on account of this unnerving insight. For humanity to experience an exuberant sense of its own unique status is to find itself tragically marooned from any amicably complicit Nature – from some answerable environment which might assure man that his purposes were valid because secretly part of itself. For a social order to demolish its own metaphysical foundation is to risk leaving its meanings and values hanging in empty space, as gratuitous as any other structure of meaning; and how then are the members of such an order to be persuaded of its authority? The urge to coopt reality by theoretical violence into one's own project may then prove well-nigh irresistible; but it is part of Kant's admirable austerity, testimony to his sober, clear-eyed realism, that he cannot wholly follow this mythological path. There is simply no verification in the procedures of reason for any such speculative hypothesis.

There are, however, few graver threats to any ideology than its sense of reality's stony indifference to its own values. Such steady recalcitrance on the world's part is bound to throw the limits of an ideology into harsh relief; and it is on a concealment of such limits that ideologies flourish, in their impulse to eternalize and universalize themselves, to present themselves as unparented and bereft of all siblings. The outrage which greeted the fiction of Thomas Hardy in late nineteenth-century England may be tracked in the end simply to Hardy's atheism: to his hard-headed refusal of the consolations of a collusive universe. By contrast, the desolate Tennyson of *In Memoriam* struggles to wrench an insensate material world back into its proper imaginary place, as ally and support of human endeavour. Kant sternly refuses to convert the heuristic fiction of a purposive universe to ideological myth; but he cannot dispense with this imaginary dimension altogether, and it is this which the aesthetic provides. When the small infant of Jacques Lacan's celebrated 'mirror stage' encounters its reflection in the glass, it finds in this image a plenitude lacking in its own body, and thus imputes to itself a fullness which in fact pertains to the representation. When the Kantian subject of taste encounters an object of beauty, it discovers in it a unity and harmony which are in fact the effect of the free play of its own faculties. In both cases, an imaginary misrecognition takes place, although with a certain reversal of subject and object from the mirror of Lacan to the mirror of Kant. The Kantian subject of aesthetic judgement, who misperceives as a quality of the object what is in fact a pleasurable coordination of its own powers, and who constitutes in a mechanistic world a figure of idealized unity, resembles the infantile narcissist of the Lacanian mirror stage, whose misperceptions Louis Althusser has taught us to regard as an indispensable structure of all ideology.[13] In the 'imaginary' of ideology, or of aesthetic taste, reality comes to seem totalized and purposive, reassuringly pliable to the centred subject, even though theoretical understanding may more bleakly inform us that this is a finality only with respect to the subject's faculty of cognition. The beauty or sublimity we perceive in aesthetic judgement is actually no more a property of the object in question than the laws of the understanding are a property of Nature; rather, in Kant's view, we ascribe to the object a felt harmony of our own creative powers, in the Freudian mechanism known as projection. It is as though we are constrained to invert Kant's 'Copernican' priority of subject and object, assigning to the object itself a power and plenitude which (so a more sober cognition informs us) belongs properly to ourselves alone. The sense that the object makes consists entirely in the sense that it makes for us. This theoretical insight, however, cannot undo our imaginary projections, which are not subject to the understanding; as in the thought of Althusser, 'theory' and 'ideology' lie on different planes, signify different registers, and to that extent do not interfere with one another even when they yield up mutually incompatible versions of reality. A social formation as known to theoretical enquiry is for Althusser nothing like a human subject, lacks organic unity and is in no way 'centred' upon individuals; but it cannot succeed in reproducing itself unless those individuals are permitted the illusion that the world 'hails' them, shows some regard for their faculties, addresses itself to them as one subject to another, and it is this fiction which ideology for Althusser exists to foster. For Kant, Nature is similarly nothing of an organic subject; but it conforms to human understanding, and it is only a small step from this to the pleasurable fantasy (one required for coherent knowledge) that it was *designed* for such understanding too. The aesthetic is thus the wan hope, in an increasingly rationalized, secularized, demythologized environment, that ultimate purpose and meaning may not be entirely lost. It is the mode of religious transcendence of a rationalistic age – the place where those apparently arbitrary, subjectivist responses which fall outside the scope of such rationalism may now be moved to the centre and granted all the dignity of an eidetic form. That which is purely residual to bourgeois rationality, the *je ne sais quoi* of taste, now comes to figure as nothing less than a parodic image of such thought, a caricature of rational law. The margins converge to the centre, since it is on those margins that quasi-transcendental intuitions have been preserved without which that centre cannot prosper. It is as though the aesthetic represents some residual feeling left over from an earlier social order, where a sense of transcendental meaning and harmony, and of the centrality of the human subject, were still active. Such metaphysical propositions cannot now withstand the critical force of bourgeois rationalism, and so must be preserved in contentless, indeterminate form, as structures of feeling rather than systems of doctrine. Unity, purpose and symmetry still exist, but they must now be thrust deep into the inwardness of the subject itself, removed from the phenomenal world. This is not to concede, however, that they can have no influence on our conduct in that realm. For to entertain the hypothesis that reality is not altogether indifferent to our own moral capacities may quicken and renew our moral consciousness, and so lead us to a finer form of life. Beauty is in this sense an aid to virtue, appearing as it does to rally support for our moral endeavours from the unlikely resource of Nature itself.

We should not, however, rejoice too soon in this apparent complicity of the universe with our purposes. For all this, in the Kantian aesthetic, happens as though by some felicitous accident. It is fortunate that the world's diversity should seem so obediently commensurate with the mind's powers; so that in the very act of revelling in this apparent prearranged harmony, in this well-nigh miraculous doubling of the structure of Nature and the structure of the subject, we are at the same time wryly conscious of its serendipity. Only in the aesthetic are we able to turn round upon ourselves, stand a little apart from our own vantage-point and begin to grasp the *relation* of our capacities to reality, in a moment of wondering self-estrangement on which the Russian Formalists will later found an entire poetics. In the routinized, automated processes of understanding, such wonder does not occur; in the aesthetic, by contrast, our faculties are suddenly foregrounded in ways which draw attention to their fittingness. But this is also to draw attention to their limitations. To be allowed a rare experience of our own peculiar point of view is, after all, to sense that it is only *our* point of view, and so one that might conceivably be transcended. In the presence of beauty, we experience an exquisite sense of adaptation of the mind to reality; but in the turbulent presence of the sublime we are forcibly reminded of the limits of our dwarfish imaginations and admonished that the world as infinite totality is not ours to know. It is as though in the sublime the 'real' itself – the eternal, ungraspable totality of things – inscribes itself as the cautionary limit of all mere ideology, of all complacent subject-centredness, causing us to feel the pain of incompletion and unassuaged desire.

Both of these operations, the beautiful and the sublime, are in fact essential dimensions of ideology. For one problem of all humanist ideology is how its centring and consoling of the subject is to be made compatible with a certain essential reverence and submissiveness on the subject's part. In making the world over to the subject, such humanism risks undermining the censorious Other which will hold humanity humbly in its place. The sublime in one of its aspects is exactly this chastening, humiliating power, which decentres the subject into an awesome awareness of its finitude, its own petty position in the universe, just as the experience of beauty shores it up. Moreover, what would be threatened by a purely 'imaginary' ideology would be the subject's desire as well as its humility. The Kantian sublime is in effect a kind of unconscious process of infinite desire, which like the Freudian unconscious continually risks swamping and overloading the pitiable ego with an excess of affects. The subject of the sublime is accordingly decentred, plunged into loss and pain, undergoes a crisis and fading of identity; yet without this unwelcome violence we would never be stirred out of ourselves, never prodded into enterprise and achievement. We would lapse back instead into the placid feminine enclosure of the imaginary, where desire is captivated and suspended. Kant associates the sublime with the masculine and the military, useful antidotes against a peace which breeds cowardice and effeminacy. Ideology must not so thoroughly centre the subject as to castrate its desire; instead we must be both cajoled and chastized, made to feel both homeless and at home, folded upon the world yet reminded that our true resting place is in infinity. It is part of the dialectic of the beautiful and the sublime to achieve this double ideological effect. It is now almost a commonplace of deconstructive thought to see the sublime as a point of fracture and fading, an abyssal undermining of metaphysical certitudes; but while there is much of value and interest in this view, it has served in effect to suppress just those modes in which the sublime also operates as a thoroughly ideological category.

The psychoanalytic register of the imaginary involves a peculiarly intimate relation of the infant to the mother's body; and it is possible to catch a glimpse of this body, suitably screened, in Kant's aesthetic representation. What else, psychoanalytically speaking, is this beautiful object which is unique yet universal, wholly designed for the subject and addressed to its faculties, which in Kant's interesting phrase

90

'relieves a want' and brings us a keenly pleasurable sense of repletion, which is miraculously self-identical and which, though sensuously particular, evokes absolutely no libidinal impulse from the subject itself? The beautiful representation, like the body of the mother, is an idealized material form safely defused of sensuality and desire, with which, in a free play of its faculties, the subject can happily sport. The bliss of the aesthetic subject is the felicity of the small child playing in the bosom of the mother, enthralled by an utterly indivisible object which is at once intimate and indeterminate, brimming with purposive life yet plastic enough to put up no resistance to the subject's own ends.

The subject can find rest in this cloistral security, but its rest is strictly temporary. For it is travelling to that higher location where it will find its true home, the phallic law of abstract reason which quite transcends the sensible. To attain full moral stature we must be wrenched from the maternal pleasures of Nature and experience in the majesty of the sublime the sense of an infinite totality to which our feeble imaginations will never be equal.[14] Yet in the very moment of being thus subdued, sharply recalled to our true finitude, we know a new kind of exultant power. When the imagination is forced up traumatically against its own limits, it finds itself straining beyond them in a movement of negative transcendence; and the giddy feeling of unboundedness which then results yields us a negative presentation of the infinity of moral Reason. In the sublime, morality and feeling for once come together, but in negative style: what we feel is how immeasurably Reason transcends the senses, and thus how radically 'unaesthetic' our true freedom, dignity and autonomy are. Morality is 'aestheticized' in the sublime as feeling, but as a feeling which, since it denigrates the sensory, is also 'anti-aesthetic'. Hurled beyond our own sensuous limits, we grasp some dim notion of the suprasensory, which is nothing less than the law of Reason inscribed within us. The pain we experience under the weight of the paternal law is thus shot through with a sense of exaltation above all merely conditioned being: we know that the sublime presentation is simply an echo of the sublimity of Reason within ourselves, and thus testimony to our absolute freedom. In this sense, the sublime is a kind of anti-aesthetic which presses the imagination to extreme crisis, to the point of failure and breakdown, in order that it may negatively figure forth the Reason that transcends it. At the very moment this immensity of

Reason threatens to overpower us, we are aware of its inscrutable imprint within ourselves. If there is finally no reason to fear the punitive phallic law of the father, it is because each of us carries the phallus securely lodged within ourselves. The subject of the imaginary, who imputes a fetishistic power to the object, must so to speak come to its senses, undo this projection and recognize that this power resides in it rather than in the object. It thus exchanges the fetish of the mother's body for the fetish of the phallic law, trading one absolute self-identity for another; but its reward for thus submitting to the pains of castration will be a kind of reconstitution of the imaginary at a higher level, as it comes to perceive that the infinity it fears in the sublime representation is in fact an infinite power within itself. This daunting totality is not ours to *know*, and to this extent the reverence and humility of the subject are preserved; but it is ours to *feel*, and to that degree the subject's autonomy is gratifyingly confirmed.

There is a difficult tension within bourgeois society between the ideology of production and the ideology of consumption. Since the former realm is generally unpleasant, sanctions and disciplines are required for the subject to buckle itself to its tasks. There is no suggestion that this world of production exists *for* the subject; but things are different in the arena of consumption, where the commodity 'hails' the individual and implies a special relationship with him. 'If the soul of the commodity which Marx occasionally mentions in jest existed,' writes Walter Benjamin, 'it would be the most empathetic ever encountered in the realm of souls, for it would have to see in everyone the buyer in whose hand and house it wants to nestle.'[15] Like Kant's aesthetic object, the commodity would seem designed especially for our faculties, addressed to us in its very being. Viewed from the standpoint of consumption, the world is uniquely ours, shaped to nestle in our palms; seen from the standpoint of production it appears, like Kantian Nature, as an impersonal domain of causal processes and autonomous laws. Capitalism continually centres the subject in the sphere of values, only to decentre it in the realm of things. One can trace something of this movement in the dialectic of the beautiful and the sublime. If things-in-themselves are beyond the reach of the subject, the beautiful will rectify this alienation by presenting reality, for a precious moment, as given spontaneously for that subject's powers. If this then seems likely to breed complacency, the sublime is always on hand with its intimidatory power; but the dangerously demoralizing effects of such power are in turn tempered by the subject's joyful consciousness that the power in question is that of its own majestic Reason.

Aesthetic judgements, Kant argues in the *Critique of Judgement*, are at once subjective and universal. They thus figure as the joker in the pack of his theoretical system, since it is hard to see on Kant's terms how the phrase 'aesthetic judgement' can be other than oxymoronic – how something can be at once a judgement, which involves subsuming particulars to a law of the understanding, and yet no more than a feeling. The grammatical form of aesthetic judgements, Kant claims, is in fact deceptive and duplicitous. In such statements as 'I am beautiful', 'You are sublime', the adjectives would appear to be predicative, but this is really an illusion: such propositions have the form, but not the real force, of referential utterances. To claim that you are sublime is not for me to identify some property in you but to report on some feeling in myself. Judgements of taste appear to be descriptions of the world but are in fact concealed emotive utterances, performatives masquerading as constatives. The grammaticality of such enunciations is at odds with their true logical status. It would, however, be quite impermissable to decode the pseudo-proposition '*x* is beautiful' as 'I like *x*', since judgements of taste are for Kant purely disinterested and have nothing to do with one's contingent inclinations or desires. Such judgements are certainly subjective; but they are so *purely* subjective, so expressive of the very essence of the subject, untainted by idiosyncratic prejudice and 'devoid of every possible condition which would necessarily distinguish the judge from other people',[16] that it is possible to speak of them also as universal. If the subject transcends its ephemeral needs and desires, then a truly subjective judgement disregards all the accidents which divide one individual from another and strikes an immediate chord in them all. Aesthetic judgements are thus, as it were, 'impersonally personal',[17] a kind of subjectivity without a subject or, as Kant has it, a 'universal subjectivity'. To judge aesthetically is implicitly to declare that a wholly subjective response is of the kind that every individual must necessarily experience, one that must elicit spontaneous agreement from them all.

The aesthetic, one might argue, is in this sense the very paradigm of the ideological. For the peculiarity of ideological propositions might be summarized by claiming, with some exaggeration, that there is in fact no such thing as an ideological proposition. Like aesthetic judgements for Kant, ideological utterances conceal an essentially emotive content within a referential form, characterizing the lived relation of a speaker to the world in the act of appearing to characterize the world. This is not to suggest that ideological discourses do not in fact contain referential propositions which may be assessed as either true or false, simply that this is not what is most specific about the ideological. Ideology does indeed importantly contain many false propositions, such as the claim that Asians are inferior to Europeans or that the Queen of England is highly intelligent; but the falsity of such claims is not what is peculiarly ideological about them, since not all false propositions are ideological and not all ideological statements are false. What makes such false claims ideological is the *motivation* of their falsity: the fact that they encode emotive attitudes relevant to the reproduction of social power. The same is true of the many ideological utterances which happen to be true, such as the claim that the Queen of England takes her job seriously and is devoted to her work. Ideology cannot primarily be characterized in terms of false statements, not, as some have held, because it does not contain more than its fair share of them, but because it is not at root a question of propositionality at all. It is a matter of wishing, cursing, fearing, reverencing, desiring, denigrating and so on – *performative* discourse, which like Kant's aesthetic judgements does not rest upon conceptual categories of truth or falsehood, even if it significantly involves them. The statement 'The Irish are inferior to the British' is a pseudo-referential encodement of the imperative: 'Down with the Irish!' This is one reason why it is notoriously difficult to argue with.

The aesthetic in Kant short-circuits the conceptual to link concrete particulars in their very immediacy to a kind of universal law, but a law which can be in no sense formulated. In the aesthetic, in contrast to the domains of pure and practical reason, the individual is not abstracted to the universal but is somehow raised to the universal in its very particularity, manifesting it spontaneously on its surface. 'In the phenomenon of the beautiful the inconceivable thing happens, that in contemplating beauty every subject remains in itself and is purely immersed in its own state, while at the same time it is absolved of all contingent particularity and knows itself to be the bearer of a total feeling which no longer belongs to "this" or "that".[18] The ideological viewpoint, somewhat similarly, is at once wholly my own and an utterly subjectless truth – at once constitutive of the very depths of the subject, who will from time to time fight and die for it, and a sort of universal law, though one which seems so self-evidently inscribed in the very material phenomena themselves as to be quite untheorizable. In ideology and the aesthetic we stay with the thing itself, which is preserved in all of its concrete materiality rather than dissolved to its abstract conditions; yet this very materiality, this uniquely unrepeatable form or body, comes mysteriously to assume all the compelling logic of a global decree. The ideologico-aesthetic is that indeterminate region, stranded somewhere between the empirical and theoretical, in which abstractions seem flushed with irreducible specificity and accidental particulars raised to pseudo-cognitive status. The loose contingencies of subjective experience are imbued with the binding force of law, but a law which can never be known in abstraction from them. Ideology constantly offers to go beyond the concrete to some debatable proposition, but that proposition constantly eludes formulation and disappears back into the things themselves. In this peculiar condition of being, the individual subject becomes the bearer of a universal, ineluctable structure which impresses itself upon it as the very essence of its identity. What is from one standpoint an absolute impersonal rightness is from another standpoint just something one happens to feel; but that 'happens' is somehow unavoidable. Ideology is on the one hand an 'everybody knows', a ragbag of tarnished adages; but this reach-me-down assemblage of tags and clichés is forceful enough to impel the subject to murder or martyrdom, so deeply does it engage the roots of a unique identity.

Just as it is illicit in Kant's view to decode the statement 'x is beautiful' as 'I like x', so it would be clearly inadequate to translate the proposition 'The Irish are inferior to the British' as 'I don't like the Irish'. If ideology were merely a question of such incidental prejudices, then it would no doubt be somewhat easier to uproot than it is. The rhetorical move which converts an emotive utterance to the grammatical form of the referential is an index of the fact that certain attitudes are at once 'merely subjective' and somehow necessary. In this sense, surprisingly enough, Kantian aesthetics move us a little way towards a materialist understanding of ideology. They define a third realm, between those propositions of theoretical reason which do not necessarily engage subjectivity at all ('two plus two equals four'), and mere whimsical predilections. Given the nature of our immutable faculties, Kant holds, it is necessary that certain subjective judgements elicit the universal consent of others, since these judgements arise from the sheer formal workings of capacities we have in common. Given certain material conditions, one might similarly claim, it is necessary that certain subjective responses be invested with all the force of universally binding propositions, and this is the sphere of the ideological.

In the business of aesthetic judgement, the nature or even existence of the referent is a matter of indifference, just as ideology is not primarily a question of the truth of certain determinate propositions. The real object makes its appearance in the aesthetic simply as an occasion for the pleasurable harmonization of our faculties. The universal quality of taste cannot spring from the object, which is purely contingent, or from any particular desire or interest of the subject, which are similarly parochial; so it must be a matter of the very cognitive structure of the subject itself, which is presumed to be invariable among all individuals. Part of what we enjoy in the aesthetic, then, is the knowledge that our very structural constitution as human subjects predisposes us to mutual harmony. It is as though, prior to any determinate dialogue or debate, we are always already in agreement, *fashioned* to concur; and the aesthetic is this experience of pure contentless consensus where we find ourselves spontaneously at one without necessarily even knowing what, referentially speaking, we are agreeing over. Once any determinate concept is removed from our grasp, we are left delighting in nothing but a universal solidarity beyond all vulgar utility. Such solidarity is a kind of *sensus communis*, which Kant opposes in his work to that fragmentary, unreflective collection of prejudices and opinions which is *doxa* or common sense. Such *doxa* is what Kant himself, had he used the word, might have termed 'ideology'; but *sensus communis* is ideology purified, universalized and rendered reflective, ideology raised to the second power, idealized beyond all mere sectarian prejudice or customary reflex to resemble the very ghostly shape of rationality itself. To establish itself as a truly universal class, the bourgeoisie will need to do more than trade in a handful of tattered maxims: its governing ideology must manifest at once the universal form of the rational and the apodictic content of the affectively immediate.

What aesthetic judgement signifies for Kant is essentially a form of altruism. In responding to an artefact, or to natural beauty, I place my own contingent aversions and appetencies in brackets, putting myself instead in everyone else's place and thus judging from the standpoint of a universal subjectivity. A portrait of cheese is not beautiful because I happen to enjoy eating the stuff. In this sense, the Kantian aesthetic challenges and confirms class-society at a stroke. On the one hand, its Olympian disinterestedness is at odds with what Kant calls 'truculent egoism', the routine selfish interests of social life. Aesthetic intersubjectivity adumbrates a utopian community of subjects, united in the very deep structure of their being. The cultural domain is in this sense for Kant distinct from the political, where individuals are bound together in purely external fashion for the instrumental pursuit of ends. Such merely extrinsic solidarity involves the ultimate back-up of coercion: social life would ultimately collapse, Kant holds, if public standards were not violently enforceable. The cultural domain, by contrast, is one of non-coercive consensus; it is of the essence of aesthetic judgements that they cannot be compelled. 'Culture' thus promotes an inward, unconstrained unity between citizens on the basis of their most intimate subjectivity. In this ethico-aesthetic sphere, 'no member shall be a mere means, but should also be an end, and seeing that he contributes to the possibility of the entire body, should have his position and function defined by the idea of the whole'.[19] Politics is restricted to public, utilitarian behaviour, marked off from that 'inner, personal interrelation between subjects as rational and feeling beings' which is the aesthetic.[20] If culture thus sketches the ghostly outline of a non-dominative social order, it does so by mystifying and legitimating actual dominative social relations. The division between the phenomenal and the noumenal is, so to speak, politicized, installed as an essential fissure within social life itself. Kant's highly formalistic ethics prove incapable of generating any distinctive political theory of their own beyond a conventional liberalism; and though such ethics proffer the dream of a community where subjects are ends in themselves, they are finally too abstract to bring this ideal home to felt experience. It is this which the aesthetic is uniquely able to provide; but in doing so it reproduces something of the very social logic it is out to resist. Kant's selfless aesthetic judge, absolved from all sensual motivation, is among other things a spiritualized version of the abstract, serialized subject of the market place, who cancels the concrete differences between himself and others as thoroughly as does the levelling, homogenizing commodity. In matters of taste, as of commodity transactions, all individuals are indifferently exchangeable; and culture is thus part of the problem to which it offers itself as a solution.

The critical philosophy, and the concept of ideology, are born at the same historical moment, as Michel Foucault notes in *The Order of Things*.[21] But whereas, as Foucault argues, the science of ideology in the hands of its founder, Destutt de Tracy, rests content with the business of representations, patiently examining the laws which organize them, the Kantian critique presses beyond this purely phenomenal space (ideology, Tracy remarks, is 'a part of zoology') to enquire into the very transcendental conditions of such representation, its object now nothing less than representability itself. What will then emerge is the ambivalently inspiring and alarming truth that all that is most precious falls outside the representational sphere. If this preserves what is most valuable from succumbing to the determined status of apples and armchairs, it also threatens to strike vacuous the very essence of the human subject. If freedom is finally unrepresentable, how is it to exert its ideological force, given that ideology is itself a question of representation? A way must consequently be found of imagining such liberty non-reductively in the empirical world, and this is one function of the Kantian aesthetic. The aesthetic is the reflection in the lower world of the higher, the place where that which finally outstrips representation altogether, as the sublime reminds us, manages nevertheless to achieve some sensuous embodiment or analogy. Humanity would see a sign; and the beautiful and the sublime conveniently supply it.

We have seen that the aesthetic in Kant fulfils a multitude of functions. It centres the human subject in an imaginary relation to a pliable, purposive reality, thereby granting it a delightful sense of its own inner coherence and confirming its status as an ethical agent. Yet it does this without ceasing to discipline and chastise the subject, recalling it to a piously submissive awareness of the infinity where it truly belongs. It ensures between human subjects a spontaneous, immediate, non-coercive consensus, providing the affective bonds which traverse the alienations of social life. It brings individuals home to each other as immediate experience, in a discourse of concrete particularity which has all the irrefragable form of a rational law but none of its rebarbative abstraction. It allows specific and universal mysteriously to coalesce, without need of conceptual mediation, and thus inscribes a global imperative on the body of the sensuously given in the manner of an hegemonic rather than a tyrannical authority. Finally, it offers an image of sheer self-determining autonomy, in which Nature, the conditioned and determined, is subtly alchemized into purposive freedom, and iron necessity miraculously reappears as absolute self-government. It thus offers an ideological paradigm for both individual subject and social order – for the aesthetic representation is a *society*, in which each constituent component is the condition of the purposive existence of every other, and finds in that felicitous totality the ground of its own identity.

In the light of this theory, it is difficult not to feel that many traditional debates about the relations between the aesthetic and the ideological – as reflection, production, transcendence, estrangement and so on – have been somewhat superfluous. From one viewpoint, the aesthetic *is* the ideological. But to claim that the reconciliation of freedom and necessity, self and others, spirit and Nature lies in the aesthetic is tantamount to confessing, gloomily enough, that it is hardly anywhere to be found. This triumphant resolution of social contradictions depends on an activity for which, as Karl Marx wryly commented, the middle class has exceedingly little time. What matters is less *art* than *aesthetics*; indeed when Theodor Adorno remarked in 1970 that 'Aesthetics today is powerless to avert its becoming a necrologue of art,'[22] it is only that 'today' that one might query. A double displacement occurs in the Enlightenment, from cultural production as such to a particular ideology of the artefact, and from that to ideology in general. For it is clear that what the ruling order requires is nothing as anaemically intellectualist as Destutt de Tracy's 'science of ideas', but a theory of ideological practice – a formalization of that which in its spontaneous immediacy would seem to evade the concept. If the ideological is primarily a question of feeling, then the aesthetic can model it a good deal more effectively than zoology. If formalizing the non-discursive would seem a peculiarly self-defeating project – if there is an oxymoronic ring to the very phrase 'theory of ideology' – then the most appropriate sign of this impossibility is the mysteriousness of art itself, which is and is not a rule-governed realm.

There is no reason to suppose, however, that 'ideology' need always be a pejorative term, and that the aesthetic stands unequivocally on the side of social oppression. Against a social philosophy founded upon egoism and appetite, Kant speaks up for a generous vision of a community of ends, finding in the freedom and autonomy of the aesthetic a prototype of human possibility equally at odds with feudal absolutism and possessive individualism. If there is no way in which this admirable ideal of mutual respect, equality and compassion can enter upon material reality, if it is necessary to rehearse in the mind what cannot be enacted in the world, this is hardly the responsibility of Kant himself.

It is within this bold vision that Marx's immanent critique will find a foothold, enquiring how it comes about that such dreams of freedom and moral dignity succeed in reproducing the conditions of violence and exploitation. 'In art, like everywhere else,' writes Adorno of idealist aesthetics, 'nothing deserved respect unless it owed its existence to the autonomous subject. What was valid and true about this for the subject was invalid and untrue for the non-subjective other: freedom for the former was unfreedom for the latter.'[23] Kant's own desperate solution to this dilemma was to split the subject down the middle, secreting its liberty at such an unsearchable depth that it becomes at once inviolable and ineffectual. Such a radical division of actual and ideal, however, will prove a constant source of ideological embarrassment; and it will be left to Hegel to draw the two realms together by the discourse of dialectics.

Notes

1 Fredric Jameson, *The Political Unconscious: Narrative as a Socially Symbolic Act* (Ithaca and London, 1981), p. 251.
2 See Jacques Derrida, 'Economimesis', *Diacritics* 11:2 (1981). It is fair to add that Kant would no doubt have thought this need to figure the non-phenomenal in phenomenal terms entirely inevitable.
3 See Georg Lukács, *History and Class Consciousness* (London, 1971), pp. 114–34. See also Lucien Goldmann, *Immanuel Kant* (London, 1971).
4 Lukács, *History and Class Consciousness*, p. 121.

5 See Walter Benjamin, *Charles Baudelaire: A Lyric Poet in the Era of High Capitalism* (London, 1973), p. 55.
6 See Charles Taylor, 'Kant's Theory of Freedom', in *Philosophy and the Human Sciences*, vol. 2 (Cambridge, 1985).
7 Karl Marx, *The People's Paper* (19 April 1856). For an account of Kant's own political views, see Howard Williams, *Kant's Political Philosophy* (Oxford, 1983).
8 See Alasdair MacIntyre, *A Short History of Ethics* (London, 1967), and *After Virtue* (London, 1981).
9 See Ernst Cassirer, *Kant's Life and Thought* (New Haven and London, 1981), pp. 246–7.
10 Sigmund Freud comments in 'The Economic Problem of Masochism' that Kant's categorical imperative 'is . . . a direct inheritance from the Oedipus complex' (*Standard Edition of the Complete Psychological Works of Sigmund Freud*, ed. J. Strachey (London, 1955–74), vol. XIX, p. 169.
11 Salim Kemal, *Kant and Fine Art* (Oxford, 1986), p. 76.
12 H. J. Paton, *The Categorical Imperative* (London, 1947), p. 256.
13 See Jacques Lacan, 'The Mirror Stage', in *Écrits: A Selection* (London, 1977), and Louis Althusser, 'Ideology and Ideological State Apparatuses', in *Lenin and Philosophy* (London, 1971).
14 For useful accounts of the sublime, see Thomas Weiskel, *The Romantic Sublime* (Baltimore and London, 1976), Part 2, and Gilles Deleuze, *Kant's Critical Philosophy* (Minneapolis, 1984), pp. 50–2. Other studies of Kant's aesthetics are Donald W. Crawford, *Kant's Aesthetic Theory* (Madison, 1974); F. Coleman, *The Harmony of Reason* (Pittsburgh, 1974); Paul Guyer, *Kant and the Claims of Taste* (Cambridge, Mass., 1979); Eva Schaper, *Studies in Kant's Aesthetics* (Edinburgh, 1979); and P. van De Pitte, *Kant as Philosophical Anthropologist* (The Hague, 1971). Two hostile accounts of Kantian aesthetics are D. S. Miall, 'Kant's Critique of Judgement: A Biased Aesthetic', *British Journal of Aesthetics*, vol. 20, no. 2 (1980), and Karl Ameriks, 'Kant and the Objectivity of Taste', *British Journal of Aesthetics*, vol. 23, no. 1 (1983).
15 Benjamin, *Charles Baudelaire*, p. 55.
16 Ted Cohen and Paul Guyer, Introduction to Cohen and Guyer (eds), *Essays in Kant's Aesthetics* (Chicago, 1982), p. 12.
17 Ibid.
18 Cassirer, *Kant's Life and Thought* p. 318.
19 Kant, *Critique of Judgement* (Oxford, 1952), Part 2, p. 23n.
20 Kemal, *Kant and Fine Art* p. 76.
21 Michel Foucault, *The Order of Things* (New York, 1973), chapter 7.
22 Theodor Adorno, *Aesthetic Theory* (London, 1984), p. 5.
23 Ibid., p. 92.

4

Schiller and Hegemony

Kant's rigorous duality of cognition and aesthetic judgement contains the seeds of its own deconstruction, as some of his successors were not slow to recognize. For if the aesthetic denotes the reference of an object to a subject, then it must, as Kant acknowledges, be present as a moment of all our knowledge. It is a necessary supposition of all our investigation of Nature that Nature is structured for, or 'shows some regard for', our cognitive faculties. Kant's 'Copernician revolution' in thought centres the world upon the human subject, and by doing so lends itself inherently to the aesthetic, making that whole register of experience seem less marginal, gratuitous or supplementary than it might otherwise appear. The harmony of faculties which is aesthetic pleasure is in fact a harmony requisite for every empirical cognition; so that if the aesthetic is in a sense 'supplementary' to our other activities of mind, it is a supplement which turns out by some Derridean logic to be more like their foundation or precondition. As Gilles Deleuze argues, 'A faculty would never take on a legislative and determining role were not all the faculties together capable of this free subjective harmony [of the aesthetic].'[1]

The root of all knowledge for Kant, as John MacMurray has pointed out, is the productive imagination; and this means to say that Kantian knowledge is always in some sense fictional.[2] This incipient aestheticization of cognition, however, must be strictly curbed, lest rationality collapse into Romantic excess; and for Kant to claim that the aesthetic does not involve determinate concepts is thus as much to safeguard rationality from this unsettling parody of itself as to account for its peculiar mode of working. The danger is that of identifying truth with what is satisfying to the mind, as the danger in the domain of ethics is to equate the good simply with what is creatively fulfilling. Such hedonism is deeply offensive to Kant's puritan austerity: truth and goodness are not so glibly come by, but require discipline and exertion. Yet practical reason, in its absolutely self-determining, self-grounding character, already resembles an 'aesthetic' phenomenon of a kind; and it will thus always be possible for others to conflate the two dimensions. The aesthetic is therefore a perilously ambivalent object for bourgeois society. On the one hand, in its subject-centredness, universality, spontaneous consensuality, intimacy, harmony and purposiveness, it offers to cater for some of that society's ideological needs superbly well; but it threatens on the other hand to escalate uncontrollably beyond this function to undercut the very foundations of rationality and moral duty. Taste, at one level sharply separate from truth and morality, seems at another level their very basis; and the terms are thus ripe for a deconstruction which will license some Romanticism to aestheticize the whole of reality. Bourgeois thought would seem confronted with an unenviable choice between preserving its rationality only at the cost of marginalizing an ideologically fruitful mode, and cultivating that mode to the point where it threatens to usurp truth and virtue themselves.

It might be claimed that Friedrich Schiller's *On the Aesthetic Education of Man* advances some way towards such a deconstruction, remaining within a Kantian problematic it simultaneously interrogates. If Kant has too severely dislocated Nature and reason, Schiller will define the aesthetic as exactly the hinge or transitional stage between the brutely sensual and the sublimely rational. In the form of the so-called 'play drive', the aesthetic condition reconciles the sense drive – the changing, shapeless, appetitive stuff of sensation and desire – with the formal drive, the active, shaping, immutable force of Kantian reason. 'The [sense drive]', writes Schiller,

> insists upon absolute reality: [man] is to turn everything which is mere form into world, and make all his potentialities fully manifest. The [formal drive] insists upon absolute formality: he is to destroy everything in himself which is mere world, and bring harmony into all his changes. In other words, he is to externalise all that is within him, and give form to all that is outside him.[3]

What brings about this resolution of sense and spirit, matter and form, change and permanence, finitude and infinity, is the aesthetic, an epistemological category which Schiller has now thoroughly anthropologized.

The aesthetic, however, is simply a way-stage or passage to the non-sensuous imperatives of practical reason, which Schiller as a good enough Kantian fully endorses. There is no question, it would seem, of his aestheticizing truth and morality out of existence: they remain humanity's loftiest goals, but goals which appear somewhat absolutist and unfeeling in their demands on sensual human nature. One can read Schiller's text, that is to say, as an essential softening up of Kant's imperious superego of reason, a tempering which carries its own ideological necessity. For if reason is simply at war with the flesh, how is it ever to take root in the body of lived experience? How is 'theory' to flesh itself out as 'ideology'? Schiller is writing with the sound of French revolutionary Terror in his ears, which might suggest one reason why he believes abstract reason to stand in need of a little compassionate moderation; but the ideological dilemma he confronts is in fact more general than this. Reason will only secure its sway if it is, in Gramscian terms, consensual rather than bluntly coercive; it must achieve hegemony in collusion with the senses it subdues, rather than trampling roughshod over them. The Kantian duality of Nature and reason simply short-circuits what we might call the question of ideological reconstruction, leaving us with little clue as to how we are to leap from the one realm to the other. Schiller, for his part, recognizes that this tension between absolute ethical injunctions, and the sordid sublunary state of bourgeois nature, must be at once sustained and relaxed; and the aesthetic is the category which will perform this difficult double operation. We shall see, however, that it succeeds in darkening the question of the transition from Nature to reason as much as illuminating it.

As a progressive refinement of sensation and desire, the aesthetic accomplishes a kind of deconstruction: it breaks down the tyrannical dominion of the sense drive not by the imposition of some external ukase, but from within. 'Through the aesthetic modulation of the psyche, then, the autonomy of reason is already opened up within the domain of sense itself, the dominion of sensation already broken within its own frontiers, and physical man refined to the point where spiritual man only needs to start developing out of the physical according to the laws of freedom' (163). On the terrain of the aesthetic, humanity must 'play the war against Matter into the very territory of Matter itself, so that [it] may be spared having to fight his dread foe on the sacred soil of Freedom' (169). It is easier, in other words, for reason to regulate sensuous Nature if it has already been busy eroding and subliming it from the inside; and it is precisely this which the aesthetic interplay of spirit and sense will achieve. The aesthetic performs in this sense an essentially propaedeutic role, processing and defusing the raw stuff of sensational life for its eventual subjugation at the hands of reason. It is as though, in the aesthetic, reason plays along with the senses, inscribes them formally from the inside as a kind of fifth columnist in the enemy camp, thereby rehearsing us in those higher states of truth and goodness towards which we are travelling. Otherwise, as creatures sunk degenerately in our desires, we are likely to experience the dictates of reason as unpleasantly absolutist and arbitrary, and so fail to comply with them. Schiller shrewdly recognizes that Kant's starkly deontological decrees are by no means the most effective ideological mechanism for subjugating a recalcitrant material world; Kant's Duty, like some paranoid absolutist monarch, reveals too little trust in the masses' generous instincts for conformity to it. This churlishly suspicious despot thus needs a touch of populist sympathy if its hegemony is to be ensured: 'Duty, stern voice of Necessity, must moderate the censorious tone of its precepts – a tone only justified by the resistance they encounter – and show greater respect for Nature through a nobler confidence in her willingness to obey them' (217). Duty must engage more closely with inclination: that moral character is defective which can assert itself only by sacrificing the natural, just as 'a political constitution will still be very imperfect if it is able to achieve unity only by suppressing variety' (19). The political allusion is apposite, since there is no doubt that the 'sense drive' for Schiller directly evokes appetitive individualism. His uncultivated 'savage', 'self-seeking, and yet without a Self; lawless, yet without Freedom' (171), is no exotic tribal specimen but the average German middle-class philistine, who sees in Nature's splendid profusion nothing but his own prey, and either devours its objects in an access of desire or thrusts them horrifiedly aside when they threaten to destroy him. The sense drive is also the proletariat, with its 'crude, lawless instincts, unleashed with the loosening of the bonds of civil order, and hastening with ungovernable fury to their animal satisfactions' (25).

What Schiller terms the 'aesthetic modulation of the psyche' in fact denotes a project of fundamental ideological reconstruction. The aesthetic is the missing mediation between a barbaric civil society given over to pure appetite, and the ideal of a well-ordered political state: 'if man is ever to solve that problem of politics in practice he will have to approach it through the problem of the aesthetic, because it is only through Beauty that man makes his way to Freedom' (9). Every progressive politics will founder as surely as Jacobinism if it fails to take a detour through the psychical and address itself to the problem of transforming the human subject. Schiller's 'aesthetic' is in this sense Gramsci's 'hegemony' in a different key, and both concepts are brought to political birth by the dismal collapse of revolutionary hopes. The only politics that will hold is one firmly rooted in a refashioned 'culture' and a revolutionized subjectivity.

The aesthetic will leave humanity, not free, moral and truthful, but inherently ready to receive and respond to these rational imperatives: 'although this [aesthetic] state can of itself decide nothing as regards either our insights or our convictions, thus leaving both our intellectual and our moral worth as yet entirely problematic, it is nevertheless the necessary pre-condition of our attaining to any insight or conviction at all. In a word, there is no other way of making sensuous man rational except by first making him aesthetic' (161). Uneasily conscious that this might seem to make reason slavishly dependent upon sensuous representation, thus undermining its self-validatory power, Schiller swerves instantly back to Kantian orthodoxy: 'Should truth and duty not be able, of and by themselves alone, to gain access to sensuous man? To which I must answer: they not only can, they positively must, owe their determining power to themselves alone . . .' (161). Beauty imparts the *power* to think and decide, and in this sense underlies truth and morality; but it has no say at all in the actual uses of these powers, which are consequently self-determining. The aesthetic is the matrix of thought and action, but exercises no dominion over that to which it gives birth; far from hubristically usurping the role of reason, it simply smooths the path for its august appearance. It is not quite, however, a ladder which we climb only to kick away; for though the aesthetic is the mere precondition of truth and virtue, it nevertheless somehow prefigures what it will produce.

Truth is by no means beauty, so Schiller stoutly maintains against the aestheticizers; but beauty nonetheless in principle contains it. A narrow pathway can thus be opened up between Kant's disabling duality of faculties on the one hand, and some aestheticist conflation of them on the other.

What does it mean to claim that the aesthetic is the essential precondition of the moral? It means, more or less, that in this peculiar condition the rigorous determination of the sense drive, and the equally despotic power of the formal drive, play ceaselessly into one other and so succeed in cancelling out each other's pressures, thus leaving us in a state of negative freedom or 'free determinability'. 'To the extent that [the play drive] deprives feelings and passions of their dynamic power, it will bring them into harmony with the ideas of reason; and to the extent that it deprives the laws of reason of their moral compulsion, it will reconcile them with the interests of the senses' (99). The aesthetic is a kind of fictive or heuristic realm in which we can suspend the force of our usual powers, imaginatively transferring qualities from one drive to another in a kind of free-wheeling experiment of the mind. Having momentarily disconnected these drives from their real-life contexts, we can enjoy the fantasy of reconstituting each by means of the other, reconstructing psychical conflict in terms of its potential resolution. This condition is not yet liberty, which consists in Kantian vein in our free conformity to the moral law; but it is a kind of sheer potential for such positive freedom, the darkly indeterminate source of all our active self-determination. In the aesthetic, we are temporarily emancipated from all determination whatsoever, either physical or moral, and pass instead through a state of utter determinability. It is a world of pure hypothesis, a perpetual 'as if', in which we experience our powers and capacities as pure formal possibilities, drained of all particularity; and it is thus a condition of being somewhat equivalent to Kant's pure aesthetic capacity for cognition, which remains untrammalled by the determination of a specific concept.

All of this, however, makes the aesthetic, that mighty force at the root of our moral humanity, sound like nothing so much as a simple *aporia*. Two strenuously antagonistic forces cancel each other out into a kind of stalemate or nullity, and this sheer suggestive nothingness is our pre-capacity for all value. There is, however, nullity and nullity – mere blank negation, and that richly potential vacuity which, as the suspension of every specific constraint, lays the fertile ground for free action. In the aesthetic condition,

[Man] must, consequently, in a certain sense, return to that negative state of complete absence of determination in which he found himself before anything at all had made an impression upon his senses. But that former condition was completely devoid of content; and now it is a question of combining such sheer absence of determination, and an equally unlimited determinability, with the greatest possible content, since directly from this condition something positive is to result. The determination he has received through sensation must therefore be preserved, because there must be no loss of reality; but at the same time it must, inasmuch as it is limitation, be annulled, since an unlimited determinability is to come into existence. The problem is, therefore, at one and the same time to destroy and to maintain the determination of the condition – and this is possible in one way only: by confronting it with another determination. The scales of the balance stand level when they are empty; but they also stand level when they contain equal weights. (141)

The aesthetic is a kind of creative impasse, a nirvanic suspension of all determinacy and desire overflowing with entirely unspecific contents. Since it nullifies the limits of sensation along with its compulsiveness, it becomes a kind of sublime infinity of possibilities. In the aesthetic state, 'man is Nought, if we are thinking of any particular result rather than of the totality of his powers, and considering the absence in him of any specific determination' (146); but this negativity is thereby everything, a pure boundless being which eludes all sordid specificity. Taken as a whole, the aesthetic condition is supremely positive; yet it is also sheer emptiness, a deep and dazzling darkness in which all determinations are grey, an infinity of nothingness. The wretched social condition which Schiller mourns – the fragmentation of human faculties in the division of labour, the specializing and reifying of capacities, the mechanizing and dissociating of human powers – must be redeemed by a condition which is, precisely, nothing in particular. As entirely indeterminate, the

108

aesthetic upbraids the drastic one-sidedness of society with its own serene playfulness of being; but its release from all determination is also a dream of absolute freedom which belongs with the bourgeois order itself. Unlimited determinability is the alert posture of one ready for anything, as well as a utopian critique of all actual, determinate being from an eternally subjunctive standpoint.

Schiller speaks of the power which is restored to humanity in the aesthetic mode as 'the highest of all bounties' (147), and in celebrated phrase remarks that man is fully human only when he plays. But if this is so, then the aesthetic must be the *telos* of human existence, not the transition to such an end. It would certainly appear more free than the domain of morality, precisely because it dissolves all ethical constraints along with physical ones. On the one hand, the aesthetic 'only offers us the possibility of becoming human beings, and for the rest leaves it to our own free will to decide how far we wish to make this a reality' (149); on the other hand, as a state of pure untrammelled possibility, a fusion of sensual and rational, it would seem superior to what it enables, a ground elevated above what rests upon it. This ambiguity reflects a real ideological dilemma. The problem with Kantian freedom is that the moral law which enshrines it would also seem to undercut it. This freedom is of a peculiarly peremptory kind, issuing its imperious decrees in apparent indifference to the needs and natures of its subjects. True freedom may thus be shifted to the aesthetic; but since this is innocent of all moral direction and concrete determinations, it is hard to see how it will do as an adequate image of social practice. The aesthetic is whatever is the other of any specific social interest; it is without bias to any definite activity, but precisely on that account a general activating capacity. Culture is the negation of all concrete claims and commitments in the name of totality – a totality which is therefore purely void because it is no more than a totalization of negated moments. The aesthetic, in brief, is mere Olympian indifferentism: 'because it takes under its protection no single one of man's faculties to the exclusion of the others, it favours each and all of them without distinction; and it favours no single one more than another for the simple reason that it is the ground of possibility of them all' (151). Unable to say one thing without saying everything, the aesthetic says nothing whatsoever, so boundlessly eloquent as to be speechless. In cultivating every possibility to the limit, it risks leaving us musclebound and immobilized. If, after aesthetic enjoyment, 'we find ourselves disposed to prefer some one particular mode of feeling or action, but unfitted or disinclined for another, this may serve as infallible proof that we have not had a purely aesthetic experience . . .' (153). As the very taproot of our moral virtue, the aesthetic is apparently invalid unless it predisposes us indifferently to martydrom or murder. It is the way we come to think and act creatively, the transcendental ground of our practice, yet all particular thought and action are a falling off from it. As soon as we suffer concrete determination we have lost this pregnant nothingness, keeling over from one absence into another. Human existence would seem a perpetual oscillation between two types of negation, as sheer aesthetic capacity lapses through action into limitation of being, only to revert again to itself. The aesthetic, in short, is socially useless, just as its philistine critics maintain: 'for beauty produces no particular result whatsoever, neither for the understanding nor for the will. It accomplishes no particular purpose, neither intellectual nor moral; it discovers no individual truth, helps us to perform no individual duty and is, in short, as unfitted to provide a firm basis for character as to enlighten the understanding' (147). But all this, precisely, is the aesthetic's crowning glory: superbly indifferent to any one-sided truth, purpose or practice, it is nothing less than the boundless infinity of our total humanity, ruined as soon as realized. Culture, it would seem, is just a perpetual openness to anything.

By the close of Schiller's text, the aesthetic is showing signs of overreaching its humble status as handmaiden of reason. The moral law it formally subserves would seem inferior to it in one major respect: it is incapable of generating positive affective bonds between individuals. The law subjects the individual will to the general, thus securing the general conditions of possibility of social life; it sets subject over against subject, curbing their inclinations, but cannot act as a dynamic source of social harmony and pleasurable intercourse. Reason implants in humanity the principles of social conduct, but beauty alone confers on this conduct a social character. 'Taste alone brings harmony into society, because it fosters harmony in the individual . . . only the aesthetic mode of communication unites society, because it relates to that which is common to all' (215). Taste, moreover, can offer all this and happiness too, as the grim strictures of morality cannot: 'Beauty alone makes the whole world happy'

(217), whereas the price of moral virtue is self-abnegation. The aesthetic is the language of human solidarity, setting its face against all socially divisive elitism and privilege: 'No privilege, no autocracy of any kind, is tolerated where taste rules' (217), and esoteric knowledge, led out by taste into the 'broad daylight of Common Sense', becomes the common possession of society as a whole. The aesthetic state, in short, is the utopian bourgeois public sphere of liberty, equality and democracy, within which everyone is a free citizen, 'having equal rights with the noblest' (219). The constrained social order of class-struggle and division of labour has already been overcome in principle in the consensual kingdom of beauty, which installs itself like a shadowy paradise within the present. Taste, with its autonomy, universality, equality and fellow-feeling, is a whole alternative politics, suspending social hierarchy and reconstituting relations between individuals in the image of disinterested fraternity. Culture is the only true social harmony, a shadowy oppositional society within the present, a noumenal kingdom of persons and ends secretly traversing the phenomenal realm of things and causes. Yet if the aesthetic thus suggests the form of a wholly different social order, its actual content, as we have seen, would seem no more than an indeterminate negation, brimming with nothing but its own inexpressible potential. The positive unity of class society, in other words, would seem to be nothing at all, potent but mysteriously elusive; any discourse capable of spanning that society's actual, multiple divisions must indeed be of remarkably low definition. As the ideal unity of a divided reality, the aesthetic is necessarily ambiguous and obscure; to see it as a matter of potential alone is to confess that in this society individuals are at odds with each other as soon as they have acted. Cultural unity must be pressed back beyond all actual self-realization, which in this order is likely to prove dominative and partial; culture exists to enable human self-determination, but is also violated by it. Its force can be preserved, then, only if its content is steadily dwindled to nothing. Culture in no sense determines what we should do; it is rather that, in continuing to do whatever we are doing, we act with an equipoise which implies we could just as easily be doing something else. It is thus a question of style, or 'grace' as Schiller would term it: we will learn best how to behave by taking our cue from a condition which involves doing nothing whatsoever.

Neither the moral law nor the aesthetic condition, then, will wholly suffice as images of the ideal society, which is why, perhaps, Schiller's work seems unwittingly torn between elevating the law above the aesthetic, and the aesthetic over the law. The law, of course, officially reigns supreme; but it can offer no sensuous representation of the freedom it signifies, and the alarming truth must be faced that morality is incapable in itself of providing the ideological bonding essential for social cohesion. In its Kantian form, it is too abstract, individualist and imperious, too sadistically desirous of submission in its subjects, to carry through these consensual tasks at all effectively. The onus of such a project therefore shifts to the aesthetic; yet if the ethical is too formulaic and unbending for such purposes, too little sensitive to individual differences, the aesthetic would seem in its own way equally empty of practical content. If the law is too astringently masculine, too implacable in its exactions, the aesthetic is too malleably feminine. Culture marks an advance on a formalistic moral ideology by its openness to the senses; yet that embrace of the sensuous takes the form of defusing its determinate contents, hence falling back into the very formalism it was out to transcend.

The aesthetic for Schiller involves the creation of semblance; and since semblance involves a creative indifference to Nature, it is through a delight in such beautiful appearance that 'savage' human beings first grope their laborious way upward from animal dependency on their environment to the freedom of the aesthetic. Humanity launches out on the path of its true liberty, effecting a breach in its biological nature, once it 'starts preferring form to substance, and jeopardising reality for the sake of semblance' (205). If this movement abandons Nature at one level, it also stays faithful to it at another – for Nature itself has prodigally lavished on its creatures more than the bare necessities of existence, and offers in this material surplus a dim prevision of the illimitability of aesthetic freedom. The aesthetic, then, is in this sense natural: we must be prodded upward into it by the power of Nature itself, since what otherwise might impel us towards it – the will – is a product of the state of freedom, not its precondition. But the aesthetic is at the same time unnatural, since in order to come into its own the imagination must make some mysteriously inexplicable leap out of this purely material super-abundance into its own fertile autonomy. The relation between Nature and freedom, in short, is aporetic: the latter breaks sharply with the former, but somehow under the former's own impulsion. Freedom cannot take off from itself, since this would suggest that there was already a will to do so, thus rendering freedom anterior to itself. But if freedom shares some kinship with Nature, how can it be free? The negative indeterminacy of the aesthetic, transitional point between Nature and freedom, necessity and reason, is thus required as a solution to the riddle of where freedom comes from, of how it could ever have possibly been born of the unfree. The enigma of the aesthetic is the solution to this puzzle – which is to say that one riddle is merely answered with another. The obscurity of Schiller's doctrine of the aesthetic is the inscrutibility of the origins of freedom in a society where rational subjectivity is the negation of all sensuousness and materiality. How freedom and necessity, subject and object, spirit and sense can possibly go together is, in such an alienated social order, theoretically impossible to say. Yet there are increasingly urgent political reasons why they should do so, and the obscurity of the aesthetic in Schiller's thought is the upshot of this impasse.

The ambiguities of Schiller's work, dutifully tidied away to 'paradoxes' by his English editors, are signs of genuine political dilemmas. Indeed the whole text is a kind of political allegory, in which the troubled relations between sense drive and formal drive, or Nature and reason, are never far from a reflection on the ideal relations between populace and ruling class, or civil society and absolutist state. Schiller draws the parallel quite explicitly himself, comparing the relation between reason (which enjoins unity) and Nature (which demands multiplicity) to the desirable relation between political state and society. The state, while its demand for unity is absolute, must nevertheless respect the 'subjective and specific character' of its materials (the populace); it must nurture and respect spontaneous impulse, and achieve its unity without suppressing plurality. Just as reason in the aesthetic realm cunningly inserts itself within the sensual, refining it from the inside into compliance with its own injunctions, so the political state 'can only become a reality inasmuch as its parts have been tuned up to the idea of the whole' (21). It is the aesthetic, as ideological reconstruction and hegemonic strategy, which will accomplish this end; so that 'once man is inwardly at one with himself, he will be able to preserve his individuality however much he may universalise his conduct, and the State will be merely the interpreter of his own finest instinct, a clearer formulation

113

of his own sense of what is right' (21). If this fails to happen, Schiller warns, if 'subjective man sets his face against objective man', then the latter (the state) will be forced into the coercive suppression of the former (civil society), and will 'ruthlessly trample underfoot such powerfully seditious individualism in order not to fall a victim to it' (21). In this bleak political condition, 'the concrete life of the Individual is destroyed in order that the abstract idea of the Whole may drag out its sorry existence, and the State remains forever a stranger to its citizens since at no point does it ever make contact with their feeling' (37).

Political power, in short, must implant itself in subjectivity itself, if its dominance is to be secure; and this process requires the production of a citizen whose ethico-political duty has been internalized as spontaneous inclination. Moral greatness, Schiller argues in his essay 'On Grace and Dignity', is a question of obeying the moral law; but moral *beauty* is the graceful disposition to such conformity, the law introjected and habituated, the reconstruction of one's entire subjecthood in its terms. It is this whole cultural life-style which is the true object of moral judgement, not, as with Kant, certain discrete actions: 'Man is intended not to perform separate moral actions, but to be a moral being. Not virtues, but virtue is his precept, and virtue is nothing else than an inclination to duty.'[4] An atomistic ethics, earnestly calculating the effects of intentions of each distinct action, is anti-aesthetic: the shift from morality to culture is one from the power of the head to the rule of the heart, from abstract decision to bodily disposition. The 'whole' human subject, as we have seen elsewhere, must convert its necessity into freedom, transfigure its ethical duty into instinctual habit, and so operate like an aesthetic artefact.

'On Grace and Dignity', like *The Aesthetic Education of Man*, makes no secret of the political foundations of this aesthetic. 'Let us suppose', Schiller writes, 'a monarchical state administered in such a way that, although all goes on according to the will of one person, each citizen could persuade himself that he governs and obeys only his own inclination, we should call that government a liberal government' (200–1). Similarly, 'If the mind is manifested in such a way through the sensuous nature subject to its empire that it executes its behests with the most faithful exactitude, or expresses its sentiments in the most perfectly speaking manner, without going in the least against that which the aesthetic sense demands from it as a phenomenon, then we shall see produced that which we call *grace*' (201). Grace is to personal life, in brief, as the spontaneous submission of the masses is to the political state. In the political as in the aesthetic order, each individual unit behaves as though it governs itself by virtue of the way it is governed by the law of the whole. The absolutist prince of reason must neither restrict all free movement of the senses which serve him, nor allow them libertine sway. Schiller takes Kant to task for unjustly setting aside the rights of sensuous nature, claiming instead that morality must couple itself with inclination and so become a kind of 'second nature'. Kant's moral theory, in other words, is damagingly incapable of becoming effective ideology. If the moral law, that most sublime witness to our human grandeur, does nothing but humiliate and accuse us, can it really be true to its Kantian status as a rational law of self-conferred liberty? And is it altogether surprising that human beings will be tempted to rebel against a juridical power which appears to be alien and indifferent to them?

The dangers of aestheticizing the law to nothing, however, remain firmly in Schiller's sights. If it is true, as he argues in 'On Grace and Dignity', that 'the moral perfection of man cannot shine forth except from this very association of his inclination with his moral conduct' (206), it is equally the case, as he reminds us in his essay 'The Moral Utility of Aesthetic Manners', that taste is in itself a dubious foundation for moral existence. Order, harmony and perfection are not in themselves virtues, even if 'taste gives a direction to the soul which disposes it to virtue' (132). Another essay, 'On the Necessary Limitations in the Use of Beauty of Form', is likewise concerned to restore the edge to the rational: here Schiller contrasts the 'body' or material dimension of a discourse, where the imagination may be permitted a certain rhetorical license, with its conceptual substance, and warns of the dangers of rhetorical signifier coming to usurp conceptual signified. Such a move assigns too high a status to the feminine, for women are concerned with the 'matter' or external medium of truth, its beauteous embellishments, rather than with truth itself. Good taste involves the regulated coupling of male and female, signified and signifier, constative and performative; but this coupling is not symmetrical, since power and priority must always lie with the former terms. Rhetoric, or the sensuous body of a discourse, must never forget that it 'carries out an order emanating from elsewhere', that it is not its own affairs it treats of; if this forgetfulness were to occur, men might end up becoming indifferent to rational substance and allow themselves to be seduced by empty appearance. Woman, in brief, is a co-partner who must know her place: 'taste must be confined to regulating the external form, while reason and experience determine the substance and the essence of conceptions' (245). Taste has its drawbacks, in short: the more it refines and sophisticates us, the more it saps our inclination to perform actions commanded by duty which revolt our sensibilities. The fact that we should not be brutes is no excuse for becoming eunuchs.

Howard Caygill has convincingly argued that Kantian aesthetics stands at the confluence of two opposed traditions: the British lineage of 'sympathy', moral sense and natural law, which believes it possible to foster a harmonious unity in bourgeois civil society independently of juridical coercion and political decree; and the German rationalist heritage flowing from Leibniz and Christian Wolff to Alexander Baumgarten, which in its concern with the universal validity and necessity of the aesthetic is bound up with the ideologies of legality of an enlightened absolutism.[5] Such German aesthetics, in its pre-occupation with law and concept as against sense and feeling, implies the dominance of state legality over the 'moral' or affective domain of civil society. Schiller's work is a significant qualification of this tendency: social unity must be generated in a sense from 'below', from an aesthetically transformed or ideologically reconstituted civil society, not legislated arbitrarily from above. Yet the reservation of 'in a sense' is significant, since the way this will come about is not through some sentimental populist faith in natural spontaneity, but, as we have seen, through reason, in the disguise of the aesthetic, smuggling itself into the enemy camp of sensation in an effort to know, and hence master, its antagonist. If, then, Schiller is on the one hand notably nervous of law, which as he writes in his essay on the pathetic tends to restrict and humiliate us, he also betrays from time to time a pathological suspicion of the senses, which threaten to clog the free soaring of rational spirit. An idealist impulse to sublimate the sensual to the point of evaporation is at odds with a more judicious materialist recognition of Nature's stubborn autonomy. But if the former project plays too readily into the hands of rationalist absolutism, the latter viewpoint acknowledges the reality of sensuous experience only at the risk of having to renounce the absolutism of reason and the transformative power of the imagination.

The aesthetic ideal, as we have seen, is an interfusion of sense and spirit, which teaches us that 'the moral freedom of man is by no means abrogated through his inevitable dependence upon physical things'.[6] Yet this felicitous partnership is by no means as mutual as it looks: 'in the realm of truth and morality, feeling may have no say whatsoever; but in the sphere of being and well-being, form has every right to exist, and the play-drive every right to command'. The deconstruction, in other words, is all one way: the form-giving potency of male reason penetrates and subdues the inchoate sensual female, but as 'feeling' she has no reciprocal voice in the sphere of truth and morality. In the highest condition of humanity – the aesthetic state – semblance will reign supreme, and 'all that is mere matter ceases to be' (217). Such beautiful appearance veils the squalour of sensual reality, and 'by a delightful illusion of freedom, conceals from us our degrading kinship with matter' (219). An idealized version of the woman as beauty is wielded against a debased image of her as sensuality. Schiller's text has arrived at the very threshold of Nietzsche's celebration of the aesthetic as life-enhancing illusion in *The Birth of Tragedy*, and a similar pessimism about material life underlies both affirmations. His aesthetic programme is on the one hand positive and constructive – an hegemonic strategy for which culture is no solitary contemplative dreaming but an active social force, offering in its utopian public sphere of civilized intercourse the missing mediation between the degraded state of civil society (Nature) and the political requirements of the absolutist state (reason). But this resourceful social project is in partial contradiction with its author's aestheticist idealism: the former involves a faith in the sensuous body and a liberal distrust of tyrannical reason too deeply qualified by the latter. The brave effort to refine matter into spirit, while somehow preserving it *as* matter, founders on the intransigent appetitive life of civil society, and can turn at crisis-point into an aestheticizing away of this whole degraded domain. In this mood, the aesthetic would seem less to transfigure material life than to cast a decorous veil over its chronic unregeneracy. Culture is at once active social remaking and ethereal realm of being, authentic freedom and the mere hallucination of happiness, a universal community which can be located 'only in some few chosen circles'

(219). If it is internally contradictory, it is because its relation to society as a whole can only be one of conflict.

Schiller's aesthetic thought provides some of the vital constituents of a new theory of bourgeois hegemony; but it also protests with magnificent passion against the spiritual devastation which that emergent social order is wreaking, and this is the aspect of it which has perhaps been most remembered.[7] 'In the very bosom of the most exquisitely developed social life', Schiller writes in the *Aesthetic Education of Man*, 'egotism has founded its system, and without ever acquiring therefrom a heart that is truly sociable, we suffer all the contagions and afflictions of society. We subject our free judgement to its despotic opinion, our feeling to its fantastic customs, our will to its seductions; only our caprice do we uphold against its sacred rights' (27). The proliferation of technical and empirical knowledges, the divisions of social and intellectual labour, have severed the 'inner unity of human nature' and set its harmonious powers at variance with one another in a 'disastrous conflict' (33). 'Everlastingly chained to a single little fragment of the Whole, man himself develops into nothing but a fragment; everlastingly in his ear the monotonous sound of the wheel that he turns, he never develops the harmony of his being, and instead of putting the stamp of humanity upon his own nature, he becomes nothing more than the imprint of his occupation or of his specialised knowledge' (35). Such one-sided development, so Schiller trusts, is a necessary stage in the progress of Reason towards some future synthesis; and this is a view he shares with Karl Marx, whose critique of industrial capitalism is deeply rooted in a Schillerian vision of stunted capacities, dissociated powers, the ruined totality of human nature. The whole radical aesthetic tradition from Coleridge to Herbert Marcuse, lamenting the inorganic, mechanistic nature of industrial capitalism, draws sustenance from this prophetic denunciation. What must then be emphasized is the contradictory nature of an aesthetic which on the one hand offers a fruitful ideological model of the human subject for bourgeois society, and on the other hand holds out a vision of human capacities by which that society can be measured and found gravely wanting. That ideal, of a rich, all-round development of human subjective powers, is inherited from a traditional, pre-bourgeois current of humanism, and stands implacably askew to possessive individualism; but there are other

118

aspects of the aesthetic which can fulfil some of that individualism's ideological needs. In its crippling lop-sidedness, bourgeois society is the enemy of aesthetic thought; but that thought recasts the relations between law and desire, reason and the body, in ways which have much to contribute to the emergent social order. The test of a truly radical aesthetics will be its ability to operate as social critique without simultaneously providing the grounds of political ratification.

Notes

1 Gilles Deleuze, *Kant's Critical Philosophy* (Minneapolis, 1984), p. 50.
2 See John MacMurray, *The Self as Agent* (London, 1969), chapter 1.
3 Friedrich Schiller, *On the Aesthetic Education of Man*, ed. Elizabeth M. Wilkinson and L. A. Willoughby (Oxford, 1967), p. 77. All subsequent references to this text will be given parenthetically after quotations.
4 'On Grace and Dignity', in *Works of Friedrich Schiller* (New York, n.d.), vol. IV, p. 200. All subsequent references to Schiller's essays refer to this volume, and are given parenthetically after quotations.
5 See Howard Caygill, 'Aesthetics and Civil Society: Theories of Art and Society 1640–1790', unpublished Ph.D thesis, University of Sussex, 1982.
6 Schiller, *On the Aesthetic Education of Man*, p. 187. Subsequent references to this text are given parenthetically after quotations.
7 See, for example, Georg Lukács, *Goethe and His Age* (London, 1968), chapters 6 & 7; Fredric Jameson, *Marxism and Form* (Princeton, 1971), chapter 2, Part 11; Margaret C. Ives, *The Analogue of Harmony* (Louvain, 1970). For other studies of Schiller's aesthetics, see S. S. Kerry, *Schiller's Writings on Aesthetics* (Manchester, 1961), and L.P. Wessell, 'Schiller and the Genesis of German Romanticism', *Studies in Romanticism*, vol. 10, no. 3 (1971).

5

The World as Artefact: Fichte, Schelling, Hegel

'Too tender for things', was how Hegel disdainfully described Kant's proto-materialist zeal to preserve the *Ding-an-sich*. For why preserve a realm about which absolutely nothing can be said? Since nothing can be predicated of it, Kant's thing-in-itself is a cypher as resistant to symbolization as the Lacanian real, more enigmatic even than God (of whom we can predicate certain qualities), the mere sign of an absence. The essence of reality can be preserved only by being removed from the realm of cognition, and so cancelled. In some fantasy of the death wish, the world will be rendered safe by being erased, insulated from the vagaries of subjectivism in the crypt of its own non-being. That which cannot be named cannot be violated; only nothingness, as Hegel himself knew, is purity of being, so blessedly free of determination that it does not even exist. Intersecting our world at every point is an entire phantasmal universe, which is the way reality might appear to us if we were not the limited creatures we are. We can say that such appearance would be different, but since we cannot say how it would be different the difference in question becomes pure, which is to say nothing whatsoever. As pure difference, the *Ding-an-sich* makes no difference at all. It is comforting, even so, to know that there is an inviolable domain of being so far removed from our life that it has all the intelligibility of a square triangle.

Hegel will have none of this effeminate cringing before the thing-in-itself, this timid last-minute withdrawal of thought from its full penetration of the object. For him, as more explicitly for Nietzsche after him, it is as though the sage of Königsberg is a pathetic old eunuch on this score, too tender and feminine by half, loitering irresolutely on the very threshold of some full possession of being without the potency to press ahead. His is at best a mere half-virility, able to conceive thought itself as active but then sundering it from its masterful appropriation of the object. Kant's Oedipal protectiveness towards the maternal body places the real reverently out of bounds, prohibiting that impious coupling of subject and object for which Hegel's dialectical programme will clamour. His system is feebly androgynous, active in respect of thought but passive with regard to sensation, a shamefaced idealism still sentimentally ensnared in empiricism. And the upshot of this unmanly compromise, as Hegel and others saw, is mere contradiction: like the maternal body, the thing-in-itself is posited and prohibited at a stroke, so utterly self-identical that language falters and swerves off from it, leaving behind it the sheer trace of a silence. Kant's epistemology mixes concept and intuition, masculine form and feminine content, but this marriage is unstable from the outset, neither fish nor fowl. Form is external to content in the realm of understanding, left without content in practical reason, and elevated to an end in itself in aesthetic judgement. Hegel, by contrast, will have the courage of his idealist virility, penetrating to the very essence of the object and delivering up its inmost secret. He will carry the contradictions of thought right into the thing itself, into the veiled and tabooed, and so will risk fissuring the reality which for Kant must remain chastely intact, dividing it against itself by the labour of the negative. But this is only possible because he already knows, in some Kleinian fantasy of reparation, that this violated being will finally be restored to itself whole and entire. The narrative of *Geist* may be one of strenuous conflict, but this dialectical activism is folded within *Geist*'s circular, womb-like enclosure, its constant tautological return upon itself. Indeed from this standpoint the sexual roles of Kant and Hegel are reversed with a vengeance. It is Kant, in the stark solitude of the ethical 'Ought', who stands austerely aloof from desire, censoring all copulation between freedom and Nature, surrendered to a reason continually at war with the flesh; and it is Hegel's dialectic which will restore to these bloodless forms their proper carnal content, sublating mere morality into the sensuous body of 'concrete ethics' (*Sittlichkeit*), returning all formal categories to the rich, fertile movement of *Geist*'s self-becoming.

Hegel's restlessly active subject, thrusting itself into Nature's most secret recesses in order to unmask her as an inferior version of himself, need have no fear that his desire will rip him from Nature and leave him bereft of a ground. For the subject's break from its imaginary communion with the world, with all the self-estrangement and unhappy consciousness which such a rupture involves, is no more than a necessary moment of Spirit's imaginary return to itself. What figures for the subject as a catastrophic lapse into the symbolic order figures for the Absolute as mere spume on the wave of its imaginary self-recuperation. The subject's fall from narcissistic self-presence to alienation is simply a strategic move within the Absolute's own brooding narcissism, a ruse of reason whereby it will finally rise to the delights of contemplating itself in the mirror of human self-consciousness. Like the Oedipal son, the subject must surrender its unmediated unity with the world, endure splitting and desolation; but its ultimate reward will be integration into reason itself, whose apparent harshness is thus merely kindness misperceived. Division and contradiction are the very constituents of a deeper imaginary identity; splitting, in a consoling fantasy, is also healing, a binding tighter of the circle of *Geist*, which as the identity of identity and non-identity will gather such difference into itself as enrichment. Its ceaseless loss of being is thus the very dynamic by which it grows to fullness.

Kant, as we have seen, distinguishes the aesthetic fiction of a world-for-the-subject from the clear-eyed realm of the understanding, which tells us that objects finally exist for themselves in a way quite beyond the reach of mind. Hegel will override this distinction at a stroke, refusing at once that dream of a Fichte in which the object is nothing apart from the ego, and the bleak condition in which it turns its back on humanity altogether. Reality for Hegel is inseparably for us and for itself, for us in the very essence of what it is. Things exist in themselves, but their truth will emerge only through the steady incorporation of their determinations in the dialectical whole of Spirit. What makes the object truly itself is simultaneously what turns its face towards humanity, for the principle of its being is at one with the root of our own subjectivity. Hegel projects Kant's aesthetic fiction into the very structure of the real, thus rescuing the subject at once from the *hubris* of subjectivism and the miseries of estrangement. The bourgeois dilemma, that what is objective escapes my possession, and what I possess ceases to be an object, is thus resolved: what is wholly mine is nevertheless entirely real, and mine precisely in that solid reality. The imaginary is elevated from the aesthetic to the theoretical, shifted up a gear from feeling to cognition. Ideology, in the shape of the identity of subject and object, is installed at the level of scientific knowledge; and Hegel can thus afford to assign art a lowly place in his system, since he has already covertly aestheticized the whole of the reality which contains it.

Hegel's great achievement, as Charles Taylor has argued, is to resolve the conflict between the bourgeois subject's drive for freedom and its desire for an expressive unity with the world.[1] He offers, in short, a formidable synthesis of Enlightenment and Romantic thought. The dilemma of the bourgeois subject is that its freedom and autonomy, the very essence of its being, put it at odds with Nature and so cut from beneath it any ground by which it might be validated. The more autonomous the subject grows, the less it can justify its existence; the more full-bloodedly it realizes its essence, the more alienated and contingent it becomes. The price of liberty is radical homelessness, as the Schlegelian doctrine of romantic irony attests: the furious dynamic of bourgeois desire exceeds any objective correlative in the world, threatening to strike all of them provisional and banal. A desire which realizes itself thus comes to seem just as futile as one which does not. So it is, as Hegel shrewdly recognizes, that the euphoric activism of the romantic subject is only ever a hair's breadth away from utter nihilism, likely at any moment to keel over into jaded disillusion, entranced as it is by the impossible dream of some pure productivity without a product. One of ideology's most fundamental requirements – that humanity should feel reasonably at home in the world, find some confirming echo of its identity in its environs – would seem tragically at odds with the libertarian ideology of the bourgeoisie. Fichte, detecting behind Kant's *Ding-an-sich* the minatory shadow of Spinozism, with its exaltation of Nature and consequent denial of freedom, will propose the absolute ego as pure subjective activity for its own sake, an ego which needs to posit Nature simply as the field and instrument of its own expression. The world is no more than a notional constraint against which the ego may flex its muscles and delight in its powers, a convenient springboard by which it can recoil onto itself. Nature as non-ego is merely a necessary moment of the ego, a temporary given instantly transcended, posited only to be abolished. Hegel sees that if this Fichtean ego is to do more than endlessly chase its own tail, if it is to be grounded and guaranteed, then it must be forced down from its unseemly megalomania to the sober terrain of Nature and history. Fichte's frenetic activism is one form of aestheticism: like the work of art, the absolute ego takes its law from itself alone, expanding its own powers simply for the sake of it. Hegel will curb Fichte's rhapsodic self-referentiality by recalling us to the object, but in doing so merely replaces one form of aestheticization with another: in the mighty artwork of *Geist*, subject and object, form and content, part and whole, freedom and necessity slide in and out of each other incessantly, and all of this, moreover, happens just for its own sake: there is no point to these subtle strategies other than Spirit's patient self-perfection.

If grounding the subject is not to negate its freedom, then history and Nature must first of all have been transformed into freedom themselves. If the subject is to unite with the object without detriment to its autonomy, subjectivity must be smuggled into the object itself. History must be imbued with all the self-determining autonomy of reason, colonized as the homeland of *Geist*. Hegel can thus resolve the Kantian antinomy of subject and object by boldly projecting one of its terms into the other, converting Kant's aesthetic fiction – the unity of subject and object in the act of judgement – into ontological myth. If the world is subjectivized, the subject can be anchored in it with impunity; the dynamic activism of Fichte's entrepreneurial ego can continue unabated, but now without fear that it will simply cancel out the object. 'Mind', remarks one of Hegel's disciples, 'is not an inert being but, on the contrary, absolute restless being, pure activity, the negating or ideality of every fixed category of the abstractive intellect.'[2] It is just that what all this frantic negating will uncover is the rational totality of the world; and for its full disclosure, human subjectivity is indispensable. If we are at home in history, it is because history has need of our freedom for its own fulfilment. Few more elegant solutions to the conflict of groundedness and autonomy could be imagined. It belongs to the freedom and necessity of the Idea that it should come to consciousness of itself, and the place where this happens is the mind of the Hegelian philosopher. Far from being pointlessly contingent, human subjectivity was reckoned into the equation since the world began. Infinity, which for Hegel could not subsist without finitude, needs us quite as much as we need it. This, so to speak, is an imaginary on the side of the object: there is that in the object itself which posits a rational subject, without which the object would lapse into non-being. It is mind, Hegel writes in the *Encyclopaedia*, which cognizes the logical Idea in Nature, and thus raises Nature to its essence. As in the small infant's dreams of immortality, the world would not exist if it itself ceased to be; what it is for reality to be autonomous is for it to centre upon us. The bourgeoisie is thus no longer caught in the Hobson's choice of clinging to its freedom but abandoning the world, or clinging to that world but sacrificing its autonomy. If reason is what estranges us from Nature – if, for Kant, it drives a wedge between being and humanity – then reason, this time as *Vernunft* rather than *Verstand*, can be turned against itself to lead us back home, the rational gains of the Enlightenment preserved but their alienatory losses liquidated. The very power that divorces us from being, given a dialectical twist, is always in the process of returning us safely to its bosom. The contradictions of bourgeois history are projected into reality itself, so that, in a cunning *coup de grâce* of the dialectic, to struggle with contradiction is by that very act to be at one with the world, which has, so to speak, just the same problems as ourselves. If the essence of reality is contradiction, then to be self-divided is to be rooted in the real.

Some human beings, Fichte suggests in the *Science of Knowledge*, remain pathetically fixated in the mirror stage, reliant for their sense of identity on external images, in flight from their own existential freedom:

> Some, who have not yet raised themselves to full conscious-ness of their freedom and absolute independence, find themselves only in the presentation of things; they have only that dispersed self-consciousness which attaches to objects, and has to be gleaned from their multiplicity. Their image is reflected back at them by things, as by a mirror; if these were taken from them, their self would be lost as well; for the sake of their self they cannot give up the belief in the independence of things, for they themselves exist only if things do . . .[3]

Hegel will rescue the subject from this benighted condition, but unlike Fichte he will not thereby maroon it on the desolate peak of its own autonomy. Instead, he will reconstruct this imaginary register at a higher theoretical level, giving the world back to the subject but this time as idea. The dialectical twists and turns by which this is accomplished are well known. The Absolute must be a subject, since otherwise it would suffer determination from the outside and thus cease to be absolute. Therefore everything that exists is a subject; but this cannot be so, as there can be no subject without an object. There must, therefore, be objects; but these objects must be peculiar kinds of subject. If this is a contradiction, that is hardly a thought likely to disturb such a mighty dialectician.

Hegel writes in his Preface to the *Phenomenology of Spirit* that he is not concerned with relating the work to the circumstances which surround it. This, the usual business of prefaces, would be so much extraneous chit-chat, inimical to the universal, self-validating character of a philosophical system. If such a system is to be complete, then the dominion it exerts over the world must be deployed at the same stroke over its own preconditions. A discourse of absolute knowledge would otherwise never be able to get off the ground, since whatever it launches off from is rendered in that act anterior to itself, and so extrinsic to its hegemony. Simply by starting, such a work risks jeopardizing its own transcendental status, undercutting its own claims in the very act of enunciating them. The system, it seems, must somehow always already have begun, or at least hang in some perpetual present, utterly coeval with its object. It must in some sense take off from a point identical with itself, opening itself to the world without for a moment relinquishing this intimate self-involvement; yet if a discourse is to begin from nothing whatsoever, spring self-complete from its own depths, how would it ever come to enunciate anything but its own act of saying? How could its content ever be anything but its form?

To say that an absolute system must take off from itself is equivalent to claiming that the first postulate which founds it, and sustains it throughout, is nothing less than the pure act of theorizing itself. The postulate of the work must be implicit in its own act of enunciation, as indissociable from it as aesthetic content from aesthetic form. What is this first postulate that we can never go back beyond? For J. G. Fichte in *The Science of Knowledge*, it can only be the subject. For though I can imagine something behind the subject which posits it, the fact remains that it is I, the subject, who am doing the imagining. The subject can never get a grip on itself from the outside, since it would already need to be a subject to do so, and this outside would thus have become an inside. Like some dizzying vista dwindling to infinity, the subject stretches back endlessly before all conceivable beginning, intolerant of all origin. 'Self-consciousness', as Schelling writes in his *System of Transcendental Idealism*, 'is the source of light for the entire system of knowledge, but it shines only forward, not backward.'[4] In the act of self-positing, for Fichte and Schelling, I know myself as infinite and absolute; and since transcendental philosophy is no more than a complex elaboration of that act, its founding absolute principle is the very gesture of self-consciousness itself. The whole theoretical enterprise becomes no more than a reprise of that primordial, incontrovertible act by which the subject posits itself, a metaphor of that infinite moment in which the subject ceaselessly emerges and re-emerges into being. What philosophy says is thus identical with what it does, its form and content quite indistinguishable, its constative character at one with its performative practice. Theory is a living image of what it speaks of, participates in what it reveals, and is thus a kind of Romantic symbol in discursive prose.

If the founding postulate of a system is to be absolute, then it must escape all objectification and so cannot be in any way determinate. For such a principle to be determinate would imply some ground beyond itself from which it could be determined, thus ruining its absolute status at a stroke. The subject is exactly this point of pure self-determination, this 'thing' sprung eternally from its own loins which is no thing at all but sheer unconceptualizable process, infinitely in excess of any degraded given. But if this is the case, how does this irrefutable first principle not simply slip through the net of knowledge, leaving theory resting on nothing at all? How can philosophy find sure anchorage in this elusive spectre of a subject, this slippery parody of a phenomenon which is gone as soon as we give name to it, this untheorizable source of all our actions which seems fully present in none of them? How is the transcendental philosopher not to end up clutching empty air each time he tries to round upon that which is the very unthinkable condition of his efforts, and which in knowing – in rendering determinate – he would strike dead? Is such transcendental thought anything more than an impossible hauling of oneself up by one's own bootstraps, a farcically self-undoing attempt to objectify a subjectivity which, simply to be what it is, must give the slip to all objectivity? All knowledge is founded upon a coincidence of subject and object; but such a claim cannot help sliding a disabling duality between the two in the very act of announcing their felicitous marriage. Knowledge of the self as an object cannot be knowledge of it as a thing, for this would be to strike determinate and conditional the very unconditional first principle of all philosophy. To know the self is instantly to undercut its transcendental authority; not to know it, however, is to be left with the vacuous transcendence of a cypher. Philosophy requires an absolute ground; yet if such a ground must be indeterminate it cannot be determined as a ground. We are confronted, it would seem, with a Hobson's choice between meaning and being, either destroying our first principle in the act of possessing it, or preserving it only in abysmal ignorance. The only way out of this dilemma would be a form of objectifying knowledge coterminous with, even constitutive of, the self – a cognitive power by which we could generate objectivity from the very depths of the subject without for a moment endangering its self-identity, a knowledge which would mime the very structure of the subject itself, rehearsing the eternal drama by which it brings itself into being.

This uniquely privileged form of cognition is the subject's intuitive presence to itself. For Fichte, the subject is no more than this inexhaustible process of self-positing; it exists exactly in so far as it appears for itself, its being and self-knowing wholly identical. The subject becomes a subject only by positing itself as an object; but this act remains entirely within the enclosure of its subjectivity, and only appears to escape it into otherness. The object as such, comments Schelling, vanishes into the act of knowing; so that in this primordial subject-object we glimpse a kind of reality which, far from preceding the subject (and so dislodging it from its transcendental status), is its very constitutive structure. The self is that special 'thing' which is in no way independent of the act of knowing it; it constitutes what it cognizes, like a poem or novel, and like the work of art too its determinate content is inseparable from the creative act of positing it. Just as the determinate objectivity of the artefact is no more than the self-generative process by which subjectivity emerges into being, so the self is that sublimely structuring source which will come to know each of its determinate aspects as mere transient moments of its infinite self-positing.

Since this infinite self-production is the very essence of the subject's freedom, philosophy, which repeats the act by which the self comes to know itself, is an emancipatory praxis. 'Freedom', writes Schelling, 'is the one principle on which everything is supported'; and objective being is no barrier to this, since 'that which in all other systems threatens the downfall of freedom is here derived from freedom itself'.[5] Being, viewed in this light, is merely 'freedom suspended'. Philosophy is thus in no sense contingent to its object, but an essential part of its self-articulation. For it is philosophy which will show how the objective being which the free subject experiences as constraint is in fact a necessary condition of its infinity, a sort of boundedness or finitude posited by the subject only to be dynamically surpassed. In the act of self-consciousness, the subject is infinite as knower but knows itself as finite; but such finitude is essential to its infinity, since, as Fichte argues, a subject which had overcome objectivity as a whole by fully realizing its freedom would merely cancel itself out, having nothing any longer to be conscious of.

In the act of theory, then, the subject attains to its deepest self-knowledge, becoming more essentially and authentically what it already is; and transcendental discourse is thus an ethical, even existential praxis rather than a fusty set of theorems, a liberatory action in which the self comes to experience at the level of full self-awareness what was implicit in its inmost structure all along. Philosophy merely writes large the founding gesture of the subject's free self-production, achieving its absoluteness by miming an utterly unconditioned reality of which it is the expressive symbol. Just as this transcendental subjectivity is quite unknowable from the outside – is, indeed, pure process or activity, a sort of sheer contentless quicksilver energy – so philosophy itself can only be known in the doing, can validate itself only in the formal process of its self-production. We know the truths of philosophy, as we know the transcendental nature of subjectivity, because we *are* it and *do* it; so that theory is just a kind of catching ourselves in the act of being subjects, a deeper appropriation of what we already are. The subject's act of transcendental freedom grounds the system, but not as some essence separable from it, since this would instantly discredit the system's aspirations to absolute self-identity. It is rather that this grounding *is* the system's own free self-production, the very form of its curving back upon itself, the gesture by which it spins itself at every point out of its own guts. The first postulate of the philosophy cannot be contended over, as this would be the ruin of its primacy; it cannot be thrust down to the lowly status of the conditioned and controversial, but must have all the intuitive self-evidence of the fact that I am at this very moment experiencing. As this principle is gradually unfolded in the discursive intricacies of theoretical argument, we shall become aware that it has never for a moment ceased to cling to the interiority of itself, that everything which can be derived from it was implicit in it from the outset, and that we are pacing the circumference of an enormous circle which is exactly the circle of our own free self-positing. We are thinking about ourselves thinking, rehearsing in the very formal structure of our acts of reading the mighty themes which lie before us on the page. It is the drama of ourselves that we find mirrored there, but now raised to the dignified level of pure self-consciousness, transparently at one both with the act of philosophical enunciation itself, and with the praxis by which the whole world comes to be. The postulate of transcendental freedom is one which, as both Fichte and Schelling remark, we must share already for any of this discourse to make the slightest sense: we have already been in on this argument, and if we have succeeded in understanding it by the time the Conclusion arrives it is because we have always been understanding it already. Just as we know our freedom only by enacting it, for anything we could objectify in a concept would by that token not be freedom, so we grasp this argument in the act of performing it, and could say no more than we could of a poem or painting how its referential force is separable from the shape of its enunciation. Philosophy is not some report on human freedom but the very practice of it, showing what it states; since freedom is not some possible object of cognition, it can be manifested only in the act of mind which refers to it. The content of the theory, as with the artefact, is indeed in that sense its form: it does what it describes, inscribes the unsayable in its very structure, and by bringing the reading subject to a certain self-illumination validates itself in the very process of its own construction. Philosophy fashions its own object as it goes along, rather than remaining slavishly reliant on some set of premises removed from the mastery of its writing: 'the whole science', as Schelling comments, 'is concerned only with its own free construction'.[6] Theory is a self-consuming artefact, striking itself redundant in the very act of bringing the subject to absolute self-knowledge.

This is to say that the self-referentiality of Kant's ethical subject or work of art has now been projected into the very structure of cognitive argument, which is always curled up on its own tail. It is as though the Kantian text is still struggling to handle in realist or representational style that utterly unrepresentable 'thing' which will finally be encircled only by a break to full-blooded philosophical 'modernism' – to the kind of theoretical work which, like the symbolist poem, generates itself up entirely out of its own substance, projects its own referent out of its formal devices, escapes in its absolute self-groundedness the slightest taint of external determination, and takes itself as its own origin, cause and end. The self-validating practical subject of Kant's philosophy is cranked up through several gears to the act of cognition itself. Kant's own carefully discriminated discourses – of pure and practical reason, and of aesthetic judgement – are conflated together at a stroke: theoretical reason, Schelling remarks, is simply imagination in the service of freedom. Fichte, for his part, will take the Kantian moral subject and project it into a kind of dynamic revolutionary activism. And this whole operation, so Kant's successors would claim, is enabled by a fatal aporia in the Kantian system itself. For that system can be read as both implying and failing to thematize a knowledge of the ego which would be neither logical nor empirical – just as it refuses to concede that a knowledge of how subject and object interact to produce cognition must itself somehow be absolute. Kant, from this viewpoint, has failed to push the issue back far enough; and his inheritors, seizing with alacrity on this apparent lapse of theoretical nerve, will accordingly fall one by one over the edge into the abyss of transcendental intuition. Kant has delivered us a Nature from which it is impossible to derive value, which must consequently become an end in itself; but some of his successors will, so to speak, put that whole process into reverse, modelling Nature itself after the freely self-generative subject, and thus grounding that subject in a world whose structure it shares. As a little work of art all in itself, its form and content miraculously unified, the subject is microcosmic of that more imposing aesthetic totality which is the universe.

For Fichte, the ego is a tendency to activity for its own sake; but when it reflects upon itself, it recognizes that this self-activity is subject to a law – the law of determining itself in accordance with the notion of self-determination. Within the ego, then, law and freedom are inseparable: to think of oneself as free is to be compelled to think of one's freedom as falling under a law, and to think that law is to be compelled to think oneself free. As in the artefact, freedom and necessity coalesce into a unitary structure. What has happened here is that the imagination, which plays a certain role in Kant's pure reason, has been grossly expanded in function. For Kant himself, the imagination provides an answer to the problem of how the data of sense intuition become subsumed under the pure concepts of the understanding, for these two realms appear quite heterogeneous to one another. It is here that the imagination intervenes as a mediatory power, producing the 'schemata' which in turn produce the images which regulate the process of applying the categories to appearances. Fichte assigns to the imagination a considerably more central role, finding in it the very source of our belief in a world independent of the ego. Fichte's megalomaniac philosophy of the ego has an evident problem in explaining why, empirically speaking, we actually believe in the existence in a reality independent of our consciousness; and this comes about, so Fichte argues, because there is within the absolute ego a kind of spontaneous, unconscious force which produces the very idea of that which is non-ego. The absolute ego somehow spontaneously limits its own restless activity and posits itself as passively affected by an object outside itself; and the power by which it does this is the imagination. Fichte can then go ahead and deduce the Kantian categories from this founding imaginative act: if apparently autonomous objects are posited, then a space and time must also be posited for them to inhabit, as well as our means of conceptually determining what they are. Pure reason or empirical knowledge, in short, can now be derived from the transcendental imagination; and the same is true of practical reason or morality. For the 'objective' world or Nature which the imagination posits is also necessary for that incessant striving of the ego which for Fichte is the basis of all ethical action; one could not speak of the ego as 'striving' unless it encountered some kind of check, and the external world is posited to provide it. The ego *feels* its impulses inhibited by something apparently beyond itself, and it is this feeling which is therefore at the root of our belief in a real world. Reality is established no longer through theoretical knowledge, but through a kind of sentiment; and

Fichte has to this extent aestheticized the very possibility of knowledge. Our knowledge of the world is just a kind of spin-off of a more fundamental unconscious force; behind the presentations of the understanding lies a spontaneous 'drive to presentation'. Moral life, in a similar way, is a kind of higher development of these unconscious instincts, in an interesting anticipation of Sigmund Freud. It thus becomes possible to deduce everything there is – the external world, morality, the categories of the understanding – from the spontaneous, unconscious drives of the absolute ego, at the basis of which we discover the imagination. The whole world has its root in an aesthetic source.

Friedrich Schelling, who starts out as a disciple of Fichte, becomes increasingly discontented with his mentor's drastically one-sided philosopy of subjectivity. For to be a subject must surely entail being conditioned by an object, and in this sense the conscious subject itself cannot be an absolute. Fichte, in other words, is unable to break out of the vicious circle of all theories of the subject's identity with itself as a reflected object: if the subject is able to recognize its objectification as its own, then it must somehow already know itself, and what was to be established is thus presupposed. It is not clear in any case how such theories are to avoid an infinite regress, as Fichte himself was to come to acknowledge: to distinguish the 'I' that thinks from the 'I' thought about would seem to posit a further 'I' which is able to do this, and so on indefinitely.[7] Schelling consequently retreats to the notion of an absolute reason or identity which transcends the duality of subject and object altogether as an 'indifference' to both, and which can itself never be objectified. This absolute then appears as a kind of unconscious force at work in the conscious subject; but in the objective idealism of Schelling's *Naturphilosophie* it becomes equally the essence of all objective being; and what most supremely incarnates this absolute identity, prior to all subject–object division, is art itself.

For the Schelling of the *System of Transcendental Idealism*, the only place in the world where we can find a true objectification of that 'intellectual intuition' by which the self produces itself is the aesthetic. 'The objective world', Schelling writes, 'is simply the original, as yet unconscious poetry of the spirit; the universal organon of philosophy – and the keystone of its entire arch – *is the philosophy of art*.'[8] The ordinary subject in the world would seem cripplingly split between conscious and unconscious: only that part of me which is limited is present to my consciousness, whereas the limiting activity of the subject itself, precisely because it is the cause of all such constraint, is bound to fall out of representation as an unspeakably transcendent power. I am aware only of my own boundedness, not of the act through which that is posited; it is only in limiting itself that the ego can come to be, but since it can thus only know itself *as* limited, it cannot in this way come to be for itself. Like bourgeois society as a whole, the self is torn between its restless, unrepresentable productivity and those determinate products (acts of self-positing) in which it finds and loses itself simultaneously. There is an aporia at the very heart of the subject which thwarts its complete self-identity: at once sheer empty energy and determinate product, the self can know *that* it is bounded but is puzzled to know *how*, since to know how would entail grasping itself from some subjectless exterior. Without limitation there could be no becoming, and hence no freedom, but the mechanisms of this process remain stubbornly unintuitable. Philosophy must therefore culminate in some concrete reconciliation of this dilemma, and the name of this unity is art. In art, the unconscious acts through and identically with consciousness; and the aesthetic intuition is thus a unique material representation of intellectual intuition in general, a process by which the subjective cognition of philosophy becomes itself objectified. 'Art', writes Schelling, 'is at once the only true and eternal organon of philosophy, which ever and again continues to speak to us of what philosophy cannot depict in external form, namely the unconscious element in acting and producing, and its original identity with the conscious.'[9] At the very peak of its powers, philosophy must logically liquidate itself into aesthetics, reversing its forward momentum and flowing back into the poetry from which it was long ago born. The philosophical is no more than a self-effacing track from one poetic condition to another, a temporary spasm or contortion in the efflorescence of spirit.

Indeed Schelling's *System*, as it nears its own closure, enacts this very rhythm of return:

We therefore close with the following observation. A system is completed when it is led back to its starting point. But this is precisely the case with our own. The ultimate ground of all harmony between subject and object could be exhibited in its original identity only through intellectual intuition; and it is precisely this ground which, by means of the work of art, has been brought forth entirely from the subjective, and rendered wholly objective, in such wise, that we have gradually led our object, the self itself, up to the very point where we ourselves were standing when we began to philosophise.[10]

Having arrived at the notion of the work of art, itself the most exemplary objectification of subjectivity, Schelling's text must logically close its own circle and curve back upon itself, becoming its own self-sealing artefact in the very act of speaking of art. By culminating in the work of art, philosophy doubles back on its own abstract subjectivism, returning to that subject spontaneously objectified in the world which was the starting-point of such reflections. At the frontier where it sublates itself into art, philosophy flips itself over and rejoins that intellectual intuition from which it originally took off. Art is superior to philosophy because whereas the latter grasps objectivity from within its own subjective principle, the former renders this whole process objective, raises it to the second power, performs it in reality as philosophy enacts it within the arcane recesses of spirit. Philosophy may unite subject and object within its own depths, but these depths must then themselves be concretely externalized. And this 'must' is, among other things, an ideological imperative. For the plain fact of the matter is that the ordinary subject-in-the-street is not quite up to the mysteries of Schellingian philosophizing, and stands in need of some more sensuously representational embodiment of it if its reconciling power is to be effective. As a materially objective medium, art is a more universally available instance of intellectual intuition than philosophy itself, which for Schelling can never as such become widely current. Intellectual intuition is confined to philosophy alone, and makes no appearance in ordinary consciousness, whereas art concretely figures it forth, at least in principle, for everyone. Take sensuous objectivity from art and it falls to the rank of philosophy; add such objectivity to philosophy and it rises to overcome itself in the aesthetic. Art, comments Schelling in Schillerian phrase, belongs to the 'whole man', whereas philosophy brings only a fraction of him with it to its lofty summit. To go beyond philosophy is thus in a sense to return to the quotidian, with art as the indispensable relay or mediation between the two.

The aesthetic, that is to say, brings theory home to everyday social experience as incarnate ideology, the place where all this fine-drawn obscurantist brooding fleshes itself out in spontaneous understanding. But if this is true, it suspends a huge question mark over the whole status of theory itself. Reason, like Schelling's own text, ends up by immolating itself, self-destructs and disappears into its own sealed circle, kicks away the conceptual ladder which, as in Wittgenstein's *Tractatus*, it has so laboriously climbed. This is not to say that Schelling's own philosophy is unnecessary, since only by the detour of theory will we be led to accede to theory's necessary demise, watching it turn its own weapons against itself. Nor is it to say that cognitive reason is finally ousted by aesthetic intuition, since it was that, in effect, all along. Indeed the irony of the entire project is that reason, to be sufficiently self-grounding, must be modelled from the outset on the aesthetic, a 'guarantee' of absoluteness which succeeds only in striking it empty. But it *is* to say that once we have read Schelling we really have no more need for philosophy – that his system, like Hegel's a little later, in this sense exerts its inexorable dominion over the future as well as the past.

Hegel, as is well known, parts company with Schelling's full-blooded aestheticization of reason, contemptuously dismissing his portentous 'intuition' as the night in which all cows are black. To lapse into such rhapsodic ramblings ('fictitious creations that are neither fish nor flesh, neither poetry nor philosophy', Hegel grumbles) is to insult the dignity of bourgeois reason, a defeatist surrender to the fear that the world may not after all be rationally intelligible. If that is so, then the bourgeoisie might as well abandon its intellectual enterprise before it has properly begun; and Romanticism seems to Hegel a dreadful instance of such theoretical suicide. His own philosophy, by contrast, represents a last-ditch, eleventh-hour, full-dress attempt to redeem society for rationality – to do all that his intuitionist colleagues do and more, yet to do it firmly from within the standpoint of reason. Kant has apparently cut the real world off from knowledge; Fichte and Schelling have restored it, but only in the vagaries of intuition; Hegel will strive to redeem the world and knowledge simultaneously. If the bourgeoisie is to establish itself as a truly universal class, at the level of culture as much as of political and economic practice, then the vacuously self-validating absolutism of a Fichte or Schelling is not only not ideologically sufficient; it also has an ominous ring, in a rather different register, of that dogmatic absolutism which the whole project of bourgeois enlightenment arose to vanquish. Philosophy is in need of some surer foundation; and the problem with intuition is that it is surer than anything in one sense and pathetically feeble in another. Nothing could be more ineluctable, self-evident, close to the eyeball; and nothing either could be more quirky, gratuitous and undemonstrable. Its very force seems inseparable from its utter emptiness; it merely *is*, which is at once its seductive power and its embarrassing uselessness. It cannot be gainsaid, but only because there is nothing articulate enough to be contradicted. In a complex, contradictory society, where contentions over value have become notably intense, the bourgeoisie yearns for the solace of the apodictic; but this will only be found at a point of formalist abstraction so tenuous that it vanishes instantly into its own purity. Achieving your goal and falling short of it thus occur in the same instant. Nobody is going to bother dissenting over a blank space; we are all united at that sublime point where absolutely nothing is at stake, where what we experience, as in the Kantian aesthetic, is just the very abstract forms of our consensus, uncontaminated by any potentially divisive content. For a theoretical system to ground itself in such a space may render it conveniently invulnerable to counter-argument, but only because it is left hanging precariously in a void. To say that one's system is rooted in transcendental intuition comes embarrassingly close to saying that it is rooted in nothing at all – that the formal emptiness of the self-justifying Kantian moral subject has been generalized throughout the system's very letter, to the point where absolute self-groundedness is indistinguishable from pointless tautology. Such theories pivot on a central blankness and so curve constantly back on themselves, inviting us to admire them as we would admire some intricately self-supporting formation of acrobats whose dubious triumph is precisely that they might at any moment come clattering to the ground.

It is hard for any theory invoking the claim of absolute intuition to avoid a certain appearance of self-contradiction. For the final truth which it will deliver us seems unavoidably at odds with the textual labour devoted to disclosing it, to the point where we cannot help suspecting that if this labour was indeed necessary, then the absolute cannot be as ineluctable as all that. In the doubled, revealing/ concealing rhythm of the symbol, the writing which uncovers ultimate truth cannot help but occlude it too, pedantically tracing in postlapsarian time what secretly belongs to eternal immediacy. In this sense, the absolute would seem distanced from us by the very discourse sent out in its pursuit. The fact that we have need of such a discourse in the first place already suggests that something has gone awry, that philosophy comes about because of a Fall which it repeats in the very act of trying to repair. If all were as well as the theory suggests, then why are we reading at all, rather than just revelling in the rich plenitude of our intuitions? If philosophy exists, then we can already deduce at least one other existent, namely contradiction or false consciousness as its essential precondition. But if that is so then no philosophy can be absolute, since the very appearance of it indicates that in relation to which it is inevitably belated. What need would there be for science at all, if reality were not already fissured and fragmented in ordinary consciousness?

Hegel's philosophy is among many other things a superbly cunning riposte to this dilemma. That there *is* conflict is made clear by philosophy's very existence; indeed Hegel himself remarks that division is the source of the need for philosophy. But philosophy will reveal that such diremptions are inherent in the very truth it has to deliver, thus projecting its own historical conditions into its spiritual substance. What brought us to this philosophy in the first place – the fact that we were sunk in some miasma of false consciousness, stumbling around for a likely exit – was always already secretly foreseen by it, as the very tangled pathway by which it would bring us patiently to itself. As in Freudian theory, these errors and blindnesses belong to the very trajectory of truth, and are to be worked through, in that therapeutic process known as reading the works of G. W. F. Hegel, rather than austerely repressed:

> In the course of its process the Idea creates that illusion, by setting an antithesis to confront it; and its action consists in getting rid of the illusion which it has created. Only out of this error does the truth arise. In this fact lies the reconciliation with error and with finitude. Error or other-being, when superseded, is still a necessary dynamic

element of truth; for truth can only be where it makes itself its own result.[11]

Truth is not just the constative propositions of theoretical enquiry but the rhetorical performance of the theory itself, entirely at one with its subtlest contortions and occasional cul-de-sacs, a practice rather than an abstractable statement. The Absolute Idea has already charitably included the reader's reifying illusions and shaky grasp of logic within itself, and thus always takes off from a point preceding both the reader and the entire history which went into his or her making. If philosophy is famously belated, the owl of Minerva which takes flight only at dusk, it is simply because the historical drama it recapitulates requires its own full-dress entry as an actor onto the scene only at a relatively late point, for reasons the Absolute, as director of the entire theatre, has foreseen from the beginning.

If division and contradiction are essential moments of the Idea's stately unfurling through time, then it is because Hegel has subsumed the historical conflicts which necessitate his theory, and so threaten to relativize it, into the theory itself, converting its preconditions into its very dialectical form. The *Phenomenology of Mind* is thus doomed to repeat the very negations its strives to overcome; and every reader of the text will have to enact this process afresh, in that ceaseless repetition which is now all that is left of philosophy. But this performance is itself an essential part of *Geist*'s global self-expansion, a post-history of the text determined by its very letter, a necessary constituent of Spirit's arrival at full self-consciousness in the mirror of the reading subject's mind. In this sense, the constative dimension of the work is not at all at odds, however much it might at first appear so, with the performative labour of tracking these issues through discursive time. There is no need for any foolish Romantic fear that to articulate the Absolute is in that moment to disarticulate it, since the Absolute, as the identity of identity and difference, knows that only by such internal rending or reading will it ever be whole. If it is true that theory is only necessary because of false consciousness, it is equally true that false consciousness is itself necessary, so that philosophy is instantly redeemed from any merely contingent status. Hegel's work takes off from loss and lack, but will demonstrate by its ways of filling them in just how intrinsic to positivity such negation is. The whole philosophy is historically essential, itself part of the upward evolution of Spirit, a free but determined moment of praxis within the global praxis it both describes and mimics; but to secure itself thus in an historical ground is not to lay itself open to external determination, since this history is itself the product of the very Spirit which impels its own discourse, and so is included within itself. The Hegelian text is thus constative in its very performativeness: it is exactly in its self-referential construction of its own principles that it manifests how the world is, for the world is just like this too. Philosophy springs from the same root as reality itself, and so in curving back meditatively upon its own construction delivers us the inner structure of everything that exists.

Such self-reflectiveness is therefore just the opposite of that of the modernist text, since although its inner strategies are deeply ironic, it expels all irony from its own relation to the real. The self-generative nature of modernist writing implies a kind of *faute de mieux*: if the text authorizes its own discourse, then this, so it wryly insinuates, is because no reliable historical authorization can any longer be assumed. The world is no longer story-shaped, and thus can provide no external determination of a textual form which is consequently thrown back on its own devices, abandoned to the tragicomic tautology of making itself up as it goes along. Self-grounding here is just another name for unmasking the arbitrariness of all foundations, demystifying the presumption of some natural starting-point somehow cued by the very structure of the given. The self-authorizing discourse of idealism, by contrast, hopes to mime the structure of the given in this very gesture: the more broodingly autotelic such language becomes, the more resolutely realist it grows. There can be no ironic play between discourse and history, precisely because the former has always already swallowed up the latter. To say that such idealist philosophy has no determinable foundations is paradoxically to grant it the deepest possible guarantee, since its foundation is then identical with the undeterminable first principle of reality itself. In starting from itself, the modernist work is ironically non-identical with itself, since it proclaims its own incapacity to validate the truths it has to communicate. It might always at any moment be something else, and casts the blighting shadow of this possibility across its actual enunciation. For Hegelian dialectics, anything at any moment actually *is* something else, but this is precisely the sign of its location within a rational totality. To think at all for Hegel is profoundly ironic, since it involves suppressing the particularity of the given with the universality of the concept, and *vice versa*; but these local ironies cannot add up *à la* modernism to one enormous one, since in relation to what would the whole be ironic? Transcendental philosophy does not validate itself *faute de mieux*: if there is no authority to which it need appeal, it is because it has always already introjected it.

The doubleness of Schellingian intuition is that it is at once experientially certain and rationally discreditable; the ambiguity of Hegelian reason is that it is internally coherent but notably hard to feel. Both models, then, have their strengths and drawbacks as ideological paradigms. The problem for Hegel is that, given the grievous complexity and contradiction of social conditions, knowledge of the whole can no longer be spontaneous; and any project of rational totalization will thus be forced into a convoluted discursivity which threatens to limit its *ideological* effectiveness. In making the world transparent to theory, Hegel runs the risk of making theory opaque to the world. We have left behind ancient Greece, a society which Hegel likens to an artefact, where a spontaneous knowledge of the whole was still routinely available. An immense dialectical labour is now on the agenda; and Hegel in a sense does his job too well – too well at least for Schelling's subject-in-the-street, who is a little more likely to be imaginatively stirred by art than to take to the streets crying 'The rational is the real!' or 'Long live the identity of identity and non-identity!' This is not to claim that Hegelianism is incapable of becoming a political force, as Marx and the Young Hegelians well enough demonstrate; but it is to suggest a certain difficulty over the question within the system of sensuous ideological representation. 'Philosophy', so Hegel argues against Schelling, 'is of its very nature, by virtue of its general mode of existence, available *for all*';[12] indeed much of Hegel's contempt for intuitionism springs not only from a fear that such dogmatic solipsism subverts all social bonds, but from his belief that only a determinate system of thought can be properly intelligible. Only what is perfectly determinate in form, he argues in the *Phenomenology of Spirit*, is at the same time exoteric, comprehensible, and capable of being learned and possessed by everybody. Hegel's baroque lucubrations, ironically enough, are intended to be in the service of a general accessibility. Intuition, with its 'horrified rejection of mediation', is desperately esoteric and so ideologically crippled from the outset; the intelligibly determinate, by contrast, is common

141

to scientific and unscientific mind alike, thus, as Hegel comments, enabling the unscientific mind to enter the domain of science. Hegel gravely underestimates the ideological force of sensuous representation, as the low status he assigns to art within his system itself testifies. 'The interruption by conceptual thought of the habit of always thinking in figurative ideas', he writes testily in the *Phenomenology of Spirit*, 'is as annoying and troubling to this [rational] way of thinking as to that process of formal intelligence which in its reasoning rambles about with no real thought to reason with.'[13]

In this austere Protestant iconoclasm, Hegel reveals himself as the true heir of Immanuel Kant, who in a celebrated passage from the *Critique of Judgement* likewise spurns the indignity of sensuous representation from the depths of a generous faith in common rationality:

> Perhaps there is no more sublime passage in the Jewish Law than the commandment: Thou shalt not make unto thee any graven image, or any likeness of any thing that is in heaven or on earth, or under the earth, etc. This commandment can alone explain the enthusiasm which the Jewish people, in their moral period, felt for their religion when comparing themselves with others, or the pride inspired by Mohammedanism. The very same holds good of our representation of the moral law and of our native capacity for morality. The fear that, if we divest this representation of everything that can commend it to the senses, it will thereupon be attended only with a cold and lifeless approbation and not with any moving force or emotion, is wholly unwarranted. The very reverse is the truth. For when nothing any longer meets the eye of sense, and the unmistakable and ineffaceable idea of morality is left in possession of the field, there would be need rather of tempering the ardour of an unbounded imagination to prevent it rising to enthusiasm, than of seeking to lend these ideas the aid of images and childish devices for fear of their being wanting in potency.[14]

Idealist philosophy, like the commodity on which so many of its categories are modelled, must suffer no degenerate lapse into sensuousness, remaining sternly aloof from the body. But if this is part of its awesome authority – that it generates itself entirely out of abstract reason – it is also what would seem to limit its ideological efficacy. The bourgeoisie would appear caught here between a rational self-apologia too subtly discursive to find appropriate sensuous representation, and an ideologically seductive form of immediacy (aesthetic intuition) which spurns all rigorous social totalization and so leaves itself notably vulnerable. It is a dilemma remarked by Schiller, who comments in one of his essays that 'sensuous presentation is, viewed in one aspect, *rich*, for in cases where only *one* condition is desired, a complete picture, an entirety of conditions, an individual is offered. But viewed in another aspect it is *limited and poor*, because it only confines to a single individual and a single case what ought to be understood as a whole sphere. It therefore curtails the understanding in the same proportion that it grants preponderance to the imagination . . .'[15] Kant has left ultimate reality unknowable, ethics a resoundingly hollow Ought, and organic purposiveness a mere hypothesis of taste; Fichte and Schelling, as though aghast at the ideological disarray into which they are thereby plunged, convert Kant's ethics into a concrete principle of revolutionary freedom and his aesthetics into a form of knowledge. But this simply means that they have spread intuition through the whole of the world, collapsing the cognitive into pure feeling. Hegel, then, must repair this dire situation, avoiding at once the bleakness of Kantian understanding and the suffocating intimacies of Romantic intuition, reuniting mind and world in a style of knowledge with all the analytic rigour of the former, but with something of the imaginative energy of the latter. This form of knowledge is the higher reason, *Vernunft* or dialectics.

Within that dialectical system, to be sure, Hegel will dexterously combine concrete and abstract, sensuous and spiritual, negating the former terms only to reinstate them at a higher level. But this does not tackle the question of the concrete representability of the system itself; and if the aesthetic is exemplary of such representation, then Hegel refuses that particular solution by consigning art to a lowly rung on the ontological ladder, below religion and philosophy. Aesthetic representations for Hegel lack philosophy's pure transparency, as their primary (material or allegorical) meanings tend to obscure their ultimate significance as expressions of Spirit. Indeed art for

Hegel is not properly representational at all, but rather an intuitive presentation which expresses a vision rather than imitates an object. It incarnates a sensuous awareness of the Absolute, abolishing all contingency and so showing forth *Geist* in all its organic necessity. As with Kant's aesthetic, this sensuousness is securely non-libidinal, freed from all desire, a beauty whose otherwise disruptive material force is defused by the spirit which informs its every part. This intimate yet idealized body, material yet miraculously undivided, wordlessly immediate yet shaped and stylized, is what Romanticism terms the symbol, and psychoanalysis the body of the mother. It is therefore not surprising that Hegel finds something obscure and enigmatic about this form of materiality, something within it troublingly resistant to the translucent power of reason. It betrays its unsettling force most obviously in the 'bad infinity' of oriental or Egyptian art, that grotesque spawning of matter, vague, groping and boundless, which threatens in its fantastic heterogeneity to swamp the pure spirit like some nightmarish creature of science fiction. Hegel finds such sublime proliferation of matter distinctly unnerving: within his system, this shapeless feminine stuff is redeemable only when impregnated by rational form, negated in its material presence and gathered into the inner unity of the Idea. The oriental stage of art is, so to speak, the child smothered by a fleshly mother; in the harmonious artefacts of ancient Greece, child and mother have achieved some symmetrical unity; and at the highest, Romantic stage of art, when the almost disembodied spirit yearns for freedom from its material encasement, the child is in the process of definitively overcoming the Oedipal crisis and taking leave of the mother altogether. We do not, then, remain with the aesthetic for long, but climb up a stage to religion, which still presents the Absolute in terms of images; and finally, if we can stay the course, we rise to the rarefied conceptual representations of philosophy itself.

Since the Hegelian system never leaves anything entirely behind, however, the charms of art and religion do not simply flee at philosophy's cold touch. They, and religion especially, remain behind to provide what we might call the ideology of this theory, its necessary if inferior incarnation in everyday life. To accuse Hegel of a rationalism wholly inimical to ideological effectiveness would be to overlook the key role played in his system by religion. Religion is the universal still enmired in the sensual, but somewhat more successful than art in its obscure straining to capture the Absolute. It fulfils for Hegel two vital ideological functions which philosophy itself cannot properly perform: it offers us that relation to the Absolute which is a matter of feeling, heart and sensibility rather than arid conceptuality; and as a *cultic* affair it belongs not simply to subjectivity but to the 'objective spirit' of institutionalized social practices. As ideology, religion crucially mediates between the affective and the practical, providing the space in which each nurtures the other; and though the political state must finally stand not on religious belief but on the firmly independent foundation of reason, it nevertheless needs religion as a cultic, affective, representational domain, a realm of ethical conviction in which rational imperatives may strike an instinctual chord. This task cannot be left to ethical culture itself, otherwise humanity's relation to the Absolute would remain narrowly parochical, caught up with the *mores* of a specific society. Religion for Hegel is the medium in which universal truths of reason are affectively represented, and so plays for him something of the role of Kant's aesthetic judgement. Humanity, desirous as it is to see a sign, will be catered for in the ideological region by religious faith, of which philosophy is the open secret.

If Hegel demotes the concept of the aesthetic to a humble position in the evolution of *Geist*, it is partly because, like Gramsci after him, he shifts the whole concept of 'culture' from its aesthetic to its everyday or anthropological sense. He thus steals an important advance on Kant, whose idea of cultural consensus remains largely rooted in the narrowness of aesthetic judgement, and so to some extent institutionally disembodied. It was Hegel, then, long before Antonio Gramsci, who helped to effect the decisive shift in political theory from problems of *ideology* to questions of *hegemony*. The latter concept is both broader than, and inclusive of, the former: it denotes, roughly speaking, all the ways in which political power secures itself through routine institutional practices, rather than, more specifically, in those signs, images and representations which we term ideology. Social cohesion, so Hegel recognizes, cannot feasibly be secured in some abstract, disinterested aesthetic intersubjectivity; it must anchor itself instead in cultural practice, in that whole densely tessellated fabric of social life which spreads outwards from the cloistral intimacy of the family to encompass the various phenomena of social class, corporations, associations and the rest. Unless the state, supreme symbol of social unity and locus of the divine will in history, is the complex sublation of these more regional, immediate, workaday institutions, it cannot hope to sustain its august universal power. Social unity can be established neither at the level of the political state alone, nor in some universalized aesthetic inwardness divorced from politics; but neither, for Kant at least, can it find a secure base in bourgeois economic practice, 'civil society' in that narrow sense, even if Kant's hope is that such practice might *ultimately* lead to human harmony. Indeed the apparent impossibility of this latter option is one of the great implicit questions to which idealist thought in general is an attempted answer. Like Kant, the question to which Hegel addresses himself in this respect is simply: How is social cohesion to be implemented in a form of social life which everywhere denies it in its most routine economic activities? If the ideological unity of bourgeois society cannot be derived from its common social practice, if the two realms are mutually inimical, then the temptation will be to project such harmony into so rarefied a region (culture, the aesthetic, absolute intuition, the state) that its power to engage common experience will be instantly short-circuited. Hegel's 'concrete ethical life', viewed as the equivalent of Gramscian 'civil society', offers an impressive solution to this quandary, as an intricate mechanism of mediation between the private domestic affections at one end and the global truths of *Geist* at the other.

Unlike Kant, Hegel does not commit the naive error of trying to found spiritual community in anything as slippery as disinterestedness. Private property and abstract right are clearly too sunk in self-interested particularism to provide a basis in themselves for ideological consensus; but it is shrewdest to begin with these unpromisingly parochial forms, and see how, *via* the mediations of the division of labour, social class and the corporations, they dialectically transcend themselves into more altruistic modes of association. The culmination of all this will be Hegel's finest aesthetic artefact, the organic 'concrete universal' of the state. And since the Hegelian state is strongly interventionist, it reaches back into society to reinforce its social bonds. Totality, in short, must emerge organically from the actual divisions of concrete social life, rather than be mapped artificially on to them; and Hegel will thus unify concrete and abstract by a process of objective social mediation, rather than merely linking the two in the act of aesthetic judgement.

In the process of society, each smaller unit dialectically generates the need for a larger one, dissolving its particularity into greater universality, in a series of progressively higher integrations; and since these institutions incarnate the individual subject's free essence, it is in this essentially practical realm, rather than in the contemplative act of aesthetic judgement, that subject and object become truly at one. Hegel's 'culture' is less a special dimension than the concrete totality of social life as viewed in the light of reason. It is into this concrete totality that he reinserts Kant's abstract morality, from which, as he sees, it is a one-sided derivation; and his social unity is thus at once more materially grounded than Kant's intersubjective consensus, and at the same time – since it can be present as a whole only to totalizing reason – in a certain sense more abstract. Confronted with an aggressively individualist social order, Kant partially separates culture from the terrain of political institutions, establishing consensus through feeling rather than through the concept; Hegel's dialectic of culture and politics represents a mutuality of feeling and concept, whereby the abstract representations of universal reason will gradually emerge from the *Lebenswelt* in which they are always dimly stirring.

The concrete ethical world is one of traditional, largely unreflective pieties and practices; and as such it manifests a kind of 'spontaneous lawfulness' or 'lawfulness without law' which makes it akin to the Kantian aesthetic. To move from here to the political state, however, involves sacrificing the immediacy of the Kantian aesthetic to the discursivity of the concept, fusing individual and society not in some intuitive intersubjectivity but laboriously, indirectly, through the complex mediations of family, class, corporations and the like. Kantian 'culture' appears from Hegel's viewpoint as excessively idealized; only by evolving social unity from the most apparently unpropitious beginnings, from the competitive struggles of civil society itself, can any political rule hope to achieve a sound enough material grounding. And only by dissolving abstract morality into the rich, largely unconscious textures of customary practice can Kant's duality of practical reason and sensibility be transcended, and political hegemony, in a directly Gramscian sense of the term, be consolidated. To aestheticize social life in one direction – to view it as a wealth of concrete capacities awaiting their full creative development – means to adopt a properly dialectical form of reason, and so to break with aestheticization in the sense of mere intuitive immediacy.

147

Hegel is surely wise to believe that political unity must find its foundation in civil society; it is just that in bourgeois society any such strategy is notably difficult to achieve. Bourgeois civil society does indeed bring individuals together, but only, as Hegel himself acknowledges, in a largely negative, objective, unconscious interdependence. The division of labour, for example, generates mutual dependency by its separating and specializing of skills; but it is no simple matter to transform this purely objective mutual reliance into community-for-itself, and Hegel anticipates much of the early Marx in his awareness of an emergent, potentially disaffected proletariat ('a rabble of paupers', as he calls them) scandalized by the extreme poles of social wealth and poverty. It is precisely because the project of evolving political harmony from a fissured civil society is at once essential and implausible that Hegel has need of philosophy, which will show individuals how such unity is attainable at the self-conscious level of the political state. Unity will finally come about if individuals read their Hegel and work to implement it.

Philosophy, in short, does not merely describe the ideal state, but is a necessary instrument for bringing it about. One of Hegel's notable achievements is thus to resolve in his own fashion the dichotomy between fact and value deeply entrenched in empiricist and Kantian thought. One way he does so is by holding, as Marxism was later to hold, that certain forms of theoretical description are inescapably normative because they provide kinds of knowledge essential to social emancipation. And this knowledge is nothing less than the whole of the Hegelian system. The constative dimension of that discourse is thus inseparable from a performative aspect: only by becoming conscious of Spirit (or more exactly by allowing it to rise to a consciousness of itself in us) will that Spirit be politically nurtured, embodied and extended. If philosophy is to be anchored in the Absolute then it must be essentially practical, since the essence of the Absolute is precisely to realize itself ceaselessly in the world. If Hegelian theory were not itself an active political force, it would lose its absolute grounding. Hegel can thus shift from fact to value, cognitive to political, epistemology to ethics, with no sense of sharp disjunction, as David Hume and his progeny cannot. *Geist* is the essence of everything that exists, and so an account of its adventures through time would appear to be purely descriptive; but it is the *essence* of all that exists in the sense of its significant inner structure or trajectory, such that an account of it provides us with norms relevant to ethical and political behaviour. No historical epoch or social order can exist outside *Geist*, which would thus appear to be no more than a mere description of the whole; but any particular epoch or order may fail to realize *Geist*'s imperatives adequately – even if, in thus falling short, it will be unwittingly contributing to its final triumph; and in this sense *Geist* stands in critical judgement over against the historical given.

If Hegel's philosophy is to be both theory and practice, part of Spirit's very dynamic rather than a mere contemplative description of it, then people must necessarily read that philosophy and come to act upon it, fashioning those political structures appropriate for the Absolute's self-realization in history. Such activity cannot be left to the spontaneous movement of history itself; there is a lack in such movement, which only the self-consciousness of philosophy can supply. The value of philosophy depends upon the limits of the spontaneous process it charts. The culmination of history is the ideal political state; but not even individuals living in that state will attain to a spontaneous knowledge of the complex social whole, since the differentiations of modern society render any such knowledge impossible. Citizens of the ideal state will relate to the social whole only mediately, through their particular corporations and estates. Hegel does not believe in the possibility of a state in which, as in ancient society, every citizen would be immediately identified with the principle of common life. Different classes within the ideal state will live their relations to the whole in different ways, and no individual will be able to unite all of these modes within his or her own person. If this is so, then Hegel's state becomes a kind of fiction, since no one individual can possibly know it. It exists only at the level of writing, which is why Hegel's own philosophy is necessary. The only place where a knowledge of the totality resides is in the philosophy of Hegel. Absolute knowledge, as Alexandre Kojève points out, exists for Hegel only as a *book*: 'The citizen is thus only fully self-conscious to the extent to which he has read (or written) the *Phenomenology of Mind.*'[16] And this is because Hegelian wisdom consists not simply in *living* a relation to the totality, but in *knowing* this totality too. The state thus exists as a whole only for the speculative theorist: it is Hegel who keeps the ideal state in existence, sustaining it by his knowledge rather as God sustains the world. The totalization of the state lies outside itself, in the mind which knows it. The political materializes the philosophical, but cannot be quite on equal terms with it; a gap is opened up between theory and political practice, such that when the state is 'lived' it is not as the complex totality present to theory, and when it is known it is not as 'lived'. Theory and ideology, meaning and being, are in this ultimately at odds.

It is finally in this sense that the Hegelian system, as Kierkegaard continually complained, cannot be *lived*. It exists as a whole only for the concept, of which there is no sensuous analogue. Reality is an organic artefact, but it cannot be spontaneously known as a whole through aesthetic intuition. Wisdom for Hegel is finally conceptual, never representational: the whole can be grasped through the labour of dialectical reason, but not *figured* there. Art and religious faith are the closest approximations we have to such concrete imaging; but both involve sensuous representations which dilute the clarity of the concept. Dialectical reason can render us reality as an indivisible unity; but in the very act of doing so it is condemned from the viewpoint of aesthetic immediacy to the division, linearity and periphrasis of all rational discourse, disarticulating the very substance it seeks to totalize. Only the *structure* of philosophical discourse can suggest something of the synchronic truth of the Idea it strives to explicate – an Idea which, as Hegel remarks, 'is the process of its own becoming, the circle which presupposes its end as its purpose, and has its end for its beginning'.[17] The principle which philosophy expresses is an 'aesthetic' one; but this is no justification for philosophy to collapse into some portentous intuitionism.

Theory in Hegel follows after practice, as the tardy flight of Minerva's owl; and to this extent it cannot meddle with that practice in ways harmful to its spontaneous wisdom. Spirit ripens within habitual, unconscious social activity, or 'culture'; when it forgets this location within concrete life and acts abstractly, prematurely, the result is revolutionary fanaticism, Jacobinistic blueprinting. The belatedness of theory preserves practice from such injurious abstraction, leaving it as the fertile soil from which self-consciousness will gradually flower. When theory finally begins to emerge from that ground, when the Idea begins gradually to come into its own, its primary posture is retrospective: casting an equable gaze back over the whole historical process which produced it, it sees that all of this was well. What prospective, performative functions theory serves work within the context of this serene retrospect: the tasks of Reason are to ensure that what has been slowly perfected is carried forward, becoming even more essentially what it already is. Yet it is, of course, no simple feat to claim that everything has been for the best. On the contrary, to argue any such grossly implausible claim will require a staggering degree of dialectical ingenuity, which then begins to foreground the operations of pure mind to a point which threatens to cut that mind off from the concrete, spontaneous history out of which it grows. Theory thus parts company with history in the very act of justifying it; and this is another sense in which the project of rescuing the world for reason involves in Hegel a degree of rarefied speculation which is notably difficult to 'naturalize' as an ideological mode.

Confronted with the problem of establishing social harmony in an unstable, conflict-ridden social order, the apologists of emergent bourgeois society find themselves caught in a cleft stick between reason and intuition, dialectics and aesthetics. It would be convenient if the unity of society could be felt as immediately as the form of an artefact – if the law of the social totality, as supposedly in ancient Greece, were somehow inscribed in the very appearances of society itself, spontaneously available to each social participant. Such aestheticized social knowledge, given the divisions and complexities of modern life, is no longer to be hoped for: the aesthetic as a form of social cognition yields nothing but rhapsodic vacuity. Society is indeed a kind of artefact, a magnificent interpenetration of subject and object, form and content, freedom and necessity; but this will become apparent only to the patient probings of dialectical reason, given the strata of false consciousness which intervene between empirical consciousness and the whole. Family, state and civil society are clasped together in intimate unity, thus allowing Hegel to found ideological consensus in the very material institutions of the existing social order. But to demonstrate the concealed linkages between family, civil society and state can be done only at the level of the concept, rather than experientially; and there is thus a difficulty concerning the relation of Hegelian thought to that system of sensuous representation which is ideology. What is actually lived out in society, even in the ideal political state, can never be the totality as such, which eludes all sensuous incarnation and lives only in writing. Confronted with these difficulties, it will not be long before some bourgeois theory abandons rational apologia altogether, and turns increasingly to rely upon the aesthetic.

Notes

1 See Charles Taylor, *Hegel and Modern Society* (Cambridge, 1979), chapter 1.
2 Quoted by Stanley Rosen, *G. W. F. Hegel* (New Haven and London, 1974), p. 51.
3 J. G. Fichte, *Science of Knowledge* (Cambridge, 1982), p. 15.
4 F. W. J. Schelling, *System of Transcendental Idealism* (Charlottesville, Virginia, 1978), p. 34.
5 Ibid., p. 35.
6 Ibid., p. 29.
7 See, for a useful discussion of these points, Peter Dews, *Logics of Disintegration* (London, 1987), chapter 1, and Rodolphe Gasché, *The Tain of the Mirror* (Cambridge, Mass., 1986), Part 1 chapter 2.
8 Schelling, *System of Transcendental Idealism*, p. 12.
9 Ibid., p. 220.
10 Ibid., p. 232.
11 G .W. F. Hegel, *The Logic* (Oxford, 1892), para 212.
12 Quoted by Charles Taylor, *Hegel* (Cambridge, 1975), p. 431.
13 G. W. F. Hegel, *The Phenomenology of Spirit* (Oxford, 1977), p. 43.
14 Immanuel Kant, *Critique of Judgement* (Oxford, 1952), pp. 127–8.
15 F. Schiller, 'On the Necessary Limitations in the Use of Beauty of Form', in *Collected Works* (New York, n.d.), vol. IV, pp. 234–5.
16 Alexandre Kojève, *Introduction à la lecture de Hegel* (Paris, 1947), p. 305.
17 Hegel, *Phenomenology of Spirit*, p. 10.

6

The Death of Desire:
Arthur Schopenhauer

Though Schopenhauer is undoubtedly one of the gloomiest philosophers who ever wrote, there is an unwitting comedy about his work which has to do with the presence of the body within it. Schopenhauer studied physiology at university, and is impressively learned about the lungs and pancreas; indeed it is a striking thought that his choice of university subjects might have reshaped the whole course of Western philosophy right up to the fashionable neo-Nietzscheanisms of our own time. For it is from Schopenhauer's coarsely materialist meditations on the pharynx and the larynx, on cramps, convulsions, epilepsy, tetanus and hydrophobia, that Nietzsche will derive much of his own ruthless physiological reductionism; and all that solemn, archaic nineteenth-century discourse on Man in terms of the ganglia and lumbar regions, which survives at least as long as Lawrence, thus forms a shady hinterland to that resurgence of theoretical interest in the body which has also, in our own epoch, rather more positive and political dimensions.

Schopenahuer is quite unembarrassed to detect his celebrated Will, that blindly persistent desire at the root of all phenomena, in yawning, sneezing and vomiting, in jerkings and twitchings of various kinds, and seems wholly oblivious of the bathos with which his language can veer without warning in the course of a page or so from high-flown reflections on free will to the structure of the spinal cord or the excrescences of the caterpillar. There is a kind of Bakhtinian bathos or Brechtian *plumpes Denken* about this sudden swooping from *Geist* to genitalia, from the oracular to the orificial, which in Bakhtin's hands at least is a political weapon against ruling-class idealism's paranoid fear of the flesh. With Schopenhauer it is less a question of political revolt than of a kind of cracker-barrel crassness, as when he solemnly illustrates the conflict between body and intellect by pointing out that people find it hard to walk and talk at the same time: 'For as soon as their brain has to link a few ideas together, it no longer has as much force left over as is required to keep the legs in motion through the motor nerves.'[1] Elsewhere he speculates that the boundless, infinite objective world 'is really only a certain movement or affection of the pulpy mass in the skull' (2, 273), or suggests that a short stature and neck are especially favourable to genius, 'because on the shorter path the blood reaches the brain with more energy' (2, 393). All of this vulgar literalism is a kind of theoretical posture in itself, a sardonic smack at high-toned Hegelianism from one who, though a full-blooded metaphysician himself, regards Hegel as a supreme charlatan and most philosophy except Plato, Kant and himself as a lot of hot air. Crotchety, arrogant and cantankerous, a scathing Juvenilian satirist who professes to believe that the Germans need their long words because it gives their slow minds more time to think, Schopenhauer's work reveals a carnivalesque coupling of the imposing and the commonplace evident in his very name.

Indeed incongruity becomes in Schopenhauer's hands the basis for a full-blown theory of comedy. The ludicrous, so he argues, springs from the paradoxical subsumption of an object under a concept in other ways heterogeneous to it, so that an Adorno-like insistence on the non-identity of object and concept can come to explain why animals cannot laugh. Humour, in this speciously generalizing view, is by and large high words and low meanings, and so like Schopenhauer's own philosophy has an ironic or dialogical structure. This is itself profoundly ironic, since the discrepancy between percept and concept which occasions the release of laughter is exactly that disjuncture between experience and intellect, or will and representation, which lies at the very core of Schopenhauer's disgusted view of humanity. The inner structure of this bleakest of visions is thus the structure of a joke. Reason, that crude, blundering servant of the imperious will, is always pathetic false consciousness, a mere reflex of desire which believes itself absurdly to present the world just as it is. Concepts, in a familiar brand of nineteenth-century irrationalism, cannot cling to the rich intricacies of experience, but appear maladroit and crudely reductive. But if this fissures the very being of humanity into illusion, so that merely to think is to be self-deceived, it also provides the elements of a Freudian theory of humour:

[Perception] is the medium of the present, of enjoyment and cheerfulness; moreover it is not associated with any exertion. With thinking the opposite holds good; it is the second power of knowledge, whose exercise always requires some, often considerable, exertion; and it is the concepts of thinking that are so often opposed to the satisfaction of our immediate desires, since, as the medium of the past, of the future, and of what is serious, they act as the vehicle of our fears, our regrets, and all our cares. It must therefore be delightful for us to see this strict, untiring, and most troublesome governess, our faculty of reason, for once convicted of inadequacy. Therefore on this account the mien or appearance of laughter is very closely related to that of joy. (2, 98)

Comedy is the will's mocking revenge on the representation, the malicious strike of the Schopenhaurian id against the Hegelian superego; and this source of hilarity is also, curiously, the root of our utter hoplessness.[2]

If humour and hopelessness lie so close together, it is because human existence for Schopenhauer is less grand tragedy than squalid farce. Writhing in the toils of the voracious will, driven on by an implacable appetite they relentlessly idealize, men and women are less tragic protagonists than pitiably obtuse. The most fitting emblem of the human enterprise is the shovel-pawed mole: 'to dig strenuously with its enormous shovel-paws is the business of its whole life; permanent night surrounds it . . . what does it attain by this course of life that is full of trouble and devoid of pleasure? Nourishment and procreation, that is, only the means for continuing and beginning again in the new individual the same melancholy course' (2, 353–4). Nothing could be more obvious to Schopenhauer than the fact that it would be infinitely preferable if the world did not exist at all, that the whole project is a ghastly mistake which should long ago have been called off, and that only some crazed idealism could possibly believe the pleasures of existence to outweigh its pains. Only the most blatant self-delusion – ideas, values, the rest of that pointless paraphernalia –

could blind individuals to this laughably self-evident truth. Sunk in its gross stupidity, humanity insists upon regarding as valuable a history which is so plainly the record of carnage, misery and wretchedness that our capacity to think it in the least tolerable must itself be explicable only as a ruse of the will, the low cunning with which it shields itself from our knowledge of its own futility. It is hard for Schopenhauer to restrain a burst of hysterical laughter at the sight of this pompously self-important race, gripped by a remorseless will-to-live which is secretly quite indifferent to any of them, piously convinced of their own supreme value, scrambling over each other in pursuit of some earnest goal which will turn instantly to ashes in their mouths. The world is one enormous market place, 'this world of constantly needy creatures who continue for a time merely by devouring one another, pass their existence in anxiety and want, and often endure terrible afflictions, until they fall at last into the arms of death' (2, 349). There is no grand *telos* to this 'battle-ground of tormented and agonized beings' (2, 581), only 'momentary gratification, fleeting pleasure conditioned by wants, much and long suffering, constant struggle, *bellum omnium*, everything a hunter and everything hunted, pressure, want, need and anxiety, shrieking and howling; and this goes on *in saecula saeculorum* or until once again the crust of the planet breaks' (2, 354). If human beings were capable of contemplating objectively for one moment this perverse attachment of theirs to unhappiness, they would necessarily abhor it. The whole race is like a diseased beggar who appeals to us for help to prolong his miserable existence, even though from an objective viewpoint his death would be altogether desirable. Only some sentimental humanism could see such a judgement as callous rather than coolly reasonable. The most fortunate life is that with endurable want and comparative painlessness, though the result of this is boredom. Boredom for Schopenhauer is the chief motive for sociality, since it is to avoid it that we seek out each other's loveless company. All of this sets the scene for high tragedy, yet even that we bungle: 'our life must contain all the woes of tragedy, and yet we cannot even assert the dignity of tragic characters, but, in the broad detail of life, are inevitably the foolish characters of a comedy' (1, 322). History is low burlesque rather than Attic solemnity: 'no-one has the remotest idea why the whole tragi-comedy exists, for it has no spectators, and the actors themselves undergo endless worry with little and merely negative enjoyment' (2, 357). Life is a grotesquely bad absurdist drama full of farcical repetition, a set of trivial variations on a shoddy script. There is something amusing about the very relentless consistency of this Schopenhauerian gloom, a perpetual grousing with all the monotonous, mechanical repetition of the condition it denounces. If comedy for Schopenhauer involves subsuming objects to inappropriate concepts, then this is ironically true of his own pessimism, which stamps everything with its own inexorable colour and so has the funniness of all monomania. Any such obsessive conversion of difference to identity is bound to be comic, however tragic the actual outlook. To see no difference between roasting a leg of lamb and roasting a baby, to view both as mere indifferent expressions of the metaphysical will, is as risible as mistaking one's left foot for the notion of natural justice. Part of our laughter at such remorseless tunnel vision is no doubt relief at the wanton parade of a monstrous egoism we ourselves have had to camouflage – though in the case of a pervasively pessimistic vision like Schopenhauer's such laughter may contain a nervously defensive quality too. His perverse ignoring of what we feel to be the more positive aspects of life is outrageous enough to be amusing, as we would smile at someone whose only interest in great painters was in how many of them had halitosis.

Schopenhauer's intense pessimism, however, is in one sense not in the least outrageous – is, indeed, no more than the sober realism he himself considers it to be. One-sided though this viewpoint may be, it is a fact that throughout class history the fate of the great majority of men and women has been one of suffering and fruitless toil. Schopenhauer may not have all of the truth; but he has a larger share of it than the romantic humanists he is out to discredit. Any more hopeful view of humanity which has not reckoned his particular narrative into account is bound to be enfeebled. The dominant tale of history to date has indeed been one of carnage, misery and oppression. Moral virtue has never flourished as the decisive force in any political culture. Where such values have taken precarious root, they have been largely confined to the private realm. The monotonous driving forces of history have been enmity, appetite and dominion; and the scandal of that sordid heritage is that it is indeed possible to ask of the lives of innumerable individuals whether they would not have been better off dead. Any degree of freedom, dignity and comfort has been confined to a tiny minority, while indigence, unhappiness and hard labour have been the lot of the vast majority. 'To enter at the age of five a cotton-spinning or other factory', Schopenhauer remarks, 'and from then on to sit there every day first ten, then twelve, and finally fourteen hours, and perform the same mechanical work, is to purchase dearly the pleasure of drawing breath' (2, 578). The dramatic mutations of human history, its epochal ruptures and upheavals, have been in one sense mere variations on a consistent theme of exploitation and oppression. Nor could any future transformation, however radical, affect this record in any substantial way. For all Walter Benjamin's efforts to raise the dead themselves with the clarion call of his eloquence, for all his urgent attempts to muster around the frail band of the living the fertilizing shades of the unjustly quelled, it remains the harsh truth that the dead can be raised only in revolutionary imagination.[3] There is no literal way in which we can compensate them for the sufferings they received at the hands of the ruling order. We cannot recall the crushed medieval peasantry or the wage-slaves of early industrial capitalism, the children who died afraid and unloved in the wretched hovels of class society, the women who broke their backs for regimes which used them with arrogance and contempt, the colonized nations which collapsed under an oppressor who found them at once sinister and charming. There is no literal way in which the shades of these dead can be summoned to claim justice from those who abused them. The pastness of the past is the simple truth that, rewrite and recuperate them as we may, the wretched of history have passed away, and will not share in any more compassionate social order we may be able to create. For all its homespun eccentricity and obdurate monomania, Schopenhauer's appalling vision is accurate in many of its essentials. He is mistaken to think that the destructive will is all there is; but there is a sense in which he is correct to see it as the *essence* of all history to date. This is not a truth particularly palatable to political radicals, even if it is in one sense the very motivation of their practice. That this intolerable narrative cannot continue is the belief which inspires their struggle, even as the crippling burden of that history would seem to bear mute witness against the feasibility of such a faith. The source of energy of a radical politics is thus always the potential source of its enervation.

Schopenhauer is perhaps the first major modern thinker to place at the centre of his work the abstract category of *desire itself*, irrespective of this or that particular hankering. It is this powerful abstraction which psychoanalysis will later inherit, though it is probable that Freud, who was said to consider Schopenhauer one of the half-dozen greatest individuals who had ever lived, came to know his work only after his own theories were already formed. Just as capitalist society is in this period evolving to the point where it will be possible for Marx to extract from it the key concept of abstract labour, a conceptual operation only possible on the basis of certain material conditions, so the determinant role and regular repetition of appetite in bourgeois society now permits a dramatic theoretical shift: the construction of desire as a thing in itself, a momentous metaphysical event or self-identical force, as against some earlier social order in which desire is still too narrowly particularistic, too intimately bound up with local or traditional obligation, to be reified in quite this way. With Schopenhauer, desire has become the protagonist of the human theatre, and human subjects themselves its mere obedient bearers or underlings. This is not only because of the emergence of a social order in which, in the form of commonplace possessive individualism, appetite is now becoming the order of the day, the ruling ideology and dominant social practice; it is more specifically because of the perceived *infinity* of desire in a social order where the only end of accumulation is to accumulate afresh. In a traumatic collapse of teleology, desire comes to seem independent of any particular ends, or at least as grotesquely disproportionate to them; and once it thus ceases to be (in the phenomenological sense) intentional, it begins monstrously to obtrude itself as a *Ding-an-sich*, an opaque, unfathomable, self-propelling power utterly without purpose or reason, like some grisly caricature of the deity. The Schopenhauerian will, as a form of purposiveness without purpose, is in this sense a savage travesty of the Kantian aesthetic, a shoddy, inferior artefact we could all well do without.

Once desire is for the first time homogenized as a singular entity, it can become the object of moral judgement as such – a move which would have seemed quite unintelligible to those moralists for whom there is no such phenomenon as 'desire', simply this or that particular appentency on which a particular judgement may be passed. If desire becomes hypostasized in this way, then it is possible, in a long Romantic-libertarian lineage from William Blake to Gilles Deleuze, to view it as supremely positive; but the preconditions of such

Romantic affirmation are also the preconditions of the Schopenhauerian denunciation of desire *tout court*, accepting the categories of Romantic humanism but impudently inverting the valuations. Like Schopenhauer, you can retain the whole totalizing apparatus of bourgeois humanism at its most affirmative – the singular central principle informing the whole of reality, the integrated cosmic whole, the stable relations of phenomena and essence – while mischievously emptying these forms of their idealized content. You can drain off the ideological substance of the system – freedom, justice, reason, progress – and fill that system, still intact, with the actual degraded materials of everyday bourgeois existence. This, precisely, is what Schopenhauer's notion of the will achieves, which structurally speaking serves just the function of the Hegelian Idea or Romantic life-force, but is now nothing more than the uncouth rapacity of the average bourgeois, elevated to cosmic status and transformed to the prime metaphysical mover of the entire universe. It is as though one retained the whole paraphernalia of the Platonic Ideas but called them Profit, Philistinism, Self-Interest and so on.

The result of this move is ambivalent. On the one hand, it naturalizes and universalizes bourgeois behaviour: everything from the forces of gravity to the blind stirrings of the polyp or rumblings of the gut is invested with futile craving, the whole world recast in the image of the market place. On the other hand, this grandly generalizing gesture serves to discredit bourgeois Man all the more thoroughly, write him repellently large, project his sordid appetites as the very stuff of the cosmos. To reduce Man to the polyp is at once to exculpate him as a helpless puppet of the will, and to insult him. This debunking shakes bourgeois ideology to the root, at the same time as its naturalizing effect removes the hope of any historical alternative. Schopenhauer's system thus stands at the cusp of bourgeois historical fortunes, still confident enough in its *forms* to unify, essentialize, universalize, but precisely through these gestures inflating to intolerable proportions the meagre *contents* of social life. Those contents are thus discredited by the very move which grants them metaphysical status. The forms of the Hegelian system are turned against that philosophy with a vengeance; totalization is still possible, but now of a purely negative kind.

This is also true in another sense. For Hegel, the free subject articulates a universal dimension of consciousness (*Geist*) which is nevertheless at the very core of its identity, that which makes it uniquely what it is. And this transcendental principle, in order to be itself, stands in need of such individuation. Schopenhauer preserves this conceptual structure but lends it a malevolent twist. What makes me what I am, the will of which I am simply a materialization, is utterly indifferent to my individual identity, which it uses merely for its own pointless self-reproduction. At the very root of the human subject lies that which is implacably alien to it, so that in a devastating irony this will which is the very pith of my being, which I can feel from the inside of my body with incomparably greater immediacy than I can know anything else, is absolutely unlike me at all, without consciousness or motive, as blankly unfeeling and anonymous as the force which stirs the waves. No more powerful image of alienation could be imagined than this malicious parody of idealist humanism, in which the Kantian *Ding-an-sich* is brought nearer to knowledge as the directly intuitable interior of the subject, but nevertheless retains all the impenetrability to reason of that Kantian realm. This impenetrability is no longer a simple epistemological fact but an inert, intolerable weight of meaninglessness that we bear inside ourselves as the very principle of our being, as though permanently pregnant with monsters. Alienation lies now not in some oppressive mechanism out there in the world, which confiscates our products and identities, but in the mildest motions of our limbs and language, in the faintest flicker of curiosity or compassion, in all that makes us living, breathing, desiring creatures. What is now irreparably flawed is nothing less than the whole category of subjectivity itself, not just some perversion or estrangement of it. It is this which touches on the guilty secret or impossible paradox of bourgeois society, that it is exactly in their freedom that men and women are most inexorably enchained, that we live immured in our bodies like lifers in a cell. Subjectivity is that which we can least call our own. There was a time when our desires, however destructive, could at least be called ours; now desire breeds in us an illusion known as reason, in order to con us that its goals are ours too.

It is not that Schopenhauer ignores the will's more creative aspects. If yawning or yodelling are expressions of the will, so are all our nobler aspirations; but since they are thus caught up with desire they are part of the problem rather than the solution. To fight injustice is to desire, and so to be complicit with that deeper injustice which is human life. Only by somehow breaking absolutely with this chain of causality, the terrible sway of teleology, could true emancipation be achieved. Every bit of the world, from doorknobs and doctoral dissertations to modes of production and the law of the excluded middle, is the fruit of some stray appetite locked into the great empire of intentions and effects; human beings themselves are just walking materializations of their parents' copulatory instincts. The world is one vast externalization of a useless passion, and that alone is real. Since all desire is founded in lack, all desire is suffering: 'All *willing* springs from lack, from deficiency, and thus from suffering' (1, 196). Riddled by the will, the human race is creased over some central absence like a man doubled up over his ulcer; and Schopenhauer is well aware of how, in modern psychoanalytical idiom, desire outstrips need. 'For one wish that is fulfilled there remain at least ten that are denied. Further, desiring lasts a long time, demands and requests go on to infinity; fulfilment is short and meted out sparingly' (1, 196). It is not therefore for the more creative impulses that we should be searching – not a matter, as with traditional morality, of ranging our desires on an evaluative scale and pitting the more positive against the more destructive. Only the quiescence of impulse itself would save us; yet to *seek* such quiescence, in a familiar Buddhist paradox, would be self-defeating.

Where then can we turn for a momentary staunching of this insatiable urge which builds the very stuff of our blood-stream and intestines? The answer for Schopenhauer is to the aesthetic, which signifies less a preoccupation with art than a transfigured attitude to reality. The intolerable tedium of existence is that we can never burst out of our own skins, never shuck off the straitjacket of our petty subjective interests. We drag our egos with us in everything we do, like some bar-room bore intruding his dreary obsessions into the most casual conversation. Desire denotes our inability to see anything straight, the compulsive referring of all objects to our own sectarian interests. Passion 'tinges the objects of knowledge with its colour' (2, 141), falsifying the given through hope, anxiety, expectation; and Schopenhauer gives us a home-spun little instance of this victory of will over intellect by gravely pointing out how, when we do our financial accounts, the unconscious slips we make are almost always to our own advantage. The aesthetic is a temporary escape from this prison-house of subjectivity, in which all desire drops away from us and we are able for a change to see the phenomenon as it really is. As we relinquish our heated claims over it, we dissolve contentedly into a pure, will-less subject of knowledge. But to become a pure subject of knowledge is paradoxically to cease to be a subject at all, to know oneself utterly decentred into the objects of one's contemplation. The gift of genius, Schopenhauer writes, is nothing more or less than the most complete objectivity. The aesthetic is what ruptures for a blessed moment the terrible sway of teleology, the tangled chain of functions and effects into which all things are locked, plucking an object for an instant out of the clammy grip of the will and savouring it purely as spectacle. (Dutch interiors, Schopenhauer argues, are flawed aesthetic objects, since their portrayal of oysters, herrings, crabs, wine and so on makes us hungry.) The world can be released from desire only by being aestheticized; and in this process the desiring subject will dwindle to a vanishing point of pure dis-interestedness. But such disinterestedness has little in common with an Arnoldian large-mindedness, impartially weighing competing interests with an eye to the affirmative whole; on the contrary, it demands nothing less than a complete self-abandonment, a kind of serene self-immolation on the subject's part.

It is really rather too easy, however, to regard this doctrine as mere escapism. For the Buddhist tradition to which Schopenhauer is here indebted, nothing could be more bafflingly elusive than this apparently straightforward matter of seeing something as it is, a naive realism or (as Heidegger might say) a 'letting of things be' which is never really within our power, and which can occur only spontaneously in a stray moment of mystical illumination. Nor is such realism for Schopenhauer any mere positivism: on the contrary, he is a full-blooded Platonist on that score, holding that to see things as they are is to grasp them in their eternal essences or species-being. It is this well-nigh impossible realism we can attain in the blessed indifference of the aesthetic – that state in which the world is transmuted to theatrical charade, its shrieking and howling stilled to so much idle stage chatter for the unmoved spectator's delighted contemplation. The aesthetic is in this sense a kind of psychical defence mechanism by which the mind, threatened with an overload of pain, converts the cause of its agony into innocuous illusion. The sublime is therefore the most typical of all aesthetic moods, allowing us as it does to contemplate hostile objects with absolute equanimity, serene in the knowledge that they can no longer harm us. In the sublime, the paranoid ego fantasizes some state of triumphal invulnerability, wreaking Olympian vengeance on the sinister forces which would hound it to death. But this ultimate mastery, in which a predatory world is disarmed to a kind of fiction, is itself, as Freud taught us, the condition of death, towards which the battered, pitiable ego is driven for its ultimate self-preservation. The Schopenhauerian subject thus masters its own murder by suicide, outwits its predators through the premature self-abnegation of the aesthetic. The Schopenhauerian aesthetic is the death drive in action, though this death is secretly a kind of life, *Eros* disguised as *Thanatos*: the subject cannot be entirely negated as long as it still delights, even if what it takes pleasure in is the process of its own dissolution. The aesthetic condition thus presents an unsurmountable paradox, as Keats knew in contemplating the nightingale: there is no way in which one can savour one's own extinction. The more exultantly the aesthetic subject experiences its own nullity before the object the more, by that very token, the experience must have failed.

Indifference for Schopenhauer is a political as well as aesthetic state of being; and to this extent he sustains, while also subverting, the classical Schillerian concept of art as social paradigm. For Schopenhauer as for his predecessors, the aesthetic is important because it speaks of more than itself. The detachment or ataraxia we attain for a precious moment in contemplating the artefact is an implicit alternative to appetitive egoism; art is no mere antithesis to society, but the most graphic instance of an ethical existence beyond the understanding of the state. Only by somehow piercing the veil of *Maya* and recognizing the fictional status of the individual ego can one behave to others with true indifference – which is to say, make no significant distinction between them and oneself. Satiric detachment is thus at the same time loving compassion, a state in which, the *principium individuationis* once unmasked for the ideological fraud it is, selves may be empathetically exchanged. Just as all true knowledge springs from the death of the subject, so too does all moral value; to act morally is not to act from a positive standpoint, but to act from no standpoint at all. The only good subject is a dead one, or at least one which can project itself by empathetic indifference into the place of every other. It is not a question of one individual behaving considerately towards the next, but of bursting beyond the whole wretched delusion of 'individuality', in a flash of what Walter Benjamin would call 'profane illumination', to some non-place unutterably far beyond it. Schopenhauer is thus led beyond the apparatus of bourgeois legality, of rights and responsibilities and obligations, since he rejects its prime datum of the individual subject. Unlike the fetishists of difference of our own day, he believes that what human beings share in common is ultimately of more substance than what distinguishes them.

Moral action, like aesthetic knowledge, would thus appear an unthinkable paradox. For there can be no practice without a subject; and with subjects come domination and desire. To speak of a compassionate subject would seem oxymoronic: even if a purely contemplative benevolence were possible, it could only realize itself in action at the cost of falling prey to the voracious will. Knowledge and practice would appear as ironically at odds for Schopenhauer as 'theory' and 'ideology' for some contemporary thought: if there can be no truth without a subject, there can be none with it either. All practice for Schopenhauer inhabits the domain of illusion: to prosecute my pity for you is in that moment to dispel it, to find myself writhing instead in the toils of self-interest. Only by transcending the diseased category of subjecthood altogether could one individual feel for another; but this very proposition cancels itself out. As William Blake knew, pity and sorrow are signs that the catastrophe has already happened, and would be unnecessary if it had not. In a society powered by appetite, where all action appears irredeemably contaminated, compassion must be banished to the realm of 'aesthetic' contemplation. In one sense, the aesthetic offers us a whole new form of social life: in its very dispassionate amorality, it teaches us to shed our disruptive desires and live humbly, ungreedily, with the simplicity of the saint. It is thus the first faint glimmerings of utopia, bearing with it a perfect, virulently misanthropic happiness. But this is not a happiness which could ever be actively realized: like the aesthetic state of a Schiller, it betrays and undoes itself as soon as it enters upon material existence.

It is in any case difficult to know how this state of disinterestedness could ever come about. It can obviously not be a product of the will, since it involves the will's momentary suspension; but it is hard to see how it can be the work of the alienated intellect either, and in

Schopenhauer's drastically reduced universe there are really no other agents available. He himself writes obscurely of the intellect achieving in these moments a certain 'temporary preponderance' over the will; but the sources of this unwonted reversal remain significantly vague. There *is* positive value in bourgeois society, but its origins are deeply mysterious. As with the early Wittgenstein, himself a devoted disciple of Schopenhauer, value cannot really be *in* the world at all, but must be transcendental of it.[4] There is, it would seem, no way of shifting from fact to value; and Schopenhauer consequently manoeuvres himself into an inexplicable duality between the torture chamber of history on the one hand, and some vaguely Humean notion of intuitive affection on the other. In such compassion for others, he writes, we recognize our 'true and innermost self'; yet we have been told time and again that this innermost self is nothing but the ravenous will.

Schopenhauer is adamant that philosophy is quite incapable of altering human conduct, and disowns all prescriptive intent in his writing. There can be no truck between the cognitive and the ethical, which partake in the eternal enmity of the representation and the will. Yet his whole philosophy can be read as an implicit disproval of this claim, suggesting against its own conscious intentions how fact and value, description and prescription may indeed be mutually articulated. In fact his indebtedness to oriental thought betrays just how ethnocentric the fact/value dichotomy is – how deeply the consequence of a technological history from which it is admittedly impossible to derive value, since its facts have been constituted from the outset as value's very negation. The Buddhist critique of the principle of individuation, by contrast, is at once descriptive and prescriptive – an account of the way the world is, as well as, indissociably, the recommendation of a certain style of moral behaviour. It is hard to see how a genuine conviction of the relative insignificance of distinctions between selves could not affect one's practical conduct. Schopenhauer would seem to agree that a recognition of the fictional nature of identity will show up in one's actions, while refusing to acknowledge that his own discourse, which speaks of these matters, might produce such ethical effects.

To do otherwise would be to concede, contrary to one of his major tenets, that reason can influence the will. On such a remorselessly instrumentalist version of reason as Schopenhauer's, this would be

166

clearly impossible. Reason is no more than a clumsy calculative device for the realization of desires which are themselves quite insulated from rational debate. The lineage from Schopenhauer and Nietzsche to contemporary pragmatism in this sense reduplicates the bourgeois model of appetitive man of Hobbes, Hume and Bentham. Reason is the mere tool of interest and slave of desire – interests and desires over which there can be fighting but no arguing. But if what Schopenhauer asserts on this score were true, his own work would be strictly speaking impossible. If he really credited his own doctrines, Schopenhauer would be unable to write. If his theory is able to dissect the insidious workings of the will, then reason must be to that extent capable of curving back on itself, scrutinizing the drives of which it proclaims itself the obedient servant. Either he has somehow given the will the slip in his theorizing, or that theorizing is just another of its futile expressions and so quite valueless.

Schopenhauer's comparison of philosophy with music suggests that he believes the former possibility to be the true one. Of all the arts, music is the most direct presentation of the will; indeed it is the will made audible, a kind of delicate, impalpable diagram of the inner life of desire, a revelation in non-conceptual discourse of the pure essence of the world. Any true philosophy is thus no more than a translation into conceptual terms of what speaks in music, performing rationally what music achieves intuitively. A theory which knew the world as it is would thus be characterized by a kind of aesthetic completion, would be an artefact all in itself, resisting discursive divisions and deferments so as to represent in its synchronic unity the cohesion of all things in the will. Philosophy must thus be transcendental; yet the only transcendental reality it seems to identify is the will itself. It cannot be that philosophy looks at the world from the vantage point of the will, for then it would be unable to pass any true comment on it; so it would appear to be inspecting the will and all its works from some other transcendental viewpoint. But since there is no such viewpoint acknowledged in Schopenhauer's writing, philosophy must be standing in a non-place, speaking from some location not included within itself. There is indeed such a non-place identified in the theory itself – the aesthetic – but this is not conceptual; and it is hard to see how it can be conceptually translated without falling instantly foul of the delusions of the intellect. In short, truth would appear to be possible, but we are quite at a loss to account for how this can be so. It can only be that the intellect, in rare, mysterious moments, seizes a precarious hold on the will of which it is no more than a manipulated plaything. These are epistemological dilemmas which Schopenhauer will bequeath to his most famous successor, Friedrich Nietzsche.

Bourgeois thought tends to construct a recurrent binary opposition between knowledge as the sheer determined reflex of desire, and knowledge as a form of sublime disinterestedness. If the former caricatures the true state of affairs of bourgeois civil society, where no reflection would seem innocent of self-interest, the latter is no more than its fantastic negation. Only a demonic desire could dream such an angelic antithesis. As an increasingly reified, fragmented social order comes gradually to discredit the idea of its own intelligibility, sublime disinterestedness must be progressively surrendered to pragmatist disenchantment. The price of this, however, is that any more ambitious ideological defence of the society as a whole, uncoupled as it is from particular interests, steadily loses its hold upon social practice. Schopenhauer and Nietzsche are transitional figures in this respect, full-blooded totalizers in one sense yet disenchanted pragmatists in another. Caught in this contradiction, Schopenhauer ends up with a kind of transcendentalism without a subject: the place of absolute knowledge is preserved, but it lacks all determinate identity. There can be no subject to fill it, for to be a subject is to desire, and to desire is to be deluded. An idealist philosophy which once dreamt of finding salvation through the subject is now forced to contemplate the unspeakable prospect that no salvation is possible without the wholesale immolation of the subject itself, the most privileged category of the entire system.

In one sense, of course, such an abject surrender of the subject is no more than a routine feature of the bourgeois social order. Schopenhauer's empathetic ethics serialize all individuals to equal exchangeability in much the same manner as the market place, if at a somewhat loftier level. In this most rampantly individualist of cultures, the individual is indeed little more than a fiction, given the blank indifference to it of the capitalist economy. It is simply that this prosaic levelling of individual specificity must now be sublated to a form of spiritual communion, disdainfully turned (as in the Kantian aesthetic) against the practical egoism which is in truth its material foundation. It is as though the cool disregard for specific identities displayed by the capitalist mode of production must be dignified to a spiritual discipline, elevated to a tender mutuality of souls. Yet if this desperate strategy mimes the problem to which it is a solution, its radicalism is at least equally striking. Once the actual bourgeois subject, rather than its high-minded idealist representation, is placed *à la* Schopenhauer at the nub of theory, there seems no way of avoiding the conclusion that it must be liquidated. There can be no question any longer of judicious reform: nothing short of that revolution of the subject which is its mystical obliteration will serve to liberate it from itself. The philosophy of subjectivity accordingly self-destructs, leaving in its wake a numinous aura of absolute value which is, precisely, nothing.

Enthusiastic Kantian though he is, the aesthetic for Schopenhauer signifies in one sense the exact opposite of what it means for his mentor. For Kant, as we have seen, the disinterested gaze which reads the world purely as form is a way of eliciting the object's enigmatic purposiveness, lifting it out of the web of practical functions in which it is enmeshed so as to endow it with something of the self-determining autonomy of a subject. It is by virtue of this crypto-subjectivity that Kant's aesthetic object 'hails' individuals, speaks meaningfully to them, assures them that Nature is not after all entirely alien to their preoccupations. For Schopenhauer, things are quite otherwise: what we glimpse in the aesthetic realm is not yet another image of our own intolerable subjectivity, but a reality benignly indifferent to our longings. If for Kant the aesthetic works within the register of the imaginary, it involves for his successor a gratifying shift to the symbolic, where we can come finally to accept that the object turns its back upon us, has no need of us, and is all the better for that. It is as though, having himself relentlessly anthropomorphized the whole of reality, discerning analogies of human appetite in the falling of a stone or the blowing of a rose, Schopenhauer's nausea with that whole monstrously humanized world compels him to imagine how delightful it would be to look at things as though we were not there. Yet this, of course, is beyond our reach: the dissolution of the grasping ego, as we have seen, is also, unavoidably, the ego's exultant fantasy of securing an eternal, uninjured existence for itself. Perhaps, then, the aesthetic is no more than the last reckless card the will to live has to play, just as for

Schopenhauer suicide is simply a sick joke by which the will craftily affirms itself through the individual's self-annihilation.

The dream of transcending one's own petty subjecthood is a familiar enough idealist fantasy; but it generally turns out to involve a flight into some higher, deeper form of subjectivity, with a corresponding gain of omnipotent mastery. One does not give the slip to the subject simply by collectivizing or universalizing it. Schopenhauer, however, sees that since the subject *is* its particular perspective, all that can be left behind when this has been surmounted is a kind of nothing: the nirvana of aesthetic contemplation. Even this nothing turns out to be a kind of something, a negative form of knowledge; but at least one has now shed the illusion of a positive mode of transcendence. All that is left to us is to take pity on the objects of the world, infected as they are by our own contagious yearnings, and save them from ourselves by some miraculous vanishing trick. What is from one viewpoint an irresponsible escapism is thus from another viewpoint the last word in moral heroism.

It is in the body, above all, that for Schopenhauer the impossible dilemmas of existence take on flesh. For it is in the body that we are most starkly confronted with the clash between the two utterly incompatible worlds in which we live simultaneously. In a rewriting of Kant's celebrated dualism, the body which we live from the inside is will, whereas the body as an object among others is representation. The human subject, that is, lives a unique double relation to its own body as at once noumenal and phenomenal; the flesh is the shadowy frontier where will and representation, inside and outside, come mysteriously, unthinkably together, converting human beings to a kind of walking philosophical conundrum. There is an unspannable gulf between our immediate presence to ourselves, and our indirect representational knowledge of everything else. This, of course, is the most banal of Romantic dichotomies; but Schopenhauer lends it an original inflection. If he privileges the inward in Romantic style, he nevertheless refuses to valorize it. This swift, unmediated knowledge of ourselves, far from signifying some ideal truth, is nothing other than our anguished apprehension of the appetitive will. There is indeed a style of cognition which by-passes the uncertain labours of the concept, but it delivers no value whatsoever. My intuitive presence to myself is the site of a problem, not of some logocentric solution; and in any case I can know the will at work within my body only phenomenally, never in itself. But if the spontaneous and immediate are thus brusquely uncoupled from creativity, one of the central aestheticizing strategies of bourgeois idealism is cancelled at a stroke. It is not, for Schopenhauer, a question of elevating a valued form of cognition over a valueless one, but of suspending the whole question of value itself, inextricably bound up as it is with the terrorism of desire. The only true value would be to abolish value altogether. This, indeed, is the valueless value of the aesthetic state – the insight that things just are eternally what they are, the mind-bending drama of an object's sheer identity with itself. To acknowledge this entails a kind of intuition; but it is intuition to the second power, a will-less overcoming of the spontaneous movement of will, which allows us to gaze unmoved for a moment into the very heart of darkness as the objects around us grow more luminously replete, more satisfyingly pointless, and we ourselves dwindle gradually away to nothing.

Despite its dispassionateness, the aesthetic would seem best figured by either weeping or laughing. If it signifies an infinite fellow-feeling for others, it is also the incredulous cackle of one who has extricated himself from the whole squalid melodrama and surveys it from an Olympian height. These antithetical responses are deeply interrelated, in the tragicomedy of the Schopenhauerian vision: I suffer with you because I know that your inner stuff, the cruel will, is also my own; but since everything is built from this lethal substance, I scorn its futility in a burst of blasphemous laughter. The aesthetic is the noblest form of cognitive and ethical truth; but what it tells us is that reason is useless and emancipation inconceivable. As an aporetic state in which one is simultaneously alive and dead, moved and unmoved, fulfilled and erased, it is a condition which has gone beyond all conditions, a solution which testifies in its very contra-dictoriness to the impossibility of a solution. Schopenhauer's work is thus the ruin of all those high hopes which bourgeois idealism has invested in the idea of the aesthetic, even though it remains faithful to the aesthetic as some ultimate redemption. A discourse which began as an idiom of the body has now become a flight from corporeal existence; a disinterestedness which promised the possibility of an alternative social order is now an alternative to history itself. By some curious logic, the aesthetic has ended up demolishing the very category of subjectivity it was intended to foster. The embarrassing rift in a Kant or Schiller between the actual and the ideal, civil society and aesthetic *Gemeinschaft*, has now been pressed to a destructive extreme, as any practical connection between the two spheres is summarily rejected. Schopenhauer tells in his own dourly universalizing way the plain, unvarnished tale of bourgeois civil society, in fine disregard for the affirmative ideological glosses; and he is clear-eyed and courageous enough to pursue the grim implications of this narrative to their scandalous, insupportable conclusions.

Notes

1 Arthur Schopenhauer, *The World as Will and Representation*, trs. E.F.J. Payne (New York, 1969), vol. 2, p. 284. All subsequent references to this work are given after quotations in the text.

2 See also, for one of numerous anticipations of Freud, Schopenhauer's comment that 'the intellect remains so much excluded from the real resolutions and secret decisions of its own will that sometimes it can only get to know them, like those of a stranger, by spying out and taking unawares; and it must surprise the will in the act of expressing itself, in order merely to discover its real intentions' (2, 209).

3 See Walter Benjamim, 'Theses on the Philosophy of History', in Hannah Arendt (ed.), *Illuminations* (London, 1970).

4 For the influence of Schopenhauer on Wittgenstein, see Patrick Gardiner, *Schopenhauer* (Harmondsworth, 1963), pp. 275–82, and Brian Magee, *The Philosophy of Schopenhauer* (Oxford, 1983), pp. 286–315. A somewhat threadbare account of Schopenhauer's aesthetics is to be found in I. Knox, *The Aesthetic Theories of Kant, Hegel, and Schopenhauer* (New York, 1958).

7

Absolute Ironies: Søren Kierkegaard

It is surprising in a sense that Søren Kierkegaard – ironist, jester, apostle of the aporetic and enemy of all totality – has not received more attention in a deconstructive age. In another sense, it is hardly surprising at all: for Kierkegaard combines his devotion to difference, sportive humour, play with pseudonyms and guerilla-raids on the metaphysical with a passionately one-sided commitment, by which few of our modern ironists are likely to feel anything but unsettled. In an era when neither existentialism nor evangelical Protestantism are in intellectual fashion, it may be worth casting a glance back at this solitary eccentric, whose power to disturb has been less weakened by those shifts in fashion than one might have supposed.[1]

One of Kierkegaard's many eccentricities is his attitude to the aesthetic. Of the major philosophers from Kant to Habermas, he is one of the few who refuse to assign it any predominant value or privileged status. He thus stands stubbornly askew to the aestheticizing currents of the modern European mind, which is not to say that the aesthetic is not from first to last one of his central preoccupations. For him as for the originators of the discourse, aesthetics refers not in the first place to art but to the whole lived dimension of sensory experience, denoting a phenomenology of daily life before it comes to signify cultural production. As such, it indicates for Kierkegaard the very homeland of inauthenticity. Aesthetic existence is empty abstract immediacy, a zone of being which predates the temporal or historical and in which the subject's actions are only dubiously its own. In this unreflective sphere, akin in some sense to the Freudian stage of early infancy, the subject lives in a state of fragmented multiplicity, too diffuse to be called a unitary self, unable to differentiate itself from an environment of which it is little more than the determined reflex. Dreaming itself sensuously at one with the world, it confounds its own existence with the sense-impression in a manner which resembles the Lacanian register of the imaginary. Most social life for Kierkegaard is no more than a higher version of this sensuous passivity – 'immediacy with the addition of a little dose of self-reflection', he remarks sardonically in *The Sickness unto Death*[2] – since few individuals can rise above their social conditioning to a state of determinate selfhood. The judgement of the world, he comments in his *Journals*, is not moral but aesthetic, admiring 'everything that has power, cunning, selfishness'.[3] Middle-class society has never come of age, as much the decentred plaything of its repetitive drives as the small infant.

The aesthetic, then, is in one of its versions Hegel's 'bad' immediacy; but it is also, contradictorily, an Hegelian 'bad' infinity of endless self-reflection. This 'higher' or reflective stage of the aesthetic represents a break with sensuous immediacy – not, however, as a movement upwards into determinate selfhood, but rather as a lapse into some abyssal specularity, where irony tumbles on the heels of irony with no more resolute centring of the subject than can be found in the 'imaginary' of bodily immediacy. Hamlet and Caliban are thus inverted mirror-images of each other; one is always, in the aesthetic, either too much or too little oneself, ensnared in actuality or adrift in possibility, lacking that dialectical tension between these realms which is defined by the ethical paradox of becoming what one is. Reflectiveness negates immediacy, but thereby shatters it to an infinite indeterminacy not wholly untypical of immediacy itself. The self-reflective subject, as radically empty as the pseudo-self of aesthetic immediacy, erases temporality and ceaselessly reinvents itself from nothing, seeking to preserve an unbounded freedom which is in truth sheer self-consuming negativity. The name of this mode of existence is irony, of which the figure of Socrates is exemplary. Socratic irony raises the subject out of its mindless communion with the world, critically unhinging it from the real; but since it yields no positive alternative truth it leaves the subject giddily suspended between actual and ideal, in and out of the world simultaneously. The actual is the ironist's element, 'but his course through actuality is hovering and etherial, scarcely touching the ground. As the authentic kingdom of ideality is still alien to him, so he has not yet emigrated but is at every moment, as it were, about to depart.'[4] Socrates's very existence is ironic, an infinite negation of the social order which is nonetheless still sub-ethical, still to arrive at determinate subjecthood. Intoxicated by endless possibility, later 'absolute' ironists such as Fichte and the Romantics posit and destroy at a stroke, living subjunctively or hypothetically and so bereft of all continuity of self. The aesthete-ironist lives actuality as sheer possibility, hubristically usurping the divine prerogative in his impotent freedom to bind and loose. The despairing subject of *The Sickness unto Death*, perversely determined to be what it is, flamboyantly refashions the whole of its finite being in the image of its arbitrary desire. Such aesthetic experimentalism ('enchanting like an oriental poem', Kierkegaard remarks) is a kind of conjuring of oneself up *ex nihilo* at every moment, airily erasing the burden of historicity and of the self's radical givenness. The panache of this artistic self-fashioning or giving of oneself the law thinly conceals its nihilism: if the subject can dissolve this elaborate fabrication to nothing at any moment, its omnipotence is at one with its nullity. The self as perpetual *acte gratuit* is a mere self-cancelling liberty: 'irony, like the old witch, constantly makes the tantalising attempt first to devour everything in sight, then to devour itself too, or, as in the case of the old witch, her own stomach.'[5] The aesthetic as free development of one's multiple powers rests upon a violent, vacuous self-willing.

'Immediate' and 'reflective' aestheticism, then, decentre the subject in opposed directions, either flattening it out into external reality or plunging it fruitlessly into its own vertiginous depths. Such contrastive modes of aesthetic existence follow from the primary condition of the Kierkegaardian self, as a contradictory synthesis of finitude and infinity. Once this precarious unity splits apart, the subject either takes flight into sensuous finitude, abandoning itself in craven conformity to the social order, or finds itself monstrously inflated and volatilized, carried drunkenly outside of itself in that 'process of infinitizing' whose insidious root is the aesthetic imagination. As an aporetic blending of necessity and possibility, the unregenerate self finds that each of these dimensions tends constantly to outrun the other: to will not to be oneself is just as spiritually desperate as to will defiantly to be it, to spurn necessity quite as catastrophic as to deny possibility.

If irony is the joker in the aesthetic pack, the fault-line or deconstructive point at which self and world are initially uncoupled, then it can be said to provide a threshold between the aesthetic and the ethical. It is the originary splitting or cutting edge which enables the subject to effect its passage from the decentred immediacy of the aesthetic 'imaginary' to the unified, differentiated state of the ethical 'symbolic order'. Socrates in *The Concept of Irony* is in this sense a liminal figure, teetering on the very brink of determinate subjecthood without yet having achieved selfhood as resolved project and autonomous decision. Only with Judaism will the law or ethical stage proper be ushered in. If the hollow infinitude of the ironic recalls the 'bad' immediacy of the aesthetic, the two conditions being akin in their utter indeterminacy, the ironic nevertheless negates that immediacy and so opens up a transition to the ethical. Since irony cannot avoid positing what it negates, it ends up by negating its own negativity and thus allowing the affirmative to appear. It is not, then, that irony is to be rejected; on the contrary, as we shall see, it provides the matrix of much of Kierkegaard's own writing. Irony is essential, but as a 'mastered moment' within the endlessly unfinished process of truth – a moment which as opposed to 'bad' infinity 'limits, renders finite, defines, and thereby yields truth, actuality and content . . .'.[6] Ironizing is not thereby itself negated, brought to an abrupt closure by the act of commitment; instead, it lives on as the very form of that commitment, which knows a wry discrepancy between its own intense inwardness and the external world with which it continues to have practical involvements. Commitment thus raises the ambivalence of irony to a higher level, preserving something of its sceptical stance towards social reality but combining it with positive belief. To that extent, irony is sublated to humour and comedy, which in debunking the world's pretensions carry with them a deeper positivity than Socratic subversion.

There is another mode of negativity in Kierkegaard which invades the otherwise replete sphere of aesthetic immediacy, and this is the experience of dread. Dread is the self's encounter with its own nothingness, or more particularly our response to that unsettling *néant* which haunts even the purest sensual lack of self-consciousness. Even aesthetic immediacy, dreaming its blissful undifferentiation, always already betrays some elusive negation, which would seem a kind of dim premonition of difference, otherness and freedom. It is as though spirit is already glimpsing its own future possibilities within the serene self-ignorance of the aesthetic – as though, in Hegelian terms, the annulment of immediacy is an immanent movement within immediacy itself. The very repleteness of the aesthetic state cannot help being sinisterly suggestive of lack – not, to be sure, lack of something specific, for then how could this state be said to be replete, but an absence necessarily entailed by its own sheer existence. One might describe this uncanny feeling in Heideggerian or Satreian terms, as that nameless anxiety we experience when the very fullness of some object unavoidably calls to mind the non-being it has contingently filled in; or one could picture it alternatively as that moment within the Lacanian imaginary – the dim presence of the mother beside the child's mirror-image, for example – which threatens to puncture its coherence. It might even be that Kierkegaardian dread has resonances of Julia Kristeva's category of the 'abject', that originary experience of nausea, horror and distaste involved in our first efforts to separate out from the pre-oedipal mother.[7] Whatever the appropriate model, it is clear that for Kierkegaard there can be no genuine aesthetic, Edenic or pre-oedipal innocence – that the Fall has always already happened, otherwise how would Adam have been able to violate God's injunction in the first place? Adam's disobedience is viewed in *The Concept of Dread* as an absurd aporia: it was from his transgression that a knowledge of difference sprang, so that in this sense it was the primordial prohibition itself, in Freudian style, which opened up desire; yet Adam could not have fallen unless some vague pre-understanding of the possibility of freedom was already at work within his prelapsarian innocence, to be catalysed by the taboo itself. Adam was thereby awakened to the pure possibility of freedom, of the simple state of being able, and this is the condition of dread. Dread, Kierkegaard comments in strikingly Schillerian terms, 'is not a determinant of necessity, but neither is it of freedom; it is a trammelled freedom, where freedom is not free in itself but trammelled, not by necessity but in itself'.[8] Like Schiller's aesthetic condition of being, dread is undecidably suspended between freedom and necessity; but what for Schiller was a supremely positive state of nameless potential is for Kierkegaard a form of ontological *angst*.

'Sin presupposes itself', Kierkegaard writes, meaning perhaps that its origins are in any temporal sense quite unthinkable. Sin has no place or source, lying as it does under the sign of contradiction. To sin is to have been always already able to do so; and sinfulness is thus as much the ruin of any rational ethics or hunt for transcendental origins as the experience of dread is the immanent negation of innocence. Certainly any mythological temporalization of the Fall, as with *Paradise Lost*, will tend to run headlong into insurmountable paradox, as *The Concept of Dread* makes clear. If Adam is the source of original sin then he did not have that taint himself, which puts him outside the race he fathered and thereby excludes him from the fruits of the Atonement. If he is the only individual to have no history, then the race stems from an individual who was not an individual, a fact which annuls the concepts of both race and individual. How could the human race have a source outside itself? And if there can be no transcendental origin which escapes contamination by the history it generates, then there is no originary innocence, and innocence thus springs into the world under the sign of its own erasure, 'comes into existence as that which was before it was annulled and is now annulled'.[9] Innocence is thus not a perfection to be recovered, 'for as soon as one wishes for it, it is lost'.[10] Like Adam, we all bring sin into the world; what is originary is not innocence but that structural possibility of transgression which must always already have been present, the anguished awareness of which is dread. Dread is a kind of floating signifier, a dim primordial sense of the possibility of difference before difference has actually occurred, what Kierkegaard calls 'freedom's appearance before itself in possibility'.[11] It is less immediacy's groping apprehension of some possibility other than itself than, as it were, the dawning of the possibility of possibility itself – less the intuition of an other than the first stirrings of the very categorial possibility of otherness. There is a paranoid dimension to this condition, since such otherness is at once intimidating and attractive in its indeterminacy, generating what Kierkegaard calls 'antipathetic sympathy'. As long as the other remains beyond the self's grasp, the subject is unable to define itself and so remains extrinsic to its own being; but the anxiety of this state is also curiously pleasurable, since for the subject to define itself in the other is to find and lose itself simultaneously. The self's own nothingness is both alluring and repellent to it, combining as it does the terrors and seductions of the sublime. It is thus not surprising to find Kierkegaard associating dread especially with women, who are similarly both fearful and tempting. Dread is a 'womanish debility in which freedom swoons',[12] embodying like the sublime 'the egoistic infinity of possibility, which does not tempt like a definite choice, but alarms and fascinates with its sweet anxiety'.[13] In her very sensuous immediacy, her aestheticist lack of spirit, woman will inspire the *néant* of dread and so figure, contradictorily, as a sublime abyss ready to engulf the timorous self. Dread is the 'inexplicable nothing' which shadows all sensuality, the faintest, purely negative trace of spirit lurking within it, and thus a suitable image of the innocent, treacherous female:

> Even that which, humanly speaking, is the most beautiful and lovable thing of all, a feminine youthfulness which is sheer peace and harmony and joy – even that is despair. For this indeed is happiness, but happiness is not a characteristic of spirit, and in the remote depths, in the most inward parts, in the hidden recesses of happiness, there dwells also the anxious dread which is despair . . . All immediacy, in spite of its illusory peace and tranquility, is dread, and hence, quite consistently, it is dread of nothing . . .[14]

The more perfect a woman is, in short, the sicker she must be – just as the sensuous cheerfulness of ancient Greece, excluding 'spirit' as it does, is for Kierkegaard overshadowed by a profound sorrow. Dread is that place where spirit will later be, and which in anticipating its arrival opens up within sensuous pleasure the empty space in which spirit will germinate. The aesthetic for Kierkegaard is thus inseparable from disease, even if such disease is the necessary harbinger of a transition to the ethical state. Sensuousness is not in itself sinful, *The Concept of Dread* insists; but without sin there is no sexuality. The recognition of difference and otherness essential for sexuality to operate are also structural possibilities of sinfulness; and since without sexuality there can be no history, sin is the precondition of both. It is in this sense, then, that sin is original – not as some transcendental source from which a postlapsarian history flows, but as that ever-present condition of freedom, difference and otherness which underlies our historical existence.

In contrast to the polymorphous indeterminacy of the aesthetic, the ethical sphere for Kierkegaard signifies antithesis, decision,

179

strenuously one-sided commitment. If the aesthetic subject inhabits a perpetual present, as a kind of lower parody of the eternal moment of faith, the ethical self, through some impassioned resolution in the present, binds its guilty past (duly acknowledged and repented of) to a future of unrealized possibilities. It is thus that it brings itself into being as a determinate, temporally consistent subject, one 'tensed' in every sense of the term. The paradox of this project is that the self both does and does not exist prior to this revolutionary crisis of self-choosing: for the word 'choice' to have meaning the self must somehow pre-exist that moment, but it is equally true that it emerges into being only through this act of decision. Once that decision is taken, as a fundamental orientation of one's being rather than as an option for this or that particular, it must be ceaselessly re-enacted; and this process of endless becoming, in which the subject binds together its history into a self-consistent project, might seem in one sense a form of aesthetic self-fashioning. What distinguishes it from such exotic auto-invention, however, is not only its radical one-sidedness, but its openness to all that in the subject which is sheerly *given*, its inescapable finitude and guilt-ridden temporality. If ethical self-determination is a kind of aesthetic construct, it is one whose unity is fraught and provisional, whose origin lies beyond its own mastery and whose end is nowhere in view. In any case, it breaks decisively with the inertia of aesthetic being for the dynamic venture of becoming, marked as it is by a passionate interestedness which spurns the ataraxy of the aesthetic as much as it denounces the lofty disinterestedness of speculative thought. (Humour, Kierkegaard remarked, was his own alternative to 'objective' thought, a more fruitful form of detachment.) To live in the ethical is to be infinitely interested in existing – 'existing' for Kierkegaard signifying a task rather than a *donnée*, something to be achieved rather than received. Aesthetic and theoretical disinterestedness will never yield access to goodness and truth; only an implacable partisanship can hope to do that. To see life truthfully is to see it neither steadily nor whole; the truth is loaded, tendentious, jealously exclusive in a way no liberal pluralism or aesthetic all-roundedness can comprehend.[15] 'That don' is Kierkegaard's contemptuous title for the Hegel who sought studiously to encompass every aspect of reality within his mighty totalization.

In so far as it is at all possible to distinguish subject and object in the sphere of aesthetic immediacy, this register of being can be said to involve a mutuality of inner and outer worlds. It is this symmetrical interchange which the 'reflective' aesthetic disrupts: the self-ironizing narcissist either ignores the external world entirely, or treats it merely as the manipulable material of his fantasies. The seducer of *Either/Or* is preoccupied with his own erotic strategies, not with the hapless object of them; his reflectiveness, so to speak, has become his immediacy. To exist ironically is to live a discrepancy between inward and external, ambiguously suspended between one's negating subjectivity and the world it confronts. To the extent that the aesthetic is conventionally viewed as a harmonious relation of subject and object, irony may thus be regarded as an anti-aesthetic mode. For Socrates, 'the outer and the inner did not form a harmonious unity, for the outer was in opposition to the inner, and only through this refracted angle is he to be apprehended.'[16] The attainment of the ethical brings with it a turn to the subject, since the only ethically pertinent issue is one's own inner reality; yet since the ethical also concerns the public sphere, the relation of the individual to the universal, it recreates a certain 'aesthetic' commensurability of subject and object at a higher level. Such, certainly, is the ethical ideology of Judge Wilhelm of *Either/Or*, who finds in marriage a prototype of the ethical life. Marriage for Wilhelm unites subjective feeling with an objective institution, and in doing so reconciles the antinomies of individual and universal, sensuous and spiritual, freedom and necessity, time and eternity. Such ethics are thus the very model of Hegelian synthesis, and as such, for Wilhelm's author, deeply suspect. 'The Hegelian philosophy', Kierkegaard writes in *Concluding Unscientific Postscript*, 'culminates in the proposition that the outward is the inward and the inward is the outward. With this Hegel virtually finishes. But this principle is essentially an aesthetic-metaphysical one, and in this way the Hegelian philosophy is happily finished, or is fraudulently finished, by lumping everything (including the ethical and the religious) indiscriminately in the aesthetic-metaphysical.'[17] Wilhelm's eminently bourgeois ethics, with their values of work, family, duty and civic obligation, blandly expel all contradiction in their obsessive mediations. As such they stand under the judgement of Kierkegaard himself in his *Journals*: 'let us not speak aesthetically, as if the ethical were a happy geniality.'[18] Wilhelm elevates the ethical above the aesthetic, yet his ethics are modelled on the very aesthetic notions they seek to transcend. For him, the ethical personality is the truly beautiful, an absolute which like the artefact contains its teleology within itself. The ethical life, as a symmetrical mediation of subject and object, inward and outward, individual and universal, is a splendidly conflict-free artefact of autonomously self-determining particulars; and it is precisely such aestheticized ethics which for Kierkegaard himself will be wrenched open and undermined by religious faith.

Such faith shatters the smooth mediations of the ethical, subverts the complacently autonomous self and stands askew to all merely civic virtue. Its intense inwardness thwarts any equitable interchange of subject and object, lacking as it does any adequate objective correlative: 'Christianity is spirit, spirit is inwardness, inwardness is subjectivity, subjectivity is essentially passion, and in its maximum an infinite, personal, passionate interest in one's eternal happiness.'[19] This ardent subjectivism is relentlessly particular, resistant to all dialectical mediation and universalization. The religion of an ethicist like Wilhelm is no more than an underpinning of the universal, part of a rational discourse of totality which for Kierkegaard is bound to shipwreck on the rock of faith. Such smugly idealizing talk is unable fully to acknowledge the realities of sin and guilt – the fact that before God we are always already in the wrong, that the self carries a crippling burden of suffering and injury which cannot be blandly sublated. Sin is the scandal or stumbling block upon which all 'philosophy' and rational ethics is bound to come a cropper: 'If ethics must include sin, its ideality is lost . . . an ethics that ignores sin is an altogether futile discipline, but once it postulates sin it has *eo ipso* gone beyond itself.'[20] The crux of Christian faith, the Incarnation, is similarly the ruin of all reason – the truth that, in some mind-warping paradox, the eternally unintelligible Other became finite and fleshly. Unlike the Hegelian Idea, God is sheer impenetrable otherness, and the claim that a man could incarnate him in time is thus wholly absurd. For Kierkegaard there is no necessary relation between time and eternity, which remain spheres quite extrinsic to each other; God does not, *pace* Hegel, need the world, temporality is no part of his necessity, and his appearance in history is therefore the breach of all immanence and continuity. Because God is not immanent in time, history is less some rational, evolutionary totality than a series of free, contingent events. It is nevertheless with this finite, degraded, empty time that the infinite has mysteriously intersected; and the faith of the individual must struggle to appropriate this objective absurdity. Such an appropriation might be seen as the effort towards a higher form of commensurability between subject and object; but both of these items are now opaque and aporetic. The relation between them is thus fraught with internal contradiction, accentuating the oppositions it momentarily overcomes. If faith reconstitutes a kind of unity, and so is to that degree 'aesthetic', it is a fissured unity always about to split apart again, and one that has therefore to be ceaselessly reappropriated in that act which Kierkegaard names 'repetition'. Faith is thus an endless task rather than a triumphant Hegelian closure – a kind of momentary paradoxical overcoming of the gap between inner and outer, holding fast to the objective in a surge of intensive inwardness: 'an objective uncertainty, held fast in the most passionate appropriation of inwardness, is the truth, the highest truth there is for an *existing individual* . . . The truth is precisely the venture which chooses an objective uncertainty with the passion of the infinite.'[21] The 'knowledge' of faith is thus a sort of unity-in-conflict, as the subject binds itself unconditionally to an objective reality it recognizes as problematic.

As such, faith involves a similarly unstable relation to the external world. In abandoning the finite for the infinite, it opens up an abyss between outer and inner; but this gesture is shadowed by a movement of hope which rediscovers a sort of workaday commensurability with the world, accepting the finite for what it is in the ironizing light of infinity. Faith, Kierkegaard comments, must grasp the eternal but also somehow hold fast to the finite after having given up: 'To have one's daily life in the decisive dialectic of the infinite, and yet to continue to live: this is both the art of life and its difficulty.'[22] Turning towards and away from reality in an endless dual movement, the subject of faith thus knows at once something of the inner/outer disjunction of the 'reflective' aesthetic, and that more harmonious interchange of subject and object which is the ethical. But this is not a condition to be comfortably inhabited or routinely lived: it can never crystallize into custom or spontaneous habit, and can establish itself as a permanant, collective, institutionalized form of life (Hegel's *Sittlichkeit*) only at the grave risk of inauthenticity. Faith for Kierkegaard can never be naturalized in this way, assimilated to the unconscious *mores* and traditions of a social order, and so resists the purposes of political hegemony. If the ethics of a Judge Wilhelm are an aestheticized version of religious belief, reflecting a pleasurable, instinctual conformity to universal law, that belief for his author is at once too dramatically individualist and too perpetually in crisis to oil the wheels of daily social life. Faith is *kairos* rather than custom, fear and trembling rather than cultural ideology. Its absolute disdains the logic of social evolution and strikes obliquely, apocalyptically into time, so that for Kierkegaard as much as for Walter Benjamin every moment is the strait gate through which the Messiah might enter.[23]

Nor does such belief, for all of its radical individualism, yield much comfort to the autonomous ego of the bourgeois ethical sphere. Religious commitment is indeed a question of free self-determination; but in choosing oneself one assumes one's personal reality in all its unregenerate facticity, as always in the wrong before God, and as an ultimately unmasterable mystery. Only the agonized acknowledgement of all this which is repentence can unmake and remake the subject, rather than some fantasy of 'free' aesthetic self-invention. The self for Kierkegaard is a unity of freedom and necessity, spirit and sense, infinity and finitude; but these antinomies cannot be thought on the model of some rational dialectic. What is at work in the moment of faith is some aporetic, undecidable relation of freedom and necessity, of the subject's utter dependency on that which it nevertheless opts for and actively appropriates. 'Freedom really only *exists* because the same instant it exists it rushes with infinite speed to bind itself unconditionally by choosing resignation, the choice of which it is true that in it there is no question of a choice.'[24] Since the commitment of faith is and is not the subject's own free act, it can be understood neither on the model of aesthetic immediacy, where the self can hardly call its actions its own, nor on the pattern of the self-fashioning bourgeois ego, which would recognize no determinants beyond its own precious liberty. The self clung to in faith will always remain an enigma for the rational ego, plagued as it is by contradictions which can be resolved only existentially rather than theoretically, leashed provisionally together in the moment-to-moment venture of existence rather than unified in the tranquillity of the concept or in some stabilized artefact. Instead of identity annulling the principle of contradiction, Kierkegaard writes in his *Concluding Unscientific Postscript*, it is contradiction that annuls identity.

To shift from the aesthetic to the ethical is not to liquidate the former. 'In choosing itself the personality chooses itself ethically and excludes absolutely the aesthetical, but since it is itself it chooses and it does not become another being by choosing itself, the whole of the aesthetical comes back again in its relativity.'[25] If it is *this* unregenerate self which the ethical transfigures, then it must have truck with the very aesthetic life-style it upbraids. Similarly, the religious by no means merely erases the ethical, but puts it, as Kierkegaard comments, into 'teleological suspension'. The figure of such suspension is the Abraham of *Fear and Trembling*, who in his fidelity to a God beyond all reason comes to stand above and outside the ethical-universal realm in a direct, unmediated relation to the absolute. For Abraham to sacrifice his son Isaac is to do nothing for the universal – would indeed, from this viewpoint, be to commit murder – and is thus an act offensive to all Kantian and Hegelian reason. Abraham travels beyond the frontiers of the ethical into that paradoxical territory of faith where language fails, since if language raises the particular to the general it is itself ineluctably on the side of the universal. What is customarily thought difficult is not to exist as an individual, but to transcend that paltry egoism and translate oneself into the universal. For Kierkegaard, however, the problem is exactly the other way round. There is a spurious aesthetic facility about the 'knight of faith' of *Fear and Trembling* who 'knows it is beautiful and benign to be the particular who translates himself into the universal, the one who so to speak makes a clear and elegant edition of himself, as immaculate as possible, and readable for all . . .'.[26] Such aestheticized ethics, speciously translucent and *lisible*, in which the individual's conduct becomes luminously intelligible in the light of the universal, knows nothing of the harsh opacity of faith and of the radical unreadability of those subsisting in contradiction. It is not in relation to the Kantian universal of practical reason that Abraham's lunatic loyalty will become decipherable, but in relation to an absolute imperative which can never be speculatively mediated.

' "Reality" cannot be conceived,' Kierkegaard reminds himself in his *Journals*;[27] and elsewhere, 'the particular cannot be thought.'[28] It is this which will be the downfall of aesthetics – of the discourse which seeks within the unique particular a kind of rational structure. The folly of such a project is just the fact that existence is radically heterogeneous to thought – that the whole notion of a thought supple enough to penetrate lived experience and deliver up its secret is an idealist chimera. The metaphysical principle of identity – the identity of the subject with itself, with objects, with other subjects – crumbles before the fact of existence itself, which is precisely the anguished separation of subject and object rather than their spontaneous unity. It follows for Kierkegaard that any trust in the immediate transparency of one human subject to another, any dream of an aesthetic intersubjectivity or empathetic communion of individuals, rests on this pernicious ideology of identity, and corresponds well enough to the abstractly equivalenced subjects of the bourgeois ethical and political domains. He writes of the 'negative unity of the mutual reciprocity of individuals' in such a social order, and of 'levelling' as the triumph of abstraction over particular lives.[29] Whatever community of love may be possible in some higher, religious sphere of beings who relate to each other through the absolute of faith, it remains true of secular history that human subjects are profoundly impenetrable and inaccessible to one another. The reality of another for me is never a given fact, only a 'possibility', which I can never mimetically appropriate as my own. That imaginative, empathetic imitation which for earlier thinkers was the very foundation of human sociality is here abruptly dismissed; there can be no direct communication between irreducibly particular individuals. No subject's inwardness can be known other than indirectly: all believers are, like Jesus, 'incognitos', caught in an ironic discrepancy between their passionate, secretive subjectivity and their bland appearance to others as citizens of the public world. Faith, and the individual, are that which cannot be represented, and so are at root anti-aesthetic. The new development of the age, Kierkegaard writes in his *Journals*, cannot be political, for politics is a question of the dialectical relation of individual and community in the representative individual, and 'in our times the individual is in the process of becoming far too reflective to be able to be satisfied with merely being *represented*.'[30] Politics and aesthetics thus fall together: both are given over to the fruitless task of seeking to subsume the specific within the abstract universal, and so simply annul what they strive to sublate.

If Kierkegaard is not to be caught in a performative contradiction, then it follows that what he asserts of the impossibility of direct communication must logically apply to his own writings too. It is this which necessitates his play of pseudonymous personae, as a set of guerilla-raids on the reader's false consciousness, a crabwise skirmishing whereby the reader must be approached obliquely, duplicitously, if genuine enlightenment is to dawn. The author cannot appear as some brash 'town crier of inwardness' but must practise instead a kind of Socratic ignorance, as the feigned or fictive precondition of the reader's true ignorance becoming revealed to him. Kierkegaard's writerly strategy thus resembles that of a revolutionary propagandist in hard political times who promulgates a stream of pamphlets which do no more than question the limits of her readership's left-leaning liberalism. Rather than confront the reader with an absolute truth which would only be rejected, Kierkegaard must covertly enter the reader's own viewpoint in order to deconstruct it from the inside, 'going along with the other's delusion', as he puts it, so as to deceive them into the religious domain. He speaks therefore of his pseudonymous works as his 'aesthetic production': 'I always stand in an altogether poetic relation to my work, and I am, therefore, a pseudonym.'[31] If the reader is presumed to inhabit the aesthetic sphere, driven by wayward impulse rather than ethically resolute, then as Kierkegaard comments in *My Point of View as an Author* it would hardly be appropriate to break rudely in on him with a direct discussion of Christianity. Instead, one invites the reader to debate aesthetics, and arrives at the truth in that sideways movement. If truth itself is resolutely subjective, then its conveyance demands some more circumspect medium than the language of scientific objectivity. That more underhand mode is the aesthetic, involving as it does 'an awareness of the form of the communication in relation to the recipient's possible misunderstanding'.[32] An aesthetic discourse is one which revises and reflects back upon itself in the very act of enunciation, an utterance raised to the second power which overhears itself in the ears of its recipients. If it is true that 'all receiving consists in producing',[33] then writing must reach out to engage the freedom of its readers to accept or reject the offered truth as they wish, thus figuring in its very structure something of the cryptic, undemonstrable, non-apodictic nature of truth itself. Writing which was not in this sense radically dialogical, constituted in its very letter by a putative readerly response, would cancel in its very form the emancipatory content of the truth it proffered. Truth and irony, passionate commitment and serpentine scepticism, are therefore for Kierkegaard accomplices rather than antitheses of one another; it is not that truth is dialogical 'in itself', but rather that its very relentless absolutism renders it unreadable for a fallen history and so constrains it to re-emerge as irony, deception and feigned ignorance. The problem is not that truth is 'indeterminate'; it is quite determinate enough, but simply absurd. As such, it can be encompassed neither by the ideology of self-identity nor by the dogmatism of an endless deconstructive irony. Nor is it the case that Kierkegaard himself has secure access to the truth but entices others into it by cunning propagandist ploys, since there can be no secure access to a truth appropriated in fear and trembling. If truth is that which can be lived but not known, then this must apply just as much to Kierkegaard's own experience of it as to that of his readers. Truth defeats all mediation and so is apprehended instantly or not at all; but since it defeats mediation there is nothing that can be directly said about it, which means that it is determinate and indeterminate, ironic and self-identical, at one and the same time.

If the content of truth is also its form – if truth exists only in the process of its free appropriation – then 'the mode of apprehension of the truth is precisely the truth',[34] which would seem to confer on truth that indissociability of form and content which belongs to the aesthetic. Process and end-product, as with the aesthetic artefact, are profoundly at one; and in this sense faith does not leave the aesthetic entirely behind, but re-enters and repossesses it like a fifth columnist for its own ulterior motives. The religious resembles the ironic or reflective aesthetic in its disproportioning of inner and outer; but it also parallels aesthetic immediacy, recreating the dense opacity of the sensuous at a higher spiritual level. Both faith and aesthetic immediacy thus resist that violent dissolution of specificity to universality which is the ethical. The subject of faith, as a kind of spontaneous relation of particular to absolute without the mediation of universal law, might therefore be said to be a sort of artefact in itself, working as it does by intuition rather than by reason; and its mysteriousness might then be read as a version of the Kantian aesthetic representation, which similarly fuses the particular with a greater 'law' while outflanking the mediatory concept. If for idealist thought the aesthetic transmutes temporal existence into the form of its eternal essence, then there is a sense in which Kierkegaardian belief might be viewed as an aesthetic mode of being; but the contrasts between the two spheres are finally more striking than the

188

analogies. For faith is always untotalized and internally fissured, agitated by paradox and contradiction in a way foreign to the achieved aesthetic product; and this state of continuous crisis and agonized renewal estranges it, as we have seen, from all mere social custom and civic virtue. Religious engagement resists all translation to the sedate milieu of a taken-for-granted cultural legacy – to the institutional space in which, living their conformity to the law as instinctual pleasure, men and women become the 'self-governing' subjects of bourgeois hegemony. Kierkegaard has nothing but contempt for the 'public opinion' or collective *mores* of bourgeois social theory, and rips Hegel's unity of morality and happiness rudely apart. The religious has nothing to do with well-being or sensuous fulfilment, and is thus a critique of the aesthetic in this sense too. The true Christian, Kierkegaard writes, is one who 'calls one away from the physical man's pleasure, life and gladness';[35] faith is 'no aesthetic emotion, but something far higher, exactly because it presupposes resignation; it is not the immediate inclination of the heart but the paradox of existence'.[36] For Kierkegaard there can be no Shaftesbury-like path from the heart's affections to the absolutes of ethics, and the religious sense has little in common with aesthetic taste. Poetry for faith is 'a beautiful and amiable jest, whose consolation religiousness nevertheless spurns, because the religious comes to life precisely in suffering'.[36] There is a kind of 'poet-existence' which, as *Fear and Trembling* insists, is 'the sin of poeticising instead of being, of standing in relation to the Good and the True through imagination instead of being that, or rather of existentially striving to be it'.[37] The poetic is idealist speculation rather than religious activism; and even the aesthetic register of the sublime is a poor image of divine transcendence.[38]

Kierkegaard's writing goes back beyond Hegel's collectivized 'ethical life', which seeks to blend duty and desire, to Kant's rigorous duality of happiness and moral rectitude; but it does so in ways which undermine both the autonomous subject of Kantian ethics, and the unity of that subject with others in the universal. We have seen already how the individual believer is no mere conferer of a rational law upon itself, swept up as it is in abject dependency upon a grace whose logic entirely defeats it. The uncompromising inwardness of this then ruptures the links between individuals, who become indecipherable at once to each other and to themselves; and in doing so it threatens to subvert any conceivable structure of sociality. The aestheticized politics of the bourgeois public sphere rests on a harmonious reflection of autonomous subjects one in the other, as the inwardness of each is mediated through 'concrete ethics' to their collective social existence and then back to the individual. It is this fluent continuity of inward and outward which Kierkegaard's ferocious individualism abruptly suspends; and the result is a shattering of that imaginary register in which individuals may find themselves reflected and reassured by the world around them. The believer can never feel ideologically centred in this way: 'finite experience', Kierkegaard writes, 'is homeless'.[39] There can be no objective correlative of a subjectivity lived at this pitch of passionate intensity; and the subject is accordingly thrust beyond the world, sustaining a merely ironic relation with it, a permanent thorn in the flesh of all purely institutional life.

The paradox of Kierkegaard's work is that it seizes upon the rampant individualism of bourgeois society and presses it to an unacceptable extreme, at which the social and ideological unity of that order begin to come apart at the seams. In a further paradoxical turn, this subversion takes place before any such individualism has installed itself in Danish society on a significant scale. That society is still in Kierkegaard's time one of monarchical absolutism, unaltered in many of its social practices since the middle ages. Denmark's entry into the nineteenth century was marked by a series of cataclysms: the physical devastation wrought by the Napoleonic wars, the state bankruptcy of 1813, the loss of Norway one year later, the economic failures and food shortages of the 1820s. By the 1830s, Frederik VI's rigidly conservative kingship held autocratic sway, brutally suppressing the slightest expression of liberal thought. Despite some earlier reformist legislation, which broke the bondage of peasant to landholder and established a rudimentary system of public education, the Denmark of Kierkegaard's day remained politically oppressive and culturally benighted, a traditionalist agrarian society still several decades away from industrialization. While church and censorship stifled intellectual life, a guild system in the townships thwarted commercial development.

Within this restrictive carapace, however, the forces of social progress were tentatively assembling. Newly aware of itself as a corporate social power, the Danish peasantry pressed for greater land reform, and through its representative association the *Bondevennernes Selskab* (Society of Friends of the Farmers) secured a limited programme of agrarian improvement in the late 1840s. Farmers' credit societies, the forerunners of Danish agricultural cooperativism, assisted peasants to purchase their own smallholdings; and this gradual liberalization of the countryside was coupled in Copenhagen with a rising tide of allegiance to the liberal trade principles of British bourgeois political economy. In 1857, reforming legislation dismantled the Danish guild system and swept away the ancient monopoly of trade in the market towns. 1844 had witnessed the arrival of railways in the country, contributing by the 1860s to a significant opening up of free internal trade. As improved popular education and cultural revival movements gradually raised the political consciousness of the peasantry, middle-class liberal intellectuals struggled throughout the 1830s and 1840s for constitutional reform, appealing to the benevolent despotism of Christian VIII for male suffrage and an elected legislature. By 1849 such a liberal constitution was finally declared, guaranteeing freedom of speech, religious tolerance and other civic liberties throughout the realm. There had been, however, no middle-class industrial revolution; indeed Denmark possessed little organized industry, and the national bourgeoisie, lacking an economic base and daunted by the leaden conservatism of church and state, pursued its own moderate interests in that spirit of timorous conformity and calculative prudence which Kierkegaard was to denounce as the sign of a passionless age.

A fierce opponent of the National Liberals, Kierkegaard himself was a full-blooded apologist for the forces of political reaction.[40] Elitist, puritanical and bitterly misogynistic, he defended censorship, church and monarchy, railed intemperately against the 'mob' and adhered to an orderly hierarchical structure which would reflect God's rule over creation. Liberal reformism's call for equality meant a mere abstract levelling, undermining concrete social bonds and annihilating the pure differences of individual life. His Lutheran combination of social conservatism and extreme individualism, that is to say, took the regressive ideological form of an impassioned plea for the socially specific individual, loyal offspring of family, profession, religion and fatherland, in the teeth of the abstractly universal subject of bourgeois social theory. In thus turning individualism against bourgeois society itself, Kierkegaard exposes that society's real anti-social character, cloaked as it is by its political and spiritual rhetoric. His social criticism springs not from insisting in idealist style on 'community' as against egoism, but from exploring that egoism at so profoundly serious a depth that the abstract individual of market society is transformed into an irreducible particular which resists all social integration. Nothing could in truth be more abstract than this solitary Kierkegaardian self, bereft of all history and culture; yet this speciously 'concrete' subject becomes the ruin of all social consensus, the stumbling block to bourgeois solidarity. Before the proper emergence of middle-class power in Denmark, Kierkegaard has already in a pre-emptive strike unmasked one of its major contradictions: the fact that its enthronement of the uniquely valuable individual in the ideological sphere is ceaselessly, ironically subverted by its reduction of that individual to an arbitrarily interchangeable cypher in the economic and political domains. In some sense, then, it is the very reactionary character of his thought – its scorn for the public sphere, its strident subjectivism, its patrician disdain (prefiguring Nietzsche and Heidegger) for the faceless 'mass man' of modern homogenized society – which turns out to be most explosively radical. Something of the same may be said of the repressive puritanism of this ascetic Dane, with his dour suspicion of the senses and bitter hostility to the body. Sensation, the life of corporeal pleasure, figures in his work as the aesthetic realm of mindless middle-class appetite, the sluggish, self-satisfied *Lebenswelt* of bourgeois Copenhagen.

As a *spiritual* individualism, Kierkegaardian faith sets itself at once against the life of degraded desire (bourgeois civil society) and against all vacuously idealist universalism (the bourgeois ethical and political spheres). His strategy, in short, is to split into two parts the conventional concept of the aesthetic, which reconciles sensory experience with the spiritually universal. The former dimension then appears in itself, shorn of all edifying universality, as the aesthetic; the latter form of abstract idealism takes up its home in the world of the ethical. In this way bourgeois society is doubly exposed, even before it has properly got under way, as both grossly particularist and vacuously unspecific. Kierkegaard's vehement anti-Hegelianism rips the sensuous from the spiritual and the particular from the universal, thereby challenging all aestheticizing solutions to social dilemmas. The Baumgartenian effort to render the sensuous particular transparent to reason – the very foundation of modern aesthetics – is thus decisively undone. To this extent Kierkegaard, for all his religious absolutism, is not entirely remote from the materialist logic he found so spiritually offensive. Nor is his work as irrelevant as might be thought to the present age, trapped as it is between the 'bad' infinity of deconstructive irony and certain too closed, over-totalizing theories of the political subject. The subject of faith, abandoning the solace of an idealist ethics, aware of itself as radically homeless and decentred, turns its horror-stricken face to its own guilty implication in the crime of history, and in that crisis of revolutionary repentence or *metanoia* is freed to seize upon certain transformative possibilities for the future. Gripped by a one-sided commitment scandalous to liberal pluralism, yet living also in the fear and trembling of irresolvable ambiguity, it is forced to acknowledge otherness and difference, the whole realm of the unmasterably particular, at the very instant that it seeks strenuously to remake itself in some fundamental, exclusive orientation of its being. At once dependent and self-determining, it appropriates its own 'nothingness' and becomes in that act, but always precariously and provisionally, an historically determinate being. If the subject lives in intense seriousness it is also necessarily comic and ironic, knowing its own revolutionary option to be mere foolishness in the world's eyes and secretly delighting in that incongruity while maintaining the gravest of public miens. Ready to abandon its identity in the trust that some unfathomable wisdom might flow from such folly, it nonetheless forgoes the 'bad' utopianism of any final synthesis for an endlessly unfinished existence. But that open-endedness is a self-resolution continually renewed, rather than a spiral of evasive self-ironizing.

It is not the one-sidedness of the age which is to be criticized, Kierkegaard remarks, but rather its *abstract* one-sidedness. Purity of heart is to will one thing; and an authentic existence must therefore reject the alluring all-roundedness of the aesthetic, the belief that the good lies in the rich, multiple unfolding of human powers. It is in this sense that commitment and the aesthetic are for Kierkegaard irreconcilable. For an alternative viewpoint – a one-sided engagement as unwavering as Kierkegaard's, but one in the cause of all-round creative development – we must turn to the work of Karl Marx.

Notes

1 Useful general studies of Kierkegaard include Louis Mackey, *Kierkegaard: A Kind of Poet* (Philadelphia, 1971); John W. Elrod, *Being and Existence in Kierkegaard's Pseudonymous Works* (Princeton, 1975); Mark C. Taylor, *Kierkegaard's Pseudonymous Authorship* (Princeton, 1975), and *Journeys to Selfhood: Hegel and Kierkegaard* (Berkeley and Los Angeles, 1980); Niels Thulstrup, *Kierkegaard's Relation to Hegel* (Princeton, 1980); and Stephen N. Dunning, *Kierkegaard's Dialectic of Inwardness* (Princeton, 1985). For an intricate critique of the abstractness of the Kierkegaardian individual, see Theodor Adorno, *Kierkegaard: Konstruktion des Ästhetischen* (Frankfurt, 1973).

2 Søren Kierkegaard, *Fear and Trembling and The Sickness unto Death*, translated with an Introduction by Walter Lowrie (New York, 1954), p. 191.

3 *The Journals of Søren Kierkegaard: A Selection*, edited and translated by Alexander Dru (London, 1938), p. 385.

4 Søren Kierkegaard, *The Concept of Irony*, translated with an Introduction by Lee M. Capel (New York, 1965), p. 158.

5 Ibid, p. 92.

6 Ibid, p. 338.

7 See Julia Kristeva, *Histoires d'amour* (Paris, 1983), pp. 27–58.

8 Søren Kierkegaard, *The Concept of Dread*, translated with an Introduction by Walter Lowrie (Princeton, 1944), p. 45.

9 Ibid., p. 33.

10 Ibid., p. 34.

11 Ibid., p. 99.

12 Ibid., p. 55.

13 Ibid., p. 55.

14 Kierkegaard, *The Sickness unto Death*, p. 158.

15 Which is not to say that liberal pluralism has not tried to appropriate Kierkegaard, as the pious flourish on which Mark C. Taylor concludes his *Journeys to Selfhood* well exemplifies: 'Unity *within* plurality; being *within* becoming; constancy *within* change; peace *within* flux; identity *within* difference: the union of union and nonunion – reconciliation *in the midst of* estrangement. The end of the journey to selfhood' (p. 276). Though it is hard to tell what this string of vacuous slogans actually means, one suspects it has more to do with contemporary North American ideology than with nineteenth-century Denmark.

16 Kierkegaard, *The Concept of Irony*, p. 50.

17 Søren Kierkegaard, *Concluding Unscientific Postscript*, introduced by Walter Lowrie (Princeton, 1941), p. 186.

18 Kierkegaard, *Journals*, pp. 186–7.
19 Kierkegaard, *Concluding Unscientific Postscript*, p. 33.
20 Kierkegaard, *The Concept of Dread*, pp. 16–17, and *Fear and Trembling*, p. 124.
21 Kierkegaard, *Concluding Unscientific Postscript*, p. 182.
22 Ibid., pp. 78–80n.
23 See Walter Benjamin, 'Theses on the Philosophy of History', in H. Arendt (ed.), *Illuminations* (London, 1973).
24 Kierkegaard, *Journals*, p. 371.
25 Søren Kierkegaard, *Either/Or*, translated by Walter Lowrie (Princeton, 1944), vol. 2, p. 150.
26 Kierkegaard, *Fear and Trembling*, p. 103.
27 Kierkegaard, *Journals*, p. 373.
28 Kierkegaard, *Concluding Unscientific Postscript*, p. 290.
29 Quoted in Taylor, *Journeys to Selfhood*, p. 57.
30 Kierkegaard, *Journals*, p. 151.
31 Ibid., p. 132.
32 Kierkegaard, *Concluding Unscientific Postscript*, p. 70.
33 Ibid., p. 72.
34 Ibid., p. 287.
35 Kierkegaard, *Journals*, p. 363.
36 Kierkegaard, *Concluding Unscientific Postscript*, p. 390.
37 Kierkegaard, *Fear and Trembling*, p. 208.
38 See Kierkegaard, *Journals*, p. 346, where he scorns the sublime as a kind of 'aesthetic accountancy'.
39 Quoted in Taylor, *Journeys to Selfhood*, p. 64.
40 A singularly unconvincing attempt to qualify Kierkegaard's reactionary politics can be found in Michael Plekon, 'Towards Apocalypse: Kierkegaard's Two Ages in Golden Age Denmark,' in Robert L. Perkins (ed.), *International Kierkegaard Commentary: Two Ages* (Macon, 1984).

8

The Marxist Sublime

In the narrative so far, the aesthetic as a kind of incipient materialism would not seem to have fared particularly well. Indeed there is a sense in which what we have seen so far as the aesthetic might more accurately be described as an anaesthetic. Kant expels all sensuousness from the aesthetic representation, leaving behind only pure form; as Pierre Bourdieu and Alain Darbel remark, Kantian aesthetic pleasure is 'an empty pleasure which contains within itself the renunciation of pleasure, a pleasure purified of pleasure'.[1] Schiller dissolves the aesthetic into some rich creative indeterminacy, at odds with a material realm it is nevertheless intended to transform. Hegel is fastidiously selective about the body, endorsing only those of its senses which seem somehow intrinsically open to idealization; while in the hands of a Schopenhauer the aesthetic ends up as an implacable refusal of material history itself. If Kierkegaard turns back to the aesthetic sphere, it is in largely negative mood: the aesthetic, once the very consummation of beauty, is now in effect synonymous with idle fantasy and degraded appetite. A discourse which set out with Baumgarten to reconcile sense and spirit has been left starkly polarized between an anti-sensuous idealism (Schopenhauer) and an unregenerate materialism (Kierkegaard).

If this is the case, then it would seem that the only fruitful strategy is to go back to the beginning and think everything through again, but this time from the standpoint of the body itself. The implicit materialism of the aesthetic might still be redeemable; but if it can be retrieved from the burden of idealism which weighs it down, it can only be by a revolution in thought which takes its starting-point from the body itself, rather than from a reason which struggles to make room for it. What if an idea of reason could be generated up from the body itself, rather than the body incorporated into a reason which is always already in place? What if it were possible, in a breathtaking wager, to retrace one's steps and reconstruct everything – ethics, history, politics, rationality – from a bodily foundation? That such a project would be fraught with perils is undeniable: how could it safeguard itself from naturalism, biologism, sensuous empiricism, from a mechanical materialism or false transcendentalism of the body every bit as disabling as the ideologies it seeks to oppose? How can the human body, itself in part a product of history, be taken as history's source? Does not the body in such an enterprise become simply another privileged anteriority, as spuriously self-grounding as the Fichtean ego?

There might, nevertheless, be some way of working laboriously upwards from the opposing thumb or the oral drive to mystical ecstasy and the military-industrial complex. And it is just this kind of project which the three greatest 'aestheticians' of the modern period – Marx, Nietzsche and Freud – will courageously launch: Marx with the labouring body, Nietzsche with the body as power, Freud with the body of desire. How one can even speak of such theorizing is then an immediate question; for what is one to say of a form of thought which denies itself? Denies itself, that is, as any autonomous reality, returning us instead to the bodily interests from which it was generated. 'The element of thought itself,' writes Karl Marx, 'the element of the vital expression of thought, *language*, is sensuous nature.'[2] If a materialist discourse does not necessarily betray its own premises in the act of articulation, it is because, as Marx suggests, theoretical reflection must itself be grasped as material practice.

'*Sense perception*', writes Marx in the *Economic and Philosophical Manuscripts* (*EPM*), 'must be the basis of all science. Only when science starts out from sense perception in the dual form of *sensuous* consciousness and *sensuous* need – i.e. only when science starts out from nature – it is *real* science. The whole of history is a preparation, a development, for "*man*" to become the object of *sensuous* consciousness and for the needs of "man as man" to become (sensuous) needs.'[3]

Almost a century after Alexander Baumgarten's proclamation of a new science, Marx calls for its reinvention. But the aesthetic, that humble prosthesis of reason, has here supplanted with a vengeance what it was supposed to supplement. Sense perception, to be sure; but as the *basis* of all knowledge? And how is this more than a vulgar empiricism? Marx will devote much of the *EPM* to thinking history and society through again, this time from the body upwards. Elaine Scarry has remarked on how Marx throughout his writings 'assumes that the world is the human being's body and that, having projected that body into the made world, men and women are themselves disembodied, spiritualised'.[4] The system of economic production, as Scarry points out, is for Marx a kind of materialized metaphor of the body, as when he speaks in the *Grundrisse* of agriculture as a conversion of the soil into the body's prolongation. Capital acts as the capitalist's surrogate body, providing him with a vicarious form of sentience; and if the ghostly essence of objects is exchange-value, then it is their material use-value, as Marx again comments in the *Grundrisse*, which endows them with corporeal existence.

The story Marxism has to tell is a classically hubristic tale of how the human body, through those extensions of itself we call society and technology, comes to overreach itself and bring itself to nothing, abstracting its own sensuous wealth to a cypher in the act of converting the world into its own bodily organ. That this tragedy should occur is not, of course, a mere question of technological overweening but of the social conditions within which such techno-logical development takes place. Since these are conditions of struggle, in which the fruits of labour are fiercely contested, there is need for a range of social institutions which will have, among other functions, the task of regulating and stabilizing these otherwise destructive conflicts. The mechanisms by which this can be accomplished – repression, sublimation, idealization, disavowal – are as familiar to psychoanalytical as to political discourse. Yet the strife over the appropriation and control of the body's powers is not so easily quelled, and will inscribe itself within the very institutions which seek to repress it. Indeed this struggle is so urgent and unremitting that it ballasts the whole of that institutional history, warping it out of true and skewing it out of shape. This process, whereby a contention over the body's powers comes to trace our intellectual and institutional life to its roots, is known to Marxism as the doctrine of base and superstructure. Like the neurotic symptom, a superstructure is that place where the repressed body succeeds in manifesting itself, for those who can read the signs. Bodies of a certain kind – 'prematurely' born, potentially communicative, needing to labour – produce, unlike other animal bodies, a history; and Marxism is the narrative of how that history slips from the body's grasp, thrusting it into contradiction with itself. To describe a particular form of body as historical is to say that it is continuously able to make something of that which makes it. Language is in this sense the very index of human historicity, as a system whose peculiarity is to enable events which transgress its own formal structure. But one aspect of this unfathomable capacity for self-transgression, on the part of the linguistically productive animal, is the power to extend its body into a web of abstractions which then violate its own sensuous nature.

If Marx can call for a sensuously based science without lapsing into commonplace empiricism, it is because the senses for him are less some isolable region, whose 'laws' might then be rationally inspected, as the form of our practical relations to reality. 'The objectivity of the possible objects of experience', writes Jürgen Habermas, 'is thus [for Marx] grounded in the identity of a natural substratum, namely that of the bodily organisation of man, which is oriented towards action, and not in an original unity of apperception . . .'.[5] Sense perception for Marx is in the first place the constitutive structure of human practice, rather than a set of contemplative organs; indeed it can become the latter only in so far as it is already the former. Private property is the 'sensuous expression' of humanity's estrangement from its own body, the dismal displacement of our sensuous plenitude onto a single drive to possess: '*all* the physical and intellectual senses have been replaced by the simple estrangement of *all* these senses – the sense of *having*. So that it might give birth to its inner wealth, human nature has been reduced to this absolute poverty.'[6]

What comes about under capitalism for the young Marx is a kind of splitting and polarizing of sensory life in two antithetical directions, each a grotesque travesty of the authentically sensuous body. At one level, capitalism reduces the bodily fullness of men and women to a 'crude and abstract simplicity of need' – abstract because, when sheer material survival is at stake, the sensuous qualities of the objects intended by such needs are not in question. In Freudian parlance, one might say that capitalist society collapses the *drives*, by which the human body transcends its own boundaries, to the *instincts* – those fixed, monotonously repetitive urges which incarcerate the body within its own frontiers:

By reducing the worker's needs to the paltriest minimum necessary to maintain his physical existence and by reducing his activity to the most abstract mechanical movement . . . the political economist declares that man has no other needs, either in the sphere of activity or in that of consumption . . . He turns the worker into a being with neither needs nor senses and turns the worker's activity into a pure abstraction from all activity.[7]

But if the capitalist strips the worker of his senses, he equally confiscates his own: 'The less you eat, drink, buy books, go to the theatre, go dancing, go drinking, think, love, theorise, sing, paint, fence, etc., the more you *save* and the greater will become the treasure which neither moths nor maggots can consume – your *capital*.'[8] The signal advantage of the capitalist over the worker is that the former operates a kind of double-displacement. Having alienated his sensory life to capital, he is then able vicariously to recuperate that estranged sensuality by the power of capital itself: 'everything which you are unable to do, your money can do for you: it can eat, drink, go dancing, go to the theatre, it can appropriate art, learning, historical curiosities, political power, it can travel, it is *capable* of doing all these things for you. . . .'[9] Capital is a phantasmal body, a monstrous *Doppelgänger* which stalks abroad while its master sleeps, mechanically consuming the pleasures he austerely forgoes. The more the capitalist forswears his self-delight, devoting his labours instead to the fashioning of this zombie-like *alter ego*, the more second-hand fulfilments he is able to reap. Both capitalist and capital are images of the living dead, the one animate yet anaesthetized, the other inanimate yet active.

If a brutal aesceticism is one aspect of capitalist society, its inverted mirror-image is a fantastic aestheticism. Sensory existence is stripped to skeletal need at one level only to be extravagantly inflated at another. The antithesis of the blindly biologistic wage-slave is the exotic idler, the self-pleasuring parasite for whom 'the realisation of man's *essential powers* is simply the realisation of his own disorderly existence, his whims and his capricious and bizarre notions'.[10] If the worker is devastated by need, the upper-class lounger is crippled by the lack of it. Desire, unconstrained by material circumstance, becomes in him perversely self-productive, a matter of 'refined, unnatural and *imaginary* appetites' which cynically luxuriate in their own supersubtlety. Such a figure is for Marx the social correlative of philosophical idealism, as indeed, paradoxically, is that most prosaically material of all phenomena, money. Money for Marx is idealist through and through, a realm of chimerical fantasy in which all identity is ephemeral and any object may be transmuted at a stroke to any other. Like the imaginary appetites of the social parasite, money is a purely aesthetic phenomenon, self-breeding, self-referential, autonomous of all material truth and able to conjure an infinite plurality of worlds into concrete existence. The human body under capitalism is thus fissured down the middle, traumatically divided between brute materialism and capricious idealism, either too wanting or too whimsical, hacked to the bone or bloated with perverse eroticism. The dialectical point, as one would expect, is that each of these opposites brings the other into existence. Narcissism and necessity, famished and exorbitant appetites, are (as Theodor Adorno might have said) the torn halves of an integral bodily freedom, to which however they do not add up.

The goal of Marxism is to restore to the body its plundered powers; but only with the supersession of private property will the senses be able to come into their own. If communism is necessary, it is because we are unable to feel, taste, smell and touch as fully as we might:

> The supersession of private property is therefore the complete *emancipation* of all human senses and attributes; but it is this emancipation because these senses and attributes have become *human*, subjectively as well as objectively. The eye has become a *human* eye, just as its object has become a social, *human* object, made by man for man. The senses have therefore become *theoreticians* in their immediate praxis. They relate to the thing for its own sake, but the thing itself is an *objective human* relation to itself and to man, and vice-versa. Need or enjoyment have therefore lost their *egoistic* nature, and nature has lost its mere *utility* in the sense that its use has become *human* use.[11]

201

Marx is most profoundly 'aesthetic' in his belief that the exercise of human senses, powers and capacities is an absolute end in itself, without need of utilitarian justification; but the unfolding of this sensuous richness for its own sake can be achieved, paradoxically, only through the rigorously instrumental practice of overthrowing bourgeois social relations. Only when the bodily drives have been released from the despotism of abstract need, and the object has been similarly restored from functional abstraction to sensuously particular use-value, will it be possible to live aesthetically. Only by subverting the state will we be able to experience our bodies. Since the subjectivity of the human senses is a thoroughly objective affair, the product of a complex material history, it is only through an objective historical transformation that sensuous subjectivity might flourish:

> Only through the objectively unfolded wealth of human nature can the wealth of subjective *human* sensitivity – a musical ear, an eye for the beauty of form, in short, *senses* capable of human gratification – be either cultivated or created. For not only the five senses, but also the so-called spiritual senses, the practical senses (will, love, etc.), in a word, the *human* sense, the humanity of the senses – all these come into being only through the existence of *their* objects, through *humanised* nature. The *cultivation* of the five senses is the work of all previous history. *Sense* which is a prisoner of crude practical need has only a *restricted* sense. For a man who is starving the human form of food does not exist, only its abstract form exists; it could just as well be present in its crudest form, and it would be hard to say how this way of eating differs from that of *animals* . . . the society that is *fully developed* produces man in all the richness of his being, the *rich* man who is *profoundly and abundantly endowed with all the senses*, as its constant reality.[12]

If bourgeois aesthetic thought suspends, for a rare moment, the distinction between subject and object, Marx preserves this distinction in the act of transgressing it. Unlike bourgeois idealism, he insists on the objective material preconditions of sensory emancipation; but the senses are already objective and subjective together, modes of material practice as well as experiential wealth. What he calls the 'history of industry' can be submitted to a double reading: what from the historian's viewpoint is an accumulation of productive forces is, phenomenologically speaking, the materialized text of the human body, the 'open book of the essential powers of man'. Sensuous capacities and social institutions are the *recto* and *verso* of one another, divergent perspectives on the same phenomenon. And just as the discourse of aesthetics evolved, with Baumgarten, as an attempt to map those sensible features which an objectivist rationality was in danger of suppressing, so Marx warns that 'a *psychology* for which this book [of the senses], the most tangible and accessible part of history, is closed, can never become a *real* science with a genuine content.'[13] What is needed is a form of knowledge which can examine the material preconditions of different sensory relations to the world: 'the sense perception of a fetish-worshipper is different from that of a Greek because his sensuous existence is different.'[14]

Marx's Paris Manuscripts thus surpass at a stroke the duality between the practical and the aesthetic which lies at the heart of philosophical idealism. By redefining the reified, commodified sense organs of that tradition as historical products and forms of social practice, Marx relocates bodily subjectivity as a dimension of an evolving industrial history. But this judicious curbing of idealist subjectivity is, ironically, all in the name of the subject: the only point of recalling that subject's objective character is so as the better to comprehend the political preconditions within which subjective powers may be exercised as sheer ends in themselves. In one sense, the 'aesthetic' and the 'practical' are indissolubly at one; in another sense, the latter exists for the sake of the former. As Margaret Rose has pointed out, Marx inverts Schiller by grasping human freedom as a question of the realization of the senses rather than as a liberation from them;[15] but he inherits the Schillerian aesthetic ideal of an all-round, many-sided human development, and like the idealist aestheticians holds strongly that human societies are, or should be, ends in themselves. Social intercourse requires no metaphysical or utilitarian grounding, but is a natural expression of human 'species being'. Just as Schiller, towards the conclusion of his *Letters on the Aesthetic Education of Man*, speaks of how human society is born for pragmatic ends but evolves beyond such utility to become a delightful end in itself, so Marx finds the lineaments of such 'aesthetic' bonding at the heart of the politically instrumental:

> When communist *workmen* gather together, their immediate aim is instruction, propaganda, etc. But at the same time they acquire a new need – a need for society – and what appears as a means has become an end. This practical development can be most strikingly observed in the gatherings of French socialist workers. Smoking, eating and drinking, etc., are no longer means of creating links between people. Company, association, conversation, which in its turn has society as its goal, is enough for them. The brotherhood of man is not a hollow phrase, it is a reality, and the nobility of man shines forth upon us from their work-worn figures.[16]

If production is an end in itself for capitalism, so is it also, in a quite different sense, for Marx. The actualization of human powers is a pleasurable necessity of human nature, needing no more functional justification than the work of art. Indeed art figures for Marx as the ideal paradigm of material production precisely because it is so evidently autotelic. 'A writer', he comments, 'does *not* regard his works as means to an end. They are an end in themselves; so little are they "means", for himself and others, that he will, if necessary, sacrifice his own existence to their existence.'[17] The *Grundrisse* speaks of medieval handicraft as 'still half artistic; it has its aim in itself';[18] and in the *EPM* Marx characterizes 'true' human production as the impulse to create in freedom from immediate need. The gratuitousness of art, its transcendence of sordid utility, contrasts with enforced labour as human desire differs from biological instinct. Art is a form of creative surplus, a radical exceeding of necessity; in Lacanian terminology, it is what remains when need is subtracted from demand.

It is in the concept of use-value, above all, that Marx deconstructs the opposition between the practical and the aesthetic. When he writes of the emancipated senses as 'theoreticians in their immediate praxis', he means that *theoria*, the pleasurable contemplation of an object's material qualities, is an active process within our functional relations with it. We experience the sensuous wealth of things by drawing them within our signifying projects – a stance which differs on the one hand from the crude instrumentalism of exchange-value, and on the other hand from some disinterested aesthetic speculation. The 'practical' for Marx already includes this 'aesthetic' responsiveness to particularity; its twin enemies are the commodifying abstraction of both object and drive, and the aestheticist fantasies of the social parasite, who severs the bond between use and pleasure, necessity and desire, and so allows the latter to consume themselves in privileged disconnection from material determinacy. In so far as this idealism converts pleasure and desire themselves to commodities, these twin enemies are secretly one; what the idle rich consume is the narcissism of their own acts of pleasurable consumption. For Marx himself, it is not the use of an object which violates its aesthetic being, but that abstraction of it to an empty receptacle which follows from the sway of exchange-value and the dehumanization of need. Classical aesthetics and commodity fetishism both purge the specificity of things, stripping their sensuous content to a pure ideality of form. It is in this sense that Marx's profoundly anti-Kantian aesthetic is also an anti-aesthetic, the ruin of all disinterested contemplation. The utility of objects is the ground, not the antithesis, of our appreciation of them, just as our delight in social intercourse is inseparable from its necessity.

If the early Marx is anti-Kantian in this sense, he is Kantian enough in another. 'It is only when objective reality universally becomes for man the reality of man's essential powers', Marx writes in the *EPM*, 'and thus the reality of his *own* essential powers, that all *objects* become for him the *objectification of himself*, objects that confirm and realise his individuality, *his* objects, i.e. *he himself* becomes the object.'[19] Nothing could be further from Kant than the politics of this assertion; but it is difficult to see how it differs epistemologically from the specular, imaginary relation between subject and object delineated in the third *Critique*. The Paris Manuscripts would seem to envisage a fundamental deconstruction of the antinomy between Nature and humanity, as the former is steadily humanized, and the latter gradually naturalized, through emancipated labour. This equitable interchange, whereby subject and object pass ceaselessly into each other, is for Marx an historical hope and for Kant a regulative hypothesis; but there is no insuperable distance between Marx's subject-confirming object, and Kant's wistful glimpse in the aesthetic representation of a purposiveness enheartening to humankind. It will be left to a later Marxist materialism to rupture this imaginary enclosure by insisting on the heterogeneity of matter to consciousness, on the material as some irreducible externality which inflicts a necessary wound on our narcissism. The theme of the specular identity of subject and object, meanwhile, will pass not into the later Marx and Engels but into Georg Lukács and some currents of Western Marxism.

If the young Marx thus stands in ambivalent relationship to Kant, he is similarly double-edged in his attitude to Schiller. Marx, as we have noted, inherits Schiller's 'disinterested' concern with the all-round realization of human powers as an end in itself;[20] but the process by which this might historically come about is as far from classical disinterestedness as one could imagine. The scandalous originality of Marx is to harness this noble Schillerian vision of a symmetrical, many-sided humanity to highly partial, particular, one-sided political forces. The means and the ends of communism are interestingly at odds: a traditionally conceived *Humanität* will be brought to birth by those whose humanity is most crippled and depleted; an aesthetic society will be the fruit of the most resolutely instrumental political action; an ultimate plurality of powers flows only from the most resolute partisanship. It is as though Marx cross-breeds Weimar humanism with the implacable *engagement* of a Kierkegaard: the disinterested emancipation of human faculties will be accomplished not by by-passing specific social interests, but by going all the way through them and coming out on the other side. Only such a move can resolve the Schillerian riddle of how an ideal culture by definition inimical to particular interests may enter upon material existence without fatally compromising itself.

The discourse of aesthetics addresses a grievous alienation between sense and spirit, desire and reason; and for Marx this alienation is rooted in the nature of class-society itself. With the increasing instrumentalization of Nature and humanity under capitalism, the labour process comes under the sway of an imposed, abstract law, which expels from it all corporeal pleasure. Enjoyment, as Marx argues in *The German Ideology*, then becomes a minor philosophical cult of the ruling class. It would appear impossible under these conditions to harmonize 'spirit' and 'sense' – to reconcile the coercive rational forms of social life with its grossly particular contents. In such a social order, a desirable 'aesthetic' identity of form and content would seem unattainable. This dichotomy then cleaves its path through the human body: while the body's productive powers are rationalized and commodified, its symbolic, libidinal drives are either abstracted to crude appetite or siphoned off as redundant. Withdrawn from the process of labour, they are channelled instead into three isolated enclaves of progressively marginal significance: art, religion and sexuality. A 'true' aesthetic practice – a relation to Nature and society which would be at once sensuous and rational – bifurcates into a brutal asceticism on the one hand, and a baroque aestheticism on the other. Expunged from material production, human creativity either dissipates into idealist fantasy or runs riot in that cynical travesty of itself known as possessive appetite. Capitalist society is at once an orgy of such anarchic desire and the reign of a supremely bodiless reason. As with some strikingly ill-achieved artefact, its sensuous contents degenerate to sheer raw immediacy, while its governing forms grow rigidly abstract and autonomous.

Aesthetics is, among other things, an attempt to rejoin these sundered social spheres, discerning in them à la Baumgarten some homologous logic. A perilously formalistic reason must reincorporate that which the capitalist system expels as so much waste material. If reason and pleasure are at loggerheads, then the artefact may proffer models of reconciliation, sensualizing the former and rationalizing the latter in the manner of Schiller's play drive. It can offer, moreover, an illuminating solution to the problem of freedom and necessity – for freedom in these social conditions has lapsed into anarchy, and necessity into iron determinism. We shall see later in the case of Nietzsche how artistic creation promises to deconstruct this opposition – how marvellously undecidable it is whether the artist in the act of production is supremely free, or governed by some inexorable logic. Aesthetics seeks to resolve in an imaginary way the problem of why, under certain historical conditions, human bodily activity generates a set of 'rational' forms by which the body itself is then confiscated. Marx himself will rejoin the sensuous and the rational in the concept of use-value; but there can be no liberation of use-value as long as the commodity reigns supreme, which is why 'the resolution of the *theoretical* antitheses themselves is possible *only* in a *practical* way.'[21] If the aesthetic is to realize itself it must pass over into the political, which is what it secretly always was. If the rift between raw appetite and disembodied reason is to be healed, it can only be through a revolutionary anthropology which tracks the roots of human rationality to their hidden source in the needs and capacities of the productive body. For in the realization of such needs and capacities, that body ceases to be identical with itself and opens out onto a shared social world, within which its own needs and desires will have to be weighed alongside those of others. It is in this way that we are led by a direct route from the creative body to such apparently abstract matters as reason, justice and morality – issues which, in bourgeois society, have succeeded in muting the inconvenient clamour of the body and its concrete interests.

Many of Marx's most vital economic categories are implicitly aesthetic; indeed Mikhail Lifshitz reminds us that Marx embarked on a detailed study of the German aesthetician Friedrich Vischer on the very threshold of his major economic work.[22] If there is one privileged place in his writing where the problem of abstract and concrete is focused with peculiar sharpness, it is surely in that celebrated metaphysical conundrum, the commodity. The commodity, one might claim, is a kind of grisly caricature of the authentic artefact, at once reified to a grossly particular object and virulently anti-material in form, densely corporeal and elusively spectral at the same time. As W. J. T. Mitchell has suggested, 'the terms that Marx uses to characterise the commodity are drawn from the lexicon of Romantic aesthetics and hermeneutics.'[23] The commodity for Marx is the site of some curious disturbance of the relations between spirit and sense, form and content, universal and particular: it is at once an object and not an object, 'perceptible and imperceptible by the senses' as he comments in *Capital*, a false concretizing but also a false abstracting of social relations. In a mystifying 'now you see it, now you don't' logic, the commodity is present and absent simultaneously, a tangible entity whose meaning is wholly immaterial and always elsewhere, in its formal relations of exchange with other objects. Its value is eccentric to itself, its soul or essence displaced to another commodity whose essence is similarly elsewhere, in an endless deferral of identity. In a profound act of narcissism, the commodity 'looks on every other commodity as but the form of appearance of its own value',[24] and is promiscuously eager to exchange both body and soul with them. It is blankly disconnected from its own body, since 'the existence of things *qua* commodities, and the value-relation between

208

the products of labour which *stamps* them as commodities, have absolutely no connection with their physical properties and with the material relations arising therefrom.'[25] The commodity is a schizoid, self-contradictory phenomenon, a mere symbol of itself, an entity whose meaning and being are entirely at odds and whose sensuous body exists only as the contingent bearer of an extrinsic form. Money, the universal commodity, as Marx writes in the *Grundrisse*, 'implies the separation between the value of things and their substance'.[26]

As the antithesis of the aesthetic object, a kind of artefact gone awry, the commodity's material being is a mere random instantiation of the abstract law of exchange. Yet if this is a case of Hegel's 'bad' universality, the commodity as fetish also exemplifies a 'bad' immediacy, negating the general social relations within which it was produced. As pure exchange-value, the commodity erases from itself every particle of matter; as alluring auratic object, it parades its own unique sensual being in a kind of spurious show of materiality. But this materiality is itself a form of abstraction, serving as it does to occlude the concrete social relations of its own production. On the one hand, the commodity spirits away the substance of those relations; on the other hand it invests its own abstractions with specious material density. In its esotericism, as well as in its rabid hostility to matter, the commodity is a parody of metaphysical idealism; but it is also, as fetish, the very type of degraded materiality. It thus forms a compact space in which the pervasive contradictions of bourgeois society bizarrely converge.

Just as much of Marx's economic thought turns on the aesthetic categories of form and content, so also does a central part of his political writing. When Marx accuses Hegel of 'political formalism' in his *Critique of Hegel's Doctrine of the State*, he suggests that Hegel's political thought is faithful to the real conditions of bourgeois society, in which the purely abstract equality of individuals within the political state sublimes and suppresses their concrete differences and inequalities in civil society. In such conditions, Marx argues in the *EPM*, 'real human beings, real society' appear simply as 'formless, inorganic matter'.[27] Once again, reified formalism and raw materialism emerge as inverted mirror-images of each other. Bourgeois society drives a fatal wedge between the subject of civil society in his or her 'sensuous, individual and *immediate* existence', and the 'abstract, artificial man, man as an *allegorical, moral* person' of the political state.[28] It is in this sense that 'the perfection of the idealism of the state [is] at the same time the perfection of the materialism of civil society.'[29] Political emancipation will be possible only when this dislocation between abstract and concrete, form and content, has been surmounted – when 'real, individual man resumes the abstract citizen into himself and as an individual man has become a *species-being* in his empirical life, his individual work and his individual relationships. . .'.[30] Only in democracy, Marx argues in the *Critique of Hegel's Doctrine of the State*, is 'the *formal* principle . . . identical with the *substantive* principle',[31] concrete particularity at one with one's public political role. Democratic society is the ideal artefact, since its form is the form of its content: 'in a democracy, the constitution, the law, i.e. the political state, is itself only a self-determination of the people and a determinate content of the people.'[32] Non-democratic societies are inept works of art, in which form remains extrinsic to substance: the law in such political conditions fails to inform the material of social life from within, and so 'is dominant, but without really dominating, i.e. without materially penetrating the content of all the non-political spheres'.[33] In the democratic state, by contrast, this abstract juridical structure will be absorbed into civil society itself, to become its living organic form. Individuals will form the substance of the state in their unique particularity, rather than as faceless public cyphers. Marx's contrast between non-democratic and democratic societies thus reproduces the Kantian distinction between a pure or practical reason which is heteronomous to the specific, and that mysterious aesthetic 'law' which is at one with the material content it organizes. The emancipated society, for Marx as much as for the Rousseau from whom he has learnt here, is an aesthetic interfusion of form and content.

An interfusion of form and content, in fact, may be taken as Marx's aesthetic ideal. He spoke of striving to achieve such a unity in his own scrupulously crafted literary style, and detested what he saw as Romanticism's disproportioning of the two, embellishing prosaic contents with exotic ornamentation. It is this discrepancy, as we shall see, which becomes the basis of his critique of the bourgeois revolutions in *The Eighteenth Brumaire of Louis Bonaparte*. In an article of 1842 on the German property laws, Marx declares that 'form is of no value unless it is the form of its content'.[34]

210

The key to this fine balance of form and content is for Marx the concept of *Mass*, meaning measure, standard, proportion, moderation, or even at times the compact inner structure of an artefact. To preserve due proportion, 'to apply to each object its inherent standard',[35] would seem Marx's aim, one which offers a convenient standpoint from which to criticize capitalism. As early as his doctoral dissertation on ancient Greece, Marx was contrasting what he called the 'dialectics of measure' with the reign of 'measurelessness'; and it is typical of his thought in general to discern in ancient society a kind of symmetry and proportion consequent upon its very backwardness. It is this belief which motivates his notorious remarks in the Introduction to the *Grundrisse* about the unrecapturable perfection of Greek art, rooted as it is in material immaturity.[36] Capitalism too is a matter of curbing and constraint, as the straitjacket of exchange-value impedes the free production of use-value; but unlike ancient society these limits lend it no internal symmetry. On the contrary, capitalism is immoderate, intemperate, one-sided, disproportionate, and thus offends Marx's aesthetic as well as his moral sense. Indeed the two faculties are deeply interrelated. The capitalist mode of production certainly deploys a measure: that of labour time. But one of the system's ironies is that, as it advances into the machinery stage, it begins progressively to undercut its own yardstick. 'Capital itself is the moving contradiction', Marx writes in the *Grundrisse*, 'in that it presses to reduce labour time to a minimum, while it posits labour time, on the other side, as the sole measure and source of wealth,'[17] Once the mass of workers have appropriated their own surplus labour, a new measure will be installed: that of the 'needs of the social individual', which will now come to determine the amount of time spent in labouring.

If this is a measure, it is a remarkably flexible one, since such needs are of course for Marx socially and historically variable. In the *Critique of the Gotha Programme* he is severe with the notion of applying an equal standard to inevitably unequal individuals, and rebukes this 'socialist' device as a hangover from bourgeois legality. If human needs are historically mutable and open-ended, then so must be Marx's measure; there is a certain measurelessness about this measure which distinguishes it from any fixed universal standard, even if Marx has little time on the other hand for the fantasy of infinitely unlimited needs. True wealth, he claims in the *Grundrisse*, is 'the absolute working-out of [human] creative potentialities, with no presupposition other than the previous historical development, which makes this totality of development, i.e. the development of all human powers as such the end in itself, not as measured on a *predetermined* yardstick'.[38] It would seem, then, that the working out of creative human capacities is somehow its own measure, transgressing any fixed or given form. If humanity is to be considered, as Marx goes on to insist, in its 'absolute movement of becoming', then it is hard to see how this ceaseless mutability, in which the only norm would seem change itself, does not throw into question the more static, classical paradigm of an equilibrium of form and content. There can certainly be no question of a '*predetermined* yardstick', of forms and standards extrinsic to the 'content' of history itself. Such content must find its own form, act as its own measure; and it is difficult to see whether this signifies the triumph of an 'organic' conception of form, or the dissolution of form altogether. What will *inform* this constantly shifting process of freely evolved powers?

One might claim, then, that there are two kinds of 'aesthetic' at work in Marx's texts, which are not wholly compatible with one another. If one can be called the beautiful, the other might be properly named the sublime. There is, to be sure, a 'bad' sublime for Marx, along the lines of Hegel's 'bad' infinity: it resides in the restless, overweening movement of capitalism itself, its relentless dissolution of forms and commingling of identities, its confounding of all specific qualities into one indeterminate, purely quantitative process. The movement of the commodity is in this sense a form of 'bad' sublimity, an unstoppable metonymic chain in which one object refers itself to another and that to another, to infinity. Like Kant's mathematical sublime, this endless accumulation of pure quantity subverts all stable representation, and money is its major signifier. 'The *quantity* of money', Marx writes in the *EPM*, 'becomes more and more its sole *important* property. Just as it reduces everything to its own form of abstraction, so it reduces itself in the course of its own movement to something *quantitative. Measurelessness* and *immeasurability* become its true standard.'[39] Once again – but now in a negative sense – Marx's measure is itself immeasurable. Money for Marx is a kind of monstrous sublimity, an infinitely spawning signifier which has severed all relation with the real, a fantastical idealism which blots out specific value as surely as those more conventional figures of sublimity – the raging ocean, the mountain crags – engulf all particular identities in their unbounded expanse. The sublime, for Marx as for Kant, is *Das Unform*: the formless or monstrous.

This 'bad' sublime, however, can be counterpointed by a 'good' one, which emerges most evidently in the *Eighteenth Brumaire*.[40] The opening pages of that text, surely Marx's major *semiotic* work, depict the great bourgeois revolutions as living just that hiatus between form and content, signifier and signified, which the classical aesthetician in Marx finds most insupportable. In a kind of historical cross-dressing, each bourgeois revolution tricks itself out in the flashy insignia of previous epochs, in order to conceal beneath these inflated forms the shameful paucity of its true social content. In the very act of fashioning a future, such insurrections find themselves compulsively repeating the past; history is the nightmare from which they seek to awaken, but which in doing so they merely dream again. Each revolution is a farcical travesty of the last, appropriating its external symbology in an intertextual chain.[41] Bourgeois revolutions are inherently theatrical, a matter of panache and breathless rhetoric, a baroque frenzy whose poetic effusions are in inverse proportion to their meagre substance. There is a kind of fictiveness in their very structure, a hidden flaw which disarticulates form and content.

These revolutionary repetitions, however, are not *merely* parodic, caricatures of what was no doubt already a caricature. On the contrary, the point of evoking the past is to summon the dead to the aid of the present, drawing from them something of their dangerous power:

> Thus the awakening of the dead in these revolutions served the purpose of glorifying the new struggles, not of parodying the old; of magnifying the given task in imagination, not of fleeing from its solution in reality; of finding once more the spirit of revolution, not of making its ghost walk about again.[42]

Only by dreaming the past can revolutionaries awaken from its nightmare, since the past is what they are made of. Only by turning back, with the horror-stricken face of Walter Benjamin's *angelus novus*, can the revolution be blown by the winds of history into the realm of the future. The past, for the bourgeois revolutionaries as for

213

Benjamin, must be pressed forcibly into the service of the present, classical traditions heretically appropriated and miswritten in order to redeem the time. The revolutionary is the offspring not only of oppressive political parents, but of ancestral brothers and sisters who usurped the patriarch in their own time and have bequeathed something of that perilous power to later generations. There is a sibling solidarity which cuts athwart the empty, homogeneous continuum of ruling-class history, and which Benjamin terms 'tradition'. Recycling the past, then, is both opiate and inspiration – a cynical thieving of its 'aura' which nonetheless, as Benjamin might have put it, suspends the smooth flow of historical time in a shocking 'constellation', allowing a sudden esoteric correspondence to flash between the political needs of the present and a redeemed moment of the past.[43]

The *Eighteenth Brumaire* goes on to contrast the semiology of bourgeois insurrection with the socialist revolution of the future:

> The social revolution of the nineteenth century cannot draw its poetry from the past, but only from the future. It cannot begin with itself before it has stripped off all superstition in regard to the past. Earlier revolutions required recollections of past world history in order to drug themselves concerning their own content. In order to arrive at its own content, the revolution of the nineteenth century must let the dead bury their dead. There the phrase went beyond the content; here the content goes beyond the phrase.[44]

What is in question here is the whole concept of a representational aesthetics. Previous revolutions have been formalistic, engrafting a factitious 'phrase' or form onto their content; but the consequence of this is a dwarfing of the signified by the signifier. The content of socialist revolution, by contrast, is excessive of all form, out in advance of its own rhetoric. It is unrepresentable by anything but itself, signified only in its 'absolute movement of becoming', and thus a kind of sublimity. The representational devices of bourgeois society are those of exchange-value; but it is precisely this signifying frame that the productive forces must break beyond, releasing a heterogeneity of use-values whose unique particularity would seem to refuse all

214

standardized representation. It is less a matter of discovering the expressive forms 'adequate to' the substance of socialism, than of rethinking that whole opposition – of grasping form no longer as the symbolic mould into which that substance is poured, but as the 'form of the content', as the structure of a ceaseless self-production.

To conceive of form in this way is not wholly incompatible with Marx's classical aesthetic; indeed it can be seen from one viewpoint as just such a unity of form and content. The content of communist society, like the Romantic artefact, must generate its own form from within, find its own level and measure. But what kind of form will this be, if communism is the all-round liberation of a multiplicity of particular use-values, where the only absolute would seem development itself? Socialism is able to prescribe the institutional forms which would be necessary if this wealth of use-values, this self-delighting plurality of human powers, were to be unlocked from the metaphysical prison-house of exchange-value; yet such unlocking releases the non-identical from the identical, and the question is one of how this non-identity is to represent itself. 'Reconciliation', writes Theodor Adorno, 'would release the non-identical, would rid it of coercion, including spiritualised coercion; it would open the road to the multiplicity of different things and strip dialectics of its power over them.'[45] Certainly the content of such a society cannot be 'read off' from the institutions set in place to produce it. 'We have to ensure the means of life, and the means of community', writes Raymond Williams in *Culture and Society 1780–1950*. 'But what will then, by these means, be lived, we cannot know or say.'[46] Marxism is not a theory of the future, but a theory and practice of how to make a future possible. As a doctrine, it belongs entirely to what Marx calls 'pre-history'; its role is simply to resolve those contradictions which currently prevent us from moving beyond that epoch to history proper. About that history proper, Marxism has little to say, and Marx himself generally maintained a symptomatic silence on this score. The only truly *historic* event would be to get history started, by clearing away the obstacles in its path. So far, nothing particularly special has occurred: history to date has simply been the same old story, a set of variations on persisting structures of oppression and exploitation. The endless recycling and recirculating of the commodity is the most recent phase of that historical deadlock, the perpetual present by which class-society implicitly denies that it was ever born, since to confess that one was born is to acknowledge that one can die. But this circuit cannot be broken by representing a future, since the means of representation belong to a superseded present, and are powerless to take the measure of that which will have transgressed them. It is in this sense, precisely, that the 'content goes beyond the phrase'.

Just as the pious Jews, so Walter Benjamin reminds us,[47] were forbidden on pain of idolatry to fashion graven images of the God of the future, so political radicals are prohibited under pain of fetishism from blueprinting their ultimate desire. This is not to denigrate the power of utopian thought, but to recall its fictive or regulative status, the limits of its representational resources. Marx began his political career in contention with what one might call the subjunctive mood of socialism, with the 'wouldn't it be nice if' kind of radical idealist; and his brusque imperative to 'let the dead bury their dead' is a reminder that all utopia springs from the past rather than the future. The true soothsayers or clairvoyants are the technical experts hired by monopoly capitalism to peer into the entrails of the system and assure its rulers that their profits are safe for another twenty years. As Walter Benjamin knew, it is not dreams of liberated grandchildren which spur men and women to revolt, but memories of enslaved ancestors. Like any emancipatory theory, Marxism is concerned with putting itself progressively out of business. It exists to bring about the material conditions which will spell its own demise, and like Moses will not pass with its people into the promised land. All emancipatory theories carry some self-destruct device within them, eagerly anticipating the moment when they can wither away. If there are still political radicals in a century's time, it will be a grim prospect. There is no way, then, in which the diverse uses to which men and women will turn their emancipated powers in a socialist future can now be imaged; such a process defies representation, and is in that sense sublime. The more recalcitrant problem, as we have seen, is to know how that process could be represented even when it is under way, given that it is of the essence of sensuous particularity to give the slip to general representational forms.

There is another sense in which Marx's classical concern to reconcile form and content is significantly qualified in his work. To distinguish between the matter (productive forces) and form (social relations) of a particular society, as G.A. Cohen has argued,

216

'discredits capital's pretension to being an irreplaceable means of creating material wealth . . . Confusion of content and form creates the reactionary illusion that physical production and material growth can be achieved only by capitalist investment.'[48] It is the bourgeois political economists who are in this sense the 'classicists', wedded to a conflation of capitalist form and productive material. Communism, Cohen comments, may be described as the 'conquest of form by matter. For in negating exchange-value communism releases the content fetishised economy imprisoned in form.'[49] Is this then to claim that communism is formless? Cohen's response to this query is to argue that human activity under communism is not unstructured, but that it is also not pre-structured. No social form is *imposed* upon it, but it does have a form. 'One might say: *the form is now just the boundary created by matter itself.*'[50] Here, once again, Marx equivocates between the classical and the sublime. The form of communism is entirely at one with its content, and to this extent one can speak of a classical symmetry or identity between the two. Certainly communism, unlike the conventional sublime, is not shapeless and amorphous. But this identity of form and content is so absolute that the former effectively disappears into the latter; and since the latter is no more than a continually self-expanding multiplicity bounded only by itself, the effect is then one of a certain sublimity.

There is another way of putting this point. Cohen writes of the structure displayed by communism as 'no more than the outline of the activities of its members, not something into which they must fit themselves';[51] and this is strongly reminiscent of the Kantian 'law' of beauty. That 'law', as we have seen, is wholly immanent to its content: it is the very form of that content's internal organization, rather than some external, abstractable regulation. What Marx has effectively done, then, is to project this immanance into Kant's alternative aesthetic state, the sublime. If Kant's beauty is too static, too harmoniously organic for Marx's political purposes, his sublime is too formless. The condition of communism could be envisaged only by some blending of the two – by a process which has all of the sublime's potentially infinite expansiveness, but which nevertheless carries its formal law within itself.

Marx's account of modern history may be fairly straightforwardly put. The capitalist mode of production is powered by the narrowest motives of profit and self-interest; but the overall product of such discreditable intentions is the greatest accumulation of productive forces that history has ever witnessed. The bourgeoisie have now brought those forces to the point where the socialist dream of a social order free of toil can in principle be realized. For only on the basis of such a high level of material development is socialism possible. Without such stored productive capacity, the only 'socialism' would be what Marx scathingly described as 'generalized scarcity'. It is arguable that men and women could seize control of the productive forces in a state of underdevelopment and expand them in a socialist direction. The case against this is that moderately hedonistic human beings would not freely submit themselves to such a back-breaking, dispiriting task, and that if they did not then it would be left to a despotic bureaucratic state to do it for them. Whatever the merits of these opposing arguments, there can be no doubt that Marx himself envisaged socialism as riding on the backs of the bourgeoisie.

This massive unleashing of productive powers is for Marx, inseparably, the unfolding of human richness. The capitalist division of labour brings with it a high refinement of individual capacities, just as the capitalist economy, in uprooting all parochial obstacles to global intercourse, lays down the conditions for international community. In a similar way, bourgeois political and cultural traditions nurture, however partially and abstractly, the ideals of freedom, equality and universal justice. Capitalism represents a felicitous Fall, even if one might believe with the Milton of *Paradise Lost* that it would have been better had it never occurred at all. There need certainly be no vulgarly teleological implication that every society must pass through this baptism of fire if it is to attain socialism; but Marx's praise for the magnificent revolutionary achievements of the bourgeoisie is a steady keynote in his work, inimical to all Romantic-radical nostalgia and moralistic polemic. It is customary these days among radicals to link the bourgeoisie with patriarchy, as equivalently oppressive formations; but this comes near to a category error, since there has never been a good word to say for patriarchy, and there is much to be admired in the history of the middle class. Through capitalism, individuality is enriched and developed, fresh creative powers are bred, and new forms of social intercourse created.

All of this, of course, is bought at the most terrible cost. 'More than any other mode of production', Marx writes in *Capital*, '[capitalism] squanders human lives, or living labour, and not only flesh and blood, but also nerve and brain. Indeed it is only through the most enormous waste of the individual development that the development of mankind is at all preserved in the epoch of history immediately preceding the conscious organization of society.'[52] This dynamic, exhilarating release of potential is also a long unspeakable human tragedy, in which the great majority of men and women are condemned to a life of wretched, fruitless toil. The division of labour maims and nourishes simultaneously, generating fresh skills and capacities but in a cripplingly one-sided way. The creative powers which enable humanity to control its environment, eradicating disease, famine, natural catastrophe, also enable it to prey upon itself. Each new medium of communication is at the same time an instrument of division and alienation. Culture is at once a document of civilization and a record of barbarism, the two as closely imbricated as the *recto* and *verso* of a sheet of paper. Capitalist development brings the individual to new heights of subtle self-awareness, to an intricate wealth of subjectivity, in the very act of producing him as a predatory egoist.

All of this, for Marx, is because of the exploitative social relations under which these otherwise life-bringing productive forces have been evolved. Those social relations were necessary in their day for such evolution, such that no simplistic dichotomy of 'forces good, relations bad' is feasible; but they have now come to act as fetters upon free productive development, and must be swept aside by socialist transformation. Under socialist relations of production, forces which currently create misery and estrangement will be deployed for the creative self-realization of all. Capitalism has generated a sumptuous wealth of capacities, but under the sign of scarcity, alienation, one-sidedness; it now remains to place as many of these capacities as possible at the disposal of each individual, convening within her powers which were historically bred in mutual isolation.

This whole problematic, of a dynamic energy blocked and thwarted by ossified institutions, would seem to place Marx squarely in the camp of Romantic humanism, with its expression/repression model of human existence. This is no longer a model which we can look upon uncritically, whatever partial truths it doubtless contains. To begin with, there is a notable difficulty in Marxist writing over the relation between the productive forces as material techniques, and the human powers and abilities which form a central part of them. The difficulty would seem to arise, in part at least, because the productive forces *include* such human powers, yet are to be developed *for the sake of them*. In one sense, productive forces and human powers would seem indissoluble; in another sense, an essentially instrumental relation holds between them. Marx himself generally brackets the two categories together, as when he writes of human wealth as 'the universality of individual needs, capacities, pleasures, productive forces etc.';[53] elsewhere in the *Grundrisse* he speaks of 'the highest development of the forces of production, hence also the richest development of individuals'.[54] G. A. Cohen comments on the 'extensive coincidence' in Marx's thought between the expansion of the productive forces and the growth of human capacities,[55] while Jon Elster remarks that the Marxist theory of history could be summarized as 'uninterrupted progress of the productive forces, interrupted progress of human development and social integration'.[56] What this means is that the development of the productive forces under capitalism, which will then permit socialism to actualize human capacities to their fullest, in fact involves the stunting and curtailing of certain capacities in the capitalist era. In this sense, the development of the productive forces and of human powers are synonymous *in the end*; but one condition of their coming to be so is the tragic mutilation of such powers under the dominance of capital. For such mutilation is inevitable under capitalism; and capitalism is essential to the development of the productive forces, which is in turn the precondition for a socialist realization of human capacities.

Art, for Marx, is a supreme instance of this irony. In his view, art flourished in conditions of social immaturity such as ancient Greece, when quality and proportion could still be preserved from the sway of the commodity. Once it enters under that quantifying influence in a more developed historical epoch, it begins to degenerate in relation to its earlier perfection. In this field of achievement human capacities and the forces of production are not only not synchronous with one another, but are actually in inverse proportion. But this is only part of the story. For the powers which capitalism breeds, once liberated from the tyranny of exchange-value, will provide the basis for a future socialist art even more splendid than its ancient predecessor. Once more, the expansion of capacities and of forces converge in the long run; but a lengthy period of regression on the part of the former is essential if this is to come about.

The relation between forces and capacities, then, is not quite as neatly homologous as some Marxist formulations, including some of Marx's own, would suggest. This is also true in another sense. It is easy to see how the expression/repression model may work for the forces of production, which have simply to burst through the integument of capitalist social relations in order to come into their own. But the model is less illuminating in the case of human powers. Socialist revolution does not simply liberate, in expressivist style, whatever capacities have been generated by capitalism, since these capacities are by no means indiscriminately positive. If the capitalist mode of production has brought forth human subjective wealth, it has also fostered the habits of domination, aggression and exploitation, which no socialist would simply want to see 'released'. We cannot, for example, easily extract the rational kernel of the control of Nature from the shell of the oppression of human beings. Marx is at his most Romantic-humanist in his apparent assumption that human capacities become morbid only by virtue of their alienation, repression, dissociation or one-sidedness. But this is surely a dangerous illusion; we must count among our capacities the power to torture and wage war. The very terms 'power' and 'capacity' have a deceptively positive ring to them, as of course does the term 'creative'. But war is a form of creation, and the building of concentration camps is a realization of human powers. These uncomfortable corollaries of Marx's doctrine can be escaped only by defining 'capacities' in so broad and nebulous a sense that the term becomes effectively vacuous.

It is possible to lodge another kind of objection to Marx's doctrine, which is that the ideal of the free realization of human powers and capacities is both masculinist and ethnocentric. It is not hard to detect within this strenuously self-producing subject the shadow of the virile Western male. Such an ethical outlook would seem to leave little space for the values of stillness and receptivity, of being creatively acted upon, of wise passiveness and all of the more positive aspects of the condition which Heidegger will later term *Gelassenheit*. There is probably in this sense a certain sexism structural to Marxist thought, as there is also perhaps in its privileging of that traditional male preserve, the sphere of production. If this is a reason to reject

Marxism, then it is equally a reason to reject almost every cultural product from the Stone Age to Star Wars. It is, nevertheless, cause for a certain critical resistance to the otherwise attractive vision of an all-round human self-actualization.

If human powers are far from spontaneously positive, then their emancipation would seem to require careful discrimination. Just the same, however, might be argued of the productive forces in general, where the expression/blockage paradigm might once more prove too simplistic. A nuclear power station is a productive force; yet many radicals would argue against its development. There is a question, in other words, of whether the expansion of the productive forces must not itself be carried on within the framework of socialist values, and in ways compatible with socialist relations of production. Jon Elster notes this potential conflict in a somewhat cursory footnote, when he comments that 'a technique that is optimal in terms of efficiency may not be so in terms of welfare.'[57] Certain forms of work might be simply incompatible with the socialist values of self-autonomy, cooperation and creative self-realization; indeed Marx himself seems to hold that some residual drudgery will always characterize the labour process, and that the expansion of the productive forces is necessary to release men and women as far as possible from such unwelcome labour. Andrew Levine and Eric Olin Wright have made the telling point that certain technological advances may have the effect of weakening working-class organization and strengthening the political and ideological power of the bourgeoisie.[58] The evolution of the productive forces, in other words, may involve an actual regression of those political capacities which need to be nourished if such forces are to be appropriate for socialism.

There are, then, two distinct cases. One sees the expansion of the productive forces as a value in itself, and views socialism simply as the appropriation and further development of them for the general good. The other case is summarized by Marx's comment that the forces of production must be developed 'under conditions most favourable to, and worthy of, human nature'.[59] The whole concept of a productive force hovers indeterminately between fact and value, rather, as we shall see, like the Nietzschean notion of the will to power. If human capacities are regarded as inherently positive, and viewed as *part* of the productive forces, then it might seem to follow that the expansion of those forces is a good in itself. If, however, the development of the forces of production is seen as *instrumental* to the realization of human capacities, then the question of which form of material development is likely best to accomplish this goal inevitably poses itself.

There remains, however, the need to discriminate among human capacities themselves, once it is granted that some may be destructive. Whence are we to derive the criteria to form such judgements? Romantic expressivism is quite unable to answer this question: if powers exist, then the only imperative is that they should be actualized. Value, so to speak, is inserted within fact: the very fact that we possess certain powers would seem to bring along with it the normative judgement that we should freely realize them. One can 'resolve' the fact/value dilemma by the simple device of projecting the latter into the former. The process of human capacities will not itself inform us of which are to be actualized and which not, will supply us with no built-in criteria of selection; and it might then be thought that such criteria have to be imported from some transcendental space. Marx is obviously hostile to such an idea, since part of his theoretical project is to abolish the whole notion of moral discourse as an area separable from history.

Whether Marx actually believed in 'moral' concepts is a controversial issue within Marxism.[60] The problem is that he would appear often enough to dismiss morality as ideological, while drawing implicitly on moral notions in his critique of class-society. The truth is that Marx does not so much reject morality, as translate it in large measure from superstructure to base. The 'moral' then becomes identified with the dynamic self-realization of human powers – projected, as it were, into the productive process itself rather than marooned as a set of superstructural institutions and ideologies. Human productive powers would not seem to require moral judgements imported from elsewhere, from a specialized ethical sphere; they would seem instead intrinsically positive, and 'immorality' would appear to consist in their thwarting, estranging and disproportioning. Marx does indeed possess an 'absolute' moral criterion: the unquestionable virtue of a rich, all-round expansion of capacities for each individual. It is from this standpoint that any social formation is to be assessed – either in its current ability to allow for such self-realization, or in its potential contribution to such a condition in the future.

This, however, leaves a number of questions unanswered. Why

should 'all-round' development be the most morally admirable goal? And what is to count as such? Is it the aim of historical struggle to balance my capacity to torture in symmetrical, proportionate relation to my capacity to love? Marx's vision would seem in this sense curiously formalistic. It would appear less a matter of *what* powers we express, than of whether we have recuperated them from their estranged, lop-sided state and actualized them as variously, fully and comprehensively as possible.[61]

There is, however, a powerful rebuttal of this whole interpretation of Marx's case. The riposte to the charge that Marx believed all human powers to be inherently positive is simply that this constitutes a Romantic misreading of his texts. Marx does indeed discriminate between different human capacities, on the basis of a doctrine which he inherited from Hegel, and which provides the foundation of a communist ethics. The discriminatory norm in question is that we should foster only those particular powers which allow an individual to realize herself through and in terms of the similar free self-realization of others. It is this, above all, which distinguishes socialism from liberalism. This constitutes an important qualification to the Romantic interpretation of Marx; but it still leaves some problems unresolved. For one thing, even if this is indeed the kernel of Marx's political creed, it remains true that he very often writes as though human capacities were indeed inherently positive, in oblivion of his own *caveat*. For another thing, any such normative concept of self-realization instantly implicates notions of justice, equality and associated moral ideas, which means that morality cannot after all belong purely to the productive 'base'. On the contrary, it is precisely for this reason that societies require 'superstructural' institutions of a juridical and ethical kind, apparatuses which regulate the complex business of deciding between more and less reasonable, creative human needs and desires. There is evidence to believe that Marx himself, despite his 'productivist' morality, acknowledged this fact, and did not simply dismiss the notion of justice, or the need for such juridical institutions, out of hand. It could be argued, however, that the ideal of self-realization through and in terms of others simply succeeds in pushing the question at issue back a stage. For Marx's vision of such reciprocal self-expression is not, for instance, that of Hegel, for whom it was fully compatible with social inequality. What are to count as desirable modes of mutual self-realization? By what criteria are they to be evaluated? Such criteria must be discursively established; and Marx, as Jürgen Habermas has argued, remains caught within a philosophy of the subject which passes over this process of intersubjective communication.[62] It is not for him so much a matter of discursively evaluating human capacities, as of actualizing them – a position which not only takes for granted the positive nature of human powers, but seems to assume that such powers and needs are intuitively present to the subject, spontaneously given by the historical process outside the context of intersubjective argumentation. But if human subjects have needs, then we know already what at least one of those needs must be, namely the need for the subject to know what its needs actually are. Given the subject's self-opacity, this is far from self-evident, which is why moral discourse becomes necessary. The problem for Marx would seem to be not moral but political: how are powers which we can presume to be potentially beneficent to be historically realized? 'By reducing the self-positing of the absolute ego to the more tangible productive activity of the species', writes Habermas, '[Marx] eliminates reflection as such as a motive force of history, even though he retains the framework of the philosophy of reflection.'[63]

If Marx inserts value within fact, a number of Second International Marxist theoreticians found themselves caught in an uncomfortable duality between the two. Marxist science could disclose the laws of history, but was incapable of assessing whether their supposedly inevitable outcome was actually desirable. A neo-Kantian ethics had therefore to be imported, to supplement an apparently non-normative positivism. But as Leszek Kolakowski has argued, Marxism 'is not a mere description of the world but the expression and self-knowledge of a social process by which the world is revolutionized, and thus the subject of that self-knowledge, i.e. the proletariat, comprehends reality in the very act of transforming it'.[64] What the fact/value dichotomy fails to account for, in short, is emancipatory knowledge – that peculiar kind of cognition which is essential for human freedom. In the critical consciousness of any oppressed group or class, the understanding and the transforming of reality, 'fact' and 'value', are not separable processes but aspects of the same phenomenon. As Kolakowski puts it: 'Since subject and object coincide in the knowledge of society: since, in this case, science is the self-knowledge of society and, by the same token, a factor in determining its situation at any stage of history; and since, in the case of the proletariat, this self-knowledge is at the same time a revolutionary movement, it follows that the proletariat cannot at any point disjoin its "ideal" from the actual process of realizing it.'[65]

If this is the case, then Marxism has its own particular answer to one of the problems to which aesthetics offers an imaginary solution. A reified reason which believes itself to view the world non-normatively will force the issue of value beyond its frontiers, and the aesthetic is then one place where that issue can take up a home. Morality, of course, is another: but the Kantian dilemma is one of how this noumenal sphere intersects with phenomenal history. Marxism, by contrast, locates the unity of 'fact' and 'value' in the practical, critical activity of men and women – in a form of understanding which is brought to birth in the first place by emancipatory interests, which is bred and deepened in active struggle, and which is an indispensable part of the realization of value. There are certain kinds of knowledge which we must at all costs obtain in order to be free; and this casts the fact/value problem in a quite different light.

Marx is in entire agreement with the Earl of Shaftesbury – an unlikely candidate, otherwise, for his approval – that human powers and human society are an absolute end in themselves. To live well is to live in the free, many-sided realization of one's capacities, in reciprocal interaction with the similar self-expression of others. We have seen some of the difficulties of this doctrine; but it remains, for all that, the single most creative aspect of the aesthetic tradition. As an aesthetician, Marx is offended by the instrumentalization of human powers, inevitable though this process may be in pre-history. He looks for his desirable moral goal to the 'absolute working out of creative potentialities . . . [with] the development of all human powers as such the end in itself'.[66] In the realm of socialism, work will remain a necessity; but beyond that horizon begins 'that development of human energy which is an end in itself, the true realm of freedom, which, however, can blossom forth only with this realm of necessity as its basis. The shortening of the working-day is its basic prerequisite.'[67] If art matters, it is as a type of that which has its end entirely in itself, and thus is most politically charged in its very autonomy.

Unlike Nietzsche and Heidegger after him, Marx does not press through this aestheticization to human cognition itself. This is not some anaemic rationalism: the goal of human life, for Marx as for Aristotle, is not truth, but happiness or well-being. His work is an extensive enquiry into what material conditions would be necessary for this goal to be realized as a general human condition, and thus belongs to the discourse of classical morality.[68] Marx is a moralist in the most traditional sense of the term, which is to say that he is concerned with the political determinations of the good life. His morality thus stands opposed to that withered modern sense of the 'moral', impoverished to interpersonal relations and 'spiritual' values alone, for which the Marxist term is 'moralism'.

It is because this labour of enquiry is historically necessary that thought, for Marx, has at least for the present to remain instrumental. Truth may not be the *telos* of history; but it nevertheless plays a vital part in securing that end. That final aestheticization of human existence which we call communism cannot be prematurely anticipated by a reason which surrenders itself wholly to the ludic and poetic, to image and intuition. Instead, a rigorously analytical rationality is needed, to help unlock the contradictions which prevent us from attaining the condition in which instrumentalism may lose its unwelcome dominance. It may well be that in some future social order theory, instrumental thought, calculative reason will no longer play a central role in human life, but will have been transformed out of recognition. To prefigure such an order now, by (for example) the deconstruction of theory and poetry, may thus be a valuable proleptic gesture. But if an aesthetic existence is to be achieved for all, thought in general must not be prematurely aestheticized. Such a move would be intolerably privileged, in societies where the freedom to play, in thought or anywhere else, is the preserve of the few. Those post-structuralist thinkers who urge that we abandon truth for dance and laughter might pause to inform us just who this 'we' is supposed to signify. Theory, as Hegel knew, is only necessary in the first place because contradictions exist; as a material event, it emerges from a certain historically produced tension between the actual and the possible. When Marx in the *Economic and Philosophical Manuscripts* designates logic as a 'currency of the mind', he means that theory is itself a kind of conceptual exchange-value, mediating and abstracting with a certain necessary disregard for sensuous specificity. He holds, however, that without such conceptual exchange-value, sensuous specificity will continue to be a minority cult. If the aesthetic is to flourish, it can only be by virtue of political transformation; and the political thus stands in a meta-linguistic relation to the aesthetic. If Marxism is a meta-language or meta-narrative, it is not because it lays claim to some absolute truth, a chimera it has consistently spurned; it is rather on account of its insistence that, for any human narrative whatsoever to get under way, certain other histories must be already in place. Of these histories, Marxism attends to the one which concerns material survival and social reproduction; but one must add to this the narrative of sexual reproduction, about which Marxism has had for the most part little of interest to say. Without these particular grand stories, every other *récit* would grind literally to a halt. It is not, however, that these histories merely provide a space within which other stories may be produced; on the contrary, they are so utterly vital, engage such enormous resources of human energy, that they leave their grim imprint on all of our more contingent tales, scarring and disfiguring them from within.

Something of the ambivalence which characterizes Marxism's attitude to the aestheticization of knowledge can be detected also in its view of morality. In one sense, as we have seen, Marx wishes to aestheticize morality, shifting it from a set of supra-historical norms to a question of the pleasurable realization of historical powers as an end in itself. In another sense, however, Marxism takes the point of Kant's austerely anti-aesthetic *Sollen*. Such a stark concept of duty need by no means be simply repressive ideology, whatever it might signify in the hands of Kant himself. On the contrary, its force can be felt in the tragic narratives of socialist struggle, where men and women have courageously sacrificed their own fulfilment for what they have hoped would be the greater happiness of others. Such self-sacrificial action, performed with little pleasure and often with less profit, is, one might claim, a kind of love; and though love and well-being may be *ultimately* at one, they can enter into tragic conflict with one another in anything less than the long term. For a general happiness to flourish, it would seem that individual gratification must sometimes be forgone. Marxism is thus not a hedonism, even though it is all about the enjoyable self-realization of individuals; indeed Marx has some acute comments on the material basis of hedonist ideology in *The German Ideology*.

'Sacrifice' is a potentially treacherous moral notion, to be handled with circumspection. It has been, for example, the traditional prerogative of women; if men have the happiness, women have the love. If the idea of self-sacrifice is to be more than oppressive and life-denying, it must be viewed in the context of a wider richness of life, and so seen under the sign of irony. In the regimes under which we live, the successful achievements we are afforded are usually somewhat trivial in contrast to the enduring reality of failure. Radicals are those who seek to preserve in some way a compact with failure, to remain faithful to it; but there is then always a dangerous temptation to fetishize it, forgetting that it is not in that, but in human plenitude and affirmation, that the end of political action lies. The tragic lesson of Marxism is that no such plentitude is attainable without having gone right the way through failure and dispossession, in order to emerge somewhere on the other side.

Marxism subsists, then, in the twilight zone between two worlds, the one too much with us, the other as yet powerless to be born. If it clings to the protocols of analytic reason, and insists upon unpleasurable political responsibilities, it does so ironically, in the awareness that these necessities are in the name of a future where they will no longer be so essential. It is in this sense that there is for Marxism both rupture and continuity between present and future, as opposed to those brands of reformism, apocalypticism or 'bad' utopianism which slacken this difficult dialectic at either pole. What one might call 'bad' or premature utopianism grabs instantly for a future, projecting itself by an act of will or imagination beyond the compromised political structures of the present. By failing to attend to those forces or fault-lines *within* the present which, developed or prised open in particular ways, might induce that condition to surpass itself into a future, such utopianism is in danger of persuading us to desire uselessly rather than feasibly, and so, like the neurotic, to fall ill with longing. A desirable but unfeasible future, one which fails to found itself in the potentialities of the present in order to bridge us beyond it, is in this sense the reverse of the future offered to us by some brands of social determinism, which is inevitable but not necessarily desirable. Once more, 'value' must be somehow extrapolable from 'fact', the outline of a future worth struggling for discerned within the practices of the degraded present. It is this, surely, which is the most vital meaning of that currently contemned term, teleology. A utopian thought which does not simply risk making us ill is one able to trace within the present that secret lack of identity with itself which is the spot where a feasible future might germinate – the place where the future overshadows and hollows out the present's spurious repleteness. The hopeful side of the narrative is exactly that 'value' is somehow derivable, historically speaking, from 'fact' – that oppressive social orders, as a matter of their routine operations, cannot help generating the kinds of forces and desires which can in principle overthrow them. The grimmer side of the narrative is then that we have, in effect, no way of undoing the nightmare of history other than with the few poor, contaminated instruments with which that history has furnished us. How can history be turned against itself? Marx's own response to this dilemma was the boldest imaginable. History would be transformed by its *most* contaminated products, by those bearing the most livid marks of its brutality. In a condition in which the powerful run insanely rampant, only the powerless can provide an image of that humanity which must in its turn come to power, and in doing so transfigure the very meaning of that term.

Notes

1 Pierre Bourdieu and Alain Darbel, *La Distinction: critique sociale du jugement* (Paris, 1979), p. 573.
2 Karl Marx, *Economic and Philosophical Manuscripts*, in *Karl Marx: Early Writings*, introduced by Lucio Colletti (Harmondsworth, 1975), p. 356. Hereafter cited as 'Colletti, *EPM*'.
3 Colletti, *EPM*, p. 355.
4 Elaine Scarry, *The Body in Pain* (Oxford, 1987), p. 244.
5 Jürgen Habermas, *Knowledge and Human Interests* (Oxford, 1987), p. 35.
6 Colletti, *EPM*, p. 352. See also I. Mészáros, *Marx's Theory of Alienation* (London, 1970), Part 2, chapter 7.
7 Ibid., p. 360.
8 Ibid., p. 361.
9 Ibid., p. 361.
10 Ibid., p. 359.
11 Ibid., p. 351.
12 Ibid., p. 353.
13 Ibid., p. 354.
14 Ibid., p. 364.
15 Margaret Rose, *Marx's Lost Aesthetic* (Cambridge, 1984), p. 74.
16 Colletti, *EPM*, p. 365.

17 Quoted by S. S. Prawer, *Karl Marx and World Literature* (Oxford, 1976), p. 41.
18 Karl Marx, *Grundrisse* (Harmondsworth, 1973), p. 511.
19 Colletti, *EPM*, pp. 352–3.
20 See David McLellan, *Marx Before Marxism* (Harmondsworth, 1972), pp. 243–4.
21 Colletti, *EPM*, p. 354.
22 See Mikhail Lifshitz, *The Philosophy of Art of Karl Marx* (London, 1973), pp. 95–6.
23 W.J.T. Mitchell, *Iconology* (Chicago, 1986), p. 188.
24 Karl Marx, *Capital*, vol. 1, Introduced by Ernest Mandeel (Harmondsworth, 1976), p. 165.
25 Ibid., p. 167.
26 Marx, *Grundrisse*, p. 149.
27 Colletti, *EPM*, p. 186.
28 Ibid., p. 234.
29 Ibid., p. 233.
30 Ibid., p. 234.
31 Ibid., p. 88.
32 Ibid., p. 89.
33 Ibid., p. 89.
34 Quoted in Prawer, *Karl Marx and World Literature*, p. 291.
35 Colletti, *EPM*, p. 329.
36 See Marx *Grundrisse*, pp. 110–11.
37 Ibid., p. 706.
38 Ibid., p. 488.
39 Colletti, *EPM*, p. 358.
40 For an interesting account of the semiotics of this text, see Jeffrey Mehlman, *Revolution and Repetition* (Berkeley, 1977). See also Jean-François Lyotard's comments on the 'Marxist sublime' in Lisa Appignanesi (ed.), *Postmodernism: ICA Documents 4* (London, 1986): 'What is the sublime in Marx? Very precisely it is to be found at the point he calls labour force . . . This is a metaphysical notion. And within metaphysics, it is a notion which designates what is not determinate. What is not present and supports presence . . . The whole theory of exploitation rests on this idea, which is sublime' (p. 11).
41 If intertextuality is the theme of the following passage, it is also its form. I have drawn here, in adapted form, on various of my previous comments on *The Eighteenth Brumaire*: from *Criticism and Ideology* (London, 1976), *Walter Benjamin, or Towards a Revolutionary Criticism* (London, 1981), 'Marxism and the Past', in *Salmagundi* (Fall 1985–Winter 1986), and 'The God that Failed', in Mary Nyquist and Margaret W. Ferguson

(eds), *Re-Membering Milton* (New York and London, 1987). I trust that this is the last time I shall write on this text.

42 *Marx and Engels: Selected Works* (London, 1968), p. 98.

43 See Walter Benjamin, 'Theses on the Philosophy of History', in Hannah Arendt (ed.), *Illuminations* (London, 1973).

44 *Marx and Engels: Selected Works*, p. 99.

45 Theodor Adorno, *Negative Dialectics* (London, 1973), p. 6.

46 Raymond Williams, *Culture and Society 1780–1950* (Harmondsworth, 1985), p. 320.

47 Benjamin, *Illuminations*, p. 266.

48 G. A. Cohen, *Karl Marx's Theory of History: A Defence* (Oxford, 1978), p. 105.

49 Ibid., p. 129.

50 Ibid., p. 131.

51 Ibid., p. 131.

52 Marx, *Capital*, vol. 3, quoted by Cohen, *Karl Marx's Theory of History*, p. 25. For an excellent account of the simultaneously emancipatory and oppressive development of capitalism, see Marshall Berman, *All That Is Solid Melts Into Air* (New York, 1982), Part 11.

53 Marx, *Grundrisse*, p. 488.

54 Ibid., p. 541.

55 Cohen, *Karl Marx's Theory of History*, p. 147.

56 Jon Elster, *Making Sense of Marx* (Cambridge, 1985), p. 304.

57 Ibid., p. 246n. Elster is admittedly writing here of the labour process itself, rather than of the productive forces proper, but the point has perhaps a more general application.

58 Andrew Levine and Eric Olin Wright, 'Rationality and Class Struggle', in *New Left Review*, no. 123 (September–October, 1980), p. 66.

59 Marx, *Capital*, vol. 3 (Moscow, 1962), pp. 799–800.

60 For the issue of morality in Marxism, see E. Kamenka, *Marxism and Ethics* (London, 1969), Kate Soper, *On Human Needs* (Brighton, 1981), Denys Turner, *Marxism and Christianity* (Oxford, 1983), Hugo Meynell, *Freud, Marx and Morals* (London, 1981), G. Brenkert, *Marx's Ethics of Freedom* (London, 1983), Steven Lukes, 'Marxism, Morality and Justice' in G. H. R. Parkinson (ed.), *Marx and Marxism* (Cambridge, 1982), Steven Lukes, *Marxism and Morality* (Oxford, 1985), B. Ollman, *Alienation* (Cambridge, 1971), Part 1, chapter 4, M. Cohen, T. Nagel and T. Scanlon (eds), *Marxism, Justice and History* (Princeton, 1980), and Norman Geras, 'On Marx and Justice', *New Left Review*, no. 150 (March–April 1985). On the question of the realization of human capacities, it is interesting that Marx wrote, and then crossed out, the

following passage in *The German Ideology* (quoted in Agnes Heller, *The Theory of Needs in Marx* (London, 1974, p. 43):

Communist organisation has a two-fold effect on the desires produced in the individual by present-day conditions: some of these desires – namely those existing under all conditions, which only change their form and direction under different social conditions – are merely altered by the communist social system, for they are given the opportunity to develop *normally*; others, however – namely those originating in a particular social system . . . – are totally deprived of their conditions of existence.

61 For a brief critique of the notion of self-realization, see Jon Elster, *An Introduction to Karl Marx* (Cambridge, 1986), chapter 3. For a more extended, detailed and illuminating account of Marx's 'productivism', see Kate Soper, *On Human Needs*, especially chapters 8 and 9.

62 See Jürgen Habermas, *Knowledge and Human Interests*, chapter 3, and *The Theory of Communicative Action*, vol. 1 (Boston, 1984), chapter 4. For an excellent critique of the 'philosophy of the subject', see Seyla Benhabib, *Critique, Norm, and Utopia* (New York, 1986), chapter 4.

63 Habermas, *Knowledge and Human Interests*, p. 44.

64 Leszek Kolakowski, *Main Currents of Marxism*, vol. 11: *The Breakdown* (Oxford, 1978), p. 271.

65 Ibid., p. 270.

66 Marx, *Grundrisse*, p. 488.

67 Marx, *Capital*, vol. 11 (New York, 1967), p. 820.

68 See Denys Turner, *Marxism and Christianity* (Oxford, 1983), Part 1.

9

True Illusions:
Friedrich Nietzsche

It is not difficult to trace certain general parallels between historical
materialism and the thought of Friedrich Nietzsche. For Nietzsche is in
his own way a full-blooded materialist, whatever scant regard he may
pay to the labour process and its social relations. One might say that
the root of all culture for Nietzsche is the human body, were it not
that the body itself is for him a mere ephemeral expression of the will
to power. He asks himself in *The Gay Science* whether philosophy has
'not been merely an interpretation of the body and a *misunderstanding
of the body*',[1] and notes with mock solemnity in the *Twilight of the Idols*
that no philosopher has yet spoken with reverence and gratitude of
the human nose. Nietzsche has more than a smack of vulgar
Schopenhauerian physiologism about him, as when he speculates that
the spread of Buddhism may be attributed to a loss of vigour
consequent on the Indian diet of rice. But he is right to identify the
body as the enormous blindspot of all traditional philosophy:
'philosophy says away with the *body*, this wretched *idée fixe* of the
senses, infected with all the faults of logic that exist, refuted, even
impossible, although it be impudent enough to pose as if it were
real!'[2] He, by contrast, will return to the body and attempt to think
everything through again in terms of it, grasping history, art and
reason as the unstable products of its needs and drives. His work thus
presses the original project of aesthetics to a revolutionary extreme,
for the body in Nietzsche returns with a vengeance as the ruin of all
disinterested speculation. The aesthetic, he writes in *Nietzsche Contra
Wagner*, is 'applied physiology'.

It is the body, for Nietzsche, which produces whatever truth we can
achieve. The world is the way it is only because of the peculiar

structure of our senses, and a different biology would deliver us a different universe entirely. Truth is a function of the material evolution of the species: it is the passing effect of our sensuous interaction with our environment, the upshot of what we need to survive and flourish. The will to truth means constructing the kind of world within which one's powers can best thrive and one's drives most freely function. The urge to knowledge is an impulse to conquer, an apparatus for simplifying and falsifying the rich ambiguity of things so that we might take possession of them. Truth is just reality tamed and tabulated by our practical needs, and logic is a false equivalencing in the interests of survival. If Kant's transcendental unity of apperception has any meaning at all, it refers not to the ghostly forms of the mind but to the provisional unity of the body. We think as we do because of the sort of bodies we have, and the complex relations with reality which this entails. It is the body rather than the mind which interprets the world, chops it into manageable chunks and assigns it approximate meanings. What 'knows' is our multiple sensory powers, which are not only artefacts in themselves – the products of a tangled history – but the sources of artefacts, generating as they do those life-enhancing fictions by which we prosper. Thought, to be sure, is more than just a biological reflex: it is a specialized function of our drives which can refine and spiritualize them over time. But it remains the case that everything we think, feel and do moves within a frame of interests rooted in our 'species being', and can have no reality independently of this. Communication itself, which for Nietzsche as for Marx is effectively synonymous with consciousness, develops only under duress, as part of a material struggle for survival, however much we may later come to delight in it as an activity in itself. The body, a 'richer, clearer, more tangible phenomenon' than consciousness,[3] figures in effect for Nietzsche as the unconscious – as the submerged sub-text of all our more finely reflective life. Thought is thus symptomatic of material force, and a 'psychology' is that sceptical hermeneutic which lays bare the lowly motives which impel it. One does not so much contest ideas as find inscribed within them the traces of humanity's hungering. Thinking is thus inherently 'ideological', the semiotic mark of a violence that now lies erased beneath it. What fascinates Nietzsche is the incessant hankering which lies at the core of reason, the malice, rancour or ecstasy which drives it on, the deployment of instinct in instinct's own repression; what he attends to in a discourse is the low murmur of the body speaking, in all of its greed or guilt, Like Marx, Nietzsche is out to bring down thought's credulous trust in its own autonomy, and above all that ascetic spirituality (whether its name is science, religion or philosophy) which turns its eyes in horror from the blood and toil in which ideas are actually born. That blood and toil is what he names 'genealogy', in contrast to the consoling evolutionism of 'history'. ('That gruesome dominion of nonsense and accident that has so far been called "history"', he scoffs in *Beyond Good and Evil*.)[4] Genealogy unmasks the disreputable origins of noble notions, the chanciness of their functions, illuminating the dark workshop where all thought is fashioned. High-toned moral values are the bloodstained fruit of a barbarous history of debt, torture, obligation, revenge, the whole horrific process by which the human animal was systematically degutted and debilitated to be rendered fit for civilized society. History is just a morbid moralization through which humanity learns to be ashamed of its own instincts, and 'every smallest step on earth has been paid for by spiritual and physical torture . . . how much blood and cruelty lies at the bottom of all "good things"!'[5] For Nietzsche as for Marx, 'morality' is not so much a matter of problems as a problem all in itself; philosophers may have queried this or that moral value, but they have not yet problematized the very concept of morality, which for Nietzsche is 'merely a sign language of the affects'.[6]

Rather as for Marx the productive forces become shackled and constrained by a set of social relations, so for Nietzsche the productive life-instincts are enfeebled and corrupted into what we know as moral subjecthood, the gutless, abstract 'herd' morality of conventional society. This is essentially a movement from coercion to hegemony: 'Morality is preceded by *compulsion*; indeed, it itself remains compulsion for some time, to which one submits to avoid disagreeable consequences. Later it becomes custom, later still free obedience, and finally almost becomes instinct: then, like every thing long customary and natural, it is linked with gratification – and now is called *virtue*.'[7] What we have seen in Rousseau and other middle-class moralists as the supremely positive 'aesthetic' transition from law to spontaneity, naked power to pleasurable habit, is for Nietzsche the last word in self-repression. The old barbaric law yields to the Judaeo-Christian invention of the 'free' subject, as a masochistic introjection of authority opens up that interior space of guilt, sickness and bad conscience which some like to call 'subjectivity'. Healthy vital instincts, unable to discharge themselves for fear of social disruption, turn inward to give birth to the 'soul', the police agent within each individual. The inward world thickens and expands, acquires depth and import, thus heralding the death of 'wild, free, prowling men'[8] who injured and exploited without a care. The new moral creature is an 'aestheticized' subject, in so far as power has now become pleasure; but it signals at the same time the demise of the old style of aesthetic human animal, which lived out its beautiful barbaric instincts in splendid unconstraint.

Such, for Nietzsche, were the warriors who originally imposed their despotic powers on a population humbly waiting to be hammered into shape. 'Their work is an instinctive creation and imposition of forms; they are the most involuntary, unconscious artists there are . . . They do not know what guilt, responsibility, or consideration are, these born organisers; they exemplify that terrible artists' egoism that has the look of bronze and knows itself justified to all eternity in its "work", like a mother in her child.'[9] It is this brutal ruling-class dominion which drives underground the free instincts of those it subjugates, creating the self-loathing life of science, religion, asceticism. But such sickly subjecthood is thus the product of a magnificent artistry, and reflects that formative discipline in its own festering masochism:

This secret self-ravishment, this artists' cruelty, this delight in imposing a form on oneself as a hard, recalcitrant, suffering material and in burning a will, a critique, a contradiction, a contempt, a no into it, this uncanny, dreadfully joyous labour of a soul voluntarily at odds with itself that makes itself suffer out of joy in making suffer – eventually this entirely *active* 'bad conscience' – you will have guessed it – as the womb of all ideal and imaginative phenomena, also brought to light an abundance of strange new beauty and affirmation, and perhaps beauty itself . . . [10]

There is no question of Nietzsche simply *regretting* the horrific birth of the humanist subject, unlike some of his less wary modern-day acolytes. In its alluring unity of discipline and spontaneity, sadistic form and malleable material, such a craven, self-punitive animal is an aesthetic artefact all of its own. If art is rape and violation, the humanist subject reaps the perverse aesthetic delights of a ceaseless self-violation, a sado-masochism Nietzsche much admires. And since art is that phenomenon which gives the law to itself, rather than receiving it passively from elsewhere, there is a sense in which the anguished moral self is a more exemplary aesthetic type than the old warrior class, who master an essentially alien material. The authentic art work is creature and creator in one, which is truer of the moral subject than of the imperious war-lord. There is something beautiful about the bad conscience: Nietzsche derives erotic stimulation from humanity's self-torture, and so, he implies, does humanity itself. Moreover, this compulsively self-ravishing creature is not only a work of art in itself, but the source of all sublimation, and so of all aesthetic phenomena. Culture has its roots in self-odium, and triumphantly vindicates that sorry condition.

All of this may seem gratifyingly remote from Marxism; but the parallel lies in a certain shared teleologism, however uncomfortably the word may ring in the ears of at least Nietzsche's present-day disciples. Teleology is a grossly unfashionable concept today even among Marxists, let alone Nietzscheans; but like many a demonized notion it is perhaps due for a little redemption. For Nietzsche, the breaking down of the old, reliable instinctual structure of the human animal is on the one hand a catastrophic loss, bringing forth the cringing, self-lacerating subject of moral ideology, and throwing humanity on the mercy of that most treacherous, deluded of all its faculties, consciousness. On the other hand, this declension marks a major advance: if the corruption of instinct makes human life more precarious, it also opens up at a stroke fresh possibilities of experiment and adventure. The repression of the drives is the basis of all great art and civilization, leaving as it does a void in human being which culture alone can fill. Moral man is thus an essential bridge or transition to the overman: only when the old savage inclinations have been sublimed by the imposition of 'herd' morality, by the craven love of the law, will the human animal of the future be able to take these propensities in hand and bend them to his autonomous will. The subject is born in sickness and subjection; but this is an essential workshop for the tempering and organizing of otherwise destructive powers, which in the shape of the overman will burst through moral formations as a new kind of productive force. The individual of the future will then buckle such powers to the task of forging himself into a free creature, releasing difference, heterogeneity and unique selfhood from the dull compulsion of a homogeneous ethics. The death of instinct and the birth of the subject is in this sense a fortunate Fall, in which our perilous reliance on calculative reason is at once an insidious softening of fibre and the advent of an enriched existence. The moral law was necessary in its day for the refining of human powers, but has now become a fetter which must be thrown off. 'Profoundest gratitude for that which morality has achieved hitherto', Nietzsche writes in *The Will to Power*, 'but now it is only a burden which may become a fatality!'[11] 'Many chains have been placed upon man', he remarks in *The Wanderer and his Shadow*, 'that he might unlearn behaving as an animal: and in point of fact he has become milder, more spiritual, more joyful, and more circumspect than any animal. But now he still suffers from having borne his chains too long . . .'[12] There can be no sovereign individual without straitjacketing custom: having been disciplined to internalize a despotic law which flattens them to faceless monads, human beings are now ready for that higher aesthetic self-government in which they will bestow the law upon themselves, each in his or her own uniquely autonomous way. One kind of introjection, in short, will yield ground to another, in which the wealth of evolved consciousness will be incorporated as a fresh kind of instinctual structure, lived out with all the robust spontaneity of the old barbaric drives.

There is surely a remote analogy between this vision and historical materialism. For Marxism, too, the transition from traditional society to capitalism involves a falsely homogenizing law – of economic exchange, or bourgeois democracy – which erodes concrete particularity to a shadow. But this 'fall' is felicitous, one upwards rather than downwards, since within this dull carapace of abstract equality are fostered the very forces which might break beyond the kingdom of necessity to some future realm of freedom, difference and excess. In necessarily fashioning the organized collective worker, and in evolving a plurality of historical powers, capitalism for Marx plants the seeds of its own dissolution as surely as the epoch of the subject in Nietzsche's eyes prepares the ground for that which will overturn it. And Marx, like Nietzsche, would sometimes seem to view this overturning as an overcoming of morality as such. When Nietzsche speaks of the way in which consciousness abstracts and impoverishes the real, his language is cognate with Marx's discourse on exchange value:

Owning to the nature of *animal consciousness*, the world of which we can become conscious is only a surface- and sign-world, a world that is made common and meaner; whatever becomes conscious *becomes* by the same token shallow, thin, relatively stupid, general, sign, herd signal; all becoming conscious involves a great and thorough corruption, falsification, reduction to superficialities, and generalization.[13]

What is true of consciousness as such, in Nietzsche's extreme nominalist view, is for Marx an effect of commodification, whereby a complex wealth of use-value is stripped to a meagre index of exchange. For both philosophers, however, history moves by its bad side: if for Marx this commodifying process emancipates humanity from the privilege and parochialism of traditional society, laying down the conditions for free, equal, universal intercourse, for Nietzsche the dreary narrative of humanity's 'becoming calculable' is a necessity of its species-being, for without such calculability it would never survive. Logic is a fiction in Nietzsche's eyes, since no two things can be identical; but like the equivalencing of exchange value, it is at once repressive and potentially emancipatory.

The present age, then, is for both Nietzsche and Marx propae-deutic to a more desirable condition, at once impeding and enabling it, a protective matrix now definitively outgrown. If the two are alike in this respect, they are also strikingly similar in others. Both scorn all anodyne idealism and otherworldliness: 'The true world,' comments Nietzsche in notably Marxist idiom, 'has been erected on a contradiction of the real world.'[14] Each lays claim to an energy – of production, 'life' or the will to power – which is the source and measure of all value but lies beyond such value. They are equally at one in their negative utopianism, which specifies the general forms of a future rather than pre-drafts its contents; and each imagines that future in terms of surplus, excess, overcoming, incommensurability, recovering a lost sensuousness and specificity through a transfigured concept of measure. Both thinkers deconstruct idealized unities into their concealed material conflictiveness, and are deeply wary of all altruistic rhetoric, beneath which they detect the fugitive motions of power and self-interest. If only those actions are moral which are done purely for the sake of others, Nietzsche remarks wryly in *Dawn*, then there are no moral actions at all. Neither theorist ascribes a high value to consciousness, which is berated for its idealist *hubris* and thrust back to its modest location within a broader field of historical determinations. For Nietzsche, consciousness as such is incurably idealist, stamping a deceptively stable 'being' on the material process of 'change, becoming, multiplicity, opposition, contradiction, war'.[15] For Marx, this metaphysical or reificatory impulse of the mind would seem to inhere in the specific conditions of commodity fetishism, where change is similarly frozen and naturalized. Both are sceptical of the category of the subject, although Nietzsche a good deal more so than Marx. For the later Marx, the subject appears simply as a support for the social structure; in Nietzsche's view the subject is a mere trick of grammar, a convenient fiction to sustain the deed.

If Nietzsche's thought can be paralleled to Marxism, it can also be deciphered by it. The contempt which Nietzsche evinces for bourgeois morality is understandable enough in the conditions of the German empire of his time, where the middle class was for the most part content to seek influence within Bismarck's autocratic regime rather than offer it a decisive political challenge. Deferential and pragmatic, the German bourgeoisie disowned its historic revolutionary role for the benefits of a capitalism installed in large measure from 'above' – by the protectionist Bismarckian state itself – and for the protection which such an accommodation to ruling-class policies might furnish against what was rapidly to become the greatest socialist party in the world. Deprived of proper political representation by Bismarck's implacable opposition to parliamentary government, thwarted and overshadowed by an arrogant aristocratism, the middle class compromised and manoeuvred within the structures of state power, timorous in its political demands on its superiors and terrified by the swelling socialist clamour of its subordinates. In the face of this inert, conformist stratum Nietzsche swaggeringly affirms the virile, free-booting values of the old nobility or warrior caste. Yet it is equally possible to see this autarchic individualism as an idealized version of the bourgeoisie itself, with all the daring, dynamism and self-sufficiency it might attain in more propitious social circumstances. The active, adventurous *Übermensch* casts a nostalgic glance backwards to the old military nobility; but in his insolently explicit enterprise he also prefigures a reconstituted bourgeois subject. 'To have and to want to have more – *growth*, in one word – that is life itself', comments Nietzsche in *The Will to Power*, in the course of an anti-socialist diatribe. If only manufacturers were noble, he reflects in *The Gay Science*, there might not be any socialism of the masses.

The project, however, is more complex and paradoxical than some Carlylean or Disraelian dream of grafting the heroic vigour of aristocracy onto a leaden bourgeoisie. It concerns, rather, an acute contradiction within the middle class itself. The problem is that the moral, religious and juridical 'superstructure' of that class is entering into conflict with its own productive energies. Conscience, duty, legality are essential foundations of the bourgeois social order; yet they also serve to impede the unbridled self-development of the bourgeois subject. That self-development is ironically at odds with the very 'metaphysical' values – absolute grounds, stable identities, unfissured continuities – upon which middle-class society trades for its political security. The dream of each entrepreneur is to be wholly unconstrained in his own activity, while receiving protection in the corporate forms of law, politics, religion and ethics from the potentially injurious activities of others of his kind. Such constraints, however, must then apply equally to himself, undermining the very autonomy they were meant to safeguard. Individual sovereignty and incommensurability are of the essence, yet would seem attainable only by a herd-like levelling and homogenizing. As sheer anarchic process or productive force, the bourgeois subject threatens in its sublimely inexhaustible becoming to undercut the very stabilizing social representations it requires. It is the bourgeois himself, if only he would acknowledge it, who is the true anarchist and nihilist, kicking away at every step the metaphysical foundation on which he depends. To realize itself fully, then, this strange, self-thwarting subject must somehow overthrow itself; and this is surely a central meaning of the self-overcoming *Übermensch*. The aesthetic as self-actualization is in conflict with the aesthetic as social harmony, and Nietzsche is recklessly prepared to sacrifice the latter to the former. Bourgeois man as moral, legal and political subject is 'more sick, uncertain, changeable, indeterminate than any other animal, there is no doubt of that – he is the *sick* animal';[16] yet he is also the bold adventurer who has 'dared more, done more new things, braved more and challenged fate more than all the other animals put together: he, the great experimenter with himself, discontented and insatiable, wrestling with animals, nature, and gods for ultimate dominion – he, still unvanquished, eternally directed toward the future, whose own restless energies never leave him in peace . . . '.[17] This magnificent self-entrepreneurship tragically entails the morbid germ of consciousness; but Nietzsche will, so to speak, lift such productive dynamism from 'base' to 'superstructure', shattering the metaphysical forms of the latter with the furious creativity of the former.

Both subjects and objects are for Nietzsche mere fictions, the provisional effects of deeper forces. Such an eccentric view is perhaps no more than the daily truth of the capitalist order: the objects which are for Nietzsche sheer transient nodes of force are as commodities no more than ephemeral points of exchange. The 'objective' world for Nietzsche, if one can speak in such terms, would seem at once turbulently vital and blankly meaningless – an accurate enough phenomenology, no doubt, of market society. The human subject, for all its ontological privilege, is likewise stripped in such conditions to the reflex of deeper, more determinant processes. It is this fact that Nietzsche will seize on and turn to advantage, hollowing out this already deconstructed figure to clear a path for the advent of the overman. As the ideal entrepreneur of the future, this bold creature has learnt to relinquish all the old consolations of soul, essence, identity, continuity, living provisionally and resourcefully, riding with the vital current of life itself. In him, the existing social order has come to sacrifice its security to its liberty, embracing the groundlessness of existence as the very source of its ceaseless self-experiment. If bourgeois society is caught in a cleft stick between energy and ontology, between prosecuting its ends and legitimating them, then the latter must yield to the former. To allow the old metaphysical subject to splinter apart is to tap directly into the will to power itself, appropriating this force to fashion a new, ungrounded, aesthetic being who carries his justification entirely in himself. In a reversal of Kierkegaard, ethics will then have given way to aesthetics, as the fiction of a stable order is swept aside for the more authentic fiction of eternal self-creation.

The most notable difference between Nietzsche and Marx is that Nietzsche is not a Marxist. Indeed he is not only not a Marxist, but a belligerent opponent of almost every enlightened liberal or democratic value. We must resist all sentimental weakness, he reminds himself: 'life itself is *essentially* appropriation, injury, overpowering of what is alien and weaker; suppression, hardness, imposition of one's own forms, incorporation, and at least, at its mildest, exploitation . . . '.[18] Much of Nietzsche's writing reads like a brochure for a youth adventure scheme, or the dyspeptic grousings at liberal effeteness of some pensioned-off Pentagon general. He desires

> spirits strengthened by war and victory, for whom conquest, adventure, danger, and even pain have become needs; it would require habituation to the keen air of the heights, to winter journeys, to ice and mountains in every sense; it would require even a kind of sublime wickedness, an ultimate, supremely self-confident mischievousness in knowledge that goes with great health.[19]

We must steel ourselves to the sufferings of others, and ride our chariots over the morbid and decadent. Sympathy and compassion as we have them are the diseased virtues of Judaeo-Christianity, symptoms of that self-odium and disgust for life which the lower orders, in their rancorous resentment, have by a stroke of genius persuaded their own masters to internalize. The poor have cunningly infected the strong with their own loathsome nihilism, so Nietzsche will speak up in turn for cruelty and delight in domination, for 'everything haughty, manly, conquering, domineering'.[20] Like William Blake, he suspects that pity and altruism are the acceptable faces of aggression, pious masks of a predatory regime; and he can see nothing in socialism but a disastrous extension of abstract levelling. Socialism is insufficiently revolutionary, a mere collectivized version of the enfeebled bourgeois virtues which fails to challenge the whole fetish of morality and of the subject. It is simply an alternative brand of social ethics, bound in this sense to its political antagonist; the only worthwhile future must involve a transvaluation of all values.

One does not have to glimpse in Nietzsche a precursor of the Third Reich to be repelled by this grovelling self-abasement before the phallus, with all its brutal misogyny and militarist fantasizing. If

Nietzsche means such talk as 'the annihilation of the decaying races' literally, then his ethics are appalling; if he intends it metaphorically, then he is recklessly irresponsible and cannot be entirely exculpated from the sinister uses to which such ugly rhetoric was later put. It is remarkable how blandly most of his present-day acolytes have edited out these more repugnant features of the Nietzschean creed, as a previous generation edited in a proto-fascist anti-Semitism. The *Übermensch*, to be sure, is not some latter-day Genghis Khan letting rip his murderous impulses but a tempered, refined individual of serenity and self-control, sensitive and magnanimous in his bearing. Indeed one proper objection to him is less that he will exterminate the poor than that he represents little advance, for all the flamboyant flourishing with which he is heralded, on the well-balanced, self-disciplined individual of a familiar cultural idealism. Even so, it is a crucial distinction between Nietzsche and Marx that the release of individual human powers from the fetters of social uniformity – a goal which both thinkers propose – is to be achieved for Marx in and through the free self-realization of all, and for Nietzsche in disdainful isolation. Nietzsche's contempt for human solidarity belongs with his fundamental values, not simply with his denunciation of a current conformism. The overman may display compassion and benevolence, but these are simply aspects of the pleasurable exercise of his powers, the noble decision of the strong to unbend magnanimously to the weak. If he decides that such compassionate unbending is inappropriate, then the weak are at his mercy. It is aesthetically gratifying from time to time for the overman to deploy his fullness of strength to succour others, always delightfully conscious that he could equally use it to crush them.

Given that the free individual cannot be the product of collective action, Nietzsche's answer to how he emerges at all must remain somewhat vacuous. It cannot be by voluntarist transformation, since Nietzsche has no time for such mental fictions as 'acts of will'. Indeed 'will power' and 'will to power' would seem effective opposites in his thought. But nor can it be by any vulgar historical evolutionism, for the overman strikes violently, unpredictably into the complacent continuum of history. It would just seem the case that certain privileged subjects such as Friedrich Nietzsche are able mysteriously to transcend the nihilism of modern life and leap at a bound into another dimension. Such a leap can certainly not occur through the exercise of critical reason, which Nietzsche believes impossible. How could the intellect, that crude, fumbling instrument of the will to power, pick itself up by its own bootstraps and reflect critically on the interests of which it is the blind expression? 'A critique of the faculty of knowledge', Nietzsche writes, 'is senseless: how should a tool be able to criticise itself when it can only use itself for the critique?'[21] Like several of his present-day followers, he would seem to assume that all such critique entails a serene disinterestedness; and then there is nothing between this impossible metalinguistic dream and a starkly Hobbesian conception of reason as the obedient slave of power. Cognition, as we have seen, is just a fictional simplification of the world for pragmatic ends: like the artefact itself, the concept edits, schematizes, disregards the inessential, in a reductive falsification essential for 'life'. There would seem no way, then, in which it could gain an analytic hold on its own operations, even if Nietzsche's own writings would appear paradoxically to do precisely this. As Jürgen Habermas has remarked, Nietzsche 'denies the critical power of reflection with and only with *the means of reflection itself*'.[22] Marx, for his part, would endorse Nietzsche's insistence on the practical nature of knowledge, its anchorage in material interests, but reject the pragmatist corollary that an overall emancipatory critique is thereby necessarily undercut. What concerns Marx are just those historically specific, 'perspectival' interests which, being what they are, can only realize themselves by passing over from their own particularity to a profoundly interested enquiry into the structure of a whole social formation. The link for Marx between local and general, pragmatic and totalizing thought, is secured in the first place by the contradictory nature of class society itself, which would require global transformation if certain highly specific demands were to find their fulfilment.

If Nietzsche is able to know that all reasoning is simply the product of the will to power, then this knowledge itself shares something of reason's classical range and authority, unlocking the very essence of the real. It is just that this essence turns out to be the truth that there are only ever sectoral interpretations, all of which are in fact false. The quarrel between Marx and Nietzsche turns not on whether there is something more fundamental than reasoning – both thinkers insist that there is – but on the consequent locus and status of reason within this more determining context. To dethrone reason from its vainglorious supremacy is not necessarily to reduce it to the function of a can-opener. Indeed just as Nietzsche at one point acknowledges that reason and passion are not simple opposites – it is mistaken, he argues in *The Will to Power*, to talk as if every passion did not possess its quantum of reason – so critical reason for Marxism is a potential within the growth of historical interests. The critical reason which might enable an overcoming of capitalism is for Marx immanent within that system rather as for Nietzsche reason is a quality immanent to desire. Marxist critique is neither parachuted into history from some metaphysical outer space, nor confined to a reflex of narrowly particular interests. Instead, it seizes insolently on the ideals of bourgeois society itself, and enquires why it is that in current conditions those ideals are curiously, persistently unrealizable.

Marxism is much preoccupied with power, but refers this issue to certain conflicts of interest bound up with material production. Nietzsche, by contrast, hypostasizes power as an end in itself, with no rationale beyond its own self-gratifying expansion. The aim of Nietzschean power is not material survival but richness, profusion, excess; it struggles for no other reason than to realize itself. Ironically, then, there is a sense in which for Nietzsche power is ultimately disinterested. On the one hand, it is wholly inseparable from the play of specific interests; on the other hand, it broods eternally upon its own being in sublime indifference to any of its localized expressions. In this as in other ways, Nietzschean power is fundamentally aesthetic: it bears its ends entirely within itself, positing them as mere points of resistance essential to its own self-actualizing. Through the contingent goals it throws up, power returns eternally to itself, and nothing can be extraneous to it. It is thus that Nietzsche can be branded by Heidegger as the last of the metaphysicians – not that the will to power is any sort of Hegelian essence behind the world (since for Nietzsche's full-blooded phenomenalism there is absolutely nothing behind 'appearances'), but that it is the sole, fundamental, universal form the world takes. Will to power means the dynamic self-enhancement of all things in their warring multiplicity, the shifting force-field by which they expand, collide, struggle and appropriate; and it is thus no kind of 'being' at all. But since it denotes that differential relation of quanta of forces which is the shape of everything, it inevitably continues to fulfil the conceptual function of such 'being'. So it is that a modern devotee of the master, Gilles

Deleuze, can write with a certain rhetorical strain that 'The will to power is plastic, inseparable from each case in which it is determined; just as the eternal return is being, but being which is affirmed of becoming, the will to power is unitary, but unity which is affirmed of multiplicity.'[23]

We have already encountered more than once the idea of a force which is 'inseparable from each case in which it is determined', and this is the law of the aesthetic. The will to power is and is not a unitary essence in just the way that the inner form of the artefact is and is not a universal law. The 'law' regulating the work of art is not of the kind that could be abstracted from it, even provisionally, to become the subject of argument and analysis; it evaporates without trace into the stuff of the artwork as a whole, and so must be intuited rather than debated. Just the same is true of the Nietzschean will, which is at once the inward shape of all there is, yet nothing but local, strategic variations of force. As such, it can provide an absolute principle of judgement or ontological foundation while being nothing of the sort, as fleeting and quicksilver as the Fichtean process of becoming. The Kantian 'law' of taste, similarly, is at once universal and particular to the object. Poised at this conveniently ambivalent point, the idea of the will to power can be used in one direction to lambaste those metaphysicians who would hunt out an essence behind appearances, and in another direction to denounce the myopic hedonists, empiricists and utilitarians who are unable to peer beyond their own (mainly English) noses to applaud the mighty cosmic drama unfolding around them. It permits Nietzsche to combine a full-blooded foundationalism, one which has searched out the secret of all existence, with a scandalous perspectivism which can upbraid as effeminate fantasy the abject will to truth. Will to power is just the universal truth that there is no universal truth, the interpretation that all is interpretation; and this paradox, not least in the hands of Nietzsche's modern inheritors, allows an iconoclastic radicalism to blend with a prudently pragmatist suspicion of all 'global' theorizing. As with Schellingian 'indifference' or Derridean 'difference', it is impossible to trump this quasi-transcendental principle because it is entirely empty.

It is worth enquiring whether the will to power is for Nietzsche a matter of 'fact' or 'value'. It would seem that it cannot be a good in itself, for if it is coterminous with everything, by what standard could this be assessed? One cannot in Nietzsche's view speak of the value or valuelessness of existence as a whole, since this would presuppose some normative criteria outside of existence itself. 'The value of life cannot be estimated', he writes in *The Twilight of the Idols;* and this is at least one sense in which he is not a nihilist. The will to power simply *is;* yet it is also at the source of all value. The sole objective measure of value, Nietzsche comments in *The Will to Power,* is enhanced and organized power; so that what is valuable is less the will to power 'in itself', whatever that might mean, than the ways it promotes and enriches itself in coordinated complexes of energy. Since human life is one such possible enrichment, Nietzsche can claim that 'life itself forces us to posit values; life itself values through us when we posit values'.[24] But the will to power would seem to promote and complexify itself anyway, by virtue of its very 'essence'. Dandelions, for instance, are a triumph of the will to power, restlessly expanding their dominion by appropriating new areas of space. If it belongs to the 'nature' of the will to power to enhance itself, then as a 'principle' it hovers indeterminately between fact and value, its sheer existence a perpetual valuation.

If the world for Nietzsche is valueless, meaningless chaos, then the point would seem to be to create one's own values in defiance of its blank indifference. Nietzsche is accordingly stern with those senti-mental moralists who hold that to live well is to live in accordance with Nature. Such thinkers merely project their own arbitrary values onto reality and then, in an act of ideological consolation, unite narcissistically with this self-image. In a subtle gesture of dominion, philosophy always fashions the world in its own likeness. Nietzsche is out to disrupt this imaginary closure, maliciously reminding us of Nature's sheer amorality:

> 'According to nature' you want to *live?* O you noble Stoics, what deceptive words these are! Imagine a being like nature, wasteful beyond measure, indifferent beyond measure, without purposes or consideration, without mercy and justice, fertile and desolate and uncertain at the same time; imagine indifference itself as a power – how *could* you live according to this indifference?[25]

Humanity, in what Nietzsche terms a 'monstrous stupidity', regards itself as the measure of all things, and considers anything to be beautiful which reflects back its own visage.[26] But the very indifference of the Nietzschean universe, in contrast to this anthropomorphism, sounds ironically close to some of his own most cherished values. He writes in *Beyond Good and Evil* of Nature's 'prodigal and indifferent magnificence which is outrageous but noble',[27] implying that Nature's indifference to value is precisely its value. The imaginary circle between humanity and world is thus ruptured with one hand only to be resealed with the other: it is the very haughty heedlessness of Nature which would seem to mirror Nietzsche's own ethics.

It is in this sense that Nietzsche, for all his mockery of the sentimentalists, is not exactly an existentialist. At one level, he would indeed appear to argue such a case: the world's lack of inherent value forbids you from taking a moral cue from it, leaving you free to generate your own gratuitous values by hammering this brutely meaningless material into aesthetic shape. The ethical here is purely decisionistic: 'Genuine philosophers . . . are commanders and legislators: they say: *thus* shall it be!'[28] But to live in this style is precisely to imitate Nature as it truly is, an achievement beyond the purveyors of the pathetic fallacy. For the way the world is is no way in particular: reality is will to power, a variable complex of self-promoting powers, and to live a life of autonomous self-realization is therefore to live in accordance with it. It is precisely by becoming an end in oneself that one most accurately mirrors the universe. Nietzsche appears to equivocate between existentialist and naturalistic cases; but this opposition can be deconstructed, to give him the best of all possible ideological worlds. The splendid ungrounded autonomy of legislating one's own values in the teeth of an amoral reality can itself be metaphysically grounded, in the way the world essentially is. 'Life' is hard, savage indifference; but this is a value as much as a fact, a form of exuberant, indestructible energy to be ethically imitated. The will to power does not dictate any *particular* values, as the sentimentalists believe of Nature; it just demands that you do what it does, namely live in a changeful, experimental, self-improvisatory style through the shaping of a multiplicity of values. In this sense it is the 'form' of the will which the overman affirms rather than any moral content, since the will has in fact no moral content. 'Content henceforth becomes something merely formal – our life included', Nietzsche writes in *The Will to Power*.[29] And this is one sense in which the will would seem at once the highest kind of value, and no value at all.

There is a problem, however, about *why* one should affirm the will to power. One cannot call it a value to *express* this force, since everything expresses it anyway. There is no point in legislating that things should do what they cannot help doing just by virtue of what they are. What is valuable is *enhancing* the will; but what is the basis of *this* value judgement, and whence do we derive the criteria which might determine what is to count as an enhancement? Do we just know this aesthetically or intuitively, as when Nietzsche speaks of the pleasurable *feeling* of power? 'What health is', remarks Heidegger ominously in his study of Nietzsche, 'only the healthy can say . . . What truth is, only one who is truthful can discern.'[30] If the will to power is itself quite amoral, what is so morally positive about enriching it? Why should one cooperate with this force, any more than with a sentimentalized Nature? It is clear that one can choose, like Schopenhauer, to deny the will to power – even though all such denials must for Nietzsche be perverted expressions of it. But it is unclear on what grounds one judges that such negation is bad, and that affirming the will is good. Unless, of course, one has already projected certain supremely positive values into this force, such that promoting it becomes an indubitable virtue. Cannot the effects of the will to power be celebrated only if one is already in possession of some criteria of value by which to assess them?

The truth, of course, is that Nietzsche does indeed smuggle certain already assumed values into the concept of the will to power, in just the circular manner for which he scorns the dewy-eyed naturalists. In a mystificatory gesture quite as deluded as theirs, he naturalizes certain quite specific social values – domination, aggression, exploitation, appropriation – as the very essence of the universe. But since such relations of conflict are not a 'thing', their essentialism is mystified in its turn. When accused of subjectivism, Nietzsche can retreat to a kind of positivism: he is not so much promoting any particular values as describing the way life is. Life is callous, wasteful, merciless, dispassionate, inimical as such to human value; but these terms are of course thoroughly normative. True value is to acknowledge that the amorality of the competitive life-struggle is the finest thing there is. The market place would seem hostile to value of a traditional spiritual kind; but this plain-minded insistence on certain brute facts of life is itself, inevitably, a value-judgement. 'My idea', writes Nietzsche, 'is that each specific body strives to become

251

master over the whole of space, and to spread out its power – its Will-to-Power – repelling whatever resists its expansion. But it strikes continually upon a like endeavour of other bodies, and ends by adjusting itself ("unifying") with them.[31] Few more explicit theorizations of capitalist competition could be imagined; but Nietzsche is out in his own way to spiritualize this predatory state. The will to power may be in one sense philosophical code for the market place, but it also delivers an 'aristocratic' rebuke to the sordid instrumentalism of such struggle, urging instead a vision of power as an aesthetic delight in itself. Such an irrationalism of power, scornful of all base purpose, dissociates itself from an ignoble utilitarianism in the very act of reflecting the irrationalism of capitalist production.

How does one come, unlike a Schopenhauer, to 'choose' the will to power? Either the act of choosing to affirm the will is an effect of the will itself, in which case it is hard to see how it can be a 'choice'; or it is not, in which case it would seem to fall, impossibly for Nietzsche, outside the will to power's cosmic scope. Nietzsche's own response to this dilemma is to deconstruct the entire opposition between free will and determinism. In the act of affirming the will, liberty and necessity blend undecidably together; and the primary Nietzschean image of this aporia is the activity of the artist. Artistic creation is no mere matter of 'volition' – a metaphysical delusion for Nietzsche if ever there was one; but it figures nonetheless as our finest instance of emancipation.

Indeed art is Nietzsche's theme from beginning to end, and the will to power is the supreme artefact.[32] This is not to say that he places much credence in classical aesthetics: if the world is a work of art it is not as an organism but as 'in all eternity chaos – in the sense not of a lack of necessity but of a lack of order, arrangement, form, beauty, wisdom, and whatever other names there are for our aesthetic anthropomorphisms'.[33] The aesthetic is not a question of harmonious representation but of the formless productive energies of life itself, which spins off sheerly provisional unities in its eternal sport with itself. What is aesthetic about the will to power is exactly this groundless, pointless self-generating, the way it determines itself differently at every moment out of its own sublimely unsearchable depths. The universe, Nietzsche comments in *The Will to Power*, is a work of art which gives birth to itself; and the artist or *Übermensch* is one who can tap this process in the name of his own free self-production. Such an aesthetics of production is the enemy of all contemplative Kantian taste – of that disinterested gaze on the reified aesthetic object which suppresses the turbulent, tendentious process of its making.

The critical eunuchs must thus be overthrown by the virile artistic practitioners. Art is ecstasy and rapture, demonic and delirious, a physiological rather than spiritual affair. It is a matter of supple muscles and sensitized nerves, an exquisite toning and refining of the body which blends sensual intoxication with effortless discipline. Nietzsche's ideal artist sounds more like a commando than a visionary. Art is sexualized to its root: 'Making music is just another way of making children.'[34] The attempt to render it disinterested is merely another castrating feminine assault on the will to power, along with science, truth and asceticism. As Heidegger notes in a shabby little comment: 'True, Nietzsche speaks against feminine aesthetics. But in doing so he speaks for masculine aesthetics, hence for aesthetics.'[35] The overman is artist and artefact, creature and creator in one, which is precisely not to suggest that he lets rip his spontaneous impulses. On the contrary, Nietzsche denounces the 'blind indulgence of an affect' as the cause of the greatest evils, and views greatness of character as a manly control of the instincts. The highest aesthetic condition is self-hegemony: after the long, degrading labour of submission to moral law, the *Übermensch* will finally attain sovereignty over his now sublimed appetites, realizing and reining them in with all the nonchalance of the superbly confident artist cuffing his materials into shape. The whole of existence is accordingly aestheticized: we must be 'poets of our lives', Nietzsche proclaims, in the minutest everyday matters.[37] The overman improvises his being from moment to moment out of a superabundance of power and high spirits, stamping form on the flux of the world, forging chaos into fleeting order. 'To become master of the chaos one is; to compel one's chaos to become form'[38] is the highest aesthetic achievement, which only the most dedicated sado-masochist can attain. The truly strong man is serene enough to submit to such lacerating self-discipline; those who resent this constraint are the weak who fear to become slaves.

The constraint in question, in fact, is of an enhancing rather than oppressive kind. What is at stake, as Heidegger puts it, is 'not the mere subjection of chaos to a form, but that mastery which enables the primal wilderness of chaos and the primordiality of law to advance under the same yoke, inevitably bound to one another with equal necessity'.[39] The law of the future human animal is of a curiously antinomian kind, utterly unique to each individual. Nothing outrages Nietzsche more than the insulting suggestion that individuals might be in some way commensurable. The law which the *Übermensch* confers on himself, like the 'law' of the artefact, is in no sense heteronomous to him, but simply the inner necessity of his incomparable self-fashioning. The aesthetic as model or principle of social consensus is utterly routed by this radical insistence on autonomy; and it is here, perhaps, that Nietzsche's thought is at its most politically subversive. The *Übermensch* is the enemy of all established social *mores*, all proportionate political forms; his delight in danger, risk, perpetual self-reconstitution recalls the 'crisis' philosophy of a Kierkegaard, as equally disdainful of meekly habitual conduct. The aesthetic as autonomous self-realization is now at loggerheads with the aesthetic as custom, *habitus*, social unconscious; or, more precisely, the latter have now been audaciously appropriated from the public domain to the personal life. The overman lives from habitual instinct, absolved from the clumsy reckonings of conscious-ness; but what is admirable in him is inauthentic in society as a whole. Hegemony is wrested from the political arena and relocated within each incommensurable subject. Nietzsche's writings betray a profoundly masochistic love of the law, an erotic joy in the severity with which artists of their own humanity wrench the materials of their being into burnished form. But the idea of a law entirely peculiar to the individual simply allows him to reconcile his disgust for morbid self-indulgence with an extreme libertarianism.

We have seen that the moral law for Nietzsche, as with the Mosaic code for St Paul, is merely a ladder to be kicked away once mounted. It forms a protective shelter within which one grows to maturity; but it must then be abandoned, in a Kierkegaardian 'suspension of the ethical', for the adventure of free self-creation. What this enterprise involves is the transmuting into instinct of all that consciousness has painfully acquired in the epoch when it reigned supreme. In that period, the human organism learnt to absorb into its structure the 'untruth' essential for it to flourish; it remains to be seen whether it can now in turn incorporate the truth – which is to say, the recognition that there is no truth. The overman is he who can assimilate and naturalize even this terrible knowledge, convert it to finely instinctual habit, dance without certainties on the brink of the abyss. For him, the very groundlessness of the world had become a source of aesthetic delight and an opportunity for self-invention. In thus living out acquired cultural values as unconscious reflex, the overman reduplicates at a higher level the barbarian who simply unleashed his drives. In a reversal of the classic aesthetic project, instinct will now incorporate reason: consciousness, duly 'aestheticized' as bodily intuition, will take over the life-sustaining functions once fulfilled by the 'lower' drives; and the consequence will be that deconstruction of the opposition between intellect and instinct, volition and necessity, of which art is the supreme prototype. 'Artists seem to have more sensitive noses in these matters', Nietzsche writes, 'knowing only too well that precisely when they no longer do anything 'voluntarily' but do everything of necessity, their feeling of freedom, subtlety, full power, of creative placing, disposing, and forming reaches its peak – in short, that necessity and "freedom of the will" then become one in them.'[40]

Nietzsche's narrative, then, begins with an original inerrancy of blind impulse, ambivalently admirable and terrible; shifts to a moral conscience which imperils but also enriches such impulses; and culminates in a higher synthesis in which body and mind are united under the aegis of the former. An originary brutal coercion gives birth to an era of moral hegemony, which in turn paves the way for the self-hegemony of the overman. This new dispensation combines, in transfigured form, the spontaneity of the first period with the legality of the second. A 'bad' introjection of the law in the ethical-subjective stage gives way to a 'good' such internalization in the coming aesthetic epoch, when freedom and governance will each find its root in the other. For such a remorselessly anti-Hegelian thinker as Nietzsche, this scenario has something of a familiar ring. Its perturbing originality is to press to a third stage the two-phase movement, familiar to aestheticizing thought, from coercion to hegemony. The concept of hegemony is retained; but the law to which one will finally yield consent is nothing but the law of one's unique being. In taking over the aesthetic model of a free appropriation of law, but in stripping that law of its uniformity and universalism, Nietzsche brings low any notion of social consensus. 'And how should there be a "common good"!', he scoffs in *Beyond Good and Evil.* 'The term contradicts itself: whatever can be common always has little value.'[41] In *The Twilight of the Idols* he dismisses conventional virtue as little more than 'mimicry', thus scornfully overturning the whole Burkeian vision of aesthetic mimesis as the basis of social mutuality. Asthetics and politics are now outright antagonists: all great periods of culture have been periods of political decline, and the whole concept of the 'culture-state', of the aesthetic as civilizing, educational, socially therapeutic, is just another dismal emasculation of art's sublimely amoral power.[42]

Nietzsche's aristocratic disdain for a common measure is by no means wholly unacceptable to bourgeois individualism. But it strikes at the root of conventional order, and so catches the bourgeoisie on its sorest point of contradiction between its dream of autonomy and demand for legality. In the end, Nietzsche is claiming that the present regime of legal and moral subjecthood simply mediates between two states of anarchy, one 'barbaric' and the other 'artistic'. If this is hardly glad tidings for orthodox society, neither is his impudent severing of all connection between art and truth. If art is 'true' for Nietzsche, it is only because its illusoriness embodies the truth that there is no truth. 'Truth is ugly,' he writes in *The Will to Power.* 'We possess art lest we perish of the truth.'[43] Art expresses the will to power; but the will to power is nothing but semblance, transient appearance, sensuous surface. Life itself is 'aesthetic' because it aims only at 'semblance, meaning, error, deception, simulation, delusion, self-delusion';[44] and art is true to this reality precisely in its falsity. It is also false to it, since it imprints an ephemeral stability of being on this meaningless warring of forces; there is no way in which the will to power can be represented without being in that moment distorted. Art expresses the brute senselessness of the will, but simultaneously conceals this lack of meaning by the fashioning of significant form. In doing so, it tricks us into a momentary belief that the world has some significant shape to it, and so fulfils something of the function of the Kantian imaginary.

The more false art is, then, the truer it is to the essential falsity of life; but since art is *determinate* illusion, it thereby conceals the truth of that falsity.[45] At a single stroke, art symptomatizes and shields us from the terrible (un)truth of the universe, and thus is doubly false. On the one hand, its consolatory forms protect us from the dreadful insight that there is actually nothing at all, that the will to power is neither real, true nor self-identical; on the other hand, the very content of those forms is the will itself, which is no more than an eternal dissembling. Art as dynamic process is true to the untruth of the will to power; art as product or appearance is untrue to this (un)truth. In artistic creation, then, the will to power is harnessed and turned for an instant against its own cruel indifference. To produce forms and values from this tumultuous force is in once sense to work against it; but it is to do so with a touch of its own dispassionate serenity, in the knowledge that all such values are purely fictive.

One might put the same point differently by claiming that art for Nietzsche is at once masculine and feminine. If it is strenuous, muscular, productive, it is also fickle, mendacious, seductive. Indeed Nietzsche's entire philosophy turns on a curious amalgam of these sexual stereotypes. This most outrageously masculinist of creeds is devoted to hymning the 'feminine' values of form, surface, semblance, elusiveness, sensuality, against the patriarchal metaphysics of essence, truth and identity. In the concept of the will to power, these two sets of sexual characteristics are subtly interwoven. To live according to the will is to live robustly, imperiously, released from all female obeisance to law into splendid phallic autonomy. But to have mastered oneself in this style is to be set free to live mischievously, pleasurably, ironically, luxuriating in a teasing sport of masks and personae, gliding in and out of every passion and subject-position with all the serene self-composure of the sage. Nietzsche is thus able to speak up for the 'feminine' principle precisely as one of the most virulent sexists of his age, a title he shares with the obsessively misogynistic Schopenhauer. If truth is indeed a woman, then the claim is complimentary to neither.

In the aftermath of Fichte and Schelling, Nietzsche is the most flamboyant example we have of a full-blooded aestheticizer, reducing everything there is – truth, cognition, ethics, reality itself – to a species of artefact. 'It is only as an *aesthetic phenomenon*', he writes in celebrated phrase, 'that existence and the world are eternally *justified*',[46] which means among other things that the blood-sport of history is at least a *sport*, which intends no harm because it intends nothing but itself. Thought itself must be aestheticized, shedding its leaden earnestness to become dance, laughter, high spirits. The key

257

ethical terms are noble and base rather than good and bad, questions of style and taste rather than of moral judgement. Right living is a matter of artistic consistency, hammering one's existence into an austerely unified style. Art itself is blessing and deification: it must be wrested from the monkish idealists and restored to the body, to orgy and festive ritual. Aesthetic value-judgements must rediscover their true foundation in the libidinal drives. Art instructs us in the profound truth of how to live superficially, to halt at the sensuous surface rather than hunt the illusory essence beneath it. Perhaps superficiality is the true essence of life, and depth a mere veil thrown over the authentic banality of things.

To claim that there is nothing but surface is to argue, in effect, that society must relinquish its traditional metaphysical justifications for what it does. It is a feature of the rationalizing, secularizing activity of middle-class society, as we have seen already, that it tends to undermine some of the very metaphysical values on which that society depends in part for its legitimation. Nietzsche's thought points one bold way out of this embarrassing contradiction: society should renounce such metaphysical pieties and live daringly, groundlessly, in the eternal truth of its material activity. It is this activity which in the concept of the will to power has been raised to the aesthetic dignity of an end in itself. Bourgeois productive energies must furnish their own foundation; the values which ratify the social order must be conjured directly out of its own vital forces, out of the 'facts' of its incessant striving and struggling, not hypocritically superadded from some supernatural source. History must learn to be self-generative and self-legitimating, open its ears to the hard lesson of the aesthetic. This whole proliferating network of dominance, aggressiveness and appropriation must confront the death of God and have the courage to be its own rationale. The death of God is the death of the superstructure; society must make do instead with the 'base' of its own productive forces, the will to power.

Viewed in this light, Nietzsche's work signals a legitimation crisis in which the brute facts of bourgeois society are no longer easily ratifiable by an inherited notion of 'culture'. We must tear aside the 'mendacious finery of that alleged reality of the man of culture',[47] acknowledging that none of the social legitimations on offer – Kantian duty, moral sense, Utilitarian hedonism and the rest – are any longer convincing. Rather than search anxiously for some

258

alternative metaphysical guarantee, we should embrace the will to power – which is to say, the metaphysical guarantee that no ultimate ground is needed, that violence and domination are just expressions of the way the universe is and require no justification beyond this. It is this that Nietzsche means by living aesthetically, celebrating power as an end in itself. But this turns out to be simply one more justification, investing life with all the glamour of the cosmic ideologies we should supposedly surpass.

Nietzsche pits the productive vitality of social life against its drive for consensus, thus turning one current of the aesthetic against another. On the one hand, a rampant aestheticization sweeps boldly across the whole of conventional society, undoing its ethics and epistemology, shattering its supernatural consolations and scientific totems, and demolishing in its radical individualism all possibility of stable political order. On the other hand, this aestheticizing force can be seen as the very life-blood of that conventional society – as the urge to infinite productivity as an end in itself, with each producer locked in eternal combat with the others. It is as though Nietzsche finds in this organized social irrationalism something of art's own splendidly autotelic nature. In contempt for the timorous bourgeois, he unveils as his ideal that violently self-willing creature, conjuring himself up anew at every moment, who was for Kierkegaard the last word in 'aesthetic' futility. But this ferocious new creation, stamping his overbearing shape on the world with all the *hauteur* of the old transcendental ego, is hardly as new as he appears. If the furious dynamism of the *Übermensch* terrifies the stout metaphysical citizen, he may also figure as his fantastic *alter ego*, in the sphere of production if not in the sacred precincts of family, church and state. To live adventurously, experimentally, may jeopardize metaphysical certitudes; but such resourceful self-improvization is hardly an unfamiliar life-style in the market place. Nietzsche is an astonishingly radical thinker, who hacks his way through the superstructure to leave hardly a strut of it standing. As far as the base goes, his radicalism leaves everything exactly as it was, only a good deal more so.

Notes

1 Friedrich Nietzsche, *The Gay Science*, translated by Walter Kaufmann (New York, 1974), p. 35.

2 Ibid., p. 18.

3 Friedrich Nietzsche, *The Will to Power*, translated by Walter Kaufmann and R. J. Hollingdale (New York, 1968), p. 270.

4 Friedrich Nietzsche, *Beyond Good and Evil*, in Walter Kaufmann (ed.), *Basic Writings of Nietzsche* (New York, 1968), p. 307. Hereafter *BW*.

5 Friedrich Nietzsche, *On the Genealogy of Morals*, *BW*, pp. 550 and 498.

6 Nietzsche, *Beyond Good and Evil*, *BW* p. 290.

7 Friedrich Nietzsche, *Human, All Too Human*, quoted by Richard Schacht, *Nietzsche* (London, 1983), p. 429.

8 Nietzsche, *Genealogy of Morals*, *BW*, p. 521.

9 Ibid., pp. 522–3.

10 Ibid., p. 523.

11 Nietzsche, *The Will to Power*, p. 404.

12 Friedrich Nietzsche, *The Wanderer and his Shadow*, quoted by Schacht, *Nietzsche*, p. 370.

13 *The Gay Science*, quoted by Schacht, *Nietzsche*, p. 190.

14 Friedrich Nietzsche, *Twilight of the Idols*, translated by A. M. Ludovici (London, 1927), p. 34.

15 Nietzsche, *The Will to Power*, p. 315.

16 Nietzsche, *Genealogy of Morals*, *BW* p. 557.

17 Ibid.

18 Nietzsche, *Beyond Good and Evil*, *BW* p. 393.

19 Nietzsche, *Genealogy of Morals*, *BW* p. 532.

20 Ibid., p. 265.

21 Nietzsche, *The Will to Power*, p. 269.

22 Jürgen Habermas, *Knowledge and Human Interests* (London, 1987), p. 299.

23 Gilles Deleuze, *Nietzsche and Philosophy* (London, 1983), pp. 85–6.

24 Nietzsche, *The Twilight of the Idols*, p. 87.

25 Nietzsche, *Beyond Good and Evil*, *BW* p. 205.

26 Nietzsche, *The Gay Science*, p. 286; *The Twilight of the Idols*, p. 75.

27 Nietzsche, *Beyond Good and Evil*, *BW* p. 291.

28 Ibid., p. 326.

29 Nietzsche, *The Will to Power*, p. 433.

30 Martin Heidegger, *Nietzsche*, vol. 1: *The Will to Power as Art* (London, 1981), p. 127.

31 Friedrich Nietzsche, *Nachlass*, quoted by Arthur C. Danto, *Nietzsche as Philosopher* (New York, 1965), p. 220.

32 For an interesting treatment of literary and artistic motifs in Nietzsche, see Alexander Nehamas, *Nietzsche: Life as Literature* (Cambridge, Mass., 1985). See also Allan Megill, *Prophets of Extremity* (Berkeley, 1985), Part 1.

33 Nietzsche, *Genealogy of Morals*, *BW* p. 521.
34 Nietzsche, *The Will to Power*, p. 421.
35 Heidegger, *Nietzsche*, p. 76.
36 Nietzsche, *The Will to Power*, p. 490.
37 Nietzsche, *The Gay Science*, quoted Danto, p. 147.
38 Nietzsche, *The Will to Power*, p. 444.
39 Heidegger, *Nietzsche*, p. 128.
40 Nietzsche, *BW* p. 196.
41 Nietzsche, *Beyond Good and Evil*, *BW* p. 330.
42 Nietzsche, *BW* p. 243.
43 Nietzsche, *The Will to Power*, p. 435.
44 Nietzsche, *The Gay Science*, p. 282.
45 See Pierre Macherey, *A Theory of Literary Production* (London, 1978), Part 1, for an interestingly parallel approach. See also Paul de Man's account of *The Birth of Tragedy* in *Allegories of Reading* (New Haven, 1979).
46 Nietzsche, *The Birth of Tragedy*, *BW* p. 132.
47 Ibid., p. 61.

10

The Name of the Father:
Sigmund Freud

If the aesthetic informs some of Karl Marx's most central political and economic categories, it also infiltrates the psychoanalytical doctrines of Sigmund Freud. Pleasure, play, dream, myth, scene, symbol, fantasy, representation: these are no longer to be conceived of as supplementary matters, aesthetic adornments to the proper business of life, but as lying at the very root of human existence, as what Charles Levin has called 'a kind of primitive substance of social process'.[1] Human life is aesthetic for Freud in so far as it is all about intense bodily sensations and baroque imaginings, inherently significatory and symbolic, inseparable from figure and fantasy. The unconscious works by a kind of 'aesthetic' logic, condensing and displacing its images with the crafty opportunism of an artistic *bricoleur*. Art for Freud is thus no privileged realm, but is continuous with the libidinal processes which go to make up daily life. If it is somehow peculiar, it is only because that daily life is itself exceedingly strange. If the aesthetic has been promoted in idealist circles as a form of sensuousness without desire, Freud will unmask the pious naivety of this view as itself a libidinal yearning. The aesthetic is what we live by; but for a Freud as opposed to a Schiller, this is at least as much catastrophe as triumph.

Nietzsche anticipated Freud's demystifying of aesthetic disinterestedness; but in one important respect Freud presses beyond the Nietzsche who so strikingly prefigures his thought. Nietzsche's will to power is unequivocally positive, and the artefacts which express it are resonant with such affirmation. It is this virile vitality, this phallic repletion, which psychoanalysis will undercut with the concept of desire. Desire insinuates a lack at the very heart of this Nietzschean robustness, slides into the will a negativity or perversity which renders it non-identical with itself. Our powers have something eternally dissatisfied about them, a motility and indeterminacy which causes them to miss the mark, go awry, swerve back upon themselves; there is a subtle flaw at the centre of power which casts a shadow over Nietzsche's repressive drive for health, sanity, integrity. It is because our bodies are not gloriously autonomous, as Nietzsche tends to imagine them, but bound up in their evolution with the bodies of others, that this treacherous faltering or deviating of our impulses comes about. If Nietzschean power plumps the body full, Freudian desire hollows it out. And this will have its effects on our view of the aesthetic artefact, which for all Freud's own somewhat traditionalist aesthetic notions can no longer dupe us as integral, well-rounded, symmetrical. Such an artefact is a covert trope of the humanist subject, which after Freud can never be the same again. What he implicitly interrogates is the whole classical aesthetic heritage, from Goethe and Schiller to Marx and Matthew Arnold, of the rich, potent, serenely balanced subject. On the contrary, Freud argues, our drives are in contradiction with one another, our faculties in a state of permanent warfare, our fulfilments fleeting and tainted. The aesthetic may be, for Freud as much as for Schiller, an imaginary consolation, but it is also the detonator of profound discharges which unmask the human subject as fissured and unfinished. The humanist dream of fullness is itself a libidinal fantasy, as indeed is the whole of traditional aesthetics. What that aesthetics yearns for is an object at once sensuous and rule-bound, a body which is also a mind, combining all the delicious plenitude of the senses with the authority of an abstract decree. It is therefore a fantasy of mother and father in one, of love and law commingled, an imaginary space in which pleasure-principle and reality-principle fuse under the aegis of the former. To become at one with the aesthetic representation is to recover for a treasured moment that primary narcissistic condition in which object-libido and ego-libido cannot be riven apart. Freud acknowledges in *Civilisation and its Discontents* that psychoanalysis has had hardly anything significant to say about aesthetic beauty, its nature and origin; but he is certain (as how would he not be?) that it derives from 'the field of sexual feeling', as a libidinal impulse inhibited in its aim, and concludes his somewhat bemused reflections with a lame comment on the unaesthetic appearance of the male genitals.[2]

To relate a Beethoven sonata to the testicles is hardly in the style of traditional aesthetics. Freud savagely demystifies culture, tracking its murky roots to the recesses of the unconscious as relentlessly as Marxism discloses its concealed source in historical barbarism. Art is infantile and regressive, a non-neurotic form of substitute satisfaction; incapable of abandoning a pleasurable object, men and women shift from toying with their faeces to tinkering with trombones. Works of art resemble dreams less than they do jokes, and the closest thing to the sublime for Freud is the ridiculous. In a brief paper entitled 'Humour', he regards humour as a kind of triumph of narcissism, whereby the ego refuses to be distressed by the provocations of reality in a victorious assertion of its invulnerability. Humour transmutes a threatening world into an occasion for pleasure; and to this extent it resembles nothing as much as the classical sublime, which similarly permits us to reap gratification from our senses of imperviousness to the terrors around us. The highest has its base in the lowest, in a gesture of Bakhtinian reversal which shatters the lying pretensions of cultural idealism. That most lofty of all Romantic categories – vision – lies embarrassingly close to those lowly libidinal sub-texts we call dreams. Idealist culture speaks the body, but rarely speaks *of* it, unable as it is to round upon its own enabling conditions. Freud will assail this noble lie in his gravely scientific, eminently respectable mien, leaving the outraged bourgeois to dismiss him as no more than a crude reductionist. If this is so, then it is puzzling why Freud himself was so deep in traditional culture, so edified and enthralled by it. Or at least it is puzzling to those who have not taken the point of William Empson's wise pastoral faith that 'the most refined desires are inherent in the plainest, *and would be false if they weren't.*'[3] Whenever anyone speaks 'badly but not ill' of human beings, remarks Nietzsche, defining them as a belly with two needs and a head with one, then 'the lover of knowledge should listen carefully and with diligence'.[4]

Freud's other implicit assault on traditional aesthetics is to deconstruct its crucial opposition between 'culture' and 'civil society'. Scandalously, he refuses to differentiate culture and civilization, the sphere of value and the realm of appetite. There is no utilitarian sphere which is innocent of the libidinal, as there is no cultural value absolved from the aggressive drives by which civilization is constructed. The bourgeois rests satisfied in his puritan belief that pleasure is one thing and reality another; but Freud will come to deconstruct the opposition between these two mighty principles, viewing the reality principle simply as a kind of detour or cunning zig-zag by which the pleasure principle comes to achieve its goals. A whole set of distinctions vital to bourgeois ideology – between enterprise and enjoyment, the practical and the pleasurable, sexual and commercial intercourse – are accordingly dismantled.

The traditional aesthetic ideal is one of a unity of spirit and sense, reason and spontaneity. The body, as we have seen, must be judiciously reinserted into a rational discourse which might otherwise wither into despotism; but this operation must be carried out with a minimum of disruption to that discourse itself. For such conventional aesthetic theory, Freud is exceedingly bad news. For his lesson is that the body is never quite at home in language, will never quite recover from its traumatic insertion into it, escaping whole and entire from the mark of the signifier. Culture and the body meet only to conflict; the scars which we bear are the traces of our bruising inruption into the symbolic order. Psychoanalysis examines what takes place when desire is given tongue, comes to speech; but speech and desire can never consort amicably together, as meaning and being continually displace one another; and if language, broadly conceived, is what opens up desire in the first place, desire is also what can bring it to stammer and fail. If this is true of human subjects, it is equally true of the discourse of psychoanalysis itself, dealing as it does with forces which threaten to play havoc with its own theoretical coherence. Desire is itself sublime, finally defeating all representation: there is a substrate in the unconscious which cannot be symbolized, even if it is in some sense turned towards language, strives for expression, from the outset.

It is precisely at this juncture, between mute force and articulate meaning, that Freudianism installs its enquiry. It is born as a discourse at the busy cross-roads between the semantic and somatic, and explores their strange inversions: organ as signifier, signifier as material practice. Meanings for Freud are certainly meanings, not the mere imprint or reflex of the drives; but once this whole textual process is so to speak flipped over, viewed through a different optic, it can be read as nothing less than a mighty warring of somatic forces, a semantic field in which the body achieves, or fails to achieve, speech. The Freudian drives lie somewhere on the frontier between the mental and the corporeal, representing the body to the mind; where we have a drive, there we have a demand placed on the mind by virtue of its connection with the body. To claim that we 'have an unconscious' is not to designate a hidden area of the self, like an invisible kidney or ghostly pancreas, but to speak of the way our consciousness is distorted from the inside by the exactions of the body upon it.

This body, however, is always for Freud a fictional representation rather than a brute material fact. Only by an intervening representation can the drives present themselves to consciousness, and even in the unconscious an instinct must be represented by an idea. To hold with Freud that the ego is essentially a bodily ego is to claim it as a kind of artefact, a figurative projection of the body, a psychic mimesis of its surfaces. The ego is a kind of shadowy inner screen which plays the newsreel of the body's complex history, its stored sensory contacts and multiple dealings with the world. Freud anchors the mind in the body, viewing reason as founded in desire and thinking as entwined with wishing; but this is not to see these things as the mere effluxes of something unimpeachably solid. For that 'solidity' is itself a psychic construct, as the ego builds up an image of the body 'after the event', so to speak, reading it within a symbolic schema as a complex of needs and imperatives, rather than simply 'reflecting' it. The relation between ego and body to that extent resembles the Althusserian relation between theory and history, as Fredric Jameson has described it:

> since for Althusser real historical time is only indirectly accessible to us, action for him would seem to be a kind of blindfolded operation, a manipulation at distance, in which we could at best watch our own performance indirectly, as though in a mirror, reading it back from the various readjustments of consciousness which result from the alteration in the external situation itself.[5]

If the male child 'reads' the female body as lacking, it is a reading launched within the law of castration, under the aegis of the signifier, not simply an empirical perception. To anchor the mind in the body is thus to lend it no secure foundation: indeed there is something elusive and unlocatable about the body which, as Paul Ricoeur has argued, makes it the most appropriate image of the unconscious:

When asked how it is possible for a meaning to exist without being conscious, the phenomenologist replies: its mode of being is that of the body, which is neither ego nor thing of the world. The phenomenologist is not saying that the Freudian unconscious is the body; he is simply saying that the mode of being of the body, neither representation in me nor thing outside of me, is the ontic model for any conceivable unconscious.[6]

It would be a mistake to equate the ego with the subject, since the drives – as in narcissism or masochism – can just as easily veer round upon it to make it their object. The drives are not in phenomenological parlance 'intentional', defined by their object; objects for Freud are contingent and exchangeable, mere ephemeral targets for instincts whose aim predominates over their end. Subject and object, as for Nietzsche, are passing products of the play of the drives; and what opens up the subject/object duality in the first place is the deeper dialectic of pleasure and unpleasure, introjection and expulsion, as the ego separates certain bits of the world from itself and masticates certain others, thus building up those primordial identifications of which it is a kind of storehouse or cemetery. If this is so, then Freud like Nietzsche deconstructs at a stroke the whole problematic within which traditional aesthetics moves – that of the encounter between self-identical subject and stable object, whose mutual estrangement may be wondrously transcended in the act of taste. It is not a question of rescuing the subject for a precious moment from its alienation; to be a subject is to be alienated anyway, rendered eccentric to oneself by the movement of desire. And if objects matter at all, they matter precisely in the place where they are absent. The desired object, as Juliet Mitchell has argued in Lacanian vein, comes into existence *as an object* only when it is lost to the baby or infant.[7] It is when that object is removed or prohibited that it lays down the trace of desire, so that its secure possession will always move under the sign of loss, its presence warped and overshadowed by the perpetual possibility of its absence. It is just this unnerving vacuity at the heart of the object, this permanent estrangeability which permeates its every aspect, which the classical aesthetic representation is out to repress in its fetishized organicism. Freud's thought, then, is in one sense wholly 'aesthetic', all to do with the theatre of sensational life. If it is the motions of pleasure and unpleasure which bring an objective world about in the first place, then all of our non-aesthetic relations with that world will continue to be saturated with this originary hedonism. Yet this hedonism, bound up as it is with egoism and murderous aggressivity, has lost all of the innocuousness of classical aesthetic pleasure, which was a respite from such base impulses rather than a product of them. Freud returns to this harmlessly defused pleasure its harsh unpleasurability, its rancour, sadism and malice, its negativity and perversity. The aesthetic attitude, he believes, may compensate for the sufferings of existence, but cannot protect us from them; if the aesthetic is conceived of as plenitude and equipoise, as a wealth of fulfilled powers, then few thinkers since Jonathan Swift have been more sceptical of such an ideal. The pleasure principle dominates the mental apparatus from start to finish, and yet is at loggerheads with the whole world; there is not the least possibility of its programme being carried through, for the intention that humanity should be happy was omitted from the plan of creation. Freud's bleak Hobbesian view of human society forbids him from envisaging it as a potentially nourishing space, or from imagining morality as emancipatory rather than oppressive; and he is thus as far as Hobbes himself from the vision of a Shaftesbury, Schiller or Marx, of a social order in which the realization of human capacities could become a delightful end in itself. In this sense he is a radical anti-aesthetician, with scant sympathy, in the words of Paul Ricoeur, 'for what might be described as an esthetic world view'.[8] Or perhaps it might be more accurate to characterize Freud as a thinker who, while inheriting something of that great tide of aestheticizing thought which we have followed throughout the nineteenth century, receives this legacy in deeply pessimistic spirit, as a heritage gone sour. There can be no returning to purely rationalist concepts, for the aesthetic has done its subversive work; but there can be little hope or joy in this aestheticizing alternative either, for a Freud as opposed to a Nietzsche or a Heidegger. If Freud remains a rationalist, though like Swift one with a profound suspicion of reason, it is among other reasons because he is dry-eyed and hard-headed enough to acknowledge the odious corollaries of that heady celebration of instinct, intuition and spontaneity of which the aestheticizing lineage, at its most callow, must stand convicted. It was, indeed, one particular historical terminus of such thought which drove him into exile.

There is a story, which Freud might have appreciated, of Moses descending Mount Sinai with the tablets of the law under his arm. 'I've got them down to ten', he shouts to the assembled Israelites, 'but adultery's still in.'

Freud regarded the law as one of his oldest enemies, and much of his therapeutic project is devoted towards tempering its sadistic brutality, which plunges men and women into madness and despair. The law for Freud is not of course *only* an enemy, since in his view to fall outside its sway is to fall sick; but it has an intemperate violence that must be countered. This law or superego, on at least one of Freud's accounts, is simply a differentiation of the id, whereby some of the voracious energy of the latter is channelled and diverted into a remorseless violence against the ego. The superego has its origin in what Freud describes in *The Ego and the Id* as an individual's first and most important identification, that with the father of his or her own personal prehistory.[9] As a result of this identification, which is prior to any object-cathexis, one part of the ego is set over against the other, to become moral ideal, voice of conscience and censorious judge. The superego is born of a splitting of the ego induced by the action of the id upon it. As an internalization of the parental prohibition, the superego is the heir to the Oedipus complex, a kind of hangover of this lurid drama; indeed it plays a decisive role in the repression of the complex, as the male child's hostility to the father modulates into an identification with his symbolic role. The superego is thus a residue of the earliest object-choices of the id; but it also represents what Freud calls an 'energetic reaction-formation' against those choices, and so springs to birth under the sign of contradiction. Exhorting the child to be like its father on the one hand, it bans it from some of the father's most enviable activities on the other. The superego is thus a kind of aporia or impossibility, a conundrum or double-bind whose commandments are incapable of being obeyed.[10] Since it is the heir to the Oedipus complex, it is therefore, as Freud argues, 'also the expression of the most powerful impulses and most important libidinal vicissitudes of the id',[11] closer to the unconscious than is the ego. In the act of mastering the Oedipus complex, then, the ego succeeds in handing itself submissively over to the id, or more exactly to that representative of the id which the superego signifies.

All of this lends the law a frightening power. The superego is as forceful as it is because it is the consequence of the first identification, which took place when the ego itself was still feeble; and because it springs out of the Oedipus complex it 'has thus introduced the most momentous objects into the ego'.[12] It is the source of all idealism, but also of all our guilt; it is at once high priest and police agent, positive and negative, the image of the desirable and the promulgator of taboos and prohibitions. As the voice of conscience it has its root in the castration threat, and is responsible for all our self-odium and self-scourging, of which Freud drily remarks that the 'normal man' is not only far more immoral, but far more moral, than he knows. This inexorable law directs what Freud calls an 'extraordinary harshness and severity' upon the timorous ego, raging against it with merciless violence; and in the condition of melancholia, or acute depression, this violence can result in the ego's extinction by suicide.[13] It is in these circumstances in particular that some of the ferocious energy of the superego can be unmasked for what it is – as nothing less, so Freud comments, than 'a pure culture of the death instinct', which it has caught up and turned to its own predatory purposes.

The superego is not only self-contradictory, but in a certain sense self-undoing. Freud posits in human beings both a primary narcissism and a primary aggressiveness; and the construction of civilization involves a sublimation of both, directing them outwards to higher goals. Part of our primary aggressiveness is thus diverted from the ego and fused with *Eros*, builder of cities, to dominate Nature and create a culture. The death drive, which lurks within our aggressivity, is thus tricked out of its nefarious intentions and harnessed to the business of establishing a social order. But this social order inevitably entails a renunciation of instinctual gratification; so that part of our aggressiveness is driven back upon the ego to become the agency of the superego, source of the law, morality and idealism essential to the operations of society. The paradox, then, is that the more civilized we become, the more we tear ourselves apart with guilt and internal aggression. Every renunciation of instinctual satisfaction strengthens the authority of the superego, intensifies its brutality and so deepens our guilt. The more admirably idealist we grow, the more we stoke up within ourselves a culture of lethal self-hatred. Moreover, the more we direct outwards part of our narcissistic libido for the construction of civilization, the more depleted we leave its internal resources, to become a prey to *Eros's* old antagonist, *Thanatos* or the death drive. Identification with the father involves a sublimation, and so a desexualization, of our erotic drives, which in Freud's stringent economy of the unconscious leaves them fatally defused and so all the less capable of holding out against their great antagonist.

It is in this sense that civilization for Freud is peculiarly self-thwarting. The superego is a deeply ambivalent formation, at once expressive of the id and a reaction-formation against it, deriving from the energy of the Oedipus complex yet turning back repressively against it. In a grim irony, it harnesses something of the id's own rabidly amoral forces to a campaign for social idealism and moral purity. To fight the id, to repress instinct, is to become all the more vulnerable to its destructiveness in a different guise; so that the ego is caught up from the outset in something of a mug's game, hedged round on all sides by mortal enemies, pulling off what poor bargains it can between them. The internal complexity of the superego, however, extends further still. For if it is at one level the product of an introjected external authority, it is at another level caught up with the ego's own primary aggressiveness towards itself – with that lethal masochism which Freud came to see in his later work as more fundamental than sadism. As Freud puts it: 'The sadism of the super-ego and the masochism of the ego supplement each other and unite to produce the same effects.'[14] If the superego is thus a peculiarly overdetermined phenomenon, it is so in another sense too. For the hostility which it unleashes upon the ego is at once that of the introjected parental function, and the child's own aggressive reaction to this agency. It is as though the child hijacks something of the parent's severity, fuses it with its own hostile reaction to such harshness, and turns both against its own ego. As Leo Bersani has put it: 'The child will ingeniously identify with that [parental] authority, not in order to continue its punishments internally, but rather in order to safely possess it, on the inside, as the object or victim of its own aggressive impulses.'[15] The superego, in short, has all the vengefulness which the child would like to direct against the punitive father; 'the curbing of aggressiveness', as Bersani comments, 'offers

271

the only realistic strategy for satisfying aggressiveness.'[16] The superego thus represents a kind of contradiction between past and present, infantilism and maturity: at the very moment that it shows us the path towards an ideal humanity, it pulls us inexorably back into childhood. 'Through the institutionalisation of the superego', writes Norman O. Brown, 'the parents are internalised and man finally succeeds in becoming father of himself, but at the cost of becoming his own child and keeping his ego infantile.'[17]

Freud's most subversive move, throughout the whole of this discourse, is to reveal the law itself as grounded in desire. The law is no more than a modality or differentiation of the id; and it can therefore no longer be a matter, as with traditional idealist thought, of envisaging a transcendental order of authority unscathed by libidinal impulse. On the contrary, this eminently rational power stands unmasked in Freud's writing as irrational to the point of insanity – as cruel, vengeful, vindictive, malicious, vain and paranoid in its authority, madly excessive in its tyrannical demands. Like the political state in the eyes of Marxism, the law would appear augustly transcendental but is in fact the sublimation of appetite, 'interested' to its roots while preserving a facade of impartial judiciousness. It is void of all realism, obtusely blind to what the ego might reasonably endure and what injunctions are simply beyond its fragile powers. 'Kant', writes Paul Ricoeur, 'spoke of the pathology of desire; Freud speaks of the pathology of duty.'[18] Indeed Freud remarks explicitly in 'The Economic Problem of Masochism' that the Kantian categorical imperative is the direct heir of the Oedipus complex. The law is a form of high-minded terrorism, which like the Mosaic code in the judgement of St Paul will merely illuminate how far short of it we have fallen, instruct us in what to avoid but give us no pedagogical aid in how to achieve the ideals it brandishes before us. As far as the prohibitory aspects of the superego are concerned, Freud would no doubt have sympathized with W. H. Auden's crack about the uselessness of a moral law which simply observes human nature and then inserts a 'Not'. Morality as we have it is a condition of permanent self-alienation; every human subject is colonized by a foreign master, a fifth columnist within the self.

The Freudian superego thus corresponds to that form of political coercion which we have contrasted in this study with the concept of hegemony. It represents that absolutist, crudely uneducative Reason

272

which for a Schiller was in dire need of some sensuous tempering. It is a form of political power appropriate to the *ancien régime,* an imperious ruler with no regard to the feelings and capacities of his subjects. The superego, as Freud remarks, 'does not trouble itself enough about the facts of the mental constitution of human beings. It issues a command and does not ask whether it is possible for people to obey it.'[19] It has all the arrogance of power but none of its craftiness, bereft of all strategic sense and psychological insight. The question, then, is how this uncouth despotism is to become hegemonized; and we shall see in a moment what answer Freud gives to this problem.

Meanwhile, it is worth noting that the fact that power has its basis in desire delivers an ambivalent political message. There is no doubt, to begin with, that it is this which renders the Freudian law as potent as it is. One reason why repressive political regimes are as tenacious and refractory as they are would be in Freud's view because they are secretly fuelled by implacable desire, characterized by all the purblind recalcitrance of the unconscious. And this is doubtless one reason among several why they are so difficult to dislodge. A power structure held together by nothing but rational consensus or conscious manipulation would be far easier to topple. If Freud is to be believed, late capitalist society sustains its rule not only by police forces and ideological apparatuses, but by raiding the resources of the death drive, the Oedipus complex and primary aggressivity. On this theory, it is because such regimes are able to tap into the very energies involved in the turbulent constitution of the human subject that they appear at times to have all the obdurate resistance to upheaval of a mountain range. The forces which sustain authority, in short, are compulsive and pathological, and will resist transformation as stubbornly as an analysand will repeat rather than remember. Civilization reproduces itself by cornering the currents of the id in order to outflank it, flexing those drives back upon themselves through the relay of a portion of the ego in a repression every bit as intemperate as the life of the unconscious itself.

That desire and the law are bedfellows as much as sworn foes can be formulated in a number of ways. The law, as we have seen, is itself desirous; it was through the law, in the shape of the originary prohibition, that desire came into the world; and it is in the nature of taboos to intensify the longings they forbid, exciting the very

273

concupiscence they frown on. This recognition, of the mutual imbrication of law and desire, has served in our own time to license a certain fashionable political pessimism; and it is surely true that no mere expression/repression model, of the kind adopted at least in part by Marx, can survive the Freudian account unscathed. If the law and desire are born at a stroke, then there can be no question of positing an intrinsically creative desire which is merely stifled in its expressiveness by a recalcitrant external power. But it is also possible to view this grim condition from another angle. If the law really were transcendentally disinterested, then the political left would most certainly be in trouble. That the law is not, ideologically speaking, how it would like to present itself is at once political obstacle and opportunity. If its grounding in desire is what deepens its virulence, it is also what renders it precarious and problematic, as a genuinely transcendental authority would not be. Marked by the sign of castration, concealing its lack beneath its logocentrism, the law has something of the instability of the unconscious as well as of its drivenness. The very excess of its zeal is the chink in its armour – not only because it signifies the brash authoritarianism of the insecure, but because it involves the law in a ceaseless self-undoing, arousing the yearnings it interdicts, spreading havoc in the name of creating order. The law is out of hand, and if its decrees become insupportable then it leaves its victims with no choice but to fall ill of neurosis or to rebel. Both courses of action have their ambiguous pains and pleasures. It was such rebellion which Freud had in mind when he wrote in *The Future of an Illusion* that if a society fails to develop beyond the point where the satisfaction of a minority depends upon the suppression of the majority, it 'neither has nor deserves the prospect of a lasting existence'.[20] In such conditions, Freud adds, one cannot expect an internalization of cultural prohibitions to take place among the oppressed – which is to say that political power would cease to be hegemonic.

If there is ambivalence in the law, a similar doubleness can be seen to lie on the side of those who languish beneath its sway. The real enemy of the political radical is less the mega-dollar than masochism – the condition in which we come to love and desire the law itself. If the superego stems from an introjection of the father, then it bears within it the child's love for that father as much as its enmity. Freud connects the ego's desire for punishment with the wish to be beaten by the father,[21] an 'erotogenic' masochism which joins with our 'moral' masochism. This psychical state is as deep-seated as it is because tenderness and respect for authority are part of the earliest manifestations of love, prior to the emergence of sexuality itself. 'By nature (that is, originally)', writes Philip Rieff, 'love is authoritarian; sexuality – like liberty – is a later achievement, always in danger of being overwhelmed by our deeper inclinations towards submissiveness and domination.'[22] Indeed Leo Bersani goes so far as to find in masochism the very 'essence' of sexuality, whose well-nigh shattering effects on the ego would be unendurable without such perverse gratification.[23] Jean Laplanche, similarly, speaks of 'the privileged role of masochism in human sexuality'.[24] Yet there is no love without ambivalence, and this respect for privileged figures is opposed in the unconscious by intensely hostile feelings towards them. Our sense of dependency on others, after all, is bound to wound our narcissistic fantasies of omnipotence, the consoling creed that we sprang fully fledged from our own loins. If the self craves its own confinement, then, it also reaps delight from seeing its gaolers brought low – even if the result of this, in an unceasing dialectic, is guilt, further submissiveness, and yet more pleasure in dethroning the despot.

The Freudian conception of law and desire would thus seem to defeat traditional political notions of coercion and hegemony. As a kind of absolutist monarch, the tyrannical superego is so cruelly unrelenting that one would expect it inevitably to instigate revolt. But what makes it as implacable as it is – its intimacy with the id – is exactly what binds us libidinally to it, thus tightening its grip. In a striking paradox, what sustains the law's coerciveness is exactly what secures its hegemony. As Freud argues about social conflict, 'the suppressed classes can be emotionally attached to their masters; in spite of their hostility to them they may see in them their ideals; unless such relations of a fundamentally satisfying kind subsisted, it would be impossible to understand how a number of civilizations have survived so long in spite of the justifiable hostility of large human masses.'[25] The transition which Freud outlines, from an external parental agency to that introjection of it which is the superego, is parallel to the political shift from absolutism to hegemony, where the latter is understood as an internalization of the law as the principle of one's own being. Yet in Freud's scenario this transition would hardly seem to temper the law's rigours at all; on the contrary, as he remarks

275

in *Civilisation and its Discontents*, it ushers in a state of 'permanent internal unhappiness', as we eagerly collude in our own misery. We renounce a heteronomous authority for fear of its violence; but we then install it securely inside us, and renounce instinctual gratification for fear of *it*. In one sense, this signifies an even deeper subjection; for this internal conscience, unlike the actual father, is omniscient, knows our faintest unconscious wishes, and will discipline us for these as well as for our actual conduct. Moreover, unlike any reasonable father, it punishes us the more we obey it. If we refrain from aggression, it simply takes over this bit of unacted violence and turns it against us. We do indeed, in hegemonic fashion, take pleasure in the law; but this deepens its despotism rather than renders its burdens sweet.

In *Totem and Taboo*, Freud offers a phylogenetic account of the transition from coercion to hegemony, to match this ontogenetic one. Civilization cannot be properly founded until the arbitrary will of the patriarchal despot is curtailed; and this is achieved by his death at the hands of the tribal horde of sons, who give the law to themselves and thus establish the bonds of community. Coercion remains, both in the form of the internalized dead father and in the necessity of work; all societies, Freud comments in Marxian vein, have at root an economic motive.[26] But if one of the ruling forces of social life is *Ananke* (necessity or coercion), the other is *Eros*, which is a matter of hegemony. *Eros* acts as the cement of social relations, rendering them libidinally gratifying and so providing the 'aesthetic' as opposed to the objectively material foundation of social unity. Civilization, Freud writes,

> aims at binding the members of the community together in a libidinal way as well and employs every means to that end. It favours every path by which strong identifications can be established between the members of the community, and so it summons up aim-inhibited libido on the largest scale so as to strengthen the communal bonds by relations of friendship. In order for these aims to be fulfilled, a restriction upon sexual life is unavoidable.[27]

If this is what sustains society, however, it is also the nub of the problem. For sexual desire and aggressiveness will conflict with these

276

social goals; civilization will threaten love; and the more *Eros* is sublimated to these worthy ends, the more vulnerable it becomes to *Thanatos*. Only a minority of men and women will be capable of effective sublimation; the masses, for Freud as for Burke, must make do with the coerced sublimation of manual work, which is never very effective. Sublimination would seem the only path by which the claims of the ego can be met without repression – but it is a precarious, unsatisfactory affair. The process of hegemony, in short, is both partial and self-undoing: what holds society together is just what is in danger of tearing it apart.

Conventional aesthetic thought, as we have seen, imagines the introjection of a transcendental law by the desiring subject. Freud's doctrine, however, deeply complicates this paradigm: for both terms in the equation are now divided, ambiguous, unstable, mutually parasitic. It is no longer a question of imprinting a benignant law upon 'sensibility', but of bringing to bear an impossibly self-contradictory power on a body which is itself hollowed and divided. We have seen that the apparently august law is not quite what it appears to be; but we must also recognize that desire itself, which seems so much more personal and immediate than the law's anonymous decrees, is itself a kind of impersonal force.

Desire, in Jacques Lacan's famous slogan, is the desire of the Other. To desire another is to desire what that other desires, since this desire is of the other's 'essence', and only by identifying with it can we therefore become one with the other. This is a paradoxical claim, however, since desire, which splits and disperses the subject, is no kind of essence at all; so that to desire the other's desire is to be as extrinsic to them as they are to themselves, caught up in the process of their own decentrement. Desire never hits its target: it becomes entangled in the other's lack and veers off beyond them. Desire curves around the body of the other to rejoin itself, now doubly lacking since it has reduplicated its own yearning in the yearning of the other. To identify with the other is to merge with what they lack, and thus in a sense to identify with nothing.

The child does not desire the mother, but desires what she desires, or at least what it imagines her to desire, which is the imaginary plenitude *it* desires. In striving to figure this plenitude for the mother, to represent for her the imaginary phallus, the child discovers that it

277

cannot succeed – that the mother's desire swerves away beyond the child and outwards. It is not the child that women desire. It is this recognition which introduces lack into the child, reduplicating the lack of the mother; the child lacks because what the mother lacks is not him. The intervention of the castrating law or Name of the Father then converts the child's lack from a specific one – his inadequacy *vis-à-vis* the mother – to a general one: with the repression of desire into the unconscious the child is now lacking not just in a particular way but in general, in excess of all particular objects. The cutting stroke of the law generalizes the child's lack to the very basis of its being.

Plunged into Oedipal crisis, the child may not be able to name his lack, but he can at least misname it. If the mother does not desire him, it must be because she desires the father. But women do not desire the man, any more than they desire the child. The woman desires not the penis but the phallus, which is to say her own imaginary wholeness. But the phallus is an imposture which does not exist, other than as an ideological figment. Having vainly sought for it in the mother's body, the child imagines that the father must possess it instead. In doing so, he mystifies the law to an imaginary plenitude, and seeks to identify with this instead as the path to his own fulfilment. The mother may be castrated, but surely the law cannot be. Perhaps the fetish of the law will block off the terrible knowledge of castration. But the law, too, is an ideological figment, and is mad with the same desire as the child. If the child misrecognizes the law, the law equally misrecognizes the child; for the child's desire is not exactly for the mother, but for the completion she symbolizes, for the imaginary phallus it deludedly locates in her body. None of these individuals desire each other in the least; it's nothing personal. Desire is purely impersonal, a process or network without end or origin in which all three protagonists are caught up, yet which stems from none of them and has none of them as its goal. The three bodies in this scenario desire past each other all the time, converging only in the field of the Other. The child plugs into the mother's desire in the vain hope that it too might thereby uncover the phallus it imagines her to want. If the child cannot be the phallus for her, it can at least join her in the ceaseless pursuit of it, thus staying with her in one sense while abandoning her in another. An identification with the mother's desire is one which leads the child beyond her, separates it from her. The child rides out beyond the mother on the current of her own desire.

The one I love may not be able to give me the imaginary plenitude I seek, but she can at least give me the most real thing she has, namely her own desire for the same plenitude. We give each other our desire, which is to say exactly that which neither of us can fulfil in the other. To say 'I love you' thus becomes equivalent to saying 'It's *you* who can't satisfy me!' How privileged and unique I must be, to remind you that it isn't me you want . . .

Desire itself, then, would seem to operate in something of an anonymous, law-like manner; and this further complicates the classical aesthetic model, where desire is generally conceived of in terms of individual needs or wishes. The truth is that Freud rejects all notion of a 'successful' introjection of the law, and this is one of his most radical challenges to the tradition of thought we have examined. It is true that he speaks of a final dissolution of the Oedipus complex; but it is doubtful how accurate such a claim is to some of his own most troubling insights. The ego will never entirely make the superego its own; it will be embroiled instead in a constant series of fatiguing trade-offs or tactical negotiations between these ideals and ukases, and the harsh reality (of both id and external world) which they catastrophically fail to take into account. The political implications of this are once more ambivalent. If Freud is right, then we can say goodbye to all possibility of utopia. The aesthetic ideal of a benign law fully internalized and appropriated as the ground of human freedom is an illusion. For one thing, the law is not in Freud's eyes benign; and for another thing such spontaneous appropriation is forestalled by our profoundly ambivalent response to it. At the same time, however, we can say goodbye to the dystopian vision of a 'total' social order which will have wholly incorporated its members, identifying their desires entirely with its rule. Such a prospect remembers only our masochistic love for the law, not our smouldering hatred of it. The law is what brings desire into being; but that desire constantly offers to outrun and disrupt it, and the lack which the law introduces into the subject is the very dynamic of this process. 'In the struggle between law and impulse', writes Philip Rieff, 'there can be neither victory nor defeat.'[28] We will never rest easy under the law, which politically speaking is both loss and gain. For some law is indeed benign, protects us from injury and creates the conditions for community between us; and the fact that in Freud's view we will

279

continue to resent the constraints of even such enlightened law poses a serious political problem. Our ability spontaneously to introject such a power, however, would also be our readiness to find in fascist dictatorship the path to unique personal fulfilment. Many individuals, of course, have done precisely that; but if Freud is to be believed it is not a condition which can be sustained without severe conflict.

Freud holds that women, for reasons associated with their particular Oedipal development, are less marked by the superego than men, and writes scornfully of their scant capacity for instinctual renunciation. There is, perhaps, some truth in this sexist comment. The historical evidence would seem to suggest that women are on the whole less likely than men to come under the thrall of transcendental signifiers, to be hypnotized by flag and fatherland, to spout of patriotism or march bravely forward into the future shouting 'Long live Life!' The reasons for this are no doubt a good deal more historical than psychical: women have not generally been in a position to engage in such activities. Yet it may be true, even so, that these social factors interact with certain psychic structures, to render women in general more oblique to the symbolic order, more sceptical of authority and more inclined than men to perceive its clay feet. Because of their social conditions, but also perhaps because of their unconscious relations to their own bodies, women are arguably more 'spontaneously materialist' than men, who, more deeply marked by the phallus, would seem chronically inclined to abstract idealism. The phallus, as Jacqueline Rose has argued, is in any case a 'fraud';[29] but there may be psychological as well as historical reasons why women are somewhat quicker than men to spot this at the level of social and political life, and so to be less easily duped by the arrogance of power.

Much of the point of psychoanalytic practice is to combat the superego's insane lack of realism, to persuade it to lay down some of its more overbearing demands, or at least to make its burden more tolerable. Such treatment must try to make the superego more tolerant and rational, to deflate its false idealism and undermine its Pharisaical pretensions. In this process, the role of the analyst, as a figure of authority who is nevertheless forbearing and non-censorious, and who withdraws as far as possible from any libidinal involvement with the analysand, is of key importance. The analyst must try to educate the patient's desire away from its regressive subjection to parental authority, releasing it for more egalitarian relationships.

Since reverence for the parent is our earliest form of identification, this shift is bound to be painful and partial. Perhaps the most we can hope for, in Freud's eyes, is to establish some *modus vivendi* with the sublime wrath of the superego, negotiating what more creative relationships we can within this forbidding framework. Psychoanalytic practice is concerned to wean us away from battles we cannot hope to win, persuade us out of our doomed *agon* with the dead so as to free those arrested energies for other ends. Of those ends themselves, Freudianism, like Marxism, has little prescriptive to say; Freud joins Marx in attempting to shift us, this time at an individual level, from pre-history to history proper, resolving those conflicts which lock us into the past. When this has been achieved – when the 'talking cure' has run its course and we are more free to determine our own future history on the basis of a revised narrative of the past – the scene of analysis, like revolutionary political practice, will wither away. In both cases, however, it is only by recollecting the terrors of the past (what Walter Benjamin would call the tradition of the oppressed) that we can emancipate ourselves from them. Capitalist society, centred on the eternal repetition of the commodity, neurotically represses the terrible truth that there was a time when it never was, in that gesture of self-delusion known as ideology.

What is involved in the scene of analysis, to put the issue in political terms, is a gradual transition from the absolutist monarch of the superego to what Freud called the 'constitutional monarch' of the ego. The ego is the terrain on which law and desire conduct their frightful warfare, but always in a fraught, unstable, contradictory alliance. Within the person of the patient, absolutist power must undergo the kind of 'aesthetic' transformation which Friedrich Schiller called for, become more responsive to the sensuous needs and wishes of the subject. For Schiller, this was to be achieved by a fruitful interpenetration of law and desire, as formal and sensual principles soften eath other's importunity in the moment of art or play. Freud has no such utopian hope; but this, one might claim, is politically all to the good. If the scene of analysis fosters a certain realistic acceptance of the truth that we can never slay the father, it also breeds a degree of critical scepticism of his exorbitant exactions. It is a question of neither denying nor appropriating the law, but of nurturing an ambivalence towards it more creative than that infantile ambivalence which causes us pain.

Freud's story of the superego is a tragic narrative, in more senses than one. The superego is responsible for inflicting upon us grotesque suffering; but it also has the implacable high-mindedness of all tragic art, an heroic mode associated with aristocratic absolutism and ascetic self-renunciation. What can be pitted against this remorseless purity is then comedy – a more tolerant, ironic, debunking form, inherently materialist and anti-heroic, which rejoices in human frailty and imperfection, wryly concedes that all ideals are flawed, and refuses to demand too much of individuals so as to avoid falling into contemptuous disillusionment. All idealism is double-edged, spurring us productively onwards while rubbing our noses in our inadequacies. Whoever dreams of a pure revolution, remarked Vladimir Lenin, will never live to see one. Comedy, like William Empson's pastoral, pays its dues to the edifying values of truth, virtue and beauty, but understands how not to permit these admirable goals to terrorize humankind, to the point where people's weaknesses become painful to them and their self-esteem dwindles to nothing. Comedy and pastoral celebrate what individuals share in common beneath the skin, and proclaim that this is ultimately more significant than what divides them. One reason why political radicals may justifiably resent our present social system is that it forces us to pay an inordinate amount of attention to divisions of class, race and gender, which are not in the end all that important. It binds our energies ineluctably to these currently vital concerns, rather than freeing them for more rewarding purposes. Comedy's mocking denigration of what divides us is often enough a reactionary mystification; but there is also about it, as Christopher Norris writes of Empson's 'complex words', 'a down-to-earth quality of healthy scepticism which . . . permits [us] to build up a trust in human nature on a shared knowledge of its needs and attendant weaknesses'.[30] Freud had little trust in human nature, and some of the jokes he tells are execrable; but he knew like Marx and Empson that no compassion for humanity which does not found itself upon a full look at the worst can be anything other than romantic sentimentalism. For all Freud's grim disenchantment, his pity for the plight of the ego, booted as it is between id, superego and external world, is not far from the spirit of comedy. What he failed to attain was the dialectical vision of his fellow victim of Nazism Bertolt Brecht, who manages as a Marxist comedian to combine an extraordinarily sensitive nose for the imperfect, unfinished state of human affairs with the most resolute revolutionary commitment. In an epoch like our own, when these two options have become increasingly polarized and exclusive, Brecht offers a not inconsiderable lesson.

None of Freud's psychoanalytic thought is finally separable from his politics. Whatever his devoted crusade against the superego, he is politically speaking a pessimistic conservative authoritarian, full of petty-bourgeois banalities about the insensate hysteria of the masses, the chronic indolence and stupidity of the working class and the need for strong charismatic leadership.[31] When Freud turns to directly political themes, a notable coarsening of his intelligence sets in; like many a bourgeois intellectual, his ideological obtusenesses are at war with his native wit. If Freud had lived through a different, more hopeful political history, much in his theoretical doctrine would no doubt have been transformed. He has little sense of morality as anything but repression; morality for him is on the whole less a matter of virtue, in the Aristotelian or Marxist sense of the quality of a whole style of living, than a set of leaden injunctions. His negative, drastically impoverished view of human society valuably demystifies romantic idealism to the precise extent that it reproduces the shop-soiled platitudes of the market place, where man is a wolf to man. He can see nothing in the Christian commandment to love all of one's neighbours than yet another overweening imperative of the superego; as far as Freud is concerned, there just isn't that much libido to go around. He holds, for example, that to love everyone involves an intellectually suicidal suspension of judgement upon them, which is no part of the Christian doctrine. As the Duke remarks to Lucio in *Measure for Measure:* 'Love talks with better knowledge, and knowledge with dearer love.' The Christian commandment to love others has little to do with libidinal cathexis, with the warm glow or the song in the heart. To love the Soviets, for example, means refusing even to consider incinerating them, even if the consequence of this is being incinerated by them ourselves. Simply to contemplate such a course of action, let alone energetically prepare for it, is morally wicked, a form of behaviour incompatible with love. It is absolutely wrong to prepare to commit genocide, the term 'absolute' here meaning wrong irrespective of any concrete historical circumstances which could be stipulated as a justificatory context for such an action. One does not need to find individual Soviets erotically attractive to subscribe to this view. If Freud alerts us to the deep relations between *Eros* and *agape*, he considers the notion of love too much in the context of the former.

Whatever his strictures on the Christian injunction, Freud certainly believes love to travel right back to the beginnings of subjective life, and sees in it one of the foundations of human civilization. Psychoanalytic practice, as Julia Kristeva has argued, is itself a form of loving;[32] and indeed for Freud love lies at the source of all our psychical dilemmas. It is because we are all 'prematurely' born that we require an unusually extended period of material and emotional care from our parental figures; and it is within this biologically essential intimacy that sexuality begins to germinate. The paradoxes of law and desire have their origin here: the fact that we are helpless and protected allows the pleasure principle untrammelled sway, as the preliminary stage of what will later become desire; but the same fact makes us wholly dependent on our parental figures, and so brings us from the very outset into a profound submission to authority. It is these two forces – what Paul Ricoeur calls 'the history of desire in its great debate with authority',[33] which will wage their deadly warfare, chase each other's tails, collude and collide on the battleground which is our bodies. But this potential catastrophe could never have occurred had we not been cared for as infants, had love not been in place, ready and waiting for us, from the very beginning. The playwright Edward Bond speaks movingly in his preface to *Lear* of the 'biological expectations' with which we are born – the expectation that the baby's 'unpreparedness will be cared for, that it will be given not only food but emotional reassurance, that its vulnerability will be shielded, that it will be born into a world waiting to receive it, and that knows *how* to receive it'.[34] This, Bond suggests, would signify a true 'culture' – which is why he refuses the term to contemporary capitalist civilization. Bond is surely right to claim that we have created a world which does not know how to receive its new members. If it understands how to warm their milk and mash their food, it is at a loss to know how to shelter them from the possibility of nuclear destruction, or from the abrasive, uncaring relations which increasingly characterize our way of life. Bond sees that we have, so to speak, a 'right' to culture, in a normative sense of that term, by virtue of our biological structure, for that structure is such that without culture we would quickly die. Human nature has an 'expectation' of culture built

284

into it, and to this degree certain kinds of values are entailed by certain sorts of facts. 'Culture' is at once a descriptive and evaluative concept: if it designates on the one hand that without which we are factually speaking unable to survive, it is also a qualitative index of the form of social life which really does shield the weak and welcome the stranger, allows us to thrive rather than simply subsist. There may here be the seeds of a political morality which has its roots in the body without being, in some naturalistic manner, reducible to it. What is most important about our biology is that it is structured around a gap or vacancy, where culture must implant itself. It is this kind of enquiry which is forestalled by the present culturalist overreaction to biologism.

As early as the *Project for a Scientific Psychology*, Freud was feeling his way towards such a theory:

> At early stages the human organism is incapable of achieving this specific action [of satisfaction]. It is brought about by extraneous help, when the attention of an experienced person has been drawn to the child's condition by a discharge . . . This path of discharge thus acquires an extremely important secondary function – viz., of bringing about an understanding with other people: and the original helplessness of human beings is thus the primal source of all moral motives.[35]

Before we have come to internalize the parental function, before the voice of conscience begins to whisper disapprovingly in our ear, the seeds of morality have already been planted, in that dialectic of demand and response between bodies which is our earliest experience, and from which sexuality is a kind of swerve or deviation. Morality has its origin not in the superego, but in the small infant's affectionate gratitude for the care of its elders. The political problem, for which Freud provides no ultimate solution, is that this affection must move within a context of biologically determined dependency, so that the infant's learning to love is inseparable both from a reverence for authority and from aggression. To acquire a more reciprocal, egalitarian style of loving is thus one of the goals of psychoanalysis, as it is of revolutionary politics.

Notes

1 Charles Levin, 'Art and the Sociological Ego: Value from a Psycho-analytic Perspective', in John Fekete (ed.), *Life After Postmodernism* (London, 1988), p. 22.
2 Sigmund Freud, *Civilisation, Society and Religion*, Pelican Freud Library, vol. 12 (Harmondsworth, 1985), p. 271.
3 William Empson, *Some Versions of Pastoral* (London, 1966), p. 114 (my emphasis).
4 Friedrich Nietzsche, *Beyond Good and Evil* (Harmondsworth, 1979), p. 40.
5 Fredric Jameson, *The Prison-House of Language* (Princeton, 1972), p. 108.
6 Paul Ricoeur, *Freud and Philosophy: An Essay on Interpretation* (New Haven and London, 1970), p. 382.
7 Juliet Mitchell and Jacqueline Rose (eds), *Feminine Sexuality: Jacques Lacan and the École Freudienne* (London, 1982), p. 6.
8 Ricoeur, *Freud and Philosophy*, p. 334.
9 See also Julia Kristeva, 'Freud and Love: Treatment and its Discontents', in Toril Moi (ed.), *The Kristeva Reader* (Oxford, 1986).
10 See Leo Bersani, *The Freudian Body* (New York, 1986), p. 97.
11 Sigmund Freud, *The Ego and the Id*, in *Sigmund Freud: On Metapsychology*, Pelican Freud Library, vol. 11 (Harmondsworth, 1984), p. 376.
12 Ibid, p. 389.
13 See Sigmund Freud, 'Mourning and Melancholia', in *Sigmund Freud: On Metapsychology*.
14 Ibid, p. 425.
15 Bersani, *The Freudian Body*, p. 22.
16 Ibid, p. 23.
17 Norman O. Brown, *Life Against Death* (London, 1968), p. 118.
18 Ricoeur, *Freud and Philosophy*, p. 185.
19 Sigmund Freud, *Civilisation and its Discontents*, in *Sigmund Freud: Civilisation, Society and Religion*, p. 337.
20 Sigmund Freud, *The Future of an Illusion*, in *Sigmund Freud: Civilisation, Society and Religion*, p. 192.
21 See Sigmund Freud, 'A Child Is Being Beaten', in *Sigmund Freud: On Psychopathology*, Pelican Freud Library, vol. 10 (Harmondsworth, 1979).
22 Philip Rieff, *Freud: The Mind of the Moralist* (Chicago and London, 1959), p. 159.
23 Bersani, *The Freudian Body*, pp. 39f.
24 Jean Laplanche, *Life and Death in Psychoanalysis* (Baltimore and London, 1976), p. 102.

25 Freud, *The Future of an Illusion*, in *Sigmund Freud: Civilisation, Society and Religion*, p. 193.

26 Sigmund Freud, *A General Introduction to Psychoanalysis* (New York, 1943), p. 273.

27 Freud, *Civilisation and its Discontents*, in *Sigmund Freud: Civilisation, Society and Religion*, p. 299.

28 Rieff, *Freud: The Mind of the Moralist*, p. 226.

29 Juliet Mitchell and Jacqueline Rose, *Feminine Sexuality*, p. 40.

30 Christopher Norris, *William Empson and the Philosophy of Literary Criticism* (London, 1978), p. 86.

31 See Sigmund Freud, *Group Psychology and the Analysis of the Ego*, in *Sigmund Freud: Civilisation, Society and Religion*.

32 Julia Kristeva, 'Freud and Love: Treatment and its Discontents', in Moi (ed.), *The Kristeva Reader*, p. 248.

33 Ricoeur, *Freud and Philosophy*, p. 179.

34 Edward Bond, *Lear* (London, 1972), p. viii. See also my essay 'Nature and Violence: the Prefaces of Edward Bond', in *Critical Quarterly*, vol. 26, nos. 1 and 2 (spring and summer, 1984).

35 Sigmund Freud, *Project for a Scientific Psychology*, in Ernst Kris (ed.), *The Origins of Psychoanalysis* (New York, 1954), p. 379.

11

The Politics of Being: Martin Heidegger

Consider what it is about any object that is at once constitutive of its being and quite hidden from view. To begin with, there is its temporality – the fact that what we see when we contemplate something is merely a kind of snapshot or frozen moment of the temporal process which goes to make up its true nature. Our dealings with things slice cross-sections into time, tearing objects away from the temporality which is of their essence and carving them into manageable synchronic chunks. If this is true of time, it is also true of space: no object ever swims into view other than against the background of some 'world', some dimly apprehended set of interlaced functions and locations. It is this network of perspectives and relations, weaving a thing through to its core, which provides the very matrix within which it becomes identifiable and intelligible. A 'world' is just the fact that there could never simply be one object – that any particular piece of reality, to be comprehensible at all, must be already caught up in a vast, sprawling web of elements to which it vaguely alludes, or (to alter the metaphor) must always be foregrounded against some horizon which is never entirely fixable by our gaze. A world is not some kind of spatial object like the things it contains, totalized and retotalized as it continually is by human practice; this is why for phenomenology it is strange to speak of the 'external' world, as though there could ever be a world in the first place without the human bodies which organize and sustain it. But this supportive context which makes possible the sighting of any particular thing is always itself elusive, fading into indeterminacy as the thing itself surges forward. It is what we squint at sideways in viewing something, rather than have directly in our sights. And it could never be grasped as a whole, trailing off as it does out of the corners of our vision, suggesting an infinity of possible connections beyond any actual horizon.

We can see something because it is present to us; but what we cannot usually see is what enabled this presentness in the first place. How does it come about that things are available to us, given over to our understanding? The objects we view and touch have a kind of implicit accessibility about them which, since it is not a material property like colour or volume, we can easily take for granted; but in doing so we erase the mystery of how things can come into our ken in any case, of what it is that makes them so radically encounterable. Not only encounterable, indeed, but intelligible, at least potentially, which one can imagine might not necessarily have been the case. What if the world were as desperately opaque to us as the impenetrable ocean of Stanislav Lem's *Solaris*, eluding the reach of our discourse and understanding? What if objects were just not the sort of thing we could readily have any comportment with, but appeared separated from us by some unbridgeable gulf? Is such speculation sheerly idle, or does it seem so only because we have succumbed to an amnesia by which we forget our astonishment at the simple ready-to-handness of reality, the fact that it is such that we can have regular dealings with it? And what is it that explains this fact? Is it enough to say that if we could not know the world we would not be here to know that we could not know it, since such knowledge is essential to our survival?

Finally, what we do not see in an object is that it might just as well never have been. As Leibniz famously enquires, why should there be anything at all, rather than just nothing? How come that this uniquely particular thing has replaced the nothingness that would otherwise have been there, a nothingness which in certain moments of boredom or anxiety we imagine that we can still get a glimpse of? Is it not astonishing that since nothing actually *needs* to exist, so many things should? And if objects are in this sense radically contingent, can they not be seen as in some way shot through with a sort of nothingness, however much their replete presences might seem to deny it? Would not things that actually had to exist, whose being was somehow necessary, be different from the random, replaceable bits and pieces we observe around us?

Such, whether as sublime insight or mystical raving, are some of the implications of what Martin Heidegger calls Being, in crude and

289

summary form. Any such bald account of course demands qualifying and developing: in *On Time and Being,* for example, Heidegger will deny that Being *is* temporal, though Being and time 'belong together' and reciprocally determine each other; and in the 'Conversation on a Country Path' he goes beyond the (still metaphysical) notion of a spatial horizon to the idea of a 'region' into which it opens. (As Heidegger pithily puts it in his all-too-imitable later manner, 'Regioning is a gathering and re-sheltering for an expanded resting in an abiding.')[1] If we can speak of Being at all, however, then at least for the early Heidegger it is because among the various entities in the world there is one in particular which, in the course of its self-realization, finds itself unavoidably raising the question of the fundamental nature of all other entities, along with itself. This 'thing' is *Dasein* – that peculiar mode of being whose essence takes the form of existence, and which lives itself most typically in and through the human. In actualizing its own possibilities, *Dasein* cannot help but make manifest the things around it, bringing them to articulation within its own enterprise; and this process, whereby *Dasein* allows the beings around it to be what they are, liberates them into self-disclosure, is for Heidegger the transcendence which opens up Being. The understanding this entails is by no means in the first place a matter of the concept – of a knowing subject confronting a knowable object which it can represent to itself. For *Dasein,* before arriving at any such cognition, finds itself always already in commerce with other things in ways which presuppose a certain primordial access to them, a practical orientation or familiarity which is already a kind of understanding before the event, and which lays the ontological foundation of all more formal knowing. To know something rationally or scientifically is dependent on some more basic availability of the thing to *Dasein*; and Being, in at least one of its various senses, is whatever it is which allows this *a priori* availability of objects to occur, that which has already handed them over to *Dasein* in a sort of pre-rational, pre-cognitive intimacy and recognition. One can think of truth in classical style as an adequation between mind and world, subject and object; but for any such correspondence to get set up a good deal must already have happened. Where did this subject and object come from, how did their very intelligibility arise, and from where do we derive the complicated procedures by which they might be somehow compared? Truth as propositional, Heidegger argues in

The Essence of Truth, must itself rely on some deeper uncovering of things, a letting of phenomena be in their presentness which is the effect of *Dasein*'s transcendence. For us to assert something presupposes a domain of 'openness' in which *Dasein* and the world have already encountered one another, have never not already encountered, were never separable in the first place. *Dasein* is that free drift of transcendence which finds itself constantly passing over from the sheer fact of other entities to the question of their very Being; and it is this transcendence which opens up what Heidegger calls the 'ontological difference' whereby we distinguish between beings and Being, understanding that the latter can never be exhausted by the former. It is as though *Dasein* locates itself in the division between the two, inserting itself there as a kind of gap, relation or 'in between'.

Being, then, is that 'clearing' or realm of encounter which is neither subject nor object but, as it were, the spontaneous availability of each to the other. If Being is what essentially determines something as it is, then the most basic feature of things, for the early Heidegger at least, is that they are able somehow to comport themselves with us long before we have achieved any determinate knowledge of them. Being is thus a response to the question: What must always already have taken place for our traffic with the world to be possible? *Dasein's* own peculiar being is to comprehend Being, to find itself always in the midst of understanding as the very medium of its practical projects. Since it is primarily Being-in-the-world it is a form of existence ineluctably referred to other things, and it is in this bound-upness with things that it brings them to self-disclosure.

There is an obvious parallel between this exotic style of thought and the transcendentalism of classical idealist philosophy. If Being is the very accessibility of objects in the first place, then it bears a clear relation to Kant's transcendental standpoint upon the world. But it also thereby bears a peculiar relation to the Kantian aesthetic, which as we have seen involves the mystery of how mind and world shape up to each other in some unspoken compact, as the basis of any particular act of cognition. Heidegger's celebrated concept of 'pre-understanding' – of the way in which, within the inescapable circularity of all interpretation, phenomena must be somehow already intuitively comprehensible in order to be known – harks back in this sense to Kant's aesthetic amazement that the world is the kind of

291

thing in general that can be understood. It is as though Heidegger has now thoroughly ontologized this aesthetic claim, so that Kant's aesthetic perception, which is yet to arrive at any definitive knowledge but is the permanent precondition of doing so, becomes in the concept of *Dasein* the persistent orientation of human existence to a mute familiarity with what surrounds it. In his work on Nietzsche, Heidegger defends the Kantian doctrine of aesthetic disinterestedness by translating it into the terms of his own thought: 'in order to find something beautiful', he argues, 'we must let what encounters us, purely as it is in itself, come before us in its own stature and worth . . . We must freely grant to what encounters us as such its way to be; we must allow and bestow upon it what belongs to it and what belongs to us.'[2] Kantian aesthetic disinterestedness thus becomes equivalent to Heideggerian Being, Kantian 'beauty' the coming forth of the object in all its ontological purity.

Human existence is thus for Heidegger 'aesthetic' in its most fundamental structures; and it is part of his criticism of Kant in *Kant and the Problem of Metaphysics* that he backs off from this subversive insight. For Kant, what mediates between sensibility and understanding is the transcendental imagination, which constructs the schemata that make all knowledge possible; it is this imagination which on Heidegger's reading of Kant 'forms in advance the aspect of the horizon of objectivity as such'.[3] The imagination is the common source of sensibility and understanding, and the root of practical reason as well. Kant has thus aestheticized the very grounds of knowledge, undermining the foundation of pure reason in the very act of laying it down; but he shies nervously away from the radicalism of his own move, loath to admit anything as lowly as the imagination (which is commonly coupled with sensibility) as the basis of reason itself. Heidegger himself will project that transcendence out of Kant's epistemological realm into the very ontology of *Dasein* itself, seeing in that the process by which *Dasein*'s routine truck with the world continually opens up a horizon within which the Being of beings becomes discernible prior to any cognitive engagement with them. If for Kant, however, the aesthetic is a kind of rounding upon or objectifying of our own cognitive capacities, no such objectification is fully possible for *Dasein*, given that radical temporality which brings it constantly to outrun or get ahead of itself.

There is in *Being and Time* an interesting tension between two different conceptions of the relations between *Dasein* and its world. On the one hand, the whole notion of *Dasein* as Being-in-the-world tends to question as a false metaphysical duality the very distinction between *Dasein* and world implicit in the term 'relation'. The world is not a space which *Dasein* is 'in', as ink is in a bottle; if it is of the very nature of *Dasein* to be wrapped up in reality, to be constituted through and through by what Heidegger calls its 'care', then existence as such trangresses any dichotomy between inner and outer, subject and object. The world is not 'external' to *Dasein*; on the contrary, there could be no 'world' without it, as opposed to some background of meaningless materiality. The world is a part or a project of *Dasein* quite as much as *Dasein* is always 'outside' itself, ec-static, constantly passing over beyond things in that movement of transcendence which opens up Being itself. As a kind of 'in between', yet nothing as substantive as a 'relation', *Dasein* (as the very term suggests) is a 'here' which is always also a 'there', always out ahead of itself, non-self-identical, and is thus no 'thing' to be inside another thing but a sheer process of going over. *Dasein* is dependent on reality, since to be bound up in it is of its very essence; and conversely the world is dependent on *Dasein*, if not for its existence (Heidegger is no subjective idealist) then for that significant self-disclosure which is its Being. If Being is that by which objects become present to *Dasein*, then there can be Being only as long as *Dasein* inrupts into the midst of things as a revelatory force. There can be no truth without *Dasein*, since Being and truth are simultaneous. *Dasein* and the world are thus correlatives of one another: if *Dasein*'s activity is necessary for there to be Being at all, then for the early Heidegger the world is centred upon *Dasein* as its ultimate reference point. *Dasein*, as Heidegger puts it, is the 'destination' of all other things, which wait mutely to be uncovered by it. Yet at the same time *Dasein* is 'referentially dependent'[4] on the things around it, in a way which prevents it from ever fully mastering them. What Heidegger calls its 'thrownness', its condition of simply finding itself propelled willy-nilly into the midst of reality, designates both its non-mastery of its own being and its reliance upon others. Just in order to exist in its own style, *Dasein*'s structure compels it to a persistent comprehension of the entities around it, projected as it is beyond any one of them towards the unattainable completeness of grasping the totality of beings as such. *Dasein* and the world, then, are centred upon one another in what one might loosely term an 'imaginary' relation: the latter cannot be made present without the former, just as one might speculate that the small infant finds it intolerable that reality could go on existing in its own absence.

Within this mutual complicity, at least for the early Heidegger of *Being and Time*, *Dasein* retains a certain ontological priority; and this betrays in the text the trace of a certain residual humanism, however much any simple identity between *Dasein* and humanity may be denied. That priority, indeed, is also a kind of cleavage between *Dasein* and its world, which provides the alternative version of the relation between them in the work. It is the tension between an 'authentic' *Dasein*, choosing its own most individual possibilities in a resolute living-towards-death, and that degraded world of prattle, idle curiosity and anonymous mass existence into which it keeps falling ('Prattle' (*Gerede*) signifies for Heidegger empty, rootless talk, such as 'Saying says sayingly what it says in its own saying', which could be a sentence from the later Heidegger). The very world which goes to constitute *Dasein* thus also poses a threat to it; and this can be read in part as a conflict between an ontological and a political sense of the term 'world'. As the realm of Being in general, the world is inseparable from *Dasein*'s very structure; as an actual social environment it is a considerably more bleak and alienating sphere, the place of the faceless '*das Man*' who confiscates one's authenticity. This discrepancy is regulated by being itself 'ontologized': inauthenticity, Heidegger grimly insists, is not only a permanent ontological possibility of *Dasein* but for the most part its most typical mode of being. 'Falling' into a degrading reality, tarnishing its purity in a set of aimless involvements in which Being is covered up and forgotten, is built into *Dasein*'s very nature, since as Being-in-the-world it realizes itself only through its wrapped-upness in things. The very source of its free self-actualization is thus also what contaminates it; it is unable to be itself without erring, incapable of recollecting its unitary being without first having forgotten it. Heidegger thus informs us that he does not intend his descriptions of *Dasein*'s inauthentic modes to be derogatory: they are part of its 'given' possibilities, without which it could not be what it is. This disclaimer is singularly unconvincing: these descriptions quite clearly *are* negative, enforcing a rigorous distinction between *Dasein* in its 'proper' and 'improper' conditions. The two states of being are held apart even as they mutually mark and implicate one another. On the one hand, *Dasein* is inseparable from its world; on the other hand it is something of a vagrant or alien in history, 'thrown' into reality in the first place as houseless and unprotected, and summoned beyond this dismal facticity into an authentic encounter with its own lonely finitude and death. In the crisis of resolution, *Dasein* chooses to be what it is, recognizes its possibilities as its own rather than as determined by the anonymous Other, and projects itself forward towards death in a movement of separation from and re-engagement with the objects of its concern. Such movement could be seen as a kind of rupturing of its 'imaginary' relations with the world – an entry into the 'symbolic order' whose structures are those of finitude, difference, individuation and death. When Heidegger is thinking in these terms, he tends to underline the apartness of *Dasein* as a form of self-referentiality: if all other essents find their destination in it, *Dasein* itself cannot be referred beyond itself but exists as its own end. Its peculiar mode of being is to be concerned about itself, even if this self-concern necessarily takes the form of an immersion in the world. Because it is essentially temporal, its working out of its own authentic 'destiny' takes the shape of being constantly out ahead of itself and to that extent non-self-identical, deflected from a brooding upon its own being by its enmeshment in reality. In a Hegelian move, however, such errancy is just the way *Dasein* ceaselessly returns to itself: the moment of 'anxiety', for instance, in which *Dasein* in the course of its mundane involvements suddenly glimpses the nullity of things, can be profoundly therapeutic, recalling it to its own inwardness away from what Heidegger describes as its 'captivation' by objects. *Being and Time* thus turns to a kind of advantage the very temporality which jeopardizes the integrity of *Dasein* with its spacings and diffusions; for this temporality is also the very medium of *Dasein's* 'anticipatory resoluteness', its unflinching orientation towards the future certainty of its own extinction. If *Dasein* can even now appropriate that future death, stark signifier of its finitude and contingency, 'retroject' it into its current existence, then it is able to bind and brace itself in this constant prolepsis. If it can embrace the contingency symbolized in its future death then it can somehow live that contingency as inner necessity; and in a similar way it can appropriate the pure givenness of its past (its 'thrownness') in order to be resolutely at every moment what it has been. This 'aesthetic' style of existence no longer simply abolishes time, reducing it to pure synchronicity in the manner of some earlier aesthetic thought; rather, it constructs from the stuff of a fallen history a more authentic mode of temporality, which has precious little to do with historicity in any received sense of the term. (Heidegger's 'authentic' history, Lukács comments in *Realism in Our Time*, is not distinguishable from ahistoricity.) It is from such 'primordial' temporality, indeed, that for Heidegger our everyday meanings of time and history are derived. *Dasein*, then, as a transfiguration of contingency into necessity, and of the facticity of life into an inwardly appropriated law, exhibits some of the features of the work of art.

Such an aestheticization, however, can only ever be partial. For we have seen already that *Dasein's* authenticity is inseparable from a certain errancy or untruth; and though it is in some sense self-referential, it can never become wholly totalized or self-determining. The rejection of such self-determination, which belongs to the transcendental subject, is the price Heidegger's thought has to pay for a refusal to 'subjectivize' *Dasein* in the manner of some anthropological humanism, which would simply be a perpetuation of metaphysical thought. The 'thrownness' of *Dasein* means that it can never be its own master, never mistake itself for the originary source of its own being. It is unfinished, dependent and in part self-opaque, unable to round upon its own process of constitution in a moment of utter self-transparency. To this extent, one might claim, *Dasein* is a non-aesthetic form of being, shot through with negativity, always eccentric to itself.

On the one hand, then, *Dasein* is continually 'captivated' *(eingenommen)* by other beings and reverberates in attunement with them, in some fundamental compact or alliance with the world which resembles Kant's aesthetic condition. On the other hand it is prior to and transcendent of that world, preserving its precarious authenticity by a ceaseless separation from it, as well as by a resolute engagement with it. If there are philosophical – and broadly political – reasons why it is no longer enough to imagine humanity as a solitary, self-enclosed subject confronting an inert object – if that now discredited form of transcendental subjectivity has been sharply decentred into material reality – then there are also good political reasons why this should not be thought to entail an uncritical celebration of 'worldliness'. Heidegger is deeply enough marked by Kierkegaard to write off the public sphere itself as inherently inauthentic: what in the early, affirmative days of bourgeois society was a realm of civilized social intercourse has now deteriorated to an alienated domain of administered processes and manipulated mass opinion. Monopoly capitalism has now penetrated into the bourgeois public sphere itself, reorganizing it in accordance with its own reificatory logic. But the monopoly capitalism which has dehumanized this public domain is also in the process of well and truly undermining the classical bourgeois conception of the free, self-determining individual; and this is one reason why Heidegger cannot espouse Kierkegaard's own alternative to '*das Man*', the intensely inward subject of spiritual faith. Or at least such inwardness must now be prised loose from the empirical individual and lifted into some ontological sphere (*Dasein*) which is, with suitable ambiguity, both a subject and not a subject. This effort to rethink traditional notions of subjectivity, and a patrician disdain for the public, both arise from a 'higher' capitalism which is eroding at once the liberal humanist subject and the civic space in which it has traditionally consorted with others of its kind. But the shared historical source of these twin doctrines in Heidegger cannot eradicate the tension between them. *Dasein* as an idea is at once a remorseless assault on the philosophy of the autonomous subject, capsizing that subject into the world in ec-static disunity with itself, and at the same time the latest in a long series of privileged, aestheticized, quasi-transcendental 'subjects' jealously protecting their integrity and autonomy from the taint of the quotidian. The two perspectives will enter into unholy alliance in Heidegger's later Nazism: the thrown, decentred subject will become the self humbly submissive to the earth, while authentic, self-referential *Dasein* will emerge as the elitist vocation of the *Herrenvolk* for the glorious self-sacrifice of death. Death, as Heidegger argues in *Being and Time*, is that which is absolutely one's own, non-relational and non-alienable, a kind of paradigm of private property which the faceless public 'they' can never steal. Death individualizes *Dasein* to its roots, tearing it away from all Being-with-others; and it is thus perhaps not surprising that such Being-with-others, supposedly an ontological structure of *Dasein*, receives relatively perfunctory treatment in *Being and Time*. Though Heidegger's capacity to derive mystified maxims from idealized peasant societies appears well-nigh inexhaustible, it is striking that *Gemeinschaft* – the organic community so favoured by the radical right – attracts somewhat scant attention in his nostalgic maunderings.

It could be claimed, then, that a central ideological dilemma of *Being and Time* is how to protect an essential subversion of the transcendental subject against an ignominious collapse of the subject into a debased 'mass' history. To put the point in a different way: how is *Dasein* to sustain the kind of imaginary relation with the world which will make it feel at home there, and which as we have seen in Kant is epitomized in the aesthetic, without losing track of its own priority and integrity? But how in turn is that priority over the world to be distinguished from a purely tragic sense of estrangement and contingency? Not to claim some privileged status for *Dasein* would seem to be to succumb to positivism, stripping the human of its distinctiveness; to do so, however, risks reproducing the very ideology of Man's dominance over Nature with which that positivism belongs. As long as the shadow of such a humanism is cast over *Being and Time*, Heidegger has still not escaped the metaphysical duality of subject and object. As Being-in-the-world, *Dasein* is supposedly prior to all such divisions, the sheer ungrounded nothingness or transcendence which opens up their possibility in the first place. Yet if its recurrent bouts of ontological anxiety – made possible by that very transcendence – illuminate the nullity of things, a fissure is bound to open up between such things and *Dasein* itself, now sternly recalled to its 'proper' task of self-realization. In this sense a division healed at the ontological level insists on breaking out again in the existential realm. It is from this duality that the Sartre of *Being and Nothingness* will take his cue, appropriating from *Being and Time* all that makes it a *tragic* text. It becomes possible, in other words, to exploit the equivocations of Heidegger by subordinating his apparent transcendence of the subject–object divide to the vision of a sense-bestowing subject set over against a reality drained of immanent meaning.[5]

Heidegger's famous turn or *Kehre* in the period after *Being and Time* represents a drastic solution to these dilemmas. To approach Being itself through the optic of *Dasein* is still a residually metaphysical manoeuvre, since metaphysics can grasp Being only from the standpoint of particular beings. Metaphysics is born of the oblivion of the difference between Being and beings, construing the former on the model of the latter. This gesture must thus be put into reverse, and *Dasein* examined from the standpoint of Being itself. In the later Heidegger, accordingly, the emphasis falls increasingly upon *Dasein* as the 'there' of Being itself, Being's own free self-revelation in a particular mode. *Dasein* is a coming to pass of Being more fundamental than humanity itself, the source or essence of the human which itself emerges out of the still more originary abyss of Being itself. Being now seizes priority over its own 'there', throwing it out or withdrawing it in accordance with the necessities of its own nature. 'Only so long as *Dasein* is, is there Being', Heidegger had written in *Being and Time*; but in the *Letter on Humanism* he will add the crucial qualification that 'the fact that the *Da*, the lighting as the truth of Being itself, comes to pass is the dispensation of Being itself'.[6] It is now Being, in short, which has the upper hand, bringing about its own illumination. 'Man' is simply a relation to Being, responsive and delivered up to it; what thinks in human thought about Being is evoked by Being itself. Thought is just a kind of acquiescence in Being, a docile letting be of it, recollecting and giving thanks for it. Throughout the work of the post-*Kehre* Heidigger, it is Being – not of course to be mistaken for anything as metaphysical as a subject!– which arrives, bestows, descends, withdraws, gathers, advances, shines forth. The role of humanity is to be simply the shepherd and preserver of this mystery, which Heidegger will progressively speak of as 'holy' and connect with 'the gods'.[7] History itself is now simply the successive epochs of Being's self-donation or self-concealment, as humanity is thrown off and gathered back to it like some ontological yo-yo.

The relation between Being and *Dasein* in the later Heidegger is thus more full-bloodedly 'imaginary' than it was in *Being and Time*. It is not only that *Dasein* is slavishly dependent on the mystery of Being; it is also that Being has a reciprocal need of *Dasein*. *Sein* requires its *Da*: it is part of Being's inner necessity to arrive at articulation, much like the Hegelian Idea, and humanity conveniently provides the place where this may happen, the 'clearing' in which Being comes partly to light. *Dasein* is Being's mouthpiece: there is a primordial complicity between 'Man' and Being, which spring together from an 'event' or *Ereignis* more fundamental than either of them. 'It is imperative', Heidegger writes in *Identity and Difference*, 'to experience simply this *Eignen* (suited, fitting), in which man and Being are *ge-eignet* (suited, fitted, en-owned) to one another . . . '.[8] Humanity and Being are 'assigned to each other', at once held apart in difference and at one. If this is crypto-mystical speculation, it is of an ideologically consoling kind. 'Being' is now taking over from 'world', so that an affinity with the former compensates for an alienation from the latter. It is not that *Dasein*'s distressing tendency to cover up and eradicate Being is any less grievous: 'technology' is the later Heidegger's vague portmanteau term for this catastrophe. But Being would now appear to bring about its own concealedness, oblivion of it being part of its own inner destiny. 'Technology is in its essence a destiny within the history of Being and of the truth of Being, a truth that lies in oblivion', comments Heidegger in the *Letter on Humanism*. Erasing and forgetting Being is as much part of it as anything else, and so as much within its 'truth'.

Heidegger had argued in *Being and Time* that the essence of *Dasein* is homelessness: it is of the nature of human existence to be estranged and deracinated. This theme continues in his later writings; but it is now 'dwelling' or 'at-homeness' which would appear more fundamental. 'Dwelling . . . is the *basic character* of Being in keeping with which mortals exist', he writes in the essay 'Building Dwelling Thinking'.[9] Whatever the depredations of technological reason, *Dasein* is essentially at home in the world. Just as *Being and Time* turned *Dasein*'s straying and lostness into valid constituents of its nature, so the later Heidegger finds in Being a claim upon humanity which will not abandon it even when it wanders off. 'We come back to ourselves from things', he writes in 'Building Dwelling Thinking', '*without ever abandoning* our stay among things. Indeed, the loss of rapport with things that occurs in states of depression would be wholly impossible if even such a state were not still what it is as a human state: that is, a staying *with* things.'[10] Whereas in *Being and Time* an involvement with the world was always a possible deviation from *Dasein*'s own authentic self-reference, it is now an abiding with things which appears most authentic, and the recoil upon oneself subsumed easily within it. The crisis of anxiety, of that dispirited sense of the nullity of objects which unhinges us from them, is blandly sublated into a more primordial at-homeness. Paradoxically, we are most in touch with reality when we transcend it in a movement of separation, for such transcendence discloses its Being, which is what is most 'near' about it. The yawning gulf which a technological capitalism has opened up between humanity and its world is covered over in a fantasy of eternal symbiosis. Being as such remains as a whole contingent: Heidegger denies it all metaphysical grounding, viewing it simply as suspended in the movement of its own nothingness. What 'grounds' Being is just this perpetual surge of its own free transcendence, which is itself a kind of no-thing. Heidegger's Being is abyssal and anchorless, a kind of groundless ground, which sustains itself like the work of art in its own free, pointless play. Yet if Being as a whole is thus contingent, *Dasein*, curiously, is not, since Being has need of it, contains an interior indigence which *Dasein* must supplement. Viewed as a *part* of Being, *Dasein* would seem to share its non-necessity; viewed in *relation* to Being, it would appear graciously dispensed from such a fate. And this is indeed welcome news for an alienated humanity, even if the heavy price paid for it is a virtual extinction of the subject as free agent and a philosophy resonant with portentous vacuities. 'One speaks', comments Theodor Adorno in *The Jargon of Authenticity*, 'from a depth which would be profaned if it were called content.'[11]

To claim that Being needs *Dasein* is actually to say no more than that the world needs an interpreter to be interpreted. Part of the function of the later Heidegger's rhetorical devices is to slide this unexceptionable case close to the mystical vision of a Being which adopts and solicits humanity in the manner of a divinity and its votaries. If the consoling ideological fiction of a world which posits and requires the human is no longer viable, it can be replaced with the alternative imaginary circuit of a Being-as-disclosure for which the existence of *Dasein* is imperative. The primary form of that disclosure, in the later Heidegger, is language.[12] Language is the privileged mode in which Being articulates itself in humanity, and poetry is its essence: 'Poetry is the saying of the unconcealedness of beings.'[13] What is expressed in language is the original unity of names and things, the primordial source where meaning and being are undivided. 'Language', Heidegger writes in his *Introduction to Metaphysics*, 'is the primordial poetry in which a people speaks "being".'[14] To live properly is to live poetically, rapt in the mystery of Being, knowing oneself to be its humble ventriloquist. In 'The Origin of the Work of Art', it is the artefact itself which has now become the obedient *Da* or 'there' of Being, the sacral locus of its self-disclosure.

This not to say that Heidegger has much time for aesthetics in its classical sense. In 'A Dialogue on Language', he dismisses such discourse as irredeemably metaphysical, bound up with the whole discredited problematic of representation.[15] The early Heidegger may be said to return instead to the aesthetic in its original Baumgartenian meaning – to a concern with that concrete life-world which hermeneutical phenomenology takes as the centre of its enquiry. If there is an 'aesthetics' in *Being and Time*, it is just this recognition of the ineluctable worldliness of all meaning, the fact that we are always already pitched into the midst of things, experiencing the world on our bodies before we come properly to formulate it in our heads. To 'know' is to rupture and estrange that spontaneous commerce with objects which our bodily structure forces upon us, and which will return to saturate our thinking in an appropriate 'mood', since for Heidegger there can be no moodless thought. All that is richest and most positive in Heidegger's philosophy flows from this profound materialism, responsible as it is for so much of the depth, imaginative fertility and adventurous originality of *Being and Time*. It is in this earlier 'aesthetic' – in this insistence on the practical, affective, pre-reflexive grounds of all cognition – that Heidegger's project consorts most productively with those of Marx and Freud. It would not be difficult, for example, to trace suggestive affinities between the structure of 'care' which typifies *Dasein* and the Marxist concept of social interests. Yet the problem is not only that these very same motifs, in Heidegger's career as a whole, belong with an extravagant over-reaction to Enlightenment rationality which will plunge him into a fascistic mythology of stout speechless peasants and aloofly laconic sages. It is also that the broader, deeper, more generous sense of the aesthetic of *Being and Time* co-habits all along with a narrowed, post-Baumgartenian sense of the term – the aesthetic as a uniquely privileged, authentic, self-referential style of being, sharply distinguished from the drably quotidian. As a general Being-in-the-world, *Dasein* has about it something of the original, phenomenological connotation of the aesthetic: even if it is hardly a *sensuous* phenomenon, it inhabits the realms of the affective and somatic, is marked by its biological finitude and runs up against a density in things irreducible to some abstract reason. At the same time, as a form of authentic self-actualization brooding upon its own unique possibilities, *Dasein* contains more than an echo of the old Romantic subject, now forced to encounter a facticity which its freedom cannot dissolve away, but nonetheless bent upon transforming that very thrownness, contingency and mortality into the ground of its heroic self-recuperation. The esoteric and the everyday, the aesthetic as both solitary splendour and mundane conduct, commingle in the very structure of *Dasein*, as they do in a different sense in Heidegger's style of writing, with its bathetic mixture of the oracular and the ordinary. His style is well practised in the device of investing humble particulars with ontological status, elevating something as empirical as bad temper into a fundamental structure of Being. In this he anticipates the Nazi conjoining of the commonplace and the sublime, homespun wisdom and heroic elitism. 'Fallenness into *Gerede* and a lostness proximally and for the most part in *Mitsein*' might be his description of a tea-break. On the one hand, this device impresses with its demotic flavour: how liberated of philosophy to stoop for its staple themes to hammers and forest paths – to allow you, as the excited young Sartre was to realize, to do philosophy by talking about the ash tray. On the other hand, these modest bits and pieces of the world win their new-found ontological dignity only at the cost of being violently naturalized, frozen to permanent fixtures. The mundane is mythologized to the precise extent to which philosophy appears to climb off its pedestal. Quoting Heidegger's belief that philosophy 'belongs right in the midst of the labour of farmers', Adorno remarks that one would like at least to know the farmers' opinion of that.[16]

What will happen in Heidegger's later work is a steady convergence of these two senses of the aesthetic, such that Being in general comes to the fore, but now imbued with all the mysterious privilege of the aesthetic in the more specialized Romantic sense. But since Being is everything, the more general sense of the aesthetic is retained: the whole world is now an artefact, a self-sustaining play of sheer becoming. In *Being and Time*, *Dasein* was the final reference point for all things but an end in itself; now this self-reference is projected into the whole of Being, whose autonomy *Dasein* merely exists to give voice to. *Dasein* no longer marks its particular difference from other essents in having its end in itself; it is just the clearing of light which reveals this to be true of all other beings as well. The whole of Being is thus aestheticized: it is the autotelic, eternally unfinished unfolding which we observed in the early *Dasein*, but without the anguished, time-ridden, crisis-rocked nature of that doomed phenomenon. Being, like the work of art, combines freedom and necessity: it is a kind of ground of all things, and so gives them the law, but since it lacks any groundedness itself it is also a sort of non-ground of pure freedom, a game which simply plays itself out. If Being is aestheticized in this way, so is the thought which thinks it, which has no result or effect and simply 'satisfies its essence in that it is'.[17] Philosophy is more like praying than proposing: it is sacred ritual rather than secular analysis, grounded in the very Being to which it returns perpetual homage and gratitude. In *Kant and the Problem of Metaphysics*, Heidegger argues that cognition for Kant is primarily intuition, that the understanding is in the service of sensibility; and his own aestheticizing of thought returns him in effect to Fichte and Schelling, whose 'absolute ego' or 'state of indifference' are likewise attempts to transcend the subject–object duality.

If Being and thought are made aesthetic matters in Heidegger, so also in a sense is ethics. There can be no question of trying to produce a concrete ethics, a project which belongs with metaphysical rationalism. *Ethos*, we are instructed in the *Letter on Humanism*, means 'abode' or 'dwelling place', and so can be instantly subsumed under Heideggerian ontology. The true law is that of Being itself, not some merely human fabrication of rules. But this reduction of ethics to ontology is made possible in the first place because Heidegger has covertly projected normative categories into Being itself, while immediately erasing this gesture. Truth is inherent in the essence of things, so that *aletheia* or the act of disclosing them is at once a question of fact and value. The descriptive and the evaluative are held together in the word 'Being': what is most significant about an object is simply what it *is*. *Dasein*, similarly, is both fact and value: that it should comprehend Being is at once just part of the kind of thing it is and an implicitly ethical injunction, warning *Dasein* against its tendency to oblivion. Such equivocation is made possible by the vagueness of such phrases as 'comprehending Being', which are in one sense straightforwardly descriptive (understanding what things are) and in another sense loaded with a whole normative freight of being enraptured by the mystery of the world. Being itself is on the one hand just what is, but on the other hand contains its own evaluative distinctions and hierarchies: 'If Being is to disclose itself', Heidegger remarks in the *Introduction to Metaphysics*, 'it must itself have and maintain a rank.'[18] It is Being's internal differentiation which determines the divisions between individual human beings as strong or weak, masterful or open to being commanded. Being, as Heidegger constantly stresses, is at once remote and near to hand: it is that to which only a fortunate elite are summoned, yet is as simple and self-evident as a pair of shoes or a wave of the sea. Being is everywhere, which is its humble or 'popular' aspect, but it is so much everywhere that we constantly forget it, so that it becomes the most rare, fragile, obscure reality of all. Hearkening to its imperious call is at once just part of what we are and possible only by dint of strenuous decision – a paradox implicit in the Heideggerian doctrine that we must actively allow things just to be themselves, resolutely liberate them into what they already are. It is as though *Dasein*'s task is to be the energetic discloser and articulator that cancels itself at every moment and permits the world to appear with the kind of pristine splendour it would have had if we had not been there to perceive it. *Dasein* is thus granted a centrality with one hand only to be humbled with the other: it represents a sort of violent intrusion into the sanctuary of Being, but one absolutely essential for Being's coming to presence. The only way that Being can be disclosed is by something that also forgets and covers it up, so that the light of human understanding continually darkens and impoverishes what it reveals, provides a place for this revelation to occur but – since it is always a partial, particular place – cannot help falsifying the very thing it brings to light. Being thus cannot be near without also being remote, for *Dasein* is bound to distance and disfigure it in the very act of unconcealing it.

Falsehood is thus inherent in Being, but this is no ethical judgement. To make falsehood intrinsic to Being is to make it simply part of what Being factually is, and so 'natural' and unalarming. The dialectic of travestying and unfolding is gathered into Being itself, which, as it were, puts out its own false appearance alongside its true essence in a ceaseless ironic rhythm. This relieves *Dasein* of the guilt of concealing Being, as well as underlining the sublime depth of the latter. Being casts the shadow of its own infinite plenitude over any particular gift of itself to humanity, and so is reassuringly transcendent of its actual incarnations. As Heidegger writes in *The Question of Being*: 'Properly considered, oblivion, the concealment of the still unrevealed being (verbal) of Being preserves untouched treasures and is the promise of a find which is only waiting for the proper search.'[19] The 'falsity' of Being is thus a kind of self-protective device on its part, a way of aloofly withholding its riches at the very moment of communicating them, rather as the *Dasein* of *Being and Time* is already in the act of moving beyond an object to its Being in the very moment of cognizing it. Being is grandly disdainful of its humble human servant yet wholly wrapped up in him; and in this way Heidegger can press to an extreme the decentring of the human subject only partly achieved in his early work, while celebrating a preordained harmony between Being and humanity. Later Heideggerian Man is in one sense more decentred, in another sense more centred, than he was in the earlier writing.

If the ethical is thus dissolved away in the post-*Kehre* Heidegger, so is it in *Being and Time*. *Dasein* there may be mostly inauthentic, but it is proper and necessary that it should be so. 'Error is the space in which history unfolds', writes Heidegger in the 'Anaximander Fragment';[20] *Dasein*'s constant self-oblivious straying into the everyday world confronts it with just that essential weight of facticity it must strive against in the struggle to become its own author. By deftly reckoning error into truth, fallenness into redemption, *Being and Time* deconstructs the antagonism between them and so protects itself at once from nihilism and hubris, despair and presumption. The old self-authoring subject has fallen on hard times, but is still alive and kicking. To squander oneself in the world is a matter of inauthenticity, but also a perfectly valid structure of one's being. There is an equivocation here once again between fact and value: *Dansein*'s 'caring' is in one sense the sheer fact of its involvement with things, in another sense a judgement on how dangerously liable it is to deviate from itself, and in a third sense an essential part of its authentic resoluteness. Similarly, 'authenticity' is clearly at one level a normative judgement, but as a question of realizing one's individual possibilities it is also no more than a kind of becoming what one is. As an injunction, it urges one simply to be oneself, without any particular moral directive, and so has the empty formalism of all existentialist ethics. As long as the possibilities one actualizes are one's own inalienable property, it is apparently a matter of indifference what they consist in. Heidegger's subject is thus the formal, abstract individual of market society, drained of ethical substance and left only with the notional 'self' as a value. In the *Introduction to Metaphysics*, he is notably curt with any talk of 'values': much of what has been published on the topic, he remarks, is a distortion and dilution of the 'inner truth and greatness' of National Socialism. His blurring of fact and value is ideologically essential: by fudging the distinction he can cling to an elitism of authenticity without openly committing himself to normative criteria, which would be to lapse back into the merely 'subjectivist' perspective he seeks to transcend. Every valuing, he writes in the *Letter on Humanism*, is a subjectivizing. Without some strong implicit normativity there could be no critique of the alienated world of prattle and mass opinion, not to mention of science, democracy, liberalism and socialism; but for Heidegger's work to have true authority it must go beyond mere *doxa* to describe things as they really are, draw its title to speak from the very nature of Being itself rather than sink into controvertible interpretations. It is in this sense that a discourse of what *Dasein* plainly and simply is operates at the same time as a rhetoric of moral exhortation. The unspoken tragedy of *Being and Time* is that there can be no transcendence without error, no freedom without its abuse. The movement by which *Dasein* moves beyond particular things to their Being is inseparable from the way it can slip restlessly, inauthentically, from this to that. This deadlock or aporia will later be violently resolved by grasping Being less as that from which humanity errs, than as that which errs from itself through humanity as part of its own necessity. And this is just another way of saying that there can be no 'real' error at all. Deviating from the path is just a way of following it, and the paths through a wood are in any case crooked. Technology is a spiritual disaster but also part of Being's own inscrutable dispensation. Values are petty subjective ornamentations on a Being which is secretly normative through and through. Freedom disrupts the old settled pieties of earth, but nothing can escape such earth-boundness in any case, and all apparent freedom is bondage to Being.

'By virtue of . . . reliability', Heidegger writes in the *Letter on Humanism*, 'the peasant woman is made privy to the silent call of the earth; by virtue of the reliability of the equipment she is sure of her world.'[21] In 1882, seven years before Heidegger's birth, 42.5 per cent of the German people still made their living by agriculture, forestry and fishery, whereas only 35.5 per cent were engaged in industry, mining and building. By 1895, when Heidegger was a small child, the latter occupations had already outstripped the former; and by 1907, when Heidegger was a student, 42.8 per cent of the German population worked in industry and only 28.6 per cent on the land.[22]

Heidegger's early life, in brief, witnesses the decisive transition of Germany from a largely rural to a mainly industrial society. It is the period in which Germany grew to become the leading industrial capitalist state in Europe, doubling its international trade between 1872 and 1900 and challenging Britain's supremacy in world markets. By 1913 Germany had overtaken Britain as a producer of steel and pig iron, supplied three quarters of the world's synthetic dyes and surpassed all competitors in the export of electrical equipment. Under the protectionist and state-interventionist policies of Bismarck, the German economy had expanded rapidly in the latter decades of the nineteenth century, despite periods of depression and falling prices. Cartels and joint stock companies dominated economic life, and major credit banks were key institutions in capital investment for industry. Germany grew remarkably in chemical products, shipbuilding and above all in its electrical industries; a Customs Union, a sound state-built communications infrastructure, draconian anti-socialist measures and government stimulation of commerce transformed the face of German society in an astonishingly brief period of time.[23] By 1914, the country had joined the ranks of the leading world traders and was expanding its overseas commerce more rapidly than any of its rivals. Heidegger's idyllic countryside was also being speedily reshaped: agriculture, swiftly expanding alongside industry, was being rationalized and scientifically remodelled, with the application of new business and technical methods at its most intensive on the large estates. Meanwhile, beneath this flurry of innovation, land remained parcelled into big and medium-sized farms, slightly more than one fifth great estates and the rest the smallholdings of the peasantry. Heidegger's sturdily independent small farmer was an untypical, increasingly marginalized phenomenon: peasants with paltry smallholdings often had little opportunity to eke out their meagre livings through work for big landowners, and imported farm labour seriously jeopardized the position of the German farm workers. They migrated, often enough, to the cities, to swell the ranks of the industrial proletariat. Conditions there were frequently dire: long hours, low wages, unemployment and poor housing were the price the German working class paid for the industrial capitalist boom. The state laid on social welfare, with an eye to weaning the working class from the Social Democrat party, then the largest socialist party in the world. In 1878 the *Reichstag* moved against this political threat, banning the party and suppressing its newspapers.

While Heidegger was cherishing his dreams of an ontologically correct peasantry, Germany had emerged on the basis of a political unity of Prussian Junkerdom and Rhenish capital into a new Empire, the fundamental structure of which was distinctively capitalist. A new class of industrial *nouveaux riches*, numbering some spectacularly wealthy individuals, shot the nation into the league of the five richest countries. Yet if this class was setting the pace of economic development, it was doing so under the shadow of the still powerful old Prussian ruling class, gladly embracing its authoritarian supremacy as an antidote to social unrest. The mores and life-style of the traditional Junkers provided a model for bourgeois emulation: wealthy merchants and industrialists aspired in English fashion to possess landed estates and mimic the nobility. The nobility, for their part, were coming to recognize the industrial bourgeoisie as their own economic base, and the state was eager to promote its fortunes in tariff and labour policies. The new Germany, then, was a capitalist social formation, but one deeply marked by its feudal heritage. The officer corps of the army swore fealty directly to the Emperor, while the Imperial Chancellor was not responsible to the *Reichstag*. Bemused by this hybrid society, in which an autocratic traditionalist state formed the carapace for industrial capitalist development, the Marx of the *Critique of the Gotha Programme* threw at it as many formulas as he could muster: Bismarckian Germany was 'nothing but a police-guarded military despotism, embellished with parliamentary forms, alloyed with a feudal admixture, already influenced by the bourgeoisie, furnished by the bureaucracy . . .'[24] Less ambivalently, Engels recognized that the new Germany, whatever its political and cultural peculiarities, had joined the ranks of the fully-fledged capitalist states.[25]

The depth and virulence of conservative reaction in the Germany of *Being and Time* may be seen in large part as a reaction to the peculiarly *traumatic* emergence of industrial capitalism, sprung as it was so swiftly from the loins of old-world Prussia. But such reaction was also nurtured by the socially amorphous nature of the society which had come to birth – by the persistence within it of strong feudal elements, the stubborn survival of ruralist ideologies and, most vitally, the fact that German industrial capitalism had taken shape partly as a state-sponsored affair, without bringing with it a flourishing middle-class liberal tradition. Before the writing of *Being and Time*, Germany had also passed through humiliating military conquest, social and economic devastation and an abortive social revolution. Whereas Nietzsche, at an earlier stage of German capitalist development, pits the image of a vigorous nobility against an inert bourgeoisie, Heidegger, at a later phase of imperial expansion and technological domination, turns to the idea of *Gelassenheit*: of a wisely passive 'releasement' of things, a vigilant, circumspect refusal to meddle with their being, of which aesthetic experience appears prototypical. This stance, which Heidegger shares with D. H. Lawrence, contains a potent criticism of Enlightenment rationality: for all his sententious ruralism, Heidegger has much of importance to say about the violence of metaphysical thought, and his sense of a meditative 'being with' things, attending responsively, non-masteringly to their shapes and textures, finds a valuable echo in some contemporary feminist and ecological politics.

In one sense, the problem of such a perspective is that it reduces both politics and ethics to ontology, and so strikes them empty: the philosophy of Being, of a reverent openness to things in their particularity, carries with it no directives about how one is to choose, act and discriminate. Ironically, it is therefore as abstract as the very thought that it opposes, levelling and homogenizing in its turn. If one should allow trees to subsist in their unique mode of being, why not typhoid as well? In another sense, this philosophy of Being is far too concrete and specific for its own good, excluding and discriminating with its own peculiar brand of violence: Being is as internally differentiated as the social rankings of the fascistic state, and in the 1930s comes for a time to be incarnate in the *Führer*. Heidegger swings with a minimum of mediation between the nebulously ontological and the sinisterly specific; the distinction between a concern with Being and a mere preoccupation with beings, so the *Introduction to Metaphysics* suggests, is the contrast between the historic mission of the German *Volk* and the technological positivism of the USA and the Soviet Union. As a way of life, *Gelassenheit* is both Keatsian and craven – a fertile receptivity to objects on the one hand, a cringing docility before the numinous power of Being on the other. The hubristic humanist subject is properly dislodged from its virile pre-eminence, but only to adopt the servile acquiescence of the lackey. Heidegger's philosophy exemplifies one destination of the idea of the aesthetic in the twentieth century, as a ruling class in grave crisis discovered in the disinterestedness of Being the very discourse it requires to mystify its own ruthlessly instrumental activity. The main currents of Heidegger's work can be highlighted by a contrast with the thought of that other fascist sympathizer, Paul de Man. Heidegger never unequivocally recanted his Nazi past; and the reason why he never recanted was perhaps because he never repented. De Man remained silent about his own affiliations, to be exposed only after his death. It is possible to read de Man's post-war work as an extreme reaction against the politics of Being, elements of which he himself had espoused in his notorious early essays. In the later de Man, all notions of language as replete with Being, of signs as organically related to things, are denounced as pernicious mystifications. Heidegger's apocalyptic conception of a teleological time brimming with destiny is steadily drained by de Man to the empty, broken temporality of allegory. Truth and authenticity, as in Heidegger's work, are seen ineluctably to involve blindness and error, but a growing emphasis on the latter is pressed to a point of bleakly disillusioned scepticism which threatens to rob the whole concept of truth of its productiveness. Art is no longer the locus of truth and Being: its high privilege is rather to be the place where an ineradicable error and delusion are finally able to name themselves for what they are, in a negative version of Heideggerian aesthetics. The subject, as with the later Heidegger, is an effect of language; but this for de Man means it is less a faithful ventriloquist of Being than a vacuous fiction, the product of a duplicitous rhetoric. All grounds, unities, identities, transcendental significations and nostalgic yearnings for origin are ruthlessly undone by the movement of irony and the undecidable. Any hint of metaphorical organicism, in self, history or sign, is undermined by the blind, aleatory working of a mechanistic metonymy. In all of these way, de Man's later work can be read as a consistent polemic against the aesthetic, which has now come to encompass all theories of a purposive, meaningful history; and this polemic blends well in its Stoic asceticism with an end-of-ideologies era.[26] The impulse behind de Man's various theoretical hostilities is so intense and unremitting that it is not difficult to discern in it a more than literary motive.

When philosophy turns positivist, the aesthetic is on hand to come to the rescue of thought. The mighty themes evacuated by a reified, purely calculative rationality, now houseless and vagrant, seek for a roof under which to shelter, and discover one in the discourse of art. If that discourse is now called upon to play the magisterial role which philosophy as such has abandoned – if it must return an answer to the question of the meaning of existence, along with the question of the significance of art – then it must expand its horizon, up its own status and oust philosophy from its traditional sovereignty. It is thus that Nietzsche and Heidegger return over the heads of Marx and Hegel to Schelling, who held that philosophy had attained its acme in art. The more conventional thought seems to do no more than reflect an alienated social existence, the more urgently, and desperately, this flight from reason to poetry gathers force. But if such a recourse marks the true limits of a debased rationality, it also suggests, most evidently with Heidegger, the solace which in an increasingly opaque social order a disinherited group of ideologues may find in a few apodictic truths, rooted in an ontology so profound as to be ultimately ineffable, and thus incontrovertible. The appeal to Being, like the moral sense of British Enlightenment theory, is at once a confession of intellectual bankruptcy and a rhetorically powerful affair. It is unutterably more fundamental and self-evident than orthodox philosophical thought, returning us relievedly to that which, beyond all social complexity and conceptual obfuscation, we feel we simply *know*; yet it admits us in the same gesture to the inner sanctum of the sages, whose insight is rare enough to penetrate through every routinized discourse of rationality to what really matters. Being, in a familiar Zen paradox, is at once tantalizingly elusive and absolutely self-evident; only a pious peasant or mandarin professor could possibly grasp it. Like the Wittgenstein with whom he has often been compared, Heidegger returns us exactly to where we are, leaving the whole structure of everydayness comfortingly in place, but allows us to do so in the flattering knowledge that we are consequently in on the deepest conceivable mystery.

If Heidegger is able to dismiss the aesthetic, it is only because he has in effect universalized it, transgressing the frontiers between art and existence in a reactionary parody of the *avant garde*. Liberated from its specialized enclave, the aesthetic can now be spread over the whole of reality: art is what brings things to be in their essential truth, and so is identical with the very movement of Being. Art, Heidegger claims in his lectures on Nietzsche, must be conceived of as the basic happening of beings, as the authentically creative movement. Poetry, art, language, truth, thought and Being thus converge in his later work into a single reality: Being is the upholder of beings, language the essence of Being, and poetry the essence of language. Each dimension shines with radiant immediacy through the other: language, which like poetry speaks only itself, nevertheless discloses the unmediated truth of Being in that very act. The aesthetic for Heidegger is less a question of art than a way of relating to the world – a relation which fatalistically accepts even the 'untruth' of that world as a gracious dispensation of Being, and which leaves the human subject rapt in paralytic reverence before a numinous presence which the concept would only defile.

If a respectful communion with Being, disowning all thought of domination, might appear to be stereotypically 'feminine', Being itself in Heidegger would seem exactly the opposite. It appears in his writing in many guises: it is Nothingness, a pair of peasant shoes, the pure movement of temporality; as that higher destiny which summons the folk implacably to self-sacrifice, it wears for a while the features of Adolf Hitler.[27] Yet buried beneath all of these images is a more ancient, uncannily familiar one, at once infinitely remote and intimately close. In the *Introduction to Metaphysics*, Heidegger argues that particular objects were seen by the ancient Greeks as a kind of 'falling away' from an originary fullness of Being, a 'tipping over' which contrasts with Being's own steadfast 'uprightness'. The Greek *physis*, so he claims, originally meant a 'standing forth' or 'coming to stand', that which unfolds, blossoms or arises. Being is a kind of 'jutting forth', and this uprightness or 'erect standing there' is a permanent one, an unfolding which will never fall down.

It would seem that this oldest of all stand-bys is indeed always ready-to-hand.

Notes

1 Martin Heidegger, *Discourse on Thinking* (New York, 1966), p. 66.
2 Martin Heidegger, *Nietzsche* (London, 1981), p. 109.
3 Martin Heidegger, *Kant and the Problem of Metaphysics* (Bloomington, 1962), p. 138.

4 The phrase is William J. Richardson's, in what is still the most magisterial study of Heidegger: *Martin Heidegger: From Phenomenology to Thought* (The Hague, 1963). Other relevant studies of Heidegger include J. L. Metha, *The Philosophy of Martin Heidegger* (New York, 1971); Laszlo Versenyi, *Heidegger, Being and Truth* (New Haven, 1965); L. M. Vail, *Heidegger and Ontological Difference* (Pennsylvania, 1972); Michael Murray (ed.), *Heidegger and Modern Philosophy: Critical Essays* (New Haven, 1978); William V. Spanos (ed.), *Martin Heidegger and the Question of Literature* (Bloomington, 1979).

5 See Joseph P. Fell, *Heidegger and Sartre: An Essay on Being and Place* (New York, 1979), especially chapters 6 and 7.

6 Martin Heidegger, 'Letter on Humanism', in David Farrell Krell (ed.), *Martin Heidegger: Basic Writings* (New York, 1977), p. 216.

7 See for example 'What are Poets for?' and 'The Thing', in *Martin Heidegger: Poetry, Language, Thought*, translated and introduced by Albert Hofstadter (New York, 1971).

8 Martin Heidegger, *Identity and Difference* (New York, 1969), p. 35.

9 Krell (ed.), *Martin Heidegger: Basic Writings*, p. 338.

10 Ibid., p. 335.

11 Theodor Adorno, *The Jargon of Authenticity* (London, 1986), p. 93.

12 See for example Heidegger, 'Language', in *Poetry, Language, Thought*, and *On the Way to Language* (New York, 1971). For a useful essay on Heidegger and language see Donald G. Marshall, 'The Ontology of the Literary Sign: Notes towards a Heideggerian Revision of Semiology', in Spanos (ed.), *Martin Heidegger and the Question of Literature*.

13 Martin Heidegger, 'The Origin of the Work of Art', in Krell (ed.), *Martin Heidegger: Basic Writings*, p. 185.

14 Heidegger, *An Introduction to Metaphysics* (New Haven, 1959), p. 171.

15 Heidegger, 'A Dialogue on Language', in *On the Way to Language*.

16 Heidegger, *The Jargon of Authenticity*, p. 54.

17 Heidegger, 'Letter on Humanism', in Krell (ed.), *Martin Heidegger: Basic Writings*, p. 236.

18 Heidegger, *An Introduction to Metaphysics*, p. 133.

19 Heidegger, *The Question of Being* (London, 1959), p. 91.

20 Heidegger, 'The Anaximander Fragment', in *Early Greek Thinking* (New York, 1975), p. 26.

21 Krell (ed.), *Martin Heidegger: Basic Writings*, p. 164.

22 See Hajo Holborn, *A History of Modern Germany 1840–1945* (Princeton, 1982), p. 370.

23 See W. O. Henderson, *The Rise of German Industrial Power 1834–1914* (London, 1975), pp. 173ff.

24 Karl Marx, 'Critique of the Gotha Programme', in *Marx and Engels: Selected Works* (London, 1968), p. 332 (translation slightly amended).
25 F. Engels, *The Role of Force in History* (London, 1968), pp. 64–5.
26 See my comments on de Man, the so-called Yale school of deconstruction and the second world war in *The Function of Criticism* (London, 1984), pp. 100–1.
27 For two instructive studies of Heidegger's Nazism, see Pierre Bourdieu, *L'ontologie politique de Martin Heidegger* (Paris, 1975), and Victor Farias, *Heidegger et le nazism* (Paris, 1987).

12

The Marxist Rabbi:
Walter Benjamin

There are intricate relations between myth, modernism and monopoly capital. Suppressed by the varieties of Victorian rationalism during the epoch of liberal capitalism, myth stages its dramatic re-entry into European culture, with Nietzsche as one of its prophetic precursors, at the point of that capitalism's gradual mutation into 'higher' corporate forms in the late nineteenth and early twentieth centuries. If a *laissez-faire* economy is now moving into more systemic modes, then there is something peculiarly apposite about the rebirth of myth – itself, as Lévi-Strauss has taught us, a highly organized 'rational' system – as an imaginative means of deciphering this new social experience. Such mythological thought belongs with a radical shift in the whole category of the subject – a rethinking which involves Ferdinand de Saussure as much as Wyndham Lewis, Freud and Martin Heidegger as well as D. H. Lawrence and Virginia Woolf. For it is really no longer possible to pretend, given the transition from market to monopoly capitalism, that the old vigorously individualist ego, the self-determining subject of classical liberal thought, is any longer an adequate model for the subject's new experience of itself under these altered social conditions. The modern subject, much like the mythological one, is less the sharply individuated source of its own actions than an obedient function of some deeper controlling structure, which now appears more and more to do its thinking and acting for it. It is no accident that the theoretical current known as structuralism has its origins in the epoch of modernism and monopoly capital – that this period witnesses a turning away on all sides from the traditional philosophy of the subject of Kant, Hegel and the younger Marx, troubledly conscious as it is of the individual as constituted to its roots by forces and processes utterly opaque to everyday consciousness. Whether one names such implacable powers Language or Being, Capital or the Unconscious, Tradition or the *élan vital*, Archetypes or the Destiny of the West, their effect is to open up a well-nigh unspannable gulf between the waking life of the old befeathered ego and the true determinants of its identity, which are always covert and inscrutable.

If the subject is accordingly fractured and dismantled, the objective world it confronts is now quite impossible to grasp as the product of the subject's own activity. What stands over against this individual is a self-regulative system which appears on the one hand thoroughly rationalized, eminently logical in its minutest operations, yet on the other hand blankly indifferent of the rational projects of human subjects themselves. This autonomous, self-determining artefact of a world then rapidly takes on all the appearances of a second nature, erasing its own source in human practice so as to seem as self-evidently given and immobilized as those rocks, trees and mountains which are the stuff of mythology.

If myth is a matter of eternal recurrence, then the recurrence which matters most in the sphere of monopoly capitalism is the eternal return of the commodity. Capitalism indeed has a history; but the dynamic of that development, as Marx ironically noted, is the perpetual recreation of its own 'eternal' structure. Each act of commodity exchange is at once uniquely differentiated and a monotonous replaying of the same old story. The epitome of the commodity is thus the cult of fashion, in which the familiar returns with some slight variation, the very old and the very new caught up together in some oxymoronic logic of identity-in-difference. It is a paradox of modernism that its exhilarated sense of fresh technological possibilities (Futurism, Constructivism, Surrealism) finds itself constantly displaced into some static, cyclical world in which all dynamic process seems permanently arrested. Coupled with this is an equally paradoxical interplay of chance and necessity. From one viewpoint, every continent bit of experience now seems secretly regulated by some underlying structure or subtext (in the case of James Joyce's *Ulysses*, the subtext of Homeric myth) of which experience itself is the manipulated product. Reality is coded to its roots, as the ephemeral working through of some deeper logic invisible to the naked eye, and randomness is accordingly banished. Yet these determining structures are now so thoroughly formal and abstract in their operations that they seem to stand at an immense distance from the realm of sensuous immediacy, superbly autonomous of the chance combinations of matter that they throw up; and to this extent the world remains fragmentary and chaotic on its surfaces, a set of fortuitous conjunctures for which the archetypal image is the two-second encounter at some busy urban cross-roads. This is surely the case with *Finnegans Wake*, a text which offers a minimum of mediation between its local units of signification and the mighty Viconian cycles which generate and enclose them. It is not difficult to perceive a similar dislocation of abstract structure and perversely idiosyncratic particular in Saussure's celebrated distinction between *langue* – the universal categories of language itself – and the apparently random, unformalizable nature of *parole* or everyday speech.

In a strange reversal or regression of historical time, capitalism's 'higher' stages would thus seem to return it to the pre-industrial world it has left behind – to a closed, cyclical, naturalized sphere of relentless fatality, of which myth is one appropriate figuration. Mythological thought is commonly associated with season-based, traditional, pre-industrial society, and historical consciousness with urban culture; but one has only to compare the work of Yeats and Joyce to see how beautifully this contrast doesn't work. For both are of course deeply mythological writers, in an age when the most primitive and the most sophisticated have somehow coalesced. Indeed this is a stock formula of modernism, whether in the shape of that atavistic avant-gardist who is Eliot's ideal poet, the role of archaic materials in art or psychoanalysis, or the uncanny double process by which Baudelaire, in Walter Benjamin's esoteric reading of him, finds himself geologically excavating the ancient in his restless hunt for the new. This 'neverchanging everchanging' world, as *Ulysses* has it, is one in which space seems both fragmentary and homogeneous; and this is the appropriate space of the commodity, the fragment of matter which levels all phenomena to a common identity. The allegorical signifier, Benjamin remarks, returns in the modern epoch as the commodity;[1] and one might claim that it is as the mythological signifier that it returns in the work of Joyce.

If myth is thus symptomatic of a reified social condition, it is also a convenient instrument for making sense of it. The steady draining of immanent meaning from objects clears the way for some marvellous new totalization, so that in a world depleted of significance and subjectivity, myth can furnish just those ordering, reductive schemas necessary to elicit unity from chaos. It thus takes over something of the traditional role of historical explanation at a point where historical forms of thought are now themselves increasingly part of the symbolic rubble, progressively hollow and discredited in the aftermath of imperialist world war. Yet if myth for a T.S. Eliot discloses some given pattern in reality, this is precisely not the case for Lévi-Strauss – nor for James Joyce, whose texts are comically aware of the arbitrariness of the allegorical signifier, and who knows that a day in Dublin must be *made* to mean the wanderings of Odysseus, wrenched into it by hermeneutical violence in the absence of any immanent correspondences between the two. Like the commodity, Joyce's writing will seize on any old content in order to perpetuate itself.

The early decades of the twentieth century witness a search for ever more formalized models of social explanation, from structural linguistics and psychoanalysis to Wittgenstein's *Tractatus* and the Husserlian *eidos*; but these are in tension with an anxious turning back to 'the things themselves', whether in this alternative dimension of Husserlian phenomenology or in that romantic pursuit of the irreducibly 'lived' which sweeps from German *Lebensphilosophie* to emerge somewhere in the doctrines of *Scrutiny*. Perhaps, then, it is myth which can provide the missing mediations between the over-formalized on the one hand and the myopically particular on the other, between that which threatens to elude language in its abstract universality and that which slips through the net of discourse in its ineffable uniqueness. Myth would then figure as a return of the Romantic symbol, a reinvention of the Hegelian 'concrete universal' in which every phenomenon is secretly inscribed by a universal law, and any time, place or identity pregnant with the burden of the cosmic whole. If this can be achieved, then a history in crisis might once more be rendered stable and significant, reconstituted as a set of hierarchical planes and correspondences.

This, however, is more easily said than done. It is true that a novel like *Ulysses,* in which every apparently random particular opens microcosmically into some portentous universal, might be seen in one sense as standard Hegelian stuff. But this would surely be to overlook the enormous irony with which this is accomplished – the way in which this paranoid totality gestures to its own artifice in its very pokerfaced exhaustiveness. The sweated Flaubertian labour needed to bring off such a *tour de force,* a labour kept steadily before our gaze, betrays the fictive or impossible nature of the whole enterprise and contains the seeds of its own dissolution. For if a world of intricate symbolic correspondences is to be constructed, some kind of mechanism or switch-gear will be necessary by which any one element of reality can become a signifier of another; and there is clearly no natural stopping place to this play of allegorical signification, this endless metamorphosis in which anything can be alchemically converted into anything else. The symbolic system, in short, carries within it the forces of its own deconstruction – which is to say in a different idiom that it operates very much by the logic of that commodity form which is partly responsible for the chaos it hopes to transcend. It is the commodity form which at once fashions some spurious identity between disparate objects and generates an unstable, open-ended flux which threatens to outrun all such scrupulously imposed symmetry. If a day in Dublin can be made meaningful through its allegorical alliance with a classical text, could not the same be equally done for a day in Barnsley or the Bronx? The textual strategies which invest a particular time or place with unwonted centrality, ridding it of its randomness and contingency, do so only to return the whole of that contingency to it. In this sense the compliment which Joyce pays to Ireland, in inscribing it so unforgettably on the international map, is of a distinctly backhanded kind. To privilege any particular experience, you must refer it to a structure which is always elsewhere; but this equivalencing of the two realms in question is enough to rob both of them of their distinctiveness. Allegory is in this sense symbolism run riot, pressed to a self-undoing extreme; if anything can now fulfil the role of a 'concrete universal', nothing is particularly remarkable.

If anywhere is everywhere, then you can scribble away in Trieste without ever having left Dublin. Modernism, as Raymond Williams has argued, is among other things a running battle between a new mode of rootless, cosmopolitan consciousness and the older, more parochial national traditions from which this consciousness has defiantly broken loose.[2] The vibrant modernist metropolis is the cultural node of a now thoroughly global capitalist system, and is in the process of both relinquishing and reinterpreting from a distance the national enclaves within which capitalist production has traditionally flourished. Ireland or Britain will thus come to figure as no more than random regional instantiations of an autonomous international nework, whose economic operations traverse particular cultures as indifferently as 'deep structures' cut across distinct languages, literary texts or individual egos. The deracinated fate of the modernist exiles and emigrés is a material condition for the emergence of a newly formalizing, universalizing thought, one which having spurned the ambiguous comforts of a motherland can now cast a bleak analytic eye, from its 'transcendental' vantage-point in some polyglot metropolis, on all such specific historical legacies, discerning the hidden global logics by which they are governed. The modernists, as Sean Golden has suggested, were never greatly hamstrung by those vested psychological interests in a specific national culture which mark a more provincial art;[3] instead, they could approach such indigenous traditions from the outside, estrange and appropriate them for their own devious ends, roam in the manner of a Joyce, Pound or Eliot across a whole span of cultures in euphoric, melancholic liberation from the Oedipal constraints of a mother tongue. If this powerfully alienating perspective on traditionalist pieties is one source of modernism's radical impact, it also betrays well enough its reluctant complicity with the world of international capitalist production, which is quite as nation-blind as *The Waste Land* or the *Cantos* and has the same scant respect for regional idiosyncrasy. To spring like Joyce or Beckett from a chronically backward colonial society was to this extent to turn political oppression to artistic advantage: if you had little enough rich national heritage in the first place, having been systematically deprived of it by the British, then you figured already as a kind of non-place and non-identity and could thus find yourself unpredictably catapulted from margins to centre, offering in your peripherality an ironic prefiguration of the destiny that would now befall even the most advanced national capitalist formations. Bereft of a stable, continuous cultural tradition, the colonized were forced to make it up as they went along; and it is exactly this effect of political dispossession which Joyce, Beckett and Flann O'Brien will put to subversive modernist use.

The pre-industrial – Ireland as a stagnant agrarian province – thus enters into a dramatic new constellation with the most developed, as 'primitive' and sophisticated once more commingle in the modernist sensibility. If Dublin is now the capital of the world, it is in part because the life-rhythms of such a parochial spot, with its set routines, recurrent habits and sense of inert enclosure, are coming to seem exemplary of the shrunken, self-sustaining, repetitive sphere of monopoly capitalism itself. The sealed circuits of the one reflect, microcosmically, those of the other. Modernism and colonialism become strange bedfellows, not least because the liberal realist doctrines from which modernism breaks free were never quite so plausible and entrenched on the colonial edges as they were in the metropolitan centres. For the subjugated subjects of empire, the individual is less the strenuously self-fashioning agent of its own historical destiny than empty, powerless, without a name; there can be little of the major realists' trust in the beneficence of linear time, which is always on the side of Caesar. Languishing within a barren social reality, the colonized subject may beat the kind of retreat into fantasy and hallucination which lends itself more evidently to modernist than to realist literary practice. And if the traditional national languages are now encountering global semiotic systems, cherished cultural heritages yielding ground to avant-garde techniques which are easily portable across national frontiers, who better placed to speak this new non-speech than those already disinherited in their own tongue?

For Joyce, then, the future lies not so much with thwarted Romantic intellectuals still ambivalently in thrall to a national heritage, as with faceless advertising agents of mixed nationhood and little domestic stability who can be at home anywhere because anywhere is everywhere. But if Leopold Bloom signifies in this sense the 'good' side of international capitalism, with its impatience of all chauvinism and provincialism, its democratic scorn for the hieratic and elitist, his vague humanitarian creed of universal brotherhood also bears witness to the impotent universalism of the bourgeois public sphere. Bloom is at once sunk in gross particularism and too abstractly cosmopolitan; and to this extent he reproduces in his own person the contradiction between form and content which pertains to the commodities he peddles. Such, at least, would be the view of a Georg Lukács, for whom the commodity form is the secret villain of this modern scenario in which abstract and concrete have been riven apart. *History and Class Consciousness* depicts a fallen world in which, under the sway of exchange-value, 'reality disintegrates into a multitude of irrational facts and over these a network of purely

322

"formal" laws emptied of content is cast.'[4] It is a reasonable description of *Ulysses*, or for that matter of much modernist art, of which Theodor Adorno comments that its formal relations are as abstract as the real relations between individuals in bourgeois society.[5] The commodity, itself a kind of embodied hiatus between use-value and exchange-value, sensuous content and universal form, is for Lukács the source of all these disabling antinomies between general and particular. The bourgeoisie is on the one hand 'held fast in the mire of immediacy',[6] but subjected on the other hand to the dominion of iron laws with all the naturalized fatality of the world of myth. The human subject is at once empirical particular and abstract transcendence, phenomenally determined but spiritually free. In such historical conditions, subject and object, form and content, sense and spirit, are broken asunder; and the breathtaking project of the central section of *History and Class Consciousness* is to fasten upon these commonplace topoi of idealist philosophy and think them through again, this time in the transfiguring light of the commodity form which for Lukács imprints that idealism in its every aspect but to which it is necessarily blinded.

There are two possible solutions to this historical situation. One is socialism, which figured in Eastern Europe as the Stalinism for which Lukács became from time to time an ambiguous apologist. The other, somewhat less taxing solution is the aesthetic, which for Lukács emerged into existence as a strategic response to the dilemmas he sketches. In the eighteenth century, the stark polarities of early bourgeois society

> conferred upon aesthetics and upon consciousness of art a philosophical importance that art was unable to lay claim to in previous ages. This does not mean that art itself was experiencing an unprecedented golden age. On the contrary, with a very few exceptions the actual artistic production during this period cannot be remotely compared to that of past golden ages. What is crucial here is the theoretical and philosophical importance which the *principle of art* acquired in this period.[7]

This principle, so Lukács claims, involves 'the creation of a concrete totality that springs from a conception of form orientated towards the concrete content of its material substratum. In this view form is therefore able to demolish the "contingent" relation of the parts to the whole and to resolve the merely apparent opposition between chance and necessity.[8] The work of art, in short, comes to the rescue of a commodified existence, equipped with everything in which the commodity is so lamentably lacking – a form no longer indifferent to its content but indissociable from it; an objectifying of the subjective which entails enrichment rather than estrangement; a deconstruction of the antithesis between freedom and necessity, as each element of the artefact appears at once miraculously autonomous yet cunningly subordinated to the law of the whole.

In the absence of socialism, then, it will prove necessary to make do with art. Just as aesthetics itself provided for early bourgeois society an imaginary resolution of real contradictions, so as the grip of Stalinism tightens Lukács is constrained to discover in art that concrete totality which a society of labour camps looks increasingly unlikely to deliver. It is thus that he promulgates his celebrated doctrine of realism, as a kind of dialecticized version of the Romantic ideology of the symbol. In the all-round, many-sided, harmonious totality of the realist work, individual particulars are entirely mediated through the structure of the whole, sublated to the 'typical' or universal with no detriment to their sensuous specificity. In his later aesthetic theory, Lukács will cite as the central category of the aesthetic the notion of *Besonderheit* or speciality, that which seamlessly mediates between individual and totality by inhering simultaneously in both.[9] For him, as for a long tradition of Romantic idealism, art signifies that privileged place where the concrete phenomena, while posing as no more than themselves, are surreptitiously recreated in the image of their universal truth. In speaking simply of itself, jealously preserving its self-identity, each facet of the artwork cannot help transmitting a lateral message about all of the others. Works of realism know the truth, but pretend in a crafty act of prestidigitation that they do not: the work must first of all abstract the essence of the real, then conceal this essence by recreating it in all of its supposed immediacy. The realist artefact is thus a kind of *tromp l'oeil*, a surface which is also a depth, a regulative law everywhere absolute yet nowhere visible. The richly specified elements of the text are at once equivalent to and less than the totality which constitutes them; and the price which these elements must pay for their privileged mediation through the whole is the loss of any real power to react critically upon it.

Lukács's aesthetics, in other words, are a left mirror-image of the dominant model of bourgeois aesthetics whose fortunes and misfortunes we have charted through this study. Lukácsian realism lends a Marxist inflection to that imbrication of law and freedom, whole and part, spirit and sense, which plays so vital a role in the construction of middle-class hegemony. Spontaneously inscribed by the law of the whole, the minute particulars of the realist artefact dance together in consort according to some self-effacing principle of unity. It is as though Lukács, having tracked the embarrassments of bourgeois society to their material roots in a style quite at odds with that society's own self-reflection, then turns and advances much the same solutions to these difficulties. It is true that for him the relations between part and whole are always subtly mediated, never a matter of some intuited coalescence; but it is nevertheless remarkable that one with his formidable powers of historical materialist analysis should come up with an aesthetics which in broad outline faithfully reproduces some of the key structures of bourgeois political power.

If this is remarkable, it is not perhaps all that surprising. It belongs to Lukács's critique of both Stalinism and leftist avant-gardism to invoke the wealth of the bourgeois humanist legacy, overvaluing the undoubted continuity between that heritage and a socialist future; and the Romantic roots of his own brand of Marxism lead him often enough to ignore the more progressive dimensions of capitalism, including the need for an aesthetics which has learnt from the commodity form rather than lapsed back into some nostalgic totality before it ever was. To say this is not to deny the admirable force and fertility of the Lukácsian theory of realism, which represents an invaluable contribution to the canon of Marxist criticism, and which a modernist Marxism has unjustly demeaned; but Lukács's failure to take Marx's point that history progresses by its bad side nevertheless constitutes a serious limitation to his thought.

Walter Benjamin, by contrast, presses Marx's dictum to a parodic extreme. His Messianic reading of history forbids him any faith in secular redemption, dismantles all teleological hope, and in an astonishingly bold dialectical stroke locates the signs of salvation in the very unregeneracy of historical life, in its postlapsarian suffering and squalor. The more history presents itself as mortified and devalued, as in the sluggish, spiritually bankrupt world of the German *Trauerspiel*, the more it becomes a negative index of some utterly inconceivable transcendence waiting patiently in the wings. Time in such conditions is folded back into space, dwindled to a repetition so agonizingly empty that some salvific epiphany might just be imagined to tremble on its brink. The profane order of a corrupt politics is a kind of negative imprint of Messianic time, which will finally emerge into its own on the day of judgement not from the womb of history but from its ruins. The very transitoriness of a history in pieces anticipates its own ultimate passing away, so that for Benjamin the ghostly traces of paradise can be detected in its sheer antithesis – in that endless series of catastrophes which is secular temporality, the storm blowing from heaven to which some give the name of progress. At the nadir of historical fortunes, in a social order grown morbid and meaningless, the figure of the just society can be glimmeringly discerned, by a heterodox hermeneutics for which the death's head is transfigured into an angelic countenance. Only such a negative political theology can stay true to the Judaic *Bilderverbot* which prohibits all graven images of future reconciliation, including those images known as art. Only the fragmentary work of art, that which refuses the lures of the aesthetic, of *Schein* and symbolic totality, can hope to figure forth truth and justice by remaining resolutely silent about them, foregrounding in their place the unredeemed torment of secular time.

Lukács opposes the artefact to the commodity; Benjamin, in another feat of dialectical impudence, conjures a revolutionary aesthetics from the commodity form itself. The blank, petrified objects of *Trauerspiel* have undergone a kind of leakage of meaning, an unhinging of signifier and signified, in a world which like that of commodity production knows only the empty, homogeneous time of eternal repetition. The features of this inert, atomized landscape then have to suffer a kind of secondary reification at the hands of the allegorical sign, itself a dead letter or piece of lifeless script. But once all intrinsic meaning has haemorrhaged from the object, in a collapse of the expressive totality which Lukács espouses, any phenomenon can come by the wily resourcefulness of the allegorist to signify absolutely anything else, in a kind of profane parody of the creative naming of God. Allegory thus mimes the levelling, equivalencing operations of the commodity but thereby releases a fresh polyvalence of meaning, as the allegorist grubs among the ruins of once integral meanings to permutate them in startling new ways. Once purged of all mystifying immanence, the allegorical referent can be redeemed into a multiplicity of uses, read against the grain and scandalously reinterpreted in the manner of Kabbala. The inherent sense which ebbs from the object under the allegorist's melancholy gaze leaves it an arbitrary material signifier, a rune or fragment retrieved from the clutches of some univocal significance and surrendered unconditionally into the allegorist's power. Such objects have already come loose from their contexts, and so can be plucked from their environs and woven together in a set of estranging correspondences. Benjamin is already familiar with this technique from Kabbalistic interpretation, and will later find resonances of it in the practice of the avant-garde, in montage, surrealism, dream imagery and epic theatre, as well as in the epiphanies of Proustian memory, the symbolic affinities of Baudelaire and his own obsessional habit of collecting. There is also a seed of inspiration here for his later doctrine of mechanical reproduction, in which the very technology which breeds alienation, given a dialectical twist, can strip cultural products of their intimidatory aura and refunction them in productive ways.

Like the commodity, the meaning of the allegorical object is always elsewhere, eccentric to its material being; but the more polyvalent it becomes, the more supple and inventive grows its forensic power of deciphering the real. The allegorical signifier shares in a sense in the frozen world of myth, whose compulsive repetitions foreshadow Benjamin's later image of an historicism for which all time is homogeneous; but it is also a force to break open this fetishized realm, inscribing its own network of 'magical' affinities across the face of an inscrutable history. Later in Benhamin's work, this will take the form of the dialectical image, the shocking confrontation in which time is arrested to a compact monad, spatialized to a shimmering field of force, so that the political present may redeem an endangered moment of the past by wrenching it into illuminating correspondence with itself. The problem of Benjamin's project, as Jürgen Habermas has pointed out, is to restore the possibility of such symbolic correlations while liquidating that world of natural mythology of which they form a part.[10] Neither the 'natural' totalizing of the symbol, nor the mere consecration of linear repetition, is an acceptable strategy. Mechanical reproduction rejects both the unique difference of the aura and the endless self-identities of myth; in levelling artefacts to a sameness subversive of the former, it frees them for distinctive functions repugnant to the latter.

These dialectical images are an instance of what Benjamin calls a 'constellation', a motif which runs from the first few pages of his book on *Trauerspiel* to the posthumously published 'Theses on the Philosophy of History'. In the ideal critical method, he writes,

> ideas are not represented in themselves, but solely and exclusively in an arrangement of concrete elements in the concept: as the configuration of these elements . . . Ideas are to objects as constellations are to stars. This means, in the first place, that they are neither their concepts nor their laws . . . It is the function of concepts to group phenomena together, and the division which is brought about within them thanks to the distinguishing power of the intellect is all the more significant in that it brings about two things at a single stroke: the salvation of phenomena and the representation of ideas.[11]

The idea is not what lies behind the phenomenon as some informing essence, but the way the object is conceptually configurated in its diverse, extreme and contradictory elements. Benjamin's dream is of a form of criticism so tenaciously immanent that it would remain entirely immersed in its object. The truth of that object would be disclosed not by referring it in rationalist style to a governing general idea, but by dismantling its component elements through the power of minutely particular concepts, then reconfigurating them in a pattern which redeemed the thing's meaning and value without ceasing to adhere to it. 'Phenomena', he writes, 'do not, however, enter into the realm of ideas whole, in their crude empirical state, adulterated by appearances, but only in their basic elements, redeemed. They are divested of their false unity so that, thus divided, they might partake of the genuine unity of truth.'[12] The thing must not be grasped as a mere instantiation of some universal essence; instead, thought must deploy a whole cluster of stubbornly specific concepts which in Cubist style refract the object in myriad directions or penetrate it from a range of diffuse angles. In this way, the phenomenal sphere is itself persuaded to yield up a kind of noumenal truth, as the microscopic gaze estranges the everyday into the remarkable.[13]

A constellatory epistemology sets its face against the Cartesian or Kantian moment of subjectivity, less concerned to 'possess' the phenomenon than to liberate it into its own sensuous being and preserve its disparate elements in all their irreducible heterogeneity. The Kantian division of empirical and intelligible is thus transcended; and this is the only way of doing methodological justice to a thing's damaged, suppressed materiality, salvaging what Adorno calls 'the waste products and blind spots which have escaped the dialectic' from the inexorable ironing out of the abstract idea.[14] The constellation refuses to clinch itself on some metaphysical essence, leaving its component parts loosely articulated in the manner of *Trauerspiel* or epic theatre; but it nevertheless prefigures that state of reconciliation which it would be both blasphemous and politically counterproductive to represent directly. In its unity of the perceptual and conceptual, its transmutation of thoughts into images, it bears a strain of that blissful Edenic condition in which word and object were spontaneously at one, as well as of that prehistoric, mimetic correspondence between Nature and humanity which pre-dated our fall into cognitive reason.

The Benjaminian notion of constellation is itself, one might claim, a constellation all of its own, rich in theoretical allusions. If it points back to Kabbala, the Leibnizian monad and Husserl's return to the phenomena, it also glances towards surrealism's estranging reconfigurations of the everyday, to Schoenberg's musical system and to a whole new style of microscopic sociology in which, as in the work of Adorno or Benjamin's own study of Paris, a transformed relation of part and whole is established.[15] In this kind of microanalysis, the individual phenomenon is grasped in all of its overdetermined complexity as a kind of cryptic code or riddling rebus to be deciphered, a drastically abbreviated image of social processes which the discerning eye will persuade it to yield up. It might be argued that the echoes of symbolic totality thus linger on within this alternative mode of thought; but it is now less a question of receiving the object as some intuitive given than of disarticulating and reconstructing it through the labour of the concept. What this method then delivers is a kind of poetic or novelistic sociology in which the whole seems to consist of nothing but a dense tessellation of graphic images; and to this extent it represents an aestheticized model of social enquiry. It springs, however, from an aesthetic conceived otherwise – not as some symbolist inherence of part in whole, nor even in Lukácsian fashion as their complex mediation, which can be accused simply of deferring and complicating the totality's firm mastery of the particular. It is a matter, rather, of constructing a stringent economy of the object which nevertheless refuses the allure of identity, allowing its constituents to light each other up in all their contradictoriness. The literary styles of Benjamin and Adorno themselves are among the finest examples of this mode.

The concept of constellation, which Benjamin elaborated in close collaboration with Adorno,[16] is perhaps the most strikingly original attempt in the modern period to break with traditional versions of totality. It represents a determined resistance to the more paranoid forms of totalizing thought on the part of thinkers who nevertheless set their faces against any mere empiricist celebration of the fragment. By revolutionizing the relations between part and whole, the constellation strikes at the very heart of the traditional aesthetic paradigm, in which the specificity of the detail is allowed no genuine resistance to the organizing power of the totality. The aesthetic is thus turned against the aesthetic: what supposedly distinguishes art from discursive thought – its high degree of specificity – is pushed to an extreme, so that specificity is no longer à la Lukács both preserved and suspended. The constellation safeguards particularity but fissures identity, exploding the object into an array of conflictive elements and so unleashing its materiality at the cost of its self-sameness. Lukács's 'type', by contrast, suffers no loss of self-identity through its immersion in the whole, but emerges with that identity deepened and enriched. His Schillerian aesthetics envisage little conflict between the various facets of the 'all-round' individual; on the contrary, the 'typical' character's inherence in some historical essence tends to resolve its various aspects into harmony. Lukács does indeed think the category of contradiction, but always under the sign of unity. The capitalist social formation is a totality of contradictions; what determines each contradiction is thus the unity it forms with others; the truth of contradiction is accordingly unity. It would be hard to think up a more blatant contradiction.

It is this essentializing of conflict which the concept of constellation

330

is out to worst, and there can be no doubt that in developing it both Benjamin and Adorno had Lukács firmly in their sights. It is not, however, an idea without severe difficulties of its own. For one thing, it circumvents the problem of *determinations* raised by some more traditional debates about totality – of the relative causal weight and efficacy of different constituents within a whole system. In breaking with a rigidly rationalistic hierarchy of values, it tends instead to equalize out all elements of the object – a method which is sometimes pressed to an extreme in the work of Benjamin, whose deliberately casual juxtapositions of a stray feature of the superstructure with a central component of the base won him a rebuke from the more soberly minded Adorno.[17] Those radicals who instinctively mistrust the notion of hierarchy should ask themselves whether they really believe aesthetics to be as important as apartheid. One of the most vital aspects of the idea of totality has been to provide us with some concrete political guidance as to which institutions are more central than others in the process of social change – to escape, in short a purely circular notion of the social formation in which, since every 'level' seems of equal valency with every other, the question of where one politically intervenes may be arbitrarily decided. Most political radicals, whether they acknowledge it or not, are committed to some notion of hierarchical determination, believing for example that racist or sexist attitudes are more durably transformed by changes of institution than by efforts to change consciousness as such. The concept of totality reminds us forcibly of the structural limitations imposed on particular courses of political action – of what must first be done, also done, or remains to be done in the pursuit of some political goal. There is no need to suspect, in some convenient straw target of totalizing thought, that our political actions are therefore simply 'given' to us spontaneously by the structure of the social whole – a fantasy which is merely the other side of the left reformist belief (shared by a good many right-wing conservatives) that there is no 'social whole' whatsoever other than one discursively constructed for pragmatic ends.

The doctrine that social life contains hierarchical determinations does not of course automatically lead to the classical Marxist view that in human history to date certain material factors have been of consistent fundamental importance. For a more pluralist vision, the dominance of such factors is a variable conjunctural matter: what is determinant in one context or perspective is not necessarily so in another. Society may thus be conceived along the lines of some Wittgensteinian game, as a rich array of strategies, moves and countermoves in which certain priorities are pragmatically appropriate from certain viewpoints. For Marxism, society is a duller, drabber, less aesthetically enthralling affair, much more prone to compulsive repetition, with a somewhat impoverished range of moves at its disposal, less like a playground than a prison. In its monotonously determinist manner, Marxism imagines that in order to listen to Bach one must first work, or get someone else to do so, and that moral philosophers could not debate unless child-rearing practices had first put them in place. It argues, moreover, that these material preconditions are not simply the *sine qua non* of what flows from them, but continue to exert a decisive force upon it.

The concept of constellation carries with it a significant ambiguity about the subjective or objective nature of such constructive activity. On the one hand, the model is advanced as an antidote to all errant subjectivism: concepts must cling to the contours of the thing itself rather than spring from the subject's arbitrary will, subduing themselves like Schoenberg's compositional practice to the immanent logic of their subject-matter. 'There is a delicate empiricism', Benjamin quotes Goethe as declaring, 'which so intimately involves itself with the object that it becomes true theory.'[18] On the other hand, the act of constellating would seem to entail an idiosyncratic free-wheeling of the imagination which recalls the devious opportunism of the allegorist. Indeed at its worst the constellation would appear an unholy mixture of positivism (what Adorno called the 'wide-eyed presentation of mere facts' of Benjamin's *Passagenarbeit*)[19] and whimsicality; and it is this combination which Adorno detects in surrealism, whose montages seem to him to involve a fetishism of immediacy yoked to an arbitrary, undialectical subjectivism.[20] He finds something of the same blend in Benjamin's Arcades project, which he chides for a certain occult positivism as well as for a psychologistic fancifulness, finding his friend's style of thought at once too exoteric and too esoteric.[21] For Adorno, both surrealism and Benjamin's work on Paris threaten to eliminate the active, critical role of the subject in the interpretative process at the same time as they permit an unbridled subjectivity. And this combination may be endemic to Benjamin's notion of allegory, the death's head symbol of which displays a 'total expressionlessness – the black of the eye-sockets – coupled to the most unbridled expression – the grinning rows of teeth'.[22]

For all its problems, the idea of constellation surely remains durable and suggestive today. But like much of Benjamin's thought it cannot be wholly abstracted from its origins in historical crisis. As fascism comes to power, there is a sense in which Benjamin's whole career becomes a kind of urgent constellating, a cobbling together of whatever unprepossessing scraps and fragments come to hand in the teeth of a history which, like the war-weary regimes of *Trauerspiel*, seems to have subsided into ruins. The image of the past which counts, he argues in the 'Theses on the Philosophy of History', is that which appears unexpectedly to a man singled out by history at a moment of danger; and this is perhaps what 'theory' means for Benjamin too, that which under extreme pressure can be hastily thrown together and kept ready to hand. His project is to blast open the lethal continuum of history with the few poor weapons available to him: shock, allegory, estrangement, heterogeneous 'chips' of Messianic time, miniaturization, mechanical reproduction, Kabbalistic interpretative violence, surrealist montage, revolutionary nostalgia, reactivated memory traces, reading which brush left-handedly against the grain. The condition of possibility of much of this astonishingly bold enterprise, as with the baroque allegorists, was that history was collapsing behind one's back into fragments – that one could grub among the ruins and scrape together some odds and ends to oppose the inexorable march of 'progress' only because the catastrophe had already happened. That catastrophe gives the lie to the complacent assumption that national formations are now definitively outmoded by international space. On the contrary, what fascism revealed was that international monopoly capitalism, far from leaving such national lineages behind it, was able to exploit them at a point of extreme political crisis for its own ends, once again drawing the old and the new into unexpected constellation. It is precisely such correspondences between the archaic and the avant garde which characterize Nazi ideology, as the sensuous specificity of blood and soil is coupled to technological fetishism and global imperialist expansion.

At a moment of ultimate danger, Benjamin overreacts to the hubristic narratives of historicism; indeed it is not hard to reject such teleologies if one views history itself, in Messianic style, as intrinsically negative. Those of Benjamin's commentators who applaud his anti-teleology may not be quite so eager to endorse the indiscriminate downgrading of the 'profane' with which it is bound up. The abundant fertility of Benjamin's historical imagination is blighted by its catastrophism and apocalypticism; if for the human being in extreme danger history has been reduced to the fortuitous flashing up of an isolated image, there are others whose emancipation involves a less aestheticized, more sober and systematic enquiry into the nature of historical development. Benjamin learned enduringly from what one might read as the implicit slogan of Bertolt Brecht's work: Use whatever you can, collect what you can since you never know when it might come in handy. But the corollary of this valuably idiosyncratic strategy can be a disabling eclecticism, which in Brecht's case shades at times into a form of left-utilitarianism. Benjamin's fascination with the detritus of history, with the offbeat, deviant and discarded, offers an essential corrective to a narrowly totalizing ideology at the same time as it risks hardening, like certain contemporary theories, into no more than that ideology's inverted mirror-image, replacing a theoretical myopia with a corresponding astigmatism.

The constellation draws together the empirical and the conceptual; and it therefore figures as a strain of old Eden, a muffled resonance of that paradisal condition in which, in the discourse of divinity, sign and object were intimately at one. In Benjamin's view, humanity has fallen from this felicitous state into a degraded instrumentalism of language; and language has thus become depleted in its expressive, mimetic resources, dwindling to the reified token of the Saussurean sign. The allegorical signifier is dire testimony to our postlapsarian plight, in which we are no longer spontaneously possessed of the object but forced to blunder our way laboriously from one sign to another, groping for significance among the shards of a now shattered totality. Yet precisely because meaning has leaked from the signifier, its materiality has become curiously heightened; the more things and meanings disengage, the more palpable become the material operations of the allegories which fumble to reunite them. The baroque allegorist accordingly takes pleasure in this somatic dimension of the sign, finding in the creatureliness of its shape and sound some purely sensuous residue which escapes the strict regime of sense to which all language is now shackled. Discourse has been forcibly leashed to logicality; but the *Trauerspiel's* preoccupation with script as against voice, its ceremonious arranging of matter-laden hieroglyphs like so many embalmed emblems, returns to us an awareness of the bodily nature of language. The point where meaning and materiality are most painfully divided reminds us by negation of a possible unity of word and world, as well as of the somatic foundations of speech. If the body is a signifier, then language is material practice. It is part of the mission of philosophy in Benjamin's view to restore to language its occluded symbolic riches, rescue it from its lapse into the impoverishment of cognition so that the word may dance once again, like those angels whose bodies are one burning flame of praise before God.

This recoupling of concept and body is a traditional preoccupation of the aesthetic. For Benjamin, language has its roots in the acting out of magical correspondences between humanity and Nature; it is thus originally a matter of sensuous images, and only subsequently of ideas. He finds traces of this expressive mimetic discourse within our more semiotic, communicative speech, as in the aesthetics of Mallarmé or the gestural language of Naples.[23] For the baroque drama, the only good body is a dead one: death is the ultimate unhinging of meaning and materiality, draining life from the body to leave it an allegorical signifier. 'In the *Trauerspiel*', Benjamin writes, 'the corpse becomes quite simply the pre-eminent emblematic property.'[24] The baroque drama revolves on a mangled body, its parts dismembered by a violence in which the plaint for a lost organicism can still be dimly heard. Since the living body presents itself as an expressive unity, it is only in its brutal undoing, its diffusion into so many torn, reified fragments, that the drama may scavenge for significance among its organs. Meaning is ripped from the ruins of the body, from the flayed flesh rather than from the harmonious figure; and one may perhaps detect here a faint analogy with the work of Freud, for which it is likewise in the dividing of the body, the disarticulating of its zones and organs, that its 'truth' may be disclosed.

It is this kind of dismemberment, in the milder form of the shocks and invasions of urban experience, which the *flâneur* of the Arcades project strives to resist. The *flâneur* or solitary city stroller, stepping out with his turtle on a lead, moves majestically against the grain of the urban masses who would decompose him to some alien meaning;

335

in this sense his very style of walking is a politics all in itself. This is the aestheticized body of the leisured pre-industrial world, of the domestic interior and non-commodified object; what modern society demands is a reconstituted body, one intimate with technology and adapted to the sudden conjunctures and disconnections of urban life. Benjamin's project, in short, is the construction of a new kind of human body; and the role of the cultural critic in this task involves his or her intervention in what he calls the 'image sphere'. In an enigmatic passage in his essay on surrealism, he writes:

> The collective is a body, too. And the *physis* that is being organised for it in technology can, through all its political and factual reality, only be produced in that image sphere to which profane illumination initiates us. Only when in technology body and image so interpenetrate that all revolutionary tension becomes bodily collective innervation, and all the bodily innervations of the collective become revolutionary discharge, has reality transcended itself to the extent demanded by the *Communist Manifesto*.[25]

A new collective body is being organized for the individual subject by political and technological change; and the function of the critic is to fashion those images by which humanity can assume this unfamiliar flesh. If the body is constructed out of images, images are in their turn forms of material practice. The *Trauerspiel*'s undoing of the body is hardly a pleasurable affair; but this may prove yet another instance of history progressing by its bad side, since the dismantling of all false organicist unity is a necessary prelude to the emergence of the mobile, functional, multipurpose body of technological socialist humanity. Just as the aesthetic for the eighteenth century involved that whole new programme of bodily disciplines we call manners, imprinting a grace and decorousness on the flesh, so for Benjamin the body must be reprogrammed and reinscribed by the power of the sensuous image. The aesthetic, once again, becomes a politics of the body, this time with a thoroughly materialistic inflection.

This whole side of Benjamin's thought smacks of an ultra-modernist technologism, of that anxiety to prove his materialist manhood in the sceptical eyes of a Brecht which sits so uneasily with the translator of Proust and the lover of Leskov. There is a strain of left functionalism and triumphalism about this aspect of Benjamin's writing, in which the body is conceived as instrument, raw material to be organized, even as machine. No greater contrast to this could be imagined than the similarly mobile, pluralized, disarticulated body of Bakhtinian carnival, which disowns all instrumentality in the name of sensuous repleteness. If the project of aesthetics begins in the Enlightenment with a judicious reinsertion of the body into a dangerously abstract discourse, we arrive with Mikhail Bakhtin at the revolutionary consummation of that logic, as the body's libidinal practice explodes the languages of reason, unity and identity into so many superfluous bits and pieces. Bakhtin presses the initial modest impulse of the aesthetic to a fantastic extreme: what began with the Earl of Shaftesbury and his fellows as the sensual well-being induced by a fine glass of port has now become a cackle of obscene laughter, as a vulgar, shameless materialism of the body – belly, anus, genitals – rides roughshod over ruling-class civilities. For a brief, politically licensed moment, the flesh makes its insurrection and refuses the inscription of reason, pitting sensation against concept and libido against law, summoning the licentious, semiotic and dialogical in the face of that monological authority whose unspoken name is Stalinism. Like the constellation, carnival involves both a return to the particular and a constant overriding of identity, transgressing the body's frontiers in a play of erotic solidarity with others. Like the constellation too, it renders things non-identical with themselves in order to adumbrate a golden age of friendship and reconciliation, but refuses all graven images of such a goal. The dialectical image sphere of carnival (birth/death, high/low, destruction/renewal) reconstitutes the body as collectivity, organizes a *physis* for it, in just the way Benjamin proposes.

For all his austerity and melancholia, this Bakhtinian vision is not entirely foreign to Benjamin, who writes of the alienation effects of epic theatre that 'there is no better starting point for thought than laughter; speaking more generally, spasms of the diaphragm generally offer better chances for thought than spasms of the soul. Epic theatre is lavish only in the occasions it offers for laughter.'[26] The alienation effect distantiates the dramatic action, thwarts any intense psychical investment in it on the part of an audience, and so permits a pleasurable economizing of affect expended in laughter. For both Bakhtin and Benjamin, laughter is the very type of expressive somatic

337

utterance, an enunciation which springs straight from the body's libidinal depths and so for Benjamin carries a resonance of the endangered symbolic or mimetic dimension of language. Indeed it is significant that when he writes in his essay on surrealism of the reconstruction of the body, he remarks of the critic who forsakes a literary career for the building of the image sphere that 'the jokes he tells are the better for it'.[27] The joke is a graphic, condensed piece of utterance tied closely to the body, and so typical of what Benjamin means by an effective image.

Humanity, Benjamin writes in his essay on mechanical reproduction, has reached such a degree of self-alienation 'that it can now experience its own destruction as an aesthetic pleasure of the first order. This is the situation of politics which fascism is rendering aesthetic. Communism responds by politicising art.'[28] This famous final phrase is surely not recommending the *displacement* of art by politics, as a certain ultra-leftist current of theory has occasionally interpreted it. On the contrary, Benjamin's own revolutionary politics are in all kinds of ways aesthetic – in the concrete particularity of the constellation, the 'auratic' *mémoire involontaire* which offers a model for revolutionary tradition, the shift from discourse to sensuous image, the restoration of the language of the body, the celebration of mimesis as a non-dominative relation between humanity and its world. Benjamin is in search of a surrealist history and politics, one which clings tenaciously to the fragment, the miniature, the stray citation, but which impacts these fragments one upon the other to politically explosive effect, like the Messiah who will transfigure the world completely by making minor adjustments to it. The Benjamin who once dreamed of writing an entire work consisting of nothing but quotations is out to rewrite the whole of Marx as a montage of arresting imagery, in which every proposition will be preserved exactly as it is yet transformed out of recognition. But if his politics are in this sense aesthetic, it is only because he has subverted almost all of traditional aesthetics' central categories (beauty, harmony, totality, appearance), starting instead from what Brecht called the 'bad new things' and discovering in the structure of the commodity, the death of storytelling, the vacancy of historical time and the technology of capitalism itself those Messianic impulses which are still feebly astir there. Like Baudelaire, Benjamin brings the very new into shocking conjunction with the very old, with atavistic memories of a society as yet unmarked by class-division, so that with Paul Klee's *angelus novus* he can be blown backwards into the future with his eyes fixed mournfully upon the past.

Notes

1 See Richard Wolin, *Walter Benjamin: An Aesthetic of Redemption* (New York, 1982), p. 130.
2 See Raymond Williams, 'Beyond Cambridge English', in *Writing in Society* (London, 1983).
3 Sean Golden, 'Post-traditional English literature: a polemic', in *The Crane Bag Book of Irish Studies* (Dublin, 1982).
4 Georg Lukács, *History and Class Consciousness* (London, 1968), p. 155.
5 Theodor Adorno, *Aesthetic Theory* (London, 1984), p. 45.
6 Lukács, *History and Class Consciousness*, p. 163.
7 Ibid., p. 137.
8 Ibid.
9 See Georg Lukács, *Die Eigenart des Ästhetischen* (Neuwied, 1963).
10 See Jürgen Habermas, 'Bewusstmachende oder rettende Kritik - die Aktualität Walter Benjamins', in Siegfried Unseld (ed.), *Zur Aktualität Walter Benjamins* (Frankfurt-am-Main, 1972), p. 205.
11 Walter Benjamin, *The Origin of German Tragic Drama* (London, 1977), p. 34.
12 Ibid., p. 33.
13 For excellent accounts of this process, see Richard Wolin, *Walter Benjamin*, chapter 3, and Susan Buck-Morss, *The Origin of Negative Dialectics* (Hassocks, 1977), chapter 6.
14 Theodor Adorno, *Minima Moralia* (London, 1974), pp. 151–2.
15 See David Frisby, *Fragments of Modernity* (Cambridge, 1985).
16 See Susan Buck-Morss, *The Origin of Negative Dialectics*, chapter 1.
17 See Theodor Adorno, 'Letters to Walter Benjamin', in Ernst Bloch *et al.*, *Aesthetics and Politics* (London, 1977), pp. 128–30.
18 Walter Benjamin, 'A Small History of Photography', in *One-Way Street* (London, 1979), p. 252.
19 Benjamin, *Aesthetics and Politics*, p. 129.
20 See Theodor Adorno, 'Der Sürrealismus', in *Noten zur Literatur*, vol. 1 (Frankfurt-am-Main, 1958).
21 See Bloch et al., *Aesthetics and Politics*, Presentation 111.
22 Benjamin, *One-Way Street*, p. 70.
23 See 'Naples', in Benjamin, *One-Way Street*.

24 Benjamin, *Origin of German Tragic Drama*, p. 218.
25 Benjamin, *One-Way Street*, p. 239.
26 Walter Benjamin, *Understanding Brecht* (London, 1973), p. 101.
27 Benjamin, *One-Way Street*, p. 238.
28 Walter Benjamin, 'The Work of Art in the Age of Mechanical Reproduction', in H. Arendt (ed.), *Illuminations* (London, 1973), p. 244.

13

Art after Auschwitz:
Theodor Adorno

An 'aesthetic' thought is one true to the opacity of its object. But if thought is conceptual, and so general, how can 'aesthetic thought' be other than an oxymoron? How can the mind not betray the object in the very act of possessing it, struggling to register its density and recalcitrance at just the point it impoverishes it to some pallid universal? It would seem that the crude linguistic instruments with which we lift a thing towards us, preserving as much as possible of its unique quality, simply succeed in pushing it further away. In order to do justice to the qualitative moments of the thing, thought must thicken its own texture, grow gnarled and close-grained; but in doing so it becomes a kind of object in its own right, sheering off from the phenomenon it hoped to encircle. As Theodor Adorno remarks: 'the consistency of its performance, the density of its texture, helps the thought to miss the mark'.[1]

Dialectical thinking seeks to grasp whatever is heterogeneous to thought as a moment of thought itself, 'reproduced in thought itself as its immanent contradiction'.[2] But since one risks eradicating that heterogeneity in the very act of reflecting upon it, this enterprise is always teetering on the brink of blowing itself up. Adorno has a kind of running solution to this dilemma, and that is style. What negotiates this contradiction is the crabbed, rebarbative practice of writing itself, a discourse pitched into a constant state of crisis, twisting and looping back on itself, struggling in the structure of every sentence to avoid at once a 'bad' immediacy of the object and the false self-identity of the concept. Dialectical thought digs the object loose from its illusory self-identity, but thereby risks liquidating it within some ghastly concentration camp of the Absolute Idea; and Adorno's provisional response to this problem is a set of guerilla raids on the inarticulable, a style of philosophizing which frames the object conceptually but manages by some cerebral acrobatics to glance sideways at what gives such generalized identity the slip. Every sentence of his texts is thus forced to work overtime; each phrase must become a little masterpiece or miracle of dialectics, fixing a thought in the second before it disappears into its own contradictions. Like Benjamin's, this style is a constellatory one, each sentence a kind of crystallized conundrum from which the next is strictly non-deducible, a tight-meshed economy of epigrammatic *aperçus* in which every part is somehow autonomous yet intricately related to its fellows. All Marxist philosophers are supposed to be dialectical thinkers; but with Adorno one can feel the sweat and strain of this mode alive in every phrase, in a language rammed up against silence where the reader has no sooner registered the one-sidedness of some proposition than the opposite is immediately proposed.

The complaint that we live in some disabling gap between concept and thing becomes in the hands of thinkers less subtle than Adorno a kind of category error. Why should thoughts be like things, any more than the notion of freedom should resemble a ferret? Behind this nominalist plaint that words violate the quiddity of things, which is far from Adorno's own reflections, lies a nostalgia for the happy garden in which every object wore its own word in much the way that every flower flaunts its peculiar scent. But the fact that language universalizes is part of what it is, not some lapse or limit from which we might hope to be cured. It is not a defect of the word 'foot' that it refers to more feet than my own two, careless of the peculiarity of my own personal pair. To mourn the non-particularism of language is as misplaced as regretting that one cannot tune into the World Cup on a washing machine. The concept of a thing is not some pale mental replica of it, damagingly bereft of the thing's sensuous life, but a set of social practices – a way of doing something with the word which denotes the thing. A concept is no more like an object than the use of a spanner is like a spanner. Poetry strives to phenomenalize language, but this, as Adorno sees, is entirely self-defeating, since the more it labours to be like the thing the more it becomes a thing in its own right, which resembles the object no more than a squirrel resembles the slave trade. Perhaps it is a pity that we lack a word to capture the unique aroma of coffee – that our speech is wizened and anaemic, remote from the taste and feel of reality. But how could a word, as opposed to a pair of nostrils, capture the aroma of anything, and is it a matter of failure that it does not?

This is not to suggest, on the other hand, that Adorno is mistaken in believing our concepts to be reified and inadequate, adrift from our sensuous practice; indeed it is precisely in his concern to return thought to the body, lend it something of the body's feel and fullness, that he is in the most traditional sense of the word an aesthetician. His work, however, heralds one momentous shift of emphasis in that tradition. For what the body signals to Adorno is not first of all pleasure but suffering. In the shadow of Auschwitz it is in sheer physical wretchedness, in human shapes at the end of their tether, that the body once more obtrudes itself into the rarefied world of the philosophers. 'If thought is not measured by the extremity that eludes the concept,' he remarks in *Negative Dialectics*, 'it is from the outset in the nature of the musical accompaniment with which the SS liked to drown out the screams of its victims.'[3] Even this intolerable agony, of course, must somehow engage the idea of pleasurable well-being, for how could we measure suffering without such an implicit norm? But if there is any basis at all for a universal history, it is not a tale of cumulative happiness but, as Adorno comments, the narrative that leads from the slingshot to the megaton bomb. 'The One and All that keeps rolling on to this day – with occasional breathing spells – would teleologically be the absolute of suffering.'[4] There is indeed, as Marx recognized, a singular global story which weaves all men and women into its fabric, from the Stone Age to Star Wars; but it is a tale of scarcity and oppression, not of success – a fable, as Adorno puts it, of permanent catastrophe. The body has lived on, despite the depredations of instrumental reason; but in the Nazi death camps those depredations have now accomplished their deadliest work. For Adorno, there can be no real history after such an event, just the twilight or aftermath in which time still moves listlessly, vacuously on, even though humanity itself has come to a full stop. For a Jew like Adorno, there can only be the guilty mystery that one is still, by some oversight, alive. Adorno's politics of the body is thus the very reverse of Bakhtinian: the only image of the body which is more than a blasphemous lie is stark and skeletal, the poor forked creature of Beckettian humanity. In the wake of the Nazis, the whole aesthetic concern with sensation, with the innocent creaturely life, has become irreversibly disfigured – for fascism, as Adorno argues in *Minima Moralia*, 'was the absolute sensation . . . in the Third Reich the abstract horror of news and rumour was enjoyed as the only stimulus sufficient to incite a momentary glow in the weakened sensorium of the masses'.[5] Sensation in such conditions becomes a matter of commodified shock-value regardless of content: everything can now become pleasure, just as the desensitized morphine addict will grab indiscriminately at any drug. To posit the body and its pleasures as an unquestionably affirmative category is a dangerous illusion, in a social order which reifies and regulates corporeal pleasure for its own ends just as relentlessly as it colonizes the mind. Any return to the body which fails to reckon this truth into its calculations will be merely naive; and it is to Adorno's credit that, conscious of this as he is, he does not flinch from trying to redeem what he calls the 'somatic moment' of cognition, that irreducible dimension which accompanies all our acts of consciousness but can never be exhausted by them. The aesthetic project must not be abandoned, even if its terms of reference have been permanently tainted by fascism and 'mass' society.

The inadequation between thing and concept is importantly two-way. If the concept can never appropriate the object without leaving a remainder, then it is also true that the object – 'freedom', for example – fails to achieve the fullness promised by its concept. What prevents us from fully possessing the world is also what invests that world with some wan hope, the lack which spurs the thing out of its self-identity so as to rise to what it might in principle become. An identity of concept and phenomenon is for Adorno 'the primal form of ideology',[6] and Auschwitz confirmed the philosopheme of pure identity as death; but for him there is always another side to the story, unlike those present-day theorists whose pluralism would seem to wear a little thin when it comes to recognizing that identity, too, can have its value. 'Living in the rebuke that the thing is not identical with the concept', Adorno writes, 'is the concept's longing to become identical with the thing. This is how the sense of non-identity contains identity. The supposition of identity is indeed the ideological element of pure thought all the way through to formal logic; but hidden in it is also the truth moment of ideology, the pledge that there should be no contradiction, no antagonism.'[7] It would be a grim prospect if the concept of liberty or equality really was identical with the poor travesty of it we observe around us. Our current conceptions of identity can be shaken not only by difference, but by an identity which would be otherwise – which belongs to the political future, but which reverberates as a faint echo or pledge of reconciliation even in our most paranoid present-day identifications. That such a thought is scandalous to the mere celebration of difference is a measure of its subversive force.

Classical dialectical thought, for which 'contradiction is non-identity under the sign of identity',[8] is perfectly capable of registering the heterogeneous: it simply measures it by its own principles of unity, thereby coolly reckoning in to itself what it has just acknowledged to be irreducibly exterior. What it extracts from the object is only what was already, in any case, a thought. Adorno, on the other hand, believes with the deconstructive theory he prefigures almost in its entirety in 'identity's dependence on the non-identical'.[9] The indissoluble must be brought into its own in concepts, not subsumed under an abstract idea in that generalized barter of the mind which mirrors the equalizing exchanges of the market place. For Adorno as for Nietzsche, identificatory thought has its source in the eyes and stomach, the limbs and mouth. The pre-history of such violent appropriation of otherness is that of the early human predator out to devour the not-I. Dominative reason is 'the belly turned mind',[10] and such atavistic rage against otherness is the hallmark of every high-minded idealism. All philosophy, even that which intends freedom, bears within itself like a primordial urge the coercion by which society prolongs its oppressive existence. But for Adorno there is always another story, and this particular argument is no exception. The coerciveness of the identity principle, installed at the heart of Enlightenment reason, is also what prevents thought from lapsing into mere licence; and in its own pathological way it parodies, as well as forestalls, some authentic reconciliation of subject and object. What is required, then, is 'a rational critique of reason, not its banishment or abolition'[11] – hardly a surprising position for one whom the abolition of reason drove into exile. The problem is how to prise loose the grip of an insane rationality without allowing the slightest opening to some barbarous irrationalism.

This project involves thinking through the relations between universal and particular once again, this time on some model other than that of the singular law which flattens all specificity to its own image and likeness. If Adorno's style is tortuous and unsettling, it is partly because these relations are themselves fraught and unquiet, forever likely to slip out of focus as he steers a precarious course between the Scylla of blind particularism and the Charybdis of the tyrannical concept. 'Unreflective nominalism', he writes, 'is as wrong as the realism that equips a fallible language with the attributes of a revealed one.'[12] The way to avoid an oppressive totality is through the constellation:

> we are not to philosophise about concrete things; we are to philosophise, rather, out of those things . . . there is no step-by-step progression from the concepts to a more general cover concept. Instead, the concepts enter into a constellation . . . By gathering around the object of cognition, the concepts potentially determine the object's interior. They attain, in thinking, what was necessarily excised from thinking.[13]

Paradoxically, however, this circumvention of totality is only possible because of it. If it is true that 'objectively – not just through the knowing subject – the whole which theory expresses is contained in the individual object to be analysed',[14] this is because in an increasingly administered, manipulated world 'the more tightly the network of general definitions covers its objects, the greater will be the tendency of individual facts to be direct transparencies of their universals, and the greater the yield a viewer obtains precisely by micrological immersion'.[15] We may forget about totality, but totality, for good or ill, will not forget about us, even in our most microscopic meditations. If we can unpack the whole from the most humble particular, glimpse eternity in a grain of sand, this is because we inhabit a social order which tolerates particularity only as an obedient instantiation of the universal. We must no longer aim thought directly at this totality, but neither should we surrender ourselves to some pure play of difference, which would be quite as monotonous as the dreariest self-identity and indeed finally indistinguishable from it.[16] We must rather grasp the truth that the individual is both more and less than its general definition, and that the principle of identity is always self-contradictory, perpetuating non-identity in damaged, suppressed form as a condition of its being.

The place where particular and universal consort most harmoniously is traditionally supposed to be art. The aesthetic, as we have seen, is that privileged condition in which the law of the whole is nothing but the interrelations of the parts. But if this is true, then each part is still governed by what is in effect a total system; and it is this chiasmus of the aesthetic which Adorno will try to outflank. In art, the emancipation of the particular would seem merely to lead to a new form of global subordination; and it is surely not difficult to see how this contradiction corresponds to the amphibious nature of bourgeois society, in which the ideal of an interchange of autonomous individuals is constantly thwarted by the persistence of exploitation. The work of art appears free from the viewpoint of its particular elements, but these elements appear unfree from the standpoint of the law which surreptitiously marshals them into unity. In a similar way, the individual subject is free from the viewpoint of the market place, but not from the perspective of the state which violently or manipulatively preserves that market place in being. Adorno seeks to recast the relations between global and specific by finding in the aesthetic an impulse to reconciliation between them which must never quite come off, a utopian yearning for identity which must deny itself under pain of fetishism and idolatry. The work of art suspends identity without cancelling it, broaches and breaches it simultaneously, refusing at once to underwrite antagonism or supply false consolation. If its movement is thus one of perpetual deferral, this is less because of some ontological condition of language than because of the Judaeo-Marxist prohibition on the fashioning of graven images of a political future which must nonetheless be remembered.

Art may thus offer an alternative to thought, which for the Adorno of *Dialectic of Enlightenment* has become inherently pathological. All rationality is now instrumental, and simply to think is therefore to violate and victimize. A valid theory could only be one which thinks against itself, undoes its every act, achieves a frail evocation of that which its own discursivity denies. Emancipatory thought is an enormous irony, an indispensable absurdity in which the concept is at once deployed and disowned, no sooner posited than surmounted, illuminating truth only in the dim glare of light by which it self-destructs. The utopia of knowledge would be to open up the non-conceptual to concepts without rendering it equivalent to them; and this involves reason somehow hauling itself up by its own bootstraps, for if thought is intrinsically violatory how has the thought which thinks this truth not already fallen victim to the very crime it denounces?

If emancipatory thought is a scandalous contradiction, so in a different sense is the dominative reason it seeks to unlock. Historically speaking, such reason helps to release the self from its enslavement to myth and Nature; but in a devastating irony the drive to this enabling autonomy itself hardens into a kind of ferocious animal compulsion, subverting the very freedom it sets in place. In repressing its own inner nature in the name of independence, the subject finds itself throttling the very spontaneity which its break with Nature supposedly set free – so that the upshot of all this strenuous labour of individuation is an undermining of the ego from within, as the self gradually implodes into some empty, mechanical conformity. The forging of the ego is thus an ambivalently emancipatory and repressive event; and the unconscious is marked by a similar duality, promising us some blissful sensuous fulfilment but threatening at every moment to thrust us back to that archaic, undifferentiated state in which we are no longer subjects at all, let alone liberated ones. Fascism then gives us the worst of all possible worlds: the torn, wounded Nature over which an imperious reason has trampled returns with a vengeance as blood, guts and soil, but in the cruellest of ironies is now harnessed to that brutally instrumental reason itself, in an unholy coupling of the atavistic and futuristic, savage irrationalism and technological dominion. For Adorno, the self is rent by an internal fissure, and the name for the experience of it is suffering. How, then, is the identity of the subject, which is a constitutive moment of its freedom and autonomy, to be combined with the sensuousness and spontaneity on which the drive to autonomy has inflicted such grievous damage?

Adorno's solution to this riddle is the aesthetic – in so far, that is, as art is now possible at all. Modernism is art forced into mute self-contradiction; and the source of this internal impasse lies in art's contradictory material status within bourgeois society. Culture is deeply locked into the structure of commodity production; but one effect of this is to release it into a certain ideological autonomy, hence allowing it to speak against the very social order with which it is guiltily complicit. It is this complicity which spurs art into protest, but which also strikes that protest agonized and ineffectual, formal gesture rather than irate polemic. Art can only hope to be valid if it provides an implicit critique of the conditions which produce it – a validation which, in evoking art's privileged remoteness from such conditions, instantly invalidates itself. Conversely, art can only be authentic if it silently acknowledges how deeply it is compromised by what it opposes; but to press this logic too far is precisely to undermine its authenticity. The aporia of modernist culture lies in its plaintive, stricken attempt to turn autonomy (the free-standing nature of the aesthetic work) against autonomy (its functionless status as commodity on the market); what warps it into non-self-identity is the inscription of its own material conditions on its interior. It would seem that art must now either abolish itself entirely – the audacious strategy of the avant garde – or hover indecisively between life and death, subsuming its own impossibility into itself.

At the same time, it is this internal slippage or hiatus within the art work, this impossibility of ever coinciding exactly with itself, which provides the very source of its critical power, in a world where objects lie petrified in their monotonously self-same being, doomed to the hell of being no more than themselves. It is as though Adorno, who was never much entranced by the avant garde and can hardly bring himself to say a polite word about Bertolt Brecht, seizes upon the dilemma of culture in late capitalism and presses it to a calculated extreme, so that in a defiant reversal it is the very impotence of an autonomous art which will be wrenched into its finest aspect, victory snatched from the jaws of defeat as art's shaming privilege and futility is carried to a Beckettian limit and at that point begins to veer on its axis to become (negative) critique. Like Beckett, Adorno maintains a compact with failure, which is where for both Jew and Irishman all authenticity must start. An artistic vacuity which is the product of social conditions, and so part of the problem, can come by some strange logic to figure as a creative solution. The more art suffers this relentless *kenosis*, the more powerfully it speaks to its historical epoch; the more it turns its back on social issues, the more politically eloquent it grows. There is something perversely self-defeating about this aesthetic, which takes it cue from a notable contradiction of 'autonomous' culture – the fact that art's independence of social life permits it a critical force which that same autonomy tends to cancel out. 'Neutralisation', as Adorno comments, 'is the social price art pays for its autonomy.'[17] The more socially dissociated

349

art becomes, the more scandalously subversive and utterly pointless it is. For art to *refer*, even protestingly, is for it to become instantly collusive with what it opposes; negation negates itself because it cannot help positing the very object it desires to destroy. Any positive enunciation is compromised by the very fact of being such; and it follows that what one is left with is the purest imprint of the gesture of negation itself, which must never stray from the elevated level of form to anything as lowly as content. So it is that Adorno comes to rehearse with a new inflection all the reactionary clichés which a committed art customarily attracts, railing at its supposed schematism and reductivism. The most profoundly political work is one that is entirely silent about politics, as for some the greatest poet is one who has never sullied his genius with anything as sordidly determinate as a poem.

For Adorno, all art contains a utopian moment: 'even in the most sublimated work of art there is a hidden "it should be otherwise" . . . as eminently constructed and produced objects, works of art, including literary ones, point to a practice from which they abstain: the creation of a just life'.[18] By their sheer presence, artefacts testify to the possibility of the non-existent, suspending a debased empirical existence and thus expressing an unconscious desire to change the world. All art is consequently radical – an optimism which is merely the other face of Adorno's political pessimism, and every bit as indiscriminate. Pope's *Essay on Man* must for Adorno be politically progressive, and perhaps more so than *Mother Courage,* since he generally fails to extend to the revolutionary avant garde the absolution from its sins of content he grants to art in general. Simply by virtue of its forms, art speaks up for the contingent, sensuous and non-identical, bears witness to the rights of the repressed against the compulsive pathology of the identity principle. It redraws the relations between the intellective and the perceptual, and in Kantian vein is similar to the concept without actually becoming one, releasing a minetic, non-conceptual potential. The artefact tips the balance between subject and object firmly on the side of the latter, ousting the imperialism of reason with a sensuous receptivity to the thing; it thus contains a memory trace of mimesis, of an equable affinity between humanity and nature, which anticipates some future reconciliation between the individual and the collective. As a 'non-regressive integration of divergences', the art work transcends the antagonisms of everyday life without promising to abolish them; it is therefore, perhaps, 'the only remaining medium of truth in an age of incomprehensible terror and suffering'.[19] In it, the hidden irrationality of a rationalized society is brought to light; for art is a 'rational' end in itself, whereas capitalism is irrationally so. Art has a kind of paratactic logicality about it, akin to those dream images which blend cogency and contingency; and it might thus be said to represent an arational reason confronting an irrational rationality. If it acts as an implicit refutation of instrumentalized reason, it is no mere abstract negation of it; rather, it revokes the violence inflicted by such reason by emancipating rationality from its present empirical confinement, and so appears as the process by which rationality criticizes itself without being able to overcome itself.

It would be quite mistaken, however, to imagine that Adorno uncritically affirms modernist culture, setting it over against a dominative society. On the contrary, art is by no means free of the principle of domination, which takes the shape within it of its regulative or constructive drive, that impulse which invests it with a provisional unity and identity. The more the work of art seeks to liberate itself from external determinations, the more it becomes subject to self-positing principles of organization, which mime and internalize the law of an administered society. Ironically, the 'purity' of the modernist work's form is borrowed from the technical, functional forms of a rationalized social order: art holds out against domination in its respect for the sensuous particular, but reveals itself again and again as an ideological ally of such oppression. The 'spiritualization' of the artefact corrects this actual oppressiveness, but is itself secretly modelled on that very structure, assimilating itself to Nature by exerting an unlimited sway over its materials. Art thus releases the specific, but represses it too: 'The ritual of dominating nature lives on in play.'[20] It is not a resolved totality; but it carries within it an impulse to smooth over discontinuities, and all artistic construction thus strains ineluctably towards ideology.

Moreover, if art is subject like everything else to the law of objectification, it cannot avoid a kind of fetishism. The transcendence of the artefact lies in its power to dislocate things from their empirical contexts and reconfigure them in the image of freedom; but this also means that art works 'kill what they objectify, tearing it away from its context of immediacy and real life'.[21] Art's autonomy is a form of reification, reproducing what it resists; there can be no critique

351

without the objectification of spirit, but critique thus lapses to the status of thinghood and so threatens to undo itself. The modernist culture Adorno espouses cannot help positing itself as independent of any conditions of material production, and so insidiously perpetuates false consciousness; but the fetishistic character of the work is also a condition of its truth, since it is its blindness to the material world of which it is a part which enables it to break the spell of the reality principle. If art is always radical, it is also always conservative, reinforcing the illusion of a separate domain of spirit 'whose practical impotence and complicity with the principle of unmitigated disaster are painfully evident'.[22] What it gains in one direction, it loses in another; if it eludes the logic of a degraded history, then it must pay a heavy price for this freedom, part of which is a reluctant reproduction of that very logic.

Art for Adorno is thus less some idealized realm of being than contradiction incarnate. Every artefact works resolutely against itself, and this in a whole variety of ways. It strives for some pure autonomy, but knows that without a heterogeneous moment it would be nothing, vanishing into thin air. It is at once being-for-itself and being-for-society, always simultaneously itself and something else, critically estranged from its history yet incapable of taking up a vantage-point beyond it. By forswearing intervention in the real, artistic reason accrues to itself a certain precious innocence; but at the same time all art resonates with social repression, and becomes culpable precisely because it refuses to intervene. Culture is truth and illusion, cognition and false consciousness, at a stroke: like all spirit, it suffers from the narcissistic delusion of existing for itself, but does so in a way which offers to negate all false claims to such self-identity in the commodified world around it. Delusion is art's very mode of existence, which is not to grant it a license to *advocate* delusion. If the content of the art work is an illusion, it is in some sense a necessary one, and so does not lie; art is true to the degree that it is an illusion of the non-illusory. In *positing* itself as illusion, it exposes the realm of commodities (of which it is one) as unreal, thus forcing illusion into the service of truth. Art is an allegory of undeluded happiness – to which it adds the fatal rider that this cannot be had, continually breaking the promise of the well-being it adumbrates.

In all of these ways, art contains truth and ideology at once. In liberating particulars from the logic of identification, it presents us with an alternative to exchange-value, but thus cons us into the gullible faith that there are things in the world which are not for exchange. As a form of play, it is progressive and regressive at the same time, raising us for a blessed moment above the constraints of practice but only to draw us back into an infantile ignorance of the instrumental. Artefacts are divided against themselves, at once determinate and indeterminate; and nowhere is this more obvious than in the discrepancy between their mimetic (sensuous-expressive) and rational (constructive-organisational) moments. One of the many paradoxes of art is how the act of making can cause the appearance of a thing unmade; the 'natural' materials which the art work mimes, and the 'rational' forms which regulate them, will always be divergent, constituting a slippage or dissonance at the very heart of the work. Mediated through one another, these two dimensions of the artefact are nevertheless non-identical, which allows art's mimetic aspect to provide an implicit criticism of the structuring forms with which it interpenetrates.[23] But this subtle mismatching, which is a question of the work's objective logic, detaches it from the mastery of a singular authorial intention, releases it into autonomy and so permits it to become an image of possible future reconciliation. In a striking irony, it is the art work's inner irreconcilability which puts it at odds with a reified empirical world and thus holds out the promise of a future social harmony. Every work of art pretends to be the totality it can never become; there is never, *pace* Lukács, any achieved mediation of particular and universal, mimetic and rational, but always a diremption between them which the work will cover up as best it can. Artefacts for Adorno are ridden with inconsistencies, pitched battles between sense and spirit, astir with fragments which stubbornly resist incorporation. Their materials will always put up a fight against the dominative rationality which rips them from their original contexts and seeks to synthesize them at the expense of their qualitatively different moments. Complete artistic determination, in which every element of the work would become of equal value, collapses into absolute contingency. The artwork is thus centripetal and centrifugal together, a portrait of its own impossibility, living testimony to the fact that dissonance is the truth of harmony.

Such a case, however, is not to be mistaken for that simple-minded hymning of the ineffable particular into which a later, less politically engaged deconstruction has sometimes degenerated. If Adorno is the apologist for difference, heterogeneity and the aporetic, he is also implicated enough in the political struggles of his time to be able to see more than metaphysical delusion in such fundamental human values as solidarity, mutual affinity, peaceableness, fruitful communication, loving kindness – values without which not even the most exploitative social order would succeed in reproducing itself, but which are singularly absent from the disenchanted, post-political discourse of a later more jejune brand of anti-totalizing thought. Adorno's theory, in other words, holds together in extreme tension positions which in contemporary cultural theory have become ritually antagonistic. Present-day deconstruction is on the whole either silent or negative about the notion of solidarity – a value without which no significant social change is even conceivable, but which deconstruction tends to conflate in Nietzschean fashion with a craven conformity to the law. On the other hand, the work of a Jürgen Habermas might be upbraided for the opposite error, placing too sanguine a trust in a normative collective wisdom. No one could outdo the anti-totalizing animus of a thinker who resoundingly declares that the whole is the false; but Adorno is too deeply dialectical a theorist to imagine that all unity or identity is thus unequivocally terroristic. The given social order is not only a matter of oppressive self-identities; it is also a structure of antagonism, to which a certain notion of identity may be critically opposed. It is because so much post-structuralist thought mistakes a conflictive social system for a monolithic one that it can conceive of consensus or collectivity only as oppressive. Adorno's own case is more nuanced: 'while firmly rejecting the appearance of reconciliation, art none the less holds fast to the idea of reconciliation in an antagonistic world . . . without a perspective on peace art would be untrue, just as untrue as it is when it anticipates a state of reconciliation'.[24] If it is true that 'the urge of the artistic particular to be submerged in the whole reflects the disintegrative death wish of nature',[25] it is also the case that a work of art which dissolved into pure manifoldness would lose 'any sense of what makes the particular really distinctive. Works that are in constant flux and have no unitary point of reference for the many become too homogeneous, too monotonous, too undifferentiated.'[26] Pure difference, in short, is as blank and tedious as pure identity. An art which fails to render its elements *determinate* in their irreconcilability would defuse its critical force; there can be no talk of difference or dissonance without some provisional configurating of the particulars in question, which would otherwise be not dissonant or conflictive but merely incommensurable. 'What we differentiate', Adorno writes in *Negative Dialectics*, 'will appear divergent, dissonant, negative for just as long as the structure of our consciousness obliges it to strive for unity: as long as its demand for totality will be its measure for whatever is not identical with it.'[27] Artefacts are internally unreconciled through a certain reconciliation, which is what leaves them irreconcilable with empirical reality: 'the determined opposition of every art work to empirical reality presupposes its inner coherence'.[28] Unless the work has some kind of fragile, provisional identity, one cannot speak of its resisting political power. Those who indiscriminately demonize such concepts as unity, identity, consensus, regulation have forgotten that there are, after all, different modalities of these things, which are not all equivalently repressive. In Adorno's view, the 'rational' form of art allows for a 'non-repressive synthesis of diverse particulars . . . it preserves them in their diffuse, divergent and contradictory condition'.[29] Non-identity is constitutive of the work of art, but this non-identity 'is opaque only for identity's claims to be total',[30] and pure singularity is sheer abstraction. The general features of the artwork emerge from its minute specifications; but this should not be taken to authorize some brusque exorcism of the concept, which would only surrender us to the spell of the brute object. The principle of individuation, Adorno reminds us, has its limits just like any other, and neither it nor its opposite should be ontologized. 'Dadaism, the deictic gesture pointing to pure thisness, was no less universal than the demonstrative pronoun "this".'[31]

Adorno takes from Kant the insight that although the work of art is indeed a kind of totality, it is not one which can be thought along customary conceptual lines. The Kantian aesthetic posits some peculiar imbrication of part and whole, an intimacy which can then be read in two directly contrary ways. Either the whole is no more than the obedient product of the particulars, ceaselessly generated up out of them; or its power is now more pervasive and well-founded than ever, inscribed within each individual element as its informing structure. From this viewpoint, the very attempt to give the slip to a 'bad' totality keels over into its opposite. Kant opens a path towards thinking totality otherwise, but remains caught within a more traditional logic; Adorno presses Kant's privileging of the particular to an extreme limit, insisting on its recalcitrance to whatever force offers to integrate it. The concept of constellation can thus be read as a political rallying cry: 'All power to the particulars!' Yet Adorno's aesthetics incorporates this radical programme of democratic self-government with a more classical dominative model, at times viewing the 'rationality' of the art-work as non-repressive, at other times underlining its collusion with bureaucracy. What might undo the 'totalitarian' implications of Kantian aesthetics is the idea of affinity or mimesis – the non-sensuous correspondences between disparate features of the artefact, or more generally the filiations of both kinship and otherness between subject and object, humanity and nature, which might provide an alternative rationality to the instrumental. One might even name this mimesis *allegory*, that figurative mode which relates through difference, preserving the relative autonomy of a set of signifying units while suggesting an affinity with some other range of signifiers. And while this model is not broached by Adorno as explicitly political, it surely carries significant political implications. It would mean, for example, that the relations between class-struggle and sexual politics could not be conceived along the lines of some Lukácsian 'expressive totality', but mimetically or allegorically, in a set of correspondences which, like the constellation, take the full measure of otherness and disparity. If such a theory gives no comfort to the symbolic totalizers, it will equally be resisted by those for whom affinity or correspondence can only be imagined as tyrannical 'closure'.

'A liberated mankind', Adorno writes, 'would by no means be a totality.'[32] Unlike many of his statements, this is an impeccably Marxist proposition. For Lukács, totality already exists in principle, but has yet to come into its own. Literary realism prefigures that fortunate day, recreating each phenomenon in the image of the essence it belies. For Adorno, things are quite the reverse: there is indeed, here and now, a total system which integrates everything relentlessly down, but to emancipate non-identity from its voracious maw would be to transform this miserable situation into some future historical 'constellation', in which rational identity would be constituted by that hiatus within each particular which opens it to the unmasterable otherness of its fellows. Such a political order would be as far from some 'totalitarian' regime as it would be from some random distribution of monads or flux of sheer difference; and in this sense there is the basis for a politics in the work of Adorno, as there is only dubiously in that of some of his theoretical successors. Adorno does not abandon the concept of totality but submits it to a materialistic mutation; and this is equivalent to transforming the traditional concept of the aesthetic, turning it against itself by redeeming as far as possible its proto-materialist aspects from its totalizing idealism. This operation is then in its turn a kind of allegory of how the promise of bourgeois Enlightenment – the equitable interrelation of free, autonomous individuals – may be salvaged from the dominative reason which is its contradictory accomplice.

In the light of this project, Jürgen Habermas's cursory judgement that negative dialectics leads to nothing is surely too harsh.[33] Indeed Habermas himself elsewhere applauds Adorno and Adorno's colleague Max Horkheimer for the judiciousness with which their critique of reason refuses to darken into an outright renunciation of what the Enlightenment, however vainly, intended by the concept of reason.[34] There are some who would argue that, given what Adorno and Horkheimer had seen that rationality amount to in Nazi Germany, this refusal of renunciation was either foolish or all the more impressive. There are others who would argue that, given what they had seen there of the lethal consequences of abandoning reason, their refusal to do so was entirely understandable. Habermas recognizes that Adorno has no desire to press beyond the uncomfortable impasse of a reason turned back upon itself; he wishes simply to endure in the performative contradiction of a negative dialectics, thus remaining faithful to the echoes of an almost forgotten non-instrumental reason which belongs to pre-history. Like his great exemplar Samual Beckett, Adorno chooses to be poor but honest; he would prefer to suffer the constraints of the tight theoretical place in which he is stuck rather than betray a more fundamental human suffering by foreclosing upon these painful manoeuvres. What tattered shreds of authenticity can be preserved after Auschwitz consist in staying stubbornly impaled on the horns of an impossible dilemma, conscious that the abandonment of utopia is just as treacherous as the hope for it, that negations of the actual are as indispensable as they are ineffectual, that art is at once precious and worthless. Adorno makes a virtue out of agonized vulnerability, as though that is all honesty can these days mean. As in the work of Paul de Man, authenticity, if it exists at all, lies only in the gesture by which one detaches oneself ironically from all inevitably inauthentic engagements, opening a space between the degraded empirical subject and what would at one time have been the transcendental subject, had the latter not now been wholly undermined by the former.[35] For de Man, an endless self-reflexive irony is now the nearest approach we can make to that classical transcendence, in an age when vertigo must serve as the index of veracity. In the shift from early to late capitalism, the liberal humanist subject has indeed fallen upon hard times, and must now be prepared to sacrifice its truth and identity to its freedom, a disseverance which the Enlightenment would have found unintelligible.

Adorno and de Man share, in fact, an important feature: their overreaction to fascism. To speak of overreacting to such a politics might seem strange, but is surely possible. Adorno was a victim of fascism; de Man, it would appear, was for a while a sympathizer. Those who argue for some continuity between de Man's earlier and later incarnations are surely right to do so; but the continuity in question is largely negative, a matter of the later de Man's extreme reaction to his earlier involvements. The later de Man, traumatized by the philosophy of transcendental signification, metaphysical groundedness and remorseless totalization with which he had earlier consorted, lapses into a jaded liberal scepticism in some ways close to Adorno's own political pessimism, though without its frail utopian impulse. Both figures would seem afflicted for quite different reasons by a paralysing historical guilt, and would prefer to court impotence, deadlock and failure rather than risk the dogmatism of affirmation. Both positions, moreover, have to some extent always already incorporated their own hopelessness, a move which among other things renders them less vulnerable to certain impatient accusations.

In *Minima Moralia*, that bizarre blend of probing insight and patrician grousing, Adorno mourns the disappearance from modern civilization of doors that close 'quietly and discreetly', in one of his tiresome bouts of *haut bourgeois* anti-technological nostalgia: 'What does it mean for the subject that there are no more casement windows to open, but only sliding frames to shove, no gentle latches but turnable handles, no forecourt, no doorstep before the street, no wall around the garden?'[36] One knows, even before the eye has travelled to the next sentence, that a reference to the Nazis will be on its way, which indeed immediately appears: 'The movements machines demand of their users already have the violent, hard-hitting, unresting jerkiness of Fascist maltreatment.' That the man who could so vigilantly sniff out instances of the banalization of fascism, from Brecht to Chaplin, should permit himself this trivializing constellation suggests that we should evaluate with some circumspection the political responses of a former victim of fascism. In one sense, nobody could command more authority and respect; in another sense, the horror of that experience lingers thoughout Adorno's later work as a distorting as well as illuminating perspective. Something of the same might be said of Paul de Man, despite the entirely different nature of his implication in the Nazi period. His later thought must be examined in the light of his earlier career in much the same way that the declarations of a positivist or behaviourist must be considered in the context of his revulsion from an earlier Evangelicalism.

It is by now widely agreed that Adorno's experience of fascism led him and other members of the Frankfurt school to travesty and misrecognize some of the specific power-structures of liberal capitalism, projecting the minatory shadow of the former sort of regime upon the quite different institutions of the latter. Much the same confusion is inherited by some post-structuralist theory, with its perilously indiscriminate conflation of widely divergent orders of power, forms of oppression and modalities of law. The breathtaking subtlety of Adorno's disquisitions on art are in inverse proportion to the two-dimensional crudity of some of his political perceptions. Indeed these two facets of his thought are closely intertwined, as a defeatist politics generates a compensatorily rich aesthetics. Even then, however, it must be remembered that Adorno's historical pessimism is always tempered by a vision, however ragged and threadbare, of the just society. 'The only philosophy which can be responsibly practised in face of despair', reads the concluding, Benjaminian section of *Minima Moralia*, 'is the attempt to contemplate all things as they would present themselves from the standpoint of redemption. Knowledge has no light but that shed on the world by redemption; all else is reconstruction, mere technique. Perspectives must be fashioned that displace and estrange the world, reveal it to be, with its rifts and crevices, as indigent and distorted as it will appear one day in the messianic light.'[37] There can be no doubt that

Adorno believes devoutly in the good society, since how otherwise could he experience the misery of its absence quite so keenly? His despair, then, is always an intricately qualified affair, just as his notorious cultural elitism is severely tempered by the readiness he shows to savage a representative of high culture alongside an avatar of the culture industry.

There are, perhaps, two different Adornos, the one somewhat more defeatist than the other. It is possible to read his work as a retreat from the nightmare of history into the aesthetic, and there is enough in his writings to make this a plausible view. It is the most easily caricatured side of his thought: Beckett and Schoenberg as the solution to world starvation and threatened nuclear destruction. This is the Adorno who deliberately offers as a solution what is clearly part of the problem, the political homeopath who will feed us sickness as cure. This Adorno asks us simply to subsist in the near-intolerable strain of an absurdist, self-imploding thought, a thought before which all hubristic system-builders must humble themselves, and which in its extreme discomfort keeps us loyal at some lofty remove to the characteristic stuff of human history. But there is also the other Adorno who still hopes that we might go through the aesthetic and come out in some unnameable place on the other side, the theorist for whom the aesthetic offers a paradigm, rather than a displacement of emancipatory political thought.[38]

In *Negative Dialectics*, Adorno speaks out explicitly against any attempt to aestheticize philosophy. 'A philosophy that tried to imitate art, that would turn itself into a work of art, would be expunging itself.'[39] A Schellingian solution, in other words, is not to be pursued; but somewhat later in the volume Adorno is writing in Schopenhauerian vein of philosophy as 'a true sister of music . . . its suspended state is nothing but the expression of its inexpressibility'.[40] As the playful and sensuous, the aesthetic is not, Adorno insists, accidental to philosophy; there is a kind of clownish element about knowing thought's remoteness from its object yet speaking as though one had that object assuredly in hand, and theory must somehow act out this tragicomic discrepancy, foregrounding its own unfinishedness. As a form of thought whose object must always elude it, there is something a little buffoonish about this monarch of the humanities. But if Adorno wants to aestheticize theory in style and form, he is not prepared to void the cognitive, for 'cogency and play are the two poles of philosophy', and '[philosophy's] affinity to art does not entitle it to borrow from art, least of all by virtue of the intuitions which barbarians take for the prerogatives of art'.[41] The theoretical concept, however, must not relinquish the sensuous yearning which animates the artistic, even if it tends to negate that yearning. 'Philosophy can neither circumvent such negation nor submit to it. It must strive, by way of the concept, to transcend the concept.'[42]

There can be no question for Adorno of aestheticizing philosophy in the sense of reducing cognition to intuition, since art for him is itself in its peculiar way a form of rationality. Where theory *is* to be aestheticized is in its approach to the particular; art does not exactly oust systematic thought, but furnishes it with a model of sensuous receptivity to the specific. This, however, poses an intriguing problem. For how can philosophy learn from the aesthetic if the whole point of the latter is to be strictly untranslatable into discursive thought? The aesthetic would seem to offer itself as a paradigm for a thought into which it refuses to be translated back. Art shows what philosophy cannot say; but either philosophy will never be able to articulate this, in which case the aesthetic is of dubious relevance to it, or it can learn to express the inexpressible, in which case it may no longer be theory but a form of art. Art would thus seem at once the consummation and the ruin of philosophy – the point to which any authentic thought must asymptotically aspire, yet where it would cease to be in any traditional sense thought at all. On the other hand, the shift from the theoretical to the aesthetic, from a dominative reason to a mimetic one, cannot involve a definitive rupture, since as we have seen art itself contains an ineluctable moment of domination. Art's deconstruction of theory is never entirely successful, so that philosophy will live on within its other.

Just as artistic modernism figures the impossibility of art, so Adorno's modernist aesthetic marks the point at which the high aesthetic tradition is pressed to an extreme limit and begins to self-destruct, leaving among its ruins a few cryptic clues as to what might lie beyond it. Yet this undermining of classical aesthetics is achieved from *within* the aesthetic, and owes much to the lineages it throws into crisis. Adorno continues to occupy the high ground of aesthetic theory, rather than descending like Habermas to the more hospitable lowlands of a communicative rationality. He would rather stifle than suffocate, and in whole reaches of his work the air feels too rarefied to sustain much biological growth. He begins neither from the good old things nor the bad new things, to adopt a remark of Brecht's, but from the bad old things, from a history which has been racked and tormented since its inception. According to *Dialectic of Enlightenment* even Odysseus was a bourgeois individualist, and Adam was no doubt another. The only authentic hope is one wrested from the knowledge that things have been atrocious for a very long time, a hope which risks suppressing that knowledge and so becoming inauthentic. Only by remaining faithful to the past can we prise loose its terrifying grip, and this fidelity is forever likely to paralyse us. It is a problem of how one alleviates and keeps faith with suffering at the same time, since the one is always threatening to undercut the other. If Adorno plies the steel he does so as a wounded surgeon, patient and physician together; and his injuries, as Wittgenstein might have said, are the bruises he has sustained from trying to run his head up against the limits of language. The only cure for our sickness is that it should grow worse – that the wounds inflicted on humanity by its own insanity should be left festering and untended, for without their silent testimony to our historical plight we will forget that a remedy is even necessary and thus escape into innocence. The ragged gap which a predatory reason has driven through our inner nature must be kept open, for it is only in this vacant space that something more creative might just germinate, and what we might stuff it with would only be illusion. Things at the worst, as *Macbeth* reminds us, will either cease or climb up again; and Adorno positions his writing at this undecidable point, prepared to back neither possibility. Like Freud, he knows that individual particulars will never rest content under the law's yoke, that the central tenet of traditional aesthetics is a lie; and this friction between part and whole is the source of both hope and despair, the rending without which nothing can be sole or whole, but which may well succeed in deferring such wholeness to judgement day. The aesthetic, which was once a kind of resolution, is now a scandalous impossibility; and Adorno's most ironic move will be to deploy this very impossibility as a device for renewing the tradition of which it is the last faint gasp. As thought must travel beyond itself so must the aesthetic transcend itself, emptying itself of its authoritarian urges and offensively affirmative instincts until it leaves behind nothing but a ghostly negative imprint of itself, which is probably the nearest we shall get to truth.

Every generation, Benjamin writes, has been endowed with a '*weak* Messianic power'.[43] The revolutionary historian scans the past for this frail salvific impulse, fanning the sparks of hope still stirring among its ashes. Adorno is Kabbalistic enough to decipher the signs of redemption in the most wildly improbable places – in the paranoia of identity-thinking, in the mechanisms of exchange-value, between the elliptical lines of a Beckett or in some sudden jarring of a Schoenberg violin. History is awash with the desire for justice and well-being, clamouring for judgement day, labouring to overthrow itself; it is shot through with weak Messianic powers, if only one learns to search for them in the least obvious places. But there is, of course, always another story. If Adorno can detect the longing for happiness in some bureaucratic edict, he is also depressingly skilful at discerning the rapaciousness which lurks within our most edifying gestures. There can be no truth without ideology, no transcendence without betrayal, no beneficence which is not bought at the cost of another's happiness. If the skein of history is meshed as fine as this, then to tug on any one thread of it is to risk unravelling some rare design in the name of unpicking an obstructive knot. Textuality, with Adorno as with some later theorists, thus becomes a rationale for political intertia; *praxis* is a crude, blundering affair, which could never live up to the exquisite many-sidedness of our theoretical insights. It is remarkable how this Arnoldian doctrine is still alive and well today, occasionally in the most 'radical' of circles.

It is no use, however, telling Adorno that Webern will never do anything for the world economy. He knows it already, better even than us, and is more concerned to rub the ridiculousness of his doctrines in our face than to defend them. In Zen-like fashion, it is only when we have grasped their absurdity that illumination might break upon us. If some later theorists have been able to practise this provocative style even more effectively than Adorno himself, it is largely because they lack his profound sense of political responsibility. Adorno recognized the necessity of that style; but he never failed to meditate on its intolerable privilege too, which is what marks him off from a post-Auschwitz generation. If he ironized and equivocated, it was not with some feckless sub-Nietzschean zest but with a heavy heart. It is ironic in its turn that this nostalgic *haut bourgeois* intellectual, with all his mandarin fastidiousness and remorseless tunnel vision, should join the ranks of Mikhail Bakhtin and Walter

Benjamin as one of the three most creative, original cultural theorists Marxism has yet produced.

Notes

1 Theodor Adorno, *Negative Dialectics* (London, 1973), p. 35.
2 Ibid., p. 146.
3 Ibid., p. 365.
4 Ibid., p. 320.
5 Theodor Adorno, *Minima Moralia* (London, 1974), p. 237.
6 Adorno, *Negative Dialectics*, p. 148.
7 Ibid., p. 149.
8 Adorno, *Negative Dialectics*, p. 5.
9 Ibid., p. 120.
10 Ibid., p. 23.
11 Ibid., p. 85.
12 Ibid., p. 111.
13 Ibid., pp. 33 and 162.
14 Ibid., p. 47.
15 Ibid., p. 83.
16 See on this point Peter Dews, *Logics of Disintegration* (London, 1987), p. 30.
17 Theodor Adorno, *Aesthetic Theory* (London, 1984), p. 325.
18 Theodor Adorno, 'Commitment', in Ernst Bloch et al., *Aesthetics and Politics* (London, 1977), p. 194.
19 Adorno, *Aesthetic Theory*, p. 27.
20 Ibid., p. 74.
21 Ibid., p. 193.
22 Ibid., p. 333.
23 An excellent account of this topic is given by Peter Osborne, 'Adorno and the Metaphysics of Modernism' in A. Benjamin (ed.), *The Problem of Modernity: Adorno and Benjamin* (London, 1988).
24 Adorno, *Aesthetic Theory*, pp. 48 and 366.
25 Ibid., p. 78.
26 Ibid., p. 273.
27 Adorno, *Negative Dialectics*, pp. 5–6.
28 Adorno, *Aesthetic Theory*, p. 225.
29 Ibid., p. 207.
30 Adorno, *Negative Dialectics*, p. 153.
31 Adorno, *Aesthetic Theory*, p. 259.

32 Theodor Adorno, Introduction to *The Positivist Dispute in German Sociology* (London, 1976), p. 12.
33 See Peter Dews (ed.), *Jürgen Habermas: Autonomy and Solidarity* (London, 1986), p. 91.
34 Ibid., pp. 154–5.
35 See Paul de Man, 'The Rhetoric of Temporality', in *Blindness and Insight* (Minneapolis, 1983), p. 214.
36 Adorno, *Minima Moralia*, p. 40.
37 Ibid., p. 247.
38 For a critical account of Adorno's use of the aesthetic as political paradigm, see Albrecht Wellmer, 'Reason, Utopia and the *Dialectic of Enlightenment*', in R. J. Bernstein (ed.), *Habermas and Modernity* (Cambridge, 1985).
39 Adorno, *Negative Dialectics*, p. 15.
40 Ibid., p. 109.
41 Ibid., p. 15.
42 Ibid., p. 15.
43 Walter Benjamin, 'Theses on the Philosophy of History', in H. Arendt (ed.), *Illuminations* (London, 1973), p. 256.

14

From the Polis
to Postmodernism

Let us tell, in crude and fabular form, a Weberian kind of story. Imagine a society sometime in the indeterminate past, before the rise of capitalism, perhaps even before the Fall, certainly before the dissociation of sensibility, when the three great questions of philosophy – what can we know? what ought we to do? what do we find attractive? – were not as yet fully distinguishable from one another. A society, that is to say, where the three mighty regions of the cognitive, the ethico-political and the libidinal-aesthetic were still to a large extent intermeshed. Knowledge was still constrained by certain moral imperatives – there were certain things you weren't supposed to know – and was not viewed as sheerly instrumental. The ethico-political question – what are we to do? – was not regarded simply as a matter of intuition or existential decision or inexplicable preference, but involved rigorous knowledge of what we were, of the structure of our social life; so that there was a way of describing what we were from which it was possible to infer what we should do or could become. Art was not sharply separated from the ethico-political, but was one of its primary media; and it was not easily distinguishable from the cognitive either, because it could be seen as a form of social knowledge, conducted within certain normative ethical frameworks. It had cognitive functions and ethico-political effects.

Then imagine, after a while, all this changing. The snake enters the garden; the middle classes start to rise; thoughts fall apart from feelings, so that nobody thinks through their fingertips any more; and history starts out on its long trek towards Mr George Bush. The three great areas of historical life – knowledge, politics, desire – are uncoupled from one another; each becomes specialized, autonomous, sealed off into its own space. Knowledge burst out of its ethical constraints and began to operate by its own internal autonomous laws. Under the name science, it no longer bore any obvious relation to the ethical or aesthetic, and so began to lose touch with value. About this time, philosophers began to discover that you could not derive a value from a fact. For classical thought, to answer the question 'what am I to do?' involved making reference to my actual place within the social relations of the *polis*, and the rights and responsibilities which that brought along with it. A normative language was bound up with a cognitive one. Now, however, the answers to why we should be moral become non-cognitivist. Either: you ought to be moral because doesn't it feel nice to be good? Or: you should be moral because it is moral to be so. Both of these responses utilize, in very different ways, the model of the aesthetic, which at about this time was also floating adrift into its own autonomous space, and so could be drawn upon as a kind of model of ethical autonomy. The moral and the aesthetic, both in deep trouble, could thus come to one another's aid. The cultural system had detached itself from the economic and political systems, and thus came to figure as an end in itself. Indeed art had to be an end in itself, because it certainly didn't seem to have much else of a purpose any more.

This story may seem yet another ritual of nostalgic remembrance for the organic society, but in fact it is not. For why should we presume that the condition in which these three discourses were intermeshed was a positive one? Liberated from cramping theological constraint, knowledge may now steam ahead and probe into what was previously taboo, relying on no authority but its own critical, sceptical powers. Science becomes a revolutionary strike against the statesmen and high priests in the name of human welfare and intellectual independence. Ethical enquiry is no longer exclusively harnessed to the ecclesial apparatus, but is free to raise questions of human justice and dignity beyond this narrow scope. Art, too, can now cease to be a mere lackey of political power, swearing fidelity only to its own law; but this is not greatly disturbing, since the very social conditions which allow this to happen – the autonomization of culture – also prevent art's potentially subversive freedom from having much of an effect on other areas of social life. Art comes to signify pure supplementarity, that marginal region of the affective/instinctual/

non-instrumental which a reified rationality finds difficulty in incorporating. But because it has become an isolated enclave, it can act as a kind of safety-valve or sublimation of these otherwise dangerous reaches of the psyche.

The moment we are speaking of is the moment of modernity, characterized by the dissociation and specialization of these three crucial spheres of activity. Art is now autonomous of the cognitive, ethical and political; but the way it came to be so is paradoxical. It became autonomous of them, curiously enough, by being *integrated* into the capitalist mode of production. When art becomes a commodity, it is released from its traditional social functions within church, court and state into the anonymous freedom of the market place. Now it exists, not for any specific audience, but just for anybody with the taste to appreciate it and the money to buy it. And in so far as it exists for nothing and nobody in particular, it can be said to exist for itself. It is 'independent' because it has been swallowed up by commodity production.

Art itself may thus be an increasingly marginal pursuit, but aesthetics is not. Indeed one might risk the rather exaggerated formulation that aesthetics is born at the moment of art's effective demise as a political force, flourishes on the corpse of its social relevance. Though artistic production itself plays less and less of a significant role in the social order (Marx reminds us that the bourgeoisie have absolutely no time for it), what it is able to bequeath to that order, as it were, is a certain ideological model which may help it out of its mess – the mess which has marginalized pleasure and the body, reified reason, and struck morality entirely empty. The aesthetic offers to reverse this division of labour, to bring these three alienated regions back into touch with one another, but the price it demands for this generosity is high: it offers to interrelate these discourses by effectively swallowing up the other two. Everything should now become aesthetic. Truth, the cognitive, becomes that which satisfies the mind, or what helps us to move around the place rather more conveniently. Morality is converted to a matter of style, pleasure and intuition. How should one live one's life properly? By turning oneself into an artefact.

There is finally the question of politics. Here the aestheticizing lineage can take either a left or a right turn. The left turn: smash truth, cognition and morality, which are all just ideology, and live luxuriantly in the free, groundless play of your creative powers. The right turn, from Burke and Coleridge to Heidegger, Yeats and Eliot: forget about theoretical analysis, cling to the sensuously particular, view society as a self-grounding organism, all of whose parts miraculously interpenetrate without conflict and require no rational justification. Think with the blood and the body. Remember that tradition is always wiser and richer than one's own poor, pitiable ego. It is this line of descent, in one of its tributaries, which will lead to the Third Reich. It all begins with the work of art, and ends up with a scarecrow in a field.

The left-aesthetic tradition, from Schiller and Marx to Morris and Marcuse, has much to be said for it: art as critique of alienation, as an exemplary realization of creative powers, as the ideal reconciliation of subject and object, universal and particular, freedom and necessity, theory and practice, individual and society. All of these notions could be equally deployed by the political right; but while the bourgeoisie is still in its progressive phase, this style of thinking comes through as a powerfully positive utopianism. From the end of the nineteenth century, however, this heritage begins to turn sour, and this is the moment of modernism. Modernism is one of the inheritors of this radical aestheticizing, but in the negative mode: art, in Adorno's pregnant phrase, as the 'negative knowledge of reality'. Modernism in art, and later the Frankfurt school and post-structuralism in theory: these are helped off the ground because the more positive aesthetic tradition has run out of steam, found the system too powerful to break. We are now moving into late capitalism, into an apparently wholly reified, rationalized, administered regime. You can't bring it to its knees with organic craftsmanship, so you have to try instead the silent scream, the scream which in Munch's famous painting rips open the blank face of the solitary figure and reverberates endlessly around the canvas. The aesthetic becomes the guerilla tactics of secret subversion, of silent resistance, of stubborn refusal. Art will pulverize traditional form and meaning, because the laws of syntax and grammar are the laws of the police. It will dance on the grave of narrative, semantics and representation, celebrate madness and delirium, speak like a woman, dissolve all social dialectics into the free flow of desire. Its form will become its content – a form which repulses all social semantics and might just allow us a glimpse of what it might conceivably be like to be free. But at the same moment this art is fearful and wretched, blank and listless, old enough to remember a time when there was order, truth and reality and still to some degree nostalgically in thrall to them.

From Romanticism to modernism, art strives to turn to advantage the autonomy which its commodity status has forced upon it, making a virtue out of grim necessity. Autonomy in the worrying sense – social functionlessness – is wrenched into autonomy in a more productive sense: art as a deliberate turning in upon itself, as a mute gesture of resistance to a social order which, in Adorno's phrase, holds a gun to its head. Aesthetic autonomy becomes a kind of negative politics. Art, like humanity, is utterly, gloriously useless, perhaps the one non-reified, non-instrumentalized form of activity left. In post-structuralist theory this will become the trace or aporia or ineffable flicker of difference which eludes all formalization, that giddy moment of failure, slippage or *jouissance* where you might just glimpse, in some necessarily empty, unspeakable way, something beyond the prison house of metaphysics. Such a truth, as Wittgenstein might have said, can be shown but not spoken; and this negative aesthetics thus proves too feeble a basis on which to found a politics.

There would then seem only one route left open, and that is an art which rejects the aesthetic. An art against itself, which confesses the impossibility of art, like those full-blown postmodernist theories which proclaim the impossibility of theory. An art, in short, which will undo all this depressing history, which will go right back even before the beginning, before the dawning of the whole category of the aesthetic, and seek to override in its own way that moment at the birth of modernity when the cognitive, ethico-political and libidinal-aesthetic became uncoupled from one another. This time, however, it will seek to do it not in the manner of the radical aestheticizers, by the aesthetic colonizing these other two regions, but by folding the aesthetic into the other two systems, in an attempt to hook art up once again with social praxis.

This is the revolutionary avant garde. The avant garde proclaims: you can't do it by aesthetics, aesthetics is part of the problem, not of the solution. The problem of art is art itself, so let's have an art which isn't art. Down with libraries and museums, paint your pictures on people's pyjamas, read your poetry through megaphones in factory yards, lead the audience on the town hall when the play is over, leave your studios and go out into the factories (as some of the Bolshevik avant garde actually did) to make useful objects for the workers.

For negative aestheticians like Adorno, this is unmitigated catastrophe. For if art smashes through the formal contours which demarcate and estrange it from ordinary life, will it not simply succeed in spilling and defusing its critical contents? How can a stoutly fashioned Constructivist rocking-chair act as critique? From this viewpoint, the avant garde is simply the latest instance of our old friend infantile ultra-leftism, rebellious children seeking to outrage their not-all-that-shockable parents.

All of this can be pictured as a kind of narrative progression. First, in a somewhat naive moment, you imagine that you might subvert the given order by certain aesthetic contents. But exactly because these are intelligible, translucent, faithful to the laws of grammar, they fall victim to the very social logic they oppose. It may be radical, but at least it's art. It may represent the unpalatable, but at least it does so with a scrupulous fidelity which assuages the middle class's pornographic appetite for the real. So you can shed content and leave only form behind, which in its more positive moment holds out a promise of happiness and organic reconciliation, and in its more negative moment traces a jagged line of inarticulable opposition to the given. Any such form, however, will fall instantly under the judgement of what Marcuse once called 'affirmative culture'. Art's very artistry, even if that is now a question of pure form, effects a spurious sort of sublimation which will bind and confiscate the very energies it hopes to release for the purposes of political change. We stumble upon the contradiction of all utopianism, that its very images of harmony threaten to hijack the radical impulses they hope to promote. So form must go too, however pure and empty. And this leaves us with anti-art, an art which is not appropriable by the ruling order because – the final cunning – it isn't art at all. The problem with this, however, is that what cannot be appropriated and institutionalized because it refuses to distance itself from social practice in the first place may by the same token abolish all critical point of purchase upon social life.

Like the left-aesthetic lineage, the avant garde has two moments, one negative and one positive. The negative aspect is perhaps the best known: shock, outrage, moustaches on the Mona Lisa. It is difficult to base a politics on it, and difficult to do it twice. This current of the avant garde takes up the negative aesthetic of modernism and

371

destroys meaning. What is it, in the end, that the bourgeoisie cannot take? Meaninglessness. Don't strike at this or that bit of ideological meaning, for if you do you stay within the orbit of orthodoxy; strike instead at the very structure and matrix of meaning, and confound ideology in this scandalous way. There is also the positive moment of the avant garde, that of Brecht rather than Dada. This proclaims: there is indeed a way of resisting incorporation by the ruling order, whatever the fashionable jeremiads about how they will simply hang Picassos on the walls of their banks. That, claims this avant garde trend, is not the point. If they can place your revolutionary artefacts in their banks then that means only one thing: not that you were not iconoclastic or experimental enough, but that either your art was not deeply enough rooted in a revolutionary political movement, or it was, but that this mass movement failed. How idealist to imagine that *art*, all by itself, could resist incorporation! The question of appropriation has to do with politics, not with culture; it is a question of who is winning at any particular time. If *they* win, continue to govern, then it is no doubt true that there is nothing which they cannot in principle defuse and contain. If *you* win, they will not be able to appropriate a thing because you will have appropriated them. The one thing which the bourgeoisie cannot incorporate is its own political defeat. Let them try hanging *that* on the walls of their banks. The negative avant garde tries to avoid such absorption by not producing an object. No artefacts: just gestures, happenings, manifestations, disruptions. You cannot integrate that which consumes itself in the moment of production. The positive avant garde understands that the question of integration stands or falls with the destiny of a mass political movement.

The avant garde's response to the cognitive, ethical and aesthetic is quite unequivocal. Truth is a lie; morality stinks; beauty is shit. And of course they are absolutely right. Truth is a White House communiqué; morality is the Moral Majority; beauty is a naked woman advertising perfume. Equally, of course, they are wrong. Truth, morality and beauty are too important to be handed contemptuously over to the political enemy.

The avant garde failed, rolled back by Stalinism and fascism.[1] Some time later, *Ulysses* entered the university syllabuses and Schoenberg sidled regularly into the concert halls. The institutionalization of modernism had set in. But the social order on which modernism turned its back was rapidly changing too. It was no longer simply 'civil society', the realm of appetite, utility and instrumental reason to be counterposed to 'culture'; with the development of consumer capitalism, it too became pervasively aestheticized. The wholesale aestheticization of society had found its grotesque apotheosis for a brief moment in fascism, with its panoply of myths, symbols and orgiastic spectacles, its repressive expressivity, its appeals to passion, racial intuition, instinctual judgement, the sublimity of self-sacrifice and the pulse of the blood. But in the post-war years a different form of aestheticization was also to saturate the entire culture of late capital, with its fetishism of style and surface, its cult of hedonism and technique, its reifying of the signifier and displacement of discursive meaning with random intensities. In its early stages, capitalism had sharply severed the symbolic from the economic; now the two spheres are incongruously reunited, as the economic penetrates deeply into the symbolic realm itself, and the libidinal body is harnessed to the imperatives of profit. We were now, so we were told, in the era of postmodernism.

From a radical viewpoint, the case for the defence of postmodernism might go roughly as follows. Postmodernism represents the latest iconoclastic upsurge of the avant garde, with its demotic confounding of hierarchies, its self-reflexive subversions of ideological closure, its populist debunking of intellectualism and elitism. If that sounds a little too euphoric, one may always try instead the case for the prosecution, drawing attention to postmodernism's consumerist hedonism and philistine anti-historicism, its wholesale abandonment of critique and commitment, its cynical erasure of truth, meaning and subjectivity, its blank, reified technologism.

It can be argued that the first description is true of certain currents of postmodernism, and the second true of certain others. This case is true as far as it goes, but somewhat boring. The more interesting case would be to claim that, in many if not all postmodernist manifestations, both descriptions apply simultaneously. Much postmodernist culture is both radical and conservative, iconoclastic and incorporated, in the same breath. This is so because of a contradiction between the economic and cultural forms of late capitalist society, or, more simply between capitalist economy and bourgeois culture. Bourgeois culture of a traditional humanistic kind tends to value hierarchy, distinction, unique identity; what threatens constantly to undermine this exquisitely well-ordered structure is not so much the political left as the cavortings of the commodity. The commodity, as we have seen in the work of Marx, is transgressive, promiscuous, polymorphous; in its sublime self-expansiveness, its levelling passion to exchange with another of its kind, it offers paradoxically to bring low the very finely nuanced superstructure – call it 'culture' – which serves in part to protect and promote it. The commodity is the ruin of all distinctive identity, craftily conserving the difference of use-value but only by dint of sublating it to that sameness-in-difference which for Walter Benjamin was fashion. It transmutes social reality to a wilderness of mirrors, as one object contemplates the abstract essence of itself in the looking glass of another, and that in another. Traversing with superb indifference the divisions of class, sex and race, of high and low, past and present, the commodity appears as an anarchic, iconoclastic force which mocks the obsessive rankings of traditional culture even as it in some sense depends upon them to secure the stable conditions for its own operations. Like much postmodernist culture, the commodity integrates high and low; but how progressive a gesture this is is radically ambiguous. For the question of an 'elitist' or a 'popular' art, one aesthetically aloof from everyday life as against one which embraces the motifs of common experience, cannot be posed in a purely formal, abstract way, in disregard for the kind of common experience at issue. An art which espouses the *Lebenswelt* of Las Vegas is not the same as one which takes to the streets of Leningrad; a postmodernism which responds to local community needs, in art or architecture, differs from one which takes its cue from the market place There is no automatic virtue in the 'integration' of culture and common life, any more than there is in their dissociation.

From Nietzsche onwards, the 'base' of capitalist society begins to enter into embarrassing contradiction with its 'superstructure'. The legitimating forms of high bourgeois culture, the versions and definitions of subjectivity which they have to offer, appear less and less adequate to the experience of late capitalism, but on the other hand cannot merely be abandoned. The mandarin culture of the high bourgeois epoch is progressively called into question by the later evolution of that very social system, but remains at certain ideological levels indispensable. It is indispensable partly because the subject as unique, autonomous, self-identical and self-determining remains a political and ideological requirement of the system, but partly because the commodity is incapable of generating a sufficiently legitimating ideology of its own. Discourses of God, freedom and family, of the unique spiritual essence of the individual, retain much of their traditional force, but come also to have something of an implausible ring to them, in a social order where the highest empirical value is clearly profit. The United States, which tends to wear its ideology on its sleeve in contrast to the more oblique and 'naturalized' ideological modes of Europe, is then a particularly striking instance of this discrepancy, in which the conflict between high-sounding metaphysical claptrap and having your fingers in the till bulks farcically large. Nietzsche's alarmingly radical solution to this dilemma – forget about the metaphysics and celebrate unashamedly the will to power – had necessarily to be rejected by the bourgeoisie, since it deprived them of too many of their traditional legitimating forms. Better to appear a hypocrite than to cut the ground from under one's feet.

The radical credentials of an assault on elitist culture, in this situation at least, are likely to be somewhat ambiguous. It is not only that such culture itself contains meanings and values which may become available for a radical critique; it it also that a transgression of the frontiers between high and low, esoteric and demotic, lies in the very nature of capitalism itself. For Marx, it is part of the emancipatory dynamic of that society to dismantle all sacred spaces, mix a plurality of idioms, and strip the object's aura of uniqueness to the compulsive repetition of mechanical reproduction. As Bertolt Brecht once remarked, it is capitalism that is radical, not communism. This is not of course to argue that all subversions of elitist culture are politically unavailing; it is simply to point up the degree of complicity between some such gestures and the capitalist system itself. Bourgeois society rates culture extremely highly and has no time for it whatsover; to assail a sequestered art may thus signify a genuinely radical strategy at the very moment it risks reproducing the logic of what it opposes. This is not, it should be said, a contradiction to which the more ebullient apologists of postmodernism seem particularly sensitive.

A work like Joyce's *Ulysses* is at its most scandalous and subversive in its critique of the bourgeois myth of immanent meaning. As the type of all anti-auratic texts, a mechanical recycling of a sacred document, *Ulysses* pulverizes this mythology by eroding the distinctions between high and low, holy and profane, past and present, authenticity and derivativeness, and does so with all the demotic vulgarity of the commodity itself. Franco Moretti has pointed out how ruthlessly *Ulysses* commodifies discourse itself, reducing the bourgeois ideology of 'unique style' to a ceaseless, aimless circulation of packaged codes without metalinguistic privilege, a polyphony of scrupulously 'faked' verbal formulae implacably hostile to the 'personal voice'.[2] What is James Joyce's style? But this grievous reification of language, with all its Flaubertian sculpting of inert verbal materials, is then exactly what licenses Joyce's Bakhtinian radicalism, his carnivalesque, dialogical impacting of one idiom on another – just as in the *Wake* a profoundly political undermining of fixed signification comes about through the movements of a promiscuous signifier which, like the commodity form itself, must always level and equalize identities in order to permutate them in startling new ways. The mechanism of exchange or locus of exchange-value is here the pun or multiple signifier, within whose inner space, as with the commodity itself, the most strikingly disparate meanings may indifferently combine. It is in this sense that Joyce, to adopt Marx's phrase, allows history to progress 'by its bad side', starting in Brechtian fashion from the bad new things rather than from the good old ones. His texts turn the economic logic of capitalist life against its hallowed cultural forms, fastening tenaciously upon a contradiction within late bourgeois society between the realm of meaning – the symbolic order in which difference, uniqueness and privilege are the order of the day – and the sphere of production, which that symbolic order ironically helps to sustain. *Ulysses* marks the historic point at which capital begins to penetrate into the very structures of the symbolic order itself, reorganizing this sacrosanct terrain in accordance with its own degraded, emancipatory logic. It is as though *Ulysses* and the *Wake* lift a protean dissolution of all stable identity from base to superstructure, passing that great circuit of desire which is capitalist productivity through the domains of language, meaning and value. And to do this is then to collapse the classical distinction between bourgeois civil society and the public space of 'culture', so that the high-minded harmony of the latter is no longer so readily available to mystify and legitimate the raw appetite of the former.

Caught like a restless ghost within the later evolution of capitalism, liberal humanism is unable either to die or return to life. The centred, autonomous human subject is no clapped-out metaphysical fantasy, to be dispersed at a touch of deconstruction, but a continuing ideological necessity constantly outstripped and decentred by the operations of the system itself. This hangover from an older liberal epoch of bourgeois society is still alive and kicking as an ethical, juridical and political category, but embarrassingly out of gear with certain alternative versions of subjectivity which arise more directly from the late capitalist economy itself. Both forms of subjecthood are ideologically essential, at different levels of the social formation; so that a postmodernist critique of the replete, monadic subject is often enough forcefully radical in one sense and not at all so in another. To turn the logic of the commodity against the imperatives of moral humanism – to pit the subject as a diffuse network of passing libidinal attachments against that strenuously self-directing agent which continues to represent the system's official ideal – is as unacceptable to the regulators of production as it is welcome to the stage managers of consumption.

A similar ambivalence hangs over the question of historicity. Is postmodernism's celebrated historical eclecticism radical or reactionary, a sportive, productive refunctioning of authoritarian tradition or a frivolous dehistoricizing which freezes history itself to so many banalized recyclable wares? It is surely impossible to answer this question without first assessing something of the significance of history for late bourgeois society itself. On the one hand, that society reveres history as authority, continuity, heritage; on the other hand it plainly has no time for it whatsoever. History, as Mr Ford remarked, is bunk, a proposition with which a Marxist would not necessarily wish to disagree. Everything depends, once again, on whether one is considering the symbolic or the productive realm: the history which plays a venerable role in the former is continually upturned by the existential Now or crudely progressivist ideologies of the latter. 'History' as a concept lacks all unitary, self-identical status in such an order, which is one reason why it is difficult to evaluate in the abstract the political force of playing around with it. Walter Benjamin was given to distinguishing between history proper and what he termed 'tradition', signifying the narrative of the dispossessed. Only by a ritual of revolutionary remembrance, lifting the Proustian *mémoire involontaire* onto the historical plane, could this dangerous, precarious power of tradition be prised free of the ruling-class lineages with which it is bound up and revived as a strategy for unlocking the political present. Revolutionary nostalgia slices sideways into time, shattering its empty continuum and, in a sudden flash of surrealist or Kabbalistic correspondence, 'constellating' a moment of the crisis-rocked present with a redeemed fragment of the tradition of the oppressed. This has, perhaps, a superficial resemblance to post-modernist eclecticism, though 'superficial' is no doubt the word. The problem is that Benjaminian tradition is not some kind of separable, autonomous history which flows silently beneath ruling-class time, ghosting it like its shadow; it is simply a set of recurrent crises or conjunctures within that official temporality, so that the delicacy of an historical hermeneutic is one of knowing how to disrupt ruling-class history without spilling the precious resources of tradition along with it. Benjamin appreciates that there are, after all, different, contradictory histories – that it can never be a question of some stark binary opposition between the dead weight of the past and some brave new present, since the past is precisely what we are made of. 'We Marxists', commented Leon Trotsky, 'have always lived in tradition'– a statement usually greeted with some bemusement by those political radicals for whom 'tradition' spontaneously signifies the House of Lords or the Changing of the Guard rather than the Chartists and the Suffragettes.

Postmodernism has been eager to interrogate traditional concep-tions of truth, and this scepticism of absolute, monological truth claims has produced some genuinely radical effects. At the same time, postmodernism has betrayed a certain chronic tendency to caricature the notions of truth adhered to by its opponents, setting up straw targets of transcendentally disinterested knowledge in order to reap the self-righteous delights of ritually bowling them over. One of the most powerful ideological ploys of liberal humanist thought has been to secure some supposedly internal relation between truth and disinterestedness, which it is important that radicals should sever. Unless we had interests of some kind, we would see no point in bothering to find out anything in the first place. But it is considerably too convenient to imagine that all dominant social ideologies necessarily operate in accordance with absolute, self-identical concepts of truth, which a touch of textuality, deconstruction or self-reflexive irony is then capable of undoing. Any such simplistic antithesis overlooks the internal complexity of such ideologies, which are well capable from time to time of enlisting irony and self-reflexivity on their side. Good liberals, as E. M. Forster knew, must be liberal enough to be suspicious of being liberals. Like the later Frankfurt school, much postmodernist theory typically entertains a vision of the hegemonic ideologies of the West as centrally reliant upon apodictic truth, totalized system, transcendental signification, metaphysical groundedness, the naturalization of historical contingency and a teleological dynamic. All of these factors play an undeniable part in ideological legitimation; but spelled out in that stark form they delineate an ideological paradigm considerably more rigid and 'extreme' than the internally differentiated, contradictory social discourses which now dominate us. The vital distinction between liberal capitalist society and its more pathological fascistic forms is thus dangerously obscured. There is no reason, for example, to assume that all dominant social ideologies involve a pervasive, systematic naturalization of history, as a whole lineage of thinkers, from Georg Lukács to Roland Barthes and Paul de Man, have apparently presupposed.

'They make a drama of something which should be trivial by now,' Jürgen Habermas remarks wearily of Adorno and Derrida, 'a fallibilist conception of truth and knowledge. Even I learnt this from Popper!'[3] If this is one problem with the postmodernist or post-structuralist concern to place the skids under truth, another is its uneasy, unwilling complicity with certain of the less palatable political realities of late bourgeois society. For nobody who has read a government communiqué can be in the least surprised that truth is no longer in fashion. Gross deception, whitewash, cover-up and lying through one's teeth: these are no longer sporadic, regrettable necessities of our form of life but permanently and structurally essential to it. In such conditions, the true facts – concealed, suppressed, distorted – can be in themselves politically explosive; and those who have developed the nervous tic of placing such vulgar terms as 'truth' and 'fact' in fastidiously distancing scare quotes should be careful to avoid a certain collusion between their own high-toned theoretical gestures and the most banal, routine political strategies of the capitalist power-structure. The beginning of the good life is to try as far as possible to see the situation as it really is. It is unwise to assume that ambiguity, indeterminacy, undecidability are always subversive strikes against an arrogantly monological certitude; on the contrary, they are the stock-in-trade of many a juridical enquiry and official investigation. The patrician disdain which the literary mind has always evinced for such prosaic phenomena as the facts is not notably more persuasive once it is elaborated into a sophisticated textual theory. Once again, then, the politics of the interrogation of truth are every bit as ambivalent as the status of truth itself within our societies. If truth reigns supreme within the cultural and symbolic order, it is dispensable enough in the market place and political forum.

Postmodernism has been equally concerned to discredit the concept of totality, and has valuably challenged the various idealist and essentialist versions of this notion which, in Marxism and elsewhere, have long been on offer. It is always difficult, however, to know quite how far this dismantling of totalization should be taken. It is possible to argue, for example, that a philosopher like Michel Foucault remains captive to a rigorously totalizing impulse, whatever his celebration of heterogeneity and plurality. Foucault would appear to believe that there exist total systems known as 'prisons', as though some unitary entity corresponded to the appellation 'Dartmoor'. But what is 'Dartmoor' other than a decentred assemblage of this or that cell, warder, disciplinary technique, hypodermic syringe? Why this remorseless urge to homogenize these diffuse, particular realities in a singular concept? An effort to elude any such totalizing metaphysics of the 'prison' would carry, of course, distinctive political implications. There could, for example, be no orienting oneself tactically to the so-called 'total institution' – no debating with the governor about the 'prison regime', no contrasting of one type of 'prison' with another, no permissible statement which designated the prisoners as a collective body. Such totalizing would be no more than an inverted reflection of the relentless homogenizings of the ruling order, if it were possible to speak of a 'ruling order', which it is not. A genuine micropolitics of the prison would be in every sense cellular.

It is always possible, in other words, to stumble across a more fervent nominalist than oneself. For all those who feel that the human body is no more than a disarticulated ensemble of this or that organ, there is always someone else who feels just the same way about the concept of organ. It is as though any thought can be made to appear as an illicit totalization from the standpoint of some other, and so on

380

in a potentially infinite regress. Whatever the argument over 'totality' is about, it surely cannot be about this. The supposed discrediting of this idea is, historically speaking, deeply ironic. For it springs from just that recent political period about which it would be highly plausible to contend that the system which radicals oppose has never, for a long time, shown itself quite as *total* – where the capillary connections between economic crisis, national liberation struggle, the resurgence of proto-fascist ideologies, the tightening hold of the state, have never been quite so palpable. It is at just this historical moment, when it is clear that what we confront is indeed in some sense a 'total system', and is sometimes recognized as such by its own rulers, that elements of the political left begin to speak of plurality, multiplicity, schizoid circuits, microstrategies and the rest.

There are, perhaps, two major reasons for this theoretical move, one rather more creditable than the other. The more creditable reason is that many of the concepts of totality traditionally to hand are indeed objectionably homogenizing and essentialistic, superiorly excluding a range of crucial political struggles which they have decided, for one reason or another, can hardly be regarded as 'central'. The undermining of *this* version of totality is thus an urgent political task. The less creditable reason for the shift is that, some twenty years ago, the political left discovered to its dismay that the system was currently too powerful, too total, to be broken. One consequence of this gloomy revelation is what is now known as post-Marxism – a name which one takes to designate those who have come right through Marxism and out somewhere the other side, rather than those middle-class liberals who, having remained exactly where they always were, now suddenly find themselves rather in fashion. Post-Marxism and postmodernism are by no means responses to a system which has eased up, disarticulated, pluralized its operations, but to precisely the opposite: to a power-structure which, being in a sense more 'total' than ever, is capable for the moment of disarming and demoralizing many of its antagonists. In such a situation, it is sometimes comforting and convenient to imagine that there is not after all, as Foucault might have said, anything 'total' to be broken. It is as though, having temporarily mislaid the breadknife, one declares the loaf to be already sliced. The term 'post', if it has any meaning at all, means business as usual, only *more so*.

Aesthetics, as we have seen, arises in part as a response to a new situation in early bourgeois society, in which values now appear to be alarmingly, mysteriously underivable. Once the actualities of social life suffer reification, they would no longer seem to offer an adequate starting-point for discourses of value, which accordingly float loose into their own idealist space. Value must now either be self-grounding, or founded in intuition; and the aesthetic, as we have seen, serves as a model for both of these strategies. Sprung from some affective or metaphysical space, values can no longer be submitted to rational enquiry and argumentation; it is difficult now, for example, to say of my desires that they are 'unreasonable', in the sense, perhaps, of illicitly impeding the just desires of others.

It is this aestheticization of value that has been inherited by the contemporary currents of postmodernism and post-structuralism. The result of this is a new kind of transcendentalism, in which desires, beliefs and interests now occupy just those *a priori* locations which were traditionally reserved for World Spirit or the absolute ego. A characteristic formulation of the case can be found in this comment by Tony Bennett: 'it seems to me that socialism can extricate itself from the mire of an epistemological and ethical relativism only by means of a political desire which functions as cause and justification of itself (although it is, of course, produced by and within the complex play of social forces and relationships)'.[4] Bennett's self-causing, self-validating political desire is not far removed from Kantian practical reason, or indeed from Spinozan Nature. This notion of a self-generative, self-legitimating force is in essence aesthetic and theological. Such a theory takes as its absolute baseline certain irreducible, rationally uncontestable imperatives, and then allows the cognitive a purely instrumental space of manoeuvre within this aprioristic field. To this extent, for all its protests against Enlightenment, it shares the problematic of a Hobbes or Hume, for whom reason is the slave of passion. Interests and desires operate in effect if not in admission as quasi-transcendental anteriorities; there can be no asking from whence they derive, or under what circumstances one would be prepared to lay them down, for such values, whatever their origin in social interaction, are as radically given as the human body. Desire, belief and commitment, as with the Sophists' reduction of them to 'nature', are simply withdrawn from the process of rational justification, as that which one can never get behind. This case subscribes implicitly to a reified, instrumentalized version of rationality, as *Verstand* rather than *Vernunft*, and then understandably wishes to disengage value from this inherently degraded medium. On the one hand there is a realm of lifeless, discrete facts, quite bereft of structure; on the other hand there are the arbitrary, competing value-perspectives of a plethora of subjects, each perspective absolutely self-sealed and self-grounded. It is not difficult to see how well this (anti-)epistemology tallies with the conditions of bourgeois society, even in its radical varieties. There is either a realm of free-floating values, a market place within which the ethical consumer makes his or her free choice, or our culture has always already in some sense chosen for us. The former position belongs with the old-fashioned decisionism of an R.M. Hare; the latter case, as in the varieties of American neo-pragmatism, complacently consecrates the given culture, protecting it under the guise of a 'radical' or faintly scandalous anti-foundationalism from fundamental critique. The reactionary nature of this position is made explicit in the genial, clubbish, laid-back, end-of-ideologies ideology of a Richard Rorty, whose surname, so the *Oxford English Dictionary* informs us, means 'fond of amusement and excitement'. It is as plain, though less candidly acknowledged, in the work of a Stanley Fish, with his phallocentric horror of ambiguity and indeterminacy. We are offered the alternatives, as with Hayden White, of old-style decision-ism or existentialism,[5] or, as with Fish, of a monistic cultural determinism as devoted to the defence of the Free World as the Pershing missile. The weakness of this case is its failure to worry political radicals unduly. If neo-pragmatists, for their own peculiar purposes, wish to characterize such actions as the socialization of industry and the dismantling of NATO as merely 'carrying on the conversation', behaving in a rule-bound fashion or being ineluctably constrained by a belief-system, then there is no reason why radicals should protest too vigorously against these descriptions as long as they are allowed to do what they wish to do. As long as such beliefs, in good pragmatist fashion, make a difference to the world, these theoretical descriptions of them need not prove particularly alarming.

The phenomenon of post-Marxism throws some interesting light on the issues at stake here. The originality of Marx and Engels's political thought, as Marx himself once commented, lay not in the discovery of the existence of social classes, which had long been known, but in the claim that an internal relation could be discerned between the struggle between such classes and the stage of development of a mode of production. The world of human beliefs and values, and the nature of material activity, were thus bound closely together. The notorious economism of the Second International travesties this doctrine by reducing class conflict to a function of economic evolution; and humanistic Marxism then overreacts to this reductionism, staking all on consciousness and the class subject. It is, ironically, the resolutely anti-humanist theory of the Althusserian school which consummates this dissevering of class struggle and mode of production, in its effective abandonment of the classical Marxist doctrine of contradiction between the forces and relations of production. Class struggle becomes a wholly conjunctural matter, a question of strategic calculation; and this position reflects the covert influence of Maoism, with its highly voluntaristic emphasis upon 'politics' as against 'economics'.[6] It then proves a small step from this position to the post-Althusserian jettisoning of the whole concept of 'mode of production', leaving class struggle hanging in the air; and for some erstwhile post-Althusserians at least, it is then only another step to the effective rejection of the centrality of class conflict, and thus of Marxism itself.

Let us turn now to two post-structuralist texts which centre upon the problem of ethics. The first is Michel Foucault's *The Use of Pleasure*, volume two of his *History of Sexuality*; the second is Jean-François Lyotard's philosophical dialogue with Jean-Loup Thébaud, *Just Gaming*. There is a curious feature about the writing of Michel Foucault that several commentators have noted, and which is at one level a question of style. Foucault habitually writes of oppressive, even horrendous practices and institutions with a carefully calculated clinical neutrality, which has even attracted the epithet 'positivist' from Jürgen Habermas.[7] Foucault's style is scrupulously non-judgemental, his commentaries purged of the least hint of normativity. This stylistic mode is not far at times from a certain perverse eroticism, as the most sensational materials – the torture of a human body, for example – are mediated through a distanced, dispassionate tone, a measured, mandarin French serenely unruffled by its own shocking contents. Pressed to an extreme, such a conflation of clinicism and sensationalism is the stuff of pornography, which is not to suggest that Foucault's own writing is pornographic. There may well be in this style an element of mischievous parody, a trumping of the scholars on their own terrain, a cool adaptation of their own bloodless discourse to entirely opposite political ends; but it is surely also the stylistic index of a genuine contradiction at the heart of post-structuralist thought. We know from Foucault's political writings that his response to the oppressive regimes he records so impassively is one of a radical, implacable refusal; but the question is one of the position from which such a refusal is to be launched. Foucault's Nietzscheanism forbids him any universal or transcendental stand-point of ethico-political judgement on the history he examines; yet as a radical political activist he is clearly unable to abandon judgement altogether. His style, which refrains from explicit judgement but in a way so marked that this very silence itself becomes eloquent, that the very lack of moral comment becomes a comment all of its own, is then an attempt to negotiate this dilemma. Any post-structuralist theory which desires to be in some sense political is bound to find itself caught on the hop between the normativity which such politics entail, and its own full-blooded cultural relativism. One can trace a similar tension in some contemporary feminist writing, which occasionally seems to argue with the one breath that truth does not exist, and with the next that men oppress women. This conflict between cultural relativism and the demands of normative moral judgement comes to a head over the question of oppressive patriarchal practices such as foot-binding or clitoridectomy, which have the sanction of age-old cultural traditions. The necessary and proper universalism of the judgement that the oppression of women in any form is always morally wrong, and that no appeal to cultural tradition can constitute a defence of such conduct, runs into headlong conflict with a cultural relativism which is reluctant to appear 'ethnocentric' in its outlook. We should seek to understand the headhunters, not to change them.

Foucault has, in fact, a kind of solution to this problem. It is not that any particular historical regime is better or worse than any other – though as we shall see he sometimes *implies* such a distinction. What is objectionable is *regime as such*. What is insupportable is the whole notion that human life should be normalized, regulated, institutional-ized. Such a situation is offensive to Foucault's extreme nominalism, which would regard the very categorizing involved in the act of naming as a violation of unique specificity. 'For Foucault', as Peter

Dews comments, 'the mere fact of becoming an object of knowledge represents a kind of enslavement.'[8]

But this claim needs instantly to be qualified. For Foucault is not of course as naive as to believe for a moment that human life could ever be anything other than institutional life, or proceed by anything other than particular disciplines and techniques. If he is in one sense a libertarian, he is not at all in another: in common with many other post-structuralists, he is deeply sceptical of the utopian dream that heterogeneity could ever be completely released from the categories and institutions, the forms of discursive and non-discursive domestication, which alone lend it social embodiment. We can never escape law, regimentation, the prison house of the metaphysical; but this does not stop one fantasizing for a moment (a moment usually reserved for one's more 'poetic' texts) of some apocalyptic moment in which all this might come to end, finding proleptic traces of such a revolution in avant-garde literary works. It is hard to criticize particular institutions without dreaming for a giddy moment of what it might be like to be emancipated from institutionality altogether. Foucault is in one sense a sort of anarchist; but he does not believe in that anarchism for a moment, for it could never possibly come about, and it would be the height of romantic libertarian folly to imagine that it could. This ambivalence then allows him to combine, in a manner typical of much post-structuralism, a kind of secret apocalyptic ultra-leftism with a dry-eyed, pragmatic political reformism. It protects him at once from the reactionary and the romantic – the latter being a vice to which French intellectuals, one might claim, are peculiarly allergic, preferring on the whole to be thought wicked rather than gullible. A form of absolute moral position is preserved – the secret refusal of regime as such – which then allows Foucault to dissociate himself in a grandly panoramic gesture from every social formation to date; but since what is objectionable about these formations is essentially the fact that they are formations, rather than the particular values they embody, a kind of knowing, sophisticated relativism may accordingly be maintained, and one is absolved from the need to make explicit the values in whose name one's critique is deployed. 'To imagine another system', Foucault comments, 'is to extend our participation in the present system.'[9] It is system itself, in a purely formalistic politics, which is the enemy; but this enemy is quite ineluctable, and like the poor will always be with us. Such a viewpoint dangerously elides the distinctions between, say, fascistic and liberal capitalist forms of society; the latter, for Foucault as much as for the late Frankfurt school, would sometimes seem as terroristic as the former. (A similar elision is effected by Foucault's mentor Althusser, whose concept of 'ideological state apparatuses' refuses as purely legalistic the vital difference between state-controlled and non-state ideological institutions.)

Foucault's work, then, represents a kind of negative or inverted ultra-leftism, in which a resolute revolutionary negation is at once clung to and disowned. The dream of liberty must be cherished, but this impulse has fallen, historically speaking, on hard times, and caustically refuses the possibility of its own realization. To this extent Foucault, along with Jacques Derrida, is exemplary of an ideology now dominant among a certain sector of the Western radical intelligentsia: libertarian pessimism. The oxymoron is instructive: libertarian, because something of the old expression/repression model lingers on in the dream of an entirely free-floating signifier, an infinite textual productivity, an existence blessedly free from the shackles of truth, meaning and sociality. Pessimistic, because whatever blocks such creativity – law, meaning, power, closure – is acknowledged to be built into it, in a sceptical recognition of the imbrication of authority and desire, madness and metaphysics, which springs from a paradigm quite other than the expression/repression model. Both models are at work in post-structuralist thought, generating some notable internal tensions. Charles Taylor has pointed out that though Foucault wishes to discredit the very notion of a liberation from power, his own concept of power does not in fact make sense without the idea of such liberation.[10]

One might trace this aporia within post-structuralist writing in a rather different way, in a kind of running conflict between its 'epistemology' and its 'ethics' – both, of course, deeply suspect terms for the practitioners of the discourse themselves. The (anti-) epistemology of post-structuralism focuses recurrently on impasse, failure, error, missing the mark, not quite-ness, to the point where an insistence that something in a text does not quite come off, has always already failed, is even now not quite failing to deviate from what it never exactly already was, has hardened into the sheerest conventional gesture. Post-structuralism shares an underdog suspicion of the success ethic, which lends it a radical flavour. But this assault on an arrogant metaphysical self-identity is made, often enough, in the name of a freeing of forces which seem in Nietzschean fashion to acknowledge no such humble hesitancy, powers which insist on their own sweet way, which dance without stumbling and laugh without a catch in the breath. Sceptical and libertarian moments are once more curiously conjoined, in an amphibious sensibility which owes much to a mixing of *soixante-huit* ecstasy with that historical moment's more disenchanted aftermath.

Part of Foucault's objection to the shackling of madness, in his early *Madness and Civilisation*, is an aesthetic one: the disciplines which regulate madness rob it of its drama and sublimity.[11] His later preoccupation with power also places him firmly in the aestheticizing tradition; for power in Foucault's work has much in common with the classical aesthetic artefact, self-grounding, self-generative and self-delighting, without origin or end, an elusive blending of governance and pleasure which is thus a kind of subject all in itself, however subjectless it may otherwise be. Indeed Foucault can even be entranced by the *organicism* of this splendid aesthetic construct, as when he comments on power as 'an extremely complex system of relations, which leads one finally to wonder how, given that no one person can have conceived it in its entirety, it can be so subtle in its distribution, its mechanisms, reciprocal controls and adjustments'.[12] The stance is that of a Victorian agnostic contemplating some disturbing evidence of design in the universe. How can such a marvellously unified artefact have arisen without an artificer? Such organicism is not of course typical of post-structuralism, which tends to retrieve the ludic, pleasurable aspects of the aesthetic while rejecting its organicist motifs for plurality, dispersal and indeterminacy. But an aesthetic gratification in the motions of power is in fact one of the more disturbing facets of Foucault's work. It is coupled with the insinuation one can sometimes detect in his writing, when he is considering the brutal violence of the *anciens régimes*, that such violence is in some way morally preferable to the pacified, tabulated, transparent subject of the humanist epoch. The horror of the old asylums, writes Ian Hacking, 'was not worse than the solemn destruction of the mad by committees of experts with their constantly changing manuals of nostrums'.[13] The irresponsibility of such a view – symptomatic, perhaps, of the romantic primitivism of the self-castigating intellectual – is at one with Foucault's occasional dangerous inclination towards absolutist coercion as against Enlightenment hegemony. Foucault evinces a well-nigh pathological aversion to the whole category of the subject, one considerably more negative than that manifested by Nietzsche himself. In his drastically undialectical attitude to Enlightenment, he eradicates at a stroke almost all of its vital civilizing achievements, in which he can see nothing but insidious techniques of subjection. His view of self-identity is monotonously self-identical. It is therefore ironic that, late in his life, he began to discover that the Enlightenment was not so unreservedly monstrous after all, denying that he was a counter-Enlightenment thinker in the sense of one who denied that we did not still in large part depend upon it.[14]

It is not, naturally, that Foucault ever celebrates the horrors of feudalist absolutism; but it is worth noting that his latent preference for a power which is evident rather than covert forms the basis of his later discussions of this topic. The early Foucault of *Madness and Civilisation*, as he himself was later to acknowledge, still operates to some degree with the 'repression' thesis, dreaming of a wild, mute, essentially healthy madness which given a chance might inrupt through oppressive practices and speak in its own tongue. The later Foucault's insistence on the productivity of power, and on the falsity of the repression thesis, then constitutes an overreaction to his own earlier romanticism. If power was initially portrayed in too negative a style, it is now grasped as rather too positive. The truth that power does indeed repress as well as enable, that it is indeed at times centralized and 'intentional' as well as diffused and subjectless, that there are conspiracies as well as self-regulative strategies, is merely erased, in a monistic vision ironically typical of this devotee of plurality and heterogeneity. Absolutist power is opposed for its despotic centralism, but sometimes surreptitiously promoted in its relative openness, physicality and non-subjectivizing over the hegemonic epoch of Man, when, as Foucault writes, 'the laws of the state and the laws of the heart are at last identical'.[15] Power is at its best, then, when it is neither centralizing nor hegemonic, and it is to this view of an 'authentic' power that Foucault will finally come through. This, indeed, is classically Nietzschean in its tripartite scenario: from brute coercion, to insidious hegemony, to a power rescued at once

389

from despotism and interiority and applauded as self-causing and self-sustaining. Like the aesthetic artefact, power is non-instrumental, non-teleological, autonomous and self-referential.

This aesthetics of power, however, is to some extent in conflict with Foucault's radical politics. For it is as if the concept of power in the Foucault of such works as *Discipline and Punish* is being made to serve simultaneously two somewhat incompatible purposes. In so far as power remains politically oppressive, it must call forth refusal and resistance; in so far as it is aestheticized, it acts as the medium of a pleasurable expansion and productivity of capacities. The claim that power is 'productive' is ambiguous in this respect: this productivity is in one sense oppressive, generating ever more refined techniques of subjection and surveillance, but there is also an unavoidable suggestion that it is productive in a rather more positive or creative sense too, a triumphant Nietzschean growth, unfolding and proliferation. The thesis that power is all-pervasive is thus more pessimistic from the political standpoint than it is from the aesthetic one. Foucault's whole attitude to power thus carries with it a profound ambivalence, which reflects his attempt to combine Nietzsche with a radical or even revolutionary politics. And this ambivalence cannot simply be resolved by pitting one of these modalities of power against the other, the aesthetic or creative against the oppressively political, for this would simply land us back in a version of the expression/repression doctrine. Power which politically oppresses is also 'aesthetic' in its very essence, wholly wrapped up in its own self-enjoyment and self-expansiveness.

This aestheticized model of power allows Foucault to distance himself at once from coercion and hegemony, as indeed is the case with Nietzsche himself. One mode of the aesthetic – the self-generative pleasures of power – is opposed to another: the hegemonic introjection of the law. This manoeuvre permits Foucault to oppose oppressiveness without losing grip on power's positivity, and without invoking a subject in whose name this opposition is executed. It is possible, in short, to have the best of both worlds: a power which has the positivity of the *ancien régime*, having not been passed through the hypocrises of hegemony, and yet which – as in the era of hegemony – lacks that regime's more offensive cruelty. The arbitrariness of absolutist power is preserved, but now displaced from the whimsical diktats of the monarch to the gratuitous fluctuations of a non-subjective field of force.

In the late writings of Foucault, the theme of aestheticization explicitly emerges. To live well is to transfigure oneself into a work of art by an intensive process of self-discipline. 'Modern man, for Baudelaire', Foucault writes, 'is not the man who goes off to discover himself, his secrets and his hidden truth: he is the man who tries to invent himself. This modernity does not "liberate man in his own being"; it compels him to face the task of producing himself.'[16] This aesthetic working upon oneself is a sort of self-hegemony; but it differs from humanistic hegemony, as in Nietzsche, in that it allows one to give the law to oneself, rather than come meekly under the sway of a heteronomous decree. This, indeed, is the project of *The Use of Pleasure*, in which Foucault is finally able to fill one of the gaping voids in his work – the question of ethics – with an aesthetic alternative to humanist morality. In antiquity, one can supposedly uncover a morality which is more oriented to 'practices of the self', in the sense of an aesthetic production of the self that 'answers to criteria of brilliance, beauty, nobility, or perfection',[17] than to universal codes of conduct in the Judaeo-Christian manner. The ethical ideal is one of an ascetic, dispassionate mastery over one's powers, 'a mode of being which could be defined by the full enjoyment of oneself, or the perfect supremacy of oneself over oneself' (p. 31). This position thus combines the best of coercion – to produce oneself involves a taxing, punitive discipline – with the best of hegemony: the subject has the autonomy of the hegemonic subject, but now in a more radically authentic manner. Aesthetic self-production is a question of explicit power, not of that treacherous dissembling of power which is hegemony; but since this power is directed upon oneself it cannot be oppressive, and so is distanced from the epoch of coercion too.

With many judicious qualifications, Foucault equates Christianity with the dominance of a fixed universal code, and the ancient world with a more conjuncturally variable kind of conduct. The abstract code remains, but there is a looser, more flexible relation between it and the particular practices it licenses, which cannot be seen as mere obedient instantiations of this general decree. There is a degree of free play between norm and practice, or between what Althusser would term 'theoretical' and 'practical' ideologies. The tyranny of the universal law is thereby tempered: the ancient Greeks, Foucault argues, did not seek to introduce a code of conduct binding upon everyone, and thus were absolved from the constraints of humanist hegemony:

> For them, reflection on sexual behaviour as a moral domain was not a means of internalising, justifying, or formalising general interdictions imposed on everyone; rather, it was a means of developing – from the smallest minority of the population, made up of free, adult males – an aesthetics of existence, the purposeful art of a freedom perceived as a power game. (pp. 252–3).

Foucault can thus redefine the relations between law and pleasure, universal and particular: there is here no naive liberationist vision of a simple relinquishing of the law, but the individual particular is now rather more oblique to it. The mighty aesthetic organism of humanist hegemony, in which all the component parts are ruled and informed by a singular principle, gives ground to a multitude of little individual artefacts, each of them relatively autonomous and self-determining, where what matters is style and *techne*, the relationship which an individual conducts with himself in a form irreducible to a general universal model.

The idea of hegemony, then, is retained, but turned into an internal relationship between parts of the self. The individual must construct a relation with the self that is one of 'domination–submission', 'command–obedience', 'mastery–docility' (p. 70). Foucault is thus able to combine the concept of individual autonomy, which stands relatively free of the law, with the pleasures of sado-masochistic power such a law involves. What is gratifying and productive about power, its discipline and dominativeness, is salvaged from political oppressiveness and installed within the self. In this way one can enjoy the gains of hegemony without denying the pleasures of power. One might question, however, how far this model really allows Foucault to escape from the lures of traditional hegemony. For the moral hegemony of the epoch of Man, as Nietzsche recognized, surely entails a kind of practice upon the self, which Nietzsche in fact much admired. Such hegemony does not come about spontaneously, without a degree of self-labour; and it is only by implicitly caricaturing it as a passive, docile receptivity to law that Foucault can effectively counterpose it to the ancient ethic he is approving. The two conditions indeed differ, since in the case of ancient society there is, we are told, no single monolithic law to be introjected; but the activity involved in that kind of hegemony, and in the self-hegemony of the ancient Greeks, are not perhaps as antithetical as Foucault would seem to consider. Indeed he actually quotes Plato's comments on the homology between this style of self-governance, which Foucault himself clearly endorses, and the imperative of maintaining the *polis*, which he clearly does not endorse. 'The ethics of pleasure', Foucault writes, 'is of the same order of reality as the political structure'; 'if the individual is like the city', comments Plato, 'the same structure must prevail in him' (p. 71). Foucault goes on to emphasize that these two forms of practice – governing oneself and governing others – will gradually separate out: 'The time would come when the art of the self would assume its own shape, distinct from the ethical conduct that was its objective' (p. 77). But it nevertheless remains an embarrassment that the aestheticization of the self which he so strongly recommends should take its origin from the need to sustain the political authority of a slave-based society.

As with Nietzsche, Foucault's vigorously self-mastering individual remains wholly monadic. Society is just an assemblage of autonomous self-disciplining agents, with no sense that their self-realization might flourish within bonds of mutuality. The ethic in question is also troublingly formalistic. What matters is one's control over and prudent distribution of one's powers and pleasures; it is in this ascetic self-restraint that true freedom lies, as the freedom of the artefact is inseparable from its self-imposed law. 'It was not a question', Foucault claims, 'of what was permitted or forbidden among the desires that one felt or the acts that one committed, but of prudence, reflection, and calculation in the way one distributed and controlled his acts' (p. 54). Foucault has now – at last! – introduced the question of critical self-reflection into desire and power, a position perhaps not wholly at one with his Nietzscheanism; but he does so only to produce a formalistic account of morality. The ancients, he writes, did not operate on the assumption that sexual acts were bad in themselves; what matters is not the mode of conduct one prefers but the 'intensity' of that practice, and so an aesthetic rather than ethical criterion. But it is surely not true that some sexual acts are not inherently vicious. Rape, or child abuse, are signal examples. Is rape morally vicious only because it signifies a certain imprudence or immoderacy on the part of the rapist? Is there nothing to be said about the victim? This is a subject-centred morality with a vengeance: 'For the wife [of Greek antiquity]' Foucault writes without the faintest sardonic flicker, 'having sexual relations only with her husband was a consequence of the fact that she was under his control. For the husband, having sexual relations only with his wife was the most elegant way of exercising his control' (p. 151). Chastity is a political necessity for women and an aesthetic flourish for men. There is no reason whatsoever to imagine that Foucault actually approves of this dire condition; but it is one odious corollary of the ethic he most certainly does endorse. It is also true that Foucault, at least at one point in his life, opposed the criminalization of rape. Part of the problem of his approach consists in taking sexuality as somehow paradigmatic of morality in general – a stance which ironically reduplicates the case of the moral conservative, for whom sex would seem to exhaust and epitomize all moral issues. How would Foucault's case work if it were transferred to, say, the act of slander? Is slander acceptable as long as I exercise my power to perform it moderately, judiciously, slandering perhaps three persons but not thirty? Am I morally admirable if I retain a certain controlled deployment of my slanderous powers, letting them out and reining them in in an elegant display of internal symmetry? Does it all come down to a question of how, in postmodernist vein, one 'stylizes' one's conduct? What would a stylish rape look like, precisely? Foucault's Greeks believe that one should temper and refine one's practices not because they are inherently good or bad, but because self-indulgence leads to a depletion of one's vital powers – a familiar male fantasy if ever there was one. The more one aesthetically restrains oneself, the richer the powers which accrue to one – which is to say that power here would seem in romantic vein an unquestioned good, a wholly undifferentiated category. The positivity of power can thus be maintained, but converted into the basis of a discriminatory ethics by virtue of adding to it the techniques of prudence and temperance. And the ethical theory which is the upshot of this – that 'the physical regimen ought to accord with the principle of a general aesthetics of existence in which the equilibrium of the body was one of the conditions of the proper hierarchy of the soul' (p. 104) – has long been familiar on the playing fields of Eton. With *The Use of Pleasure*, Foucault completes his long trek from the hymning of madness to the public school virtues.

The ethical techniques with which Foucault is concerned in this book are ones of subjectivization; but how far the long-despised subject actually makes its belated appearance in these pages is a moot point. It is clear that Foucault's repressive hostility to subjectivity, which he can usually see only as self-incarceration, deprives him of all basis for an ethics or a politics, leaving his rebellion a useless passion; and this volume is among other things an attempt to plug that disabling gap. But he still cannot quite bring himself to address the question of the subject as such. What we have here, rather than the subject and its desires, is the body and its pleasures – a half-way, crab-wise, aestheticizing move towards the subject which leaves love as technique and conduct rather than as tenderness and affection, as praxis rather than interiority. It is symptomatic in this respect that the practice closest to sexuality in the book is that of eating. A massive repression, in other words, would still seem operative, as the body stands in for the subject and the aesthetic for the ethical. In one sense, the sudden appearance of the autonomous individual in this work, after an intellectual career devoted to systematically scourging it, comes as something of a surprise; but this individual is a matter, very scrupulously, of surface, art, technique, sensation. We are still not permitted to enter the tabooed realms of affection, emotional intimacy and compassion, which are not particularly notable among the public school virtues.

If Foucault's attempt to aestheticize social life in *The Use of Pleasure* is a radically unsatisfactory affair, much the same can be said of Jean-François Lyotard's project in *Just Gaming*. Lyotard's problem, like Foucault's, is that he wishes to maintain a post-structuralist discourse which is somehow politically engaged. This is not a problem which has ever apparently caused much loss of sleep to Jacques Derrida, whose political profile has always been remarkably low and indeterminate. But Lyotard is a former socialist militant and veteran of class struggle, an erstwhile leading ideologue of *Socialisme ou Barbarie*, who is properly reluctant to ditch notions of social justice altogether but must discover, with the supposed collapse of the old meta-narratives, a fresh way of grounding them. It is this which *Just Gaming* sets out to accomplish; and its 'grounding' of the concept of justice consists essentially in an unholy *mélange* of Kant and Sophistic conventionalism. In *The Postmodern Condition*, a work which despite its nervousness of totalities is immodestly sub-titled 'A Report on Knowlege', Lyotard urges us to abandon the *grands récits* of the Enlightenment and model our knowledge instead on the self-legitimating narratives of the Cashinahua Indians of the upper Amazon, whose stories, so we are told, apparently certify their own truth in the pragmatics of their transmission. It is difficult, therefore, to see how there can be for Lyotard any real distinction between truth, authority and rhetorical seductiveness: the one who has the smoothest tongue or the raciest story has the power. It is also hard to see how this move would not, for example, authorize the narratives of Nazism, provided they are grippingly enough recounted. Nazism, for Lyotard as for some other postmodern thinkers, is one lethal destination of the Enlightenment's *grands récits*, the tragic consummation of a terroristic Reason and totality. He does not understand it as the upshot of a barbarous anti-Enlightenment irrationalism which, like certain aspects of postmodernism, junked history, refused argumentation, aestheticized politics and staked all on the charisma of those who told the stories. There is no comment in *The Postmodern Condition* on the contemporary women's movement, which in its simultaneous belief in political emancipation, and in the need to be liberated from a dominative male rationality, somewhat complicates any simple response to the Enlightenment. Nor is there any consideration of the national liberation movements which, since the American defeat in Vietnam, have inflicted on global imperialism a series of staggering rebuffs, and which often enough operate by the 'metalanguages' of freedom, justice and truth. These movements have not, apparently, heard of postmodernism, or of the epistemological illusions of meta-narrative. There is an interesting parallel in *The Postmodern Condition* between a 'good' pragmatism and a 'bad' one: just as those succeed best who tell the finest stories, so (as Lyotard himself remarks) he who has the fattest research grant is most likely to be right. The Confederation of British Industry, did they but know it, are postmodernists to a man.

Lyotard begins his discussion of justice in *Just Gaming*, unpropitiously enough, with a straightforward espousal of intuitionism. We must judge 'without criteria . . . It is decided, and that is all that can be said . . . I mean that, in each instance, I have a feeling, that is all . . . But if I am asked by what criteria do I judge, I will have no answer to give.'[18] Later in the volume, Lyotard will remark that an aesthetic politics cannot be adequate, no doubt with a backward glance at the amoral philosophy of libidinal 'intensities' of his own earlier *Économie Libidinale*; but all he has done here is to substitute one sense of the aesthetic – intuition – for another. He is compelled into this dogmatic intuitionism because he believes it impermissible to derive the prescriptive from the descriptive, to base a politics on an analytical theory of society. Such an approach would suggest just the possibility of a 'meta-view' of society which he is out to deny. This is also the position of the later Foucault, who writes that

> it's not at all necessary to relate ethical problems to scientific knowledge . . . For centuries we have been convinced that between our ethics, our personal ethics, our everyday life, and the great political and social and economic structures, there were analytical relations . . . I think we have to get rid of this idea of an analytical or necessary link between ethics and other social or economic or political structures.[19]

Both men, that is to say, spontaneously reinvent David Hume, having perhaps never read him, and hold out for a rigorous delimitation between fact and value, the antithetical language games of description and prescription. In Lyotard's case, this view is clearly influenced by the Sophists, who denied all connection between moral and social knowledge.

Such a rigid duality of discourses is, one might think, a curious move for a post-structuralist to make. In a travesty of the later Wittgenstein, Lyotard claims that each language game must be conducted in its autonomous singularity, its 'purity' scrupulously preserved. Injustice comes about when one such language game imposes itself upon another. There is no recollection here of Wittgenstein's insistence on those complex 'family resemblances' which, like the overlapping fibres of a rope, interweave our various language games in real but non-essentialistic ways. Nor does Lyotard seem to appreciate that all prescriptions necessarily implicate claims about the way the world is. There is no point in my clamouring for the overthrow of capitalism if the system sank without trace a good century ago and I have simply not noticed. Prescriptions for Lyotard are thus left hanging in the air, cut off from any rational knowledge of society. There is no such thing as political knowledge, whatever the African National Congress may think it is up to. Thus suspended in vacant space, the prescriptive or political is left to the mercies of intuitionism, decisionism, conventionalism, consequentialism, sophistry and casuistry, all of which Lyotard tries on from time to time in a gamut of intriguing permutations.

Lyotard is somewhat wary of ethical conventionalism, these days perhaps the most fashionable substitute for classical moral theory. This is partly because like most post-structuralists he has a purely formalist suspicion of social consensus as such, whatever its particular content, but partly because in this text he now more clearly recognizes that a view of the moral good as *doxa*, opinion, what most people happen to hold, in principle lets in fascism. What he turns to most regularly, then, is a curious amalgam of Sophism and Kantianism – the latter operating as a kind of politicized version of the *Critique of Judgement* in which moral or political judgement can occur 'without going through a conceptual system that could serve as a criterion for practice' (p. 18). Such judging without concepts is clearly a derivative of Kant's aesthetic taste. Judgement is to be based not on concepts, principles or general theories, but on a kind of Kantian productive imagination, a future-oriented maximization of possibilities which eludes the concept, continually invents new games and moves, and has its closest analogy in avant-garde artistic experiment or in the so-called 'paralogical' science which Lyotard celebrates in *The Postmodern Condition*. It is thus to Kant's third *Critique* that Lyotard has recourse, not to the *Critique of Practical Reason*; for that work centres upon the idea of an autonomous will, and any such autonomy is for Lyotard an illusion. Indeed he mentions *en passant* that because of this rejection of the autonomous subject he has come to discard the political goal of self-management. The post-structuralist decentring of the subject, in other words, results here in a dismissal of the belief that men and women in society should as far as possible control and determine their own conditions of life.

Prescriptives, Lyotard proclaims, cannot be justified. The law, as with the Mosaic code, is utterly mysterious, promulgated out of an empty transcendence; we have no idea who is sending us the messages in question. There is no way of answering the question of why we are on one political side rather than another. 'If you asked me why I am on that side, I think that I would answer that I do not have an answer to the question "why?" and that this is of the order of . . . transcendence. That is, here I feel a prescription to oppose a given thing, and I think that it is a just one' (p. 69). It seems a strange way of running an election campaign. What obligates us, as with Kantian moral law, is 'something absolutely beyond our intelligence' (p. 71). The Kantian regulative Idea 'guides us in knowing what is just and not just. But guides us without, in the end, really guiding us, that is, without telling us what is just' (p. 77). Rather like Foucaultian power, the regulative Idea is utterly indeterminate, void of specific content; yet it is on this, apparently, that we should base our decisions to ban immigration, unleash genocide or feed the hungry. What is valuable about this Idea is that it permits us to think 'outside of habit', of received opinion, which is no doubt as accurate a characterization of Mussolini as it is of Mayakovsky.

If there is a type of Kantian categorical imperative which Lyotard would be willing to accept, it would be: 'One must maximise as much as possible the multiplication of small narratives' (p. 59). The problem with this case is that it is a sentimental illusion to believe that small is always beautiful. What small narratives does Lyotard have in mind? The current, gratifyingly minor tributary of British fascism? Plurality, in short, as for post-structuralism in general, is a good in itself, quite regardless of its ethical or political substance. What is morally just is to generate as many language games as possible, all of them strictly incommensurable. Lyotard has all the suspicion of the will of the majority of a John Stuart Mill, and cannot advance politically beyond this highly traditional liberal pluralism. There is a problem, however, in squaring such pluralism with the regulative Idea of judgement, for in Kant himself that Idea involves the dreaded notion of totality. 'Is it possible to decide in a just way in, and according to, this multiplicity?' Lyotard muses, and returns an appropriately indeterminate response to his own question: 'And here I must say that I don't know' (p. 94). The only justice is that no one minority should prevail over any other – a position which strictly interpreted would mean that a minority of socialists would not be permitted to persuade the majority of society to forbid a minority of anti-Semites from stirring up religious hatred. Lyotard's solution to the ills of capitalist society comes down in the end to computerized data banks, a stimulation of multiplicity regardless of its political content, and the narratives of the Cashinahua Indians. Judgement, he tells us casuistically, must always be case by case – a claim which is either trivial or false. In one sense of the phrase, nobody can judge in any other way; but if this is to be taken to mean that we must never deploy general criteria in our particular judgements, then it would be interesting to see what a particular judgement wholly innocent of general criteria would look like. How could we do this, and still use language? Lyotard confuses a kind of moral rationalism – the simple *deduction* of particular judgements from general principles – with the inevitable involvement of some kind of general criteria in any concrete act of judgement.

Whatever the real problems inherent in the sorts of moral and political cases which Lyotard opposes, they can hardly be the source of as much calamitous confusion, slippage and obscurantism as in this work. As with postmodernist theory in general, Lyotard is out to sever the connections between truth and justice – though unlike some of the more reckless manifestations of that position he does not deny that truth is possible. Theoretical and descriptive discourses certainly exist; but they are now blankly disconnected from normative questions. We are back, in other words, with the familiar couplet of positivism and idealism, against which dialectical thought (now comfortingly consigned by Lyotard to 'dinosaur' status) has always struggled. John Locke, father of English liberalism and devout racist, held in his doctrine of anti-essentialism that no particular feature of reality could be said to be in itself more important than any other; and it follows from this that there is no more reason why an individual's colour of skin should not be regarded as an essential feature of her, than why it should.[20] Lyotard's divorce of the descriptive and the normative is exactly in line with this tradition of thought.

'We want to know', writes Denys Turner, 'because we want to be free; and from time to time we learn to call by the name of "knowledge" those forms of enquiry which we need if we are at all to free ourselves from those time-encrusted conceptions which, in the course of history, have degenerated into the anachronism of ideology.'[21] Morality, Turner claims, is as classically conceived 'a scientific investigation of the social order that can generate norms for action'.[22] This, in brief, is the alternative political case to Lyotard; and it is worth turning now to a highly innovative, if deeply problematic attempt in our own time to articulate the given and the desirable together.

The aesthetic began with Baumgarten as a modest assertion of the claims of the *Lebenswelt* upon an abstract reason; and it is just this project, now inflected as a radical critique of capitalist society, which Jürgen Habermas takes up in our own time. What has come about in the later development of capitalist society, so Habermas argues, is a progressive conflict between 'system' and 'life-world', as the former penetrates more and more deeply into the latter, reorganizing its practices in accordance with its own rationalizing, bureaucratizing logic.[23] As these anonymous political and economic structures invade and colonize the life-world, they begin to instrumentalize forms of human activity which require for their effective operation a rationality of a quite different kind: a 'communicative rationality' which involves practical and moral agencies, democratic and participatory processes, and the resources of cultural tradition. Such a rationality, bound up as it is with subjectivity, cultural know-how and the sphere of the affective, will never submit without a struggle to such remorseless systematization; and in imposing its own alien logic upon it, late capitalism risks eroding some of the very cultural resources essential for its own legitimation. Systems integration poses a threat to social integration, undermining the consensual foundations of social interaction. As the state reaches its long arm into the economic realm, it also spreads into the socio-cultural system, enfeebling with its organizational rationality some of the values and habits which guarantee its own continued rule. And given the expansion of the state's activity in social affairs, those guarantees are all the more necessary at precisely the point where they are more difficult to come by. The *Lebenswelt* or cultural system is peculiarly resistant to administrative control; and that control may well have the uncomfortable effect of thematizing and publicizing issues which once could safely be taken for granted. In the classical phase of capitalism, the so-called 'public sphere' – private individuals engaged in a public discourse of critical reason – exercised a vital function in mediating between the essentially distinct realms of state and civil society; but as this distinction is gradually eroded, with the spreading of state activity into social existence as a whole, the public sphere becomes itself shrunken and desiccated, in what Habermas terms a 'refeudalization' of public life. This conflict, between system and life-world, then produces within the latter certain pathological symptoms, of which the current resurgence of reactionary moral campaigns in the Western world could be seen as an example. Terrorism, for Habermas, would be another such instance – what he calls 'the attempt to introduce aesthetically expressive elements into politics, like a small-scale underground'.[24] Such terrorism, he claims, is in its own way an attempt 'to reaffirm politics in the face of pure administration'.[25]

The politics which Habermas himself affirms are probably little more viable than terrorism. Like Lyotard, if for quite different reasons, he has abandoned the goal of workers' self-management, effectively jettisoned the idea of class struggle, and can offer no convincing programme by which his ideal of radical democracy might be achieved. Habermas's is an academicist mind, aloofly remote from the sphere of political action; but his work nevertheless represents a political strike for the life-world against administrative rationality, without for a moment romantically disowning the necessity of systems and systems theory as such. What he wishes to speak up for is 'the structure of a rationality which is immanent in everyday communicative practice, and which brings the stubbornness of life-forms into play against the functional demands of autonomized economic and administrative systems'.[26] In the broadest sense of the term, he thus writes as a political 'aesthetician', defending the lived against the logical, *phronēsis* against *epistēmē*. Indeed art itself is for Habermas one crucial place where the jeopardized resources of moral and affective life may be crystallized; and in the critical discussion of such art, a kind of shadowy public sphere may be reestablished, contemplating the implications of such experiences for political life and so mediating between the separate Kantian spheres of the cognitive, moral and aesthetic.

It is this 'aesthetic' dimension of Habermas's work which the customary, sometimes merited criticism of his excessive rationalism frequently overlooks. What gives rise to that criticism, in part, is Habermas's belief that for the life-world to be brought effectively to bear on a reified public system, its workings must be formalized as far as possible by what he calls a 'reconstructive science'. The domain of communicative rationality works by the tacit assumptions, under-standings and know-how of acting, speaking subjects, who would not themselves usually be capable of thematizing this pre-theoretical knowledge; but for the life-world to act as radical political resource, its inner logic must for Habermas be disengaged from this tacitness and theoretically formalized. In this sense his work is in line with the classical aesthetic tradition, which as we have seen in the case of a Baumgarten similarly seeks, if with quite different political effects, to chart a kind of alternative rationality at work within everyday bodily experience, and to bring this rationality into relation with the operations of abstract reason. For Baumgarten, of course, such an aesthetic logic is an inferior mode, which it is not for Habermas; indeed the latter inverts these traditional priorities, insisting that a technico-instrumental reasoning be conducted within the constraints of a communicative rationality.[27]

The 'aesthetic', then, can be shifted up a level to theoretical thematization; but the consequent charge of rationalism or intellectu-alism against Habermas, justified in several senses, overlooks the fact that for him there is no theoretical answer to the question of *why* this should be done, of the motive of the whole enterprise. As far as such motivation goes, we are returned in a sense to the issue of the aesthetic, which makes its appearance again at a 'higher' level. In a reply to some of his critics, Habermas comments favourably on these remarks on his work by Joel Whitebrook:

> It is somewhat ironic that Habermas, who is so often accused of hyper-rationalism by the hermeneuticists, requires so large an element of judgement at the very base of his scheme. The way in which one 'comes to terms' with the transcendental standpoint ultimately bears a closer resemblance to aesthetic taste or Aristotelian phronesis than to emphatic philosophical proof.[28]

Habermas renounces all ultimate foundations; and as Whitebrook sees this leaves open a certain space for the return of the aesthetic.

The reconstructive science by which Habermas will seek to lay bare the inner logic of the life-world is that of universal pragmatics, the aim of which is to reconstruct the invariable structures of every conceivable speech situation. Habermas's faith is that language, however distorted and manipulative, always has consensus or understanding as its inner *telos*. We speak to others in order to be understood, even if the content of our enunciations is imperious or offensive; and if this were not the case we would not bother to speak at all. In every act of speech, however debased, certain validity claims arc implicitly raised and reciprocally recognized: claims to truth, intelligibility, sincerity and performative appropriateness. It is therefore possible to project from this condition the contours of an ideal communicative situation, implicitly anticipated in every actual act of dialogue, in which discourse would be as far as possible unconstrained by external or internal deformations, and in which for all possible participants there would be a symmetrical distribution of chances to choose and apply speech acts. If, in other words, we extrapolate from our actual acts of communication and stylize their enabling conditions, we can recover the political values of autonomy, mutuality, equality, freedom and responsibility from their most routinized structures. 'The truth of statements', Habermas is thus able to proclaim, 'is linked in the last analysis to the intention of the good and the true life.'[29]

To claim to detect a *promesse de bonheur* in an exchange of obscene insults would seem either ridiculously gullible or faintly perverse – akin, perhaps, to Fredric Jameson's startling claim to discern a proleptic image of utopia in any human collectivity whatsoever, which would presumably encompass racist rallies.[30] Do not such proposals move at such a rarefied level of abstraction as to be effectively worthless? Can a political ideal really be projected from the supposedly invariable, universal 'deep structures' of human conversation? These are serious reservations; yet there are ways of grasping these apparently naive propositions which perhaps make them a little less implausible. Raymond Williams, whose intricate connections of the ideas of communication and community in some sense parallel Habermas's own work, is given to arguing that when a writer 'disengages', he or she stops writing. In *Modern Tragedy*, Williams quotes approvingly Albert Camus's dictum that 'if despair prompts speech or reasoning, and above all if it results in writing, fraternity is established, natural objects are justified, love is born'.[31] The worst is not, as Edgar comments in *King Lear*, as long as we can say: 'this is the worst'. On this hypothesis, the very act of speech or dialogue, however brutal or sterile, cannot help bearing with it a tacit commitment to reason, truth and value, establishing a reciprocity, however grossly inequitable, within which it is open to us to glimpse the possibility of full human mutuality, and so the dim lineaments of an alternative form of society. 'I believe', writes Habermas, 'that I can show that a species that depends for its survival on the structures of linguistic communication and cooperative, purposive-rational action, must *of necessity* rely on reason'.[32] Reason thus has its roots in our social and biological condition, however systematically crippled and deluded our actual discourses. Truth for Habermas means that sort of proposition which would, did the discursive conditions allow it, command the free consent of anyone who could enter unconstrained into the relevant discussion; and in this sense truth remains something to be anticipated rather than fully secured in the present. Only in the context of radical democracy, where social institutions had been so transformed as to ensure in principle the full, equal participation of all in the definition of meanings and values, would truth properly flourish; and what truth we can negotiate now, in a state of unequal, dominative, systematically distorted communication, refers itself forward in some sense to this idealized future condition. If we wish to know the truth, we have to change our way of life.

It is possible to see in Habermas's ideal speech community an updated version of Kant's community of aesthetic judgement. Just as Habermas holds that communication is naturally oriented to agreement, so Kant proposes some deep spontaneous consensus built into our faculties, which the act of aesthetic taste most clearly exemplifies. And just as taste is entirely unconstrained, so Habermas's discursive community must be absolved as far as possible from all distorting powers and interests, relying on the force of the better argument alone. This community 'virtualizes' the constraints of practical interests, suspends them, like the work of art, for a privileged moment, puts out of play all motives other than the will to a rationally grounded agreement. In this sense it bears something of the relation to our common, interest-ridden social life that the work of art bears to the practical, instrumental realm of bourgeois civil society. The ideal speech community suspends judgement on the givenness of certain norms or even the existence of certain states of affairs, hypothesizing the whole of this in rather the way that the actual existence of the aesthetic referent is a matter of indifference for Kantian taste. The community has a social function, as the democratic forum in which matters vital to public policy are decided; but within its own frontiers a pervasive disinterestedness rules, in the sense of a readiness to suspend one's immediate interests in the name of the better argument. If the Kantian aesthetic representation is an image of 'purposiveness without purpose', the Habermasian community is a matter of purposeful disinterestedness. It might seem that the more obvious Kantian parallel would be with the domain of practical reason, which like Habermas's model is concerned with the formation of a pure will free of all pathological interests; but Kant's moral agent is a solitary, monological subject, and to that extent an inadequate image of a truth which for Habermas is always intrinsically dialogical. His paradigm of communicative rationality can thus be seen to combine elements of Kant's second and third *Critiques*, superadding the communitarian structures of the latter to the will-formation of the former.

Habermas has been at pains to deny that the forms of communicative rationality can simply be projected forward as a utopian future. The concept is, he claims, a fiction or 'illusion', but one which is effectively operative in the act of communication and so an unavoidable supposition. He also claims to be peculiarly unentranced by the dream of a unified, homogenized, wholly transparent society.[33] On the contrary, his work has always insisted on the necessary differentation of the cognitive, moral and cultural spheres, which he wishes to see interrelated but not conflated. His intention, he comments in an interview, is 'not to mix questions of truth with questions of justice or taste'[34] – to resist, in short, that wholesale aestheticization of knowledge and morality typical of some postmodernist thought, while pointing at the same time to the damage inflicted by the Enlightenment's rigid separation of these areas. Indeed one might argue that it is some postmodernists who are the true levellers and homogenizers in this respect, for all their cult of the heterogeneous: the aesthetic imperializes its neighbouring territories, modelling them upon itself with scant regard for their discursive specificity. Unlike a Lyotard, and in the teeth of all emotivism and decisionism, Habermas believes that normative statements admit of truth just as theoretical ones do – that they too must be submitted to the test of public argumentation.[35]

Universal pragmatics have justly come in for a good deal of sharp criticism. There is a doubt, for example, about how 'aesthetic' the ideal speech community really is – how far, in Seyla Benhabib's terms, it acknowledges the 'concrete' as well as the 'generalized' other, engages with bodily needs and individual particularities.[36] Its Kantian provenance augurs ill in this respect, since as we have seen Kant's community of taste rigorously excludes the body. In his more recent work, Habermas has limited somewhat the political reach of his model, suggesting that it applies to questions of justice rather than to evaluative issues of the good life.[37] The whole model would indeed seem considerably too juridical and legalistic, unable to sustain the weight of the concrete, conflictive histories of interest which its participants necessarily bring to it from the life-world, and ambiguous in its gestures of accommodation of what Habermas calls the 'aesthetic-expressive'. Despite these critical judgements, the model displays one particularly bold and original feature: its attempt to span the poles of fact and value, theoretical and normative discourses, which in the case of Lyotard are held so rigorously separate. Whatever the undoubted vulnerability of his project, Habermas understands that a desirable future must be somehow a dialectical function of the present – just as, so Denys Turner has argued, the 'true desires' to which a currently self-deluded person might attain must somehow be a function of what he or she does now actually want.[38] A socialist-feminist future is in this sense both continuous and discontinuous with the present, in opposition to apocalypticism on the one hand and evolutionism on the other. Unless we are able to show that a desirable future society is in some way already immanent within the present system, extrapolable from a certain imaginative reconstruction of our current practices, we lapse into the amalgam of disillusionment and 'bad' utopianism with which the later Frankfurt school, before Habermas assumed its mantle, came to be afflicted. Disillusionment and 'bad' utopia in one: for on the one hand such a political vision, in its paranoid perception of the given social order as wholly incorporative and devoid of contradiction, can locate no dynamic in the present which might feasibly lead to what it desires; utopian in the bad sense, because it must therefore discover its ideal values in some sphere largely disconnected from the major social forces of the given power-structure. In the case of Adorno, this sphere is modernist art.

If a 'bad' utopianism arbitrarily tacks an ideal onto a degraded present, forms of left triumphalism tend to see the future as bulking too palpably and robustly in the present – in the conception, for example, of a working class which is always inherently revolutionary or pre-revolutionary, which is merely held back by social democratic or Stalinist betrayers, and which is even now on the point of coming into its own, as for the New Testament the kingdom of God is even now striking into history had we but eyes to see it. Habermas steers neatly, if for many unconvincingly, between this particular Scylla and Charybdis, partly by virtue of the high degree of formalism of his universal pragmatics. It is the 'deep' structures of our communicative rationality, not any particular substantive content, which can form the basis of a certain conception of radical democratic institutions; and this formalism is meant to safeguard his theory against any too positive or programmatic utopian thought. On the other hand, his hope is that the transhistorical set of criteria which this universal pragmatics yields him will protect him equally from cultural relativism. How successful this project actually is is questionable: it is arguable, for instance, that the norms of communicative rationality are too minimalist and indeterminate, too compatible with a whole range of possible ethical theories, to be of much help. Whatever its grievous flaws, however, the general *tenor* of the theory remains interesting and valuable. Habermas believes, perhaps too sentiment-ally, that what it is to live well is somehow already secretly embedded in that which makes us most distinctively what we are: language. The good life shadows our every discursive gesture, running beneath our wranglings like a silent, unbroken sub-text. Our dialogues, simply by virtue of what they are, point implicitly beyond themselves. As Thomas McCarthy puts it: 'the idea of truth points ultimately to a form of interaction that is free from all distorting influences'.[39]

The moral, *pace* the pragmatists and pluralists, does not importantly consist in choosing here and now a life-style, maximizing current possibilities or simply carrying on the given conversation with one or two baroque flourishes. It consists primarily, as Habermas and Marxism recognize, in creating the material conditions in which a communication about these matters as free as possible from domination could be established, so that individuals, given full participatory access to the processes by which common meanings and values are formulated, could then select and exercise a plurality of values and styles in ways not currently available to them. Viewed in

408

this light, Habermas's theoretical enterprise has much in common with the work of Raymond Williams – though Williams's subtle sense of the complex mediations between such necessarily universal formations as social class, and the lived particularities of place, region, Nature, the body, contrasts tellingly with Habermas's universalist rationalism. Williams's social theory refuses at once a 'bad' universalism and what he liked to term a 'militant particularism', holding together a deeply pluralistic commitment, a keen recognition of complexity, specificity and unevenness, with what became as he developed a more and more resolute emphasis upon the centrality of social class. For Williams as for Habermas, however, morality is most importantly conceived as the material, political movement towards the goal of a humane society, and thus as a bridge between present and future about which the struggles of the past have much to instruct us. The postmodernist preoccupation with a plurality of life-styles too often turns its eyes from the quite specific historical conditions which, in certain areas of the globe, now permit of such a plurality, and averts its eyes too from the stringent, often invisible limitations imposed upon any such plurality by our present conditions of life.

The hubristic doctrine that human beings are infinitely plastic in their powers belongs essentially to the epoch of bourgeois Romanticism, and has sometimes been uncritically appropriated by political radicals. Karl Marx, as it happens, was not of this number; as Norman Geras has argued, Marx held firmly throughout his work to a concept of human nature, and was quite right to do so.[40] If Marx sometimes seems to regard human powers as unequivocally positive, he does not consider them infinitely transformable. It is mistaken to believe that the idea of a human nature is inherently reactionary. It is true that it has often enough been used for such ends; but it has also proved in its time a revolutionary rallying cry, as the reactionary powers of late eighteenth-century Europe learned to their cost. There is no reason to suppose that a denial of the infinite plasticity of human beings, or of the utter relativity of their cultures, entails an assertion of their rigid unalterability. No necessary comfort is given by this belief to the various reactionary brands of biologism or other more metaphysical notions of a static human nature. Paradoxically, a certain open-endedness and transformability is part of our natures, built into what we are; that the human animal is able to 'go beyond', make something creative and unpredictable of what makes it, is the condition of historicity and the consequence of a 'lack' in our biological structure which culture, if we are to survive at all, has at all costs to fill. But such creative self-making is carried out within given limits, which are finally those of the body itself. Human societies, by virtue of the biological structure of that body, all need to engage in some form of labour and some kind of sexual reproduction; all human beings require warmth, rest, nourishment and shelter, and are inevitably implicated by the necessities of labour and sexuality in various forms of social association, the regulation of which we name the political. Human society is in this sense natural, even if all particular societies are artefacts. All human beings are frail, mortal and needy, vulnerable to suffering and death. The fact that these transhistorical truths are always culturally specific, always variably instantiated, is no argument against their transhistoricality. For a materialist, it is these particular biologically determined facts which have so far bulked largest in the course of human history, and have set their imprint upon what, in a narrower sense, we call culture.

Because human beings are weak and unprotected, especially in their infancy, they are in biological need of the care and emotional sustenance of others. It is here, as Freud recognized, that the first glimmerings of morality are to be found, in the materially compassionate bonds beween the young and their elders. 'Fact' and 'value', biologically essential practices and affectionate fellow-feeling, are not dissociable in the 'pre-history' of human individuals. Such compassionate feeling, however, has to struggle hard in the course of our personal and historical development against a whole range of threatening factors – not only, if Freud is to be believed, against our originary aggressiveness and hostility, but also against the harsh conditions imposed by the need to labour, and the conflict and domination which arise when the appropriation of a surplus from the fruits of that labour lays down the conditions for class-society. Our shared material conditions bind us ineluctably together, and in doing so open up the possibilities of friendship and love; it is not necessary to argue in a nuclear age that friendship and biological survival go hand in hand, that we must, as Auden puts it, 'love one another or die'. But the history we must evolve, by virtue of our biological structure, also divides us and thrusts us into enmity with one another. Communication, understanding, a certain reciprocity are essential for our material survival, but can always be deployed for the purposes of oppression and exploitation. The language which releases us from the monotony of a purely biological existence also weakens the intra-specific inhibitions which constrain our mutual destructiveness. If we are to survive at all, it is necessary that we separate ourselves to some extent from Nature in order to control and regulate its threats to our existence; but the same gesture opens up a distance between the self and others, which is at once the ground of all genuine relationship and the possibility of exploitation. The autonomy of the other is at once the condition of creative relationship, and a source of violence and insecurity.

Work, sexuality and sociality all bring with them the possibility of gratification. The pleasure of the small baby is at first inseparable from the satisfaction of biological need. But just as, for Freud, sexual desire is born as a kind of swerving away from such instinctual need, so in the course of social development the processes of pleasure and fantasy come to separate themselves out to a certain extent from the fulfilling of material wants, in the phenomenon we know as culture. Once the economic surplus permits, a minority can be released from labour to enjoy such culture as an end in itself, in dissociation from the exigencies of labour, sexual reproduction and political regulation. 'Value', in this sense, comes to distinguish itself from 'fact', and finally comes to deny its roots in material practice altogether. This culture is often enough employed as an escape from or sublimation of unpalatable necessity, and as a means of mystifying and legitimating it; but it can also offer a prefigurative image of a social condition in which such pleasurable creativity might become available in principle to all. The political struggle which arises at this point is between those who wish to divert the forces of production to the end of allowing social life to become a gratifying end in itself, and those who, having much to lose from this prospect, resist it by violence and manipulation. In the service of this manipulation, certain aspects of culture can be exploited so as to redefine the concepts of power, law, freedom and subjectivity in ways which contribute to the maintenance of the given social system. A conflict accordingly sets in between two opposing notions of the aesthetic, one figuring as an image of emancipation, the other as ratifying domination.

The idea of human nature, or 'species being' as Marx calls it, moves on the frontier between fact and value. Needs which human beings have as an essential part of their biological nature – for food,

411

shelter, association, protection from injury and so on – can serve as a norm of political judgement and practice. That something is a fact of our nature, however, does not of course entail that its fulfilment or enactment is automatically a value. And there is much in the way that we have historically developed which is clearly not desirable, as the problem of evil attests. Evil is not simply a matter of immorality, but of an active, sadistic delight in human misery and destruction which apparently indulges in such destructiveness as an end in itself. One of the most mind-shaking aspects of the Nazi concentration camps is that they were entirely unnecessary, and indeed from the Nazis' own military and economic viewpoint counterproductive. Evil is revolted by the very sight of virtue, unable to see truth or meaning as anything but pretentious shams with which human beings pathetically conceal from themselves the utter vacuousness of their existence. It is thus closely related to cynicism, a mocking cackle at the high-minded claptrap of human idealism. Fortunately, evil is an extremely rare condition, outside the upper echelons of fascist organizations; but in its strangely autotelic character it has an unnerving affinity with the aesthetic. It shares with the aesthetic a certain low estimate of the utilitarian; and this may be one reason why we should approach the doctrine of autotelism rather more cautiously than we might otherwise be inclined to do.

The idea of a human nature does not suggest that we should realize any capacity which is natural, but that the highest values we *can* realize spring from part of our nature, and are not arbitrary choices or constructs. They are not natural in the sense of being obvious or easy to come by, but in the sense that they are bound up with what we materially are. If we do not live in such a way that the free self-realization of each is achieved in and through the free self-realization of all, then we are very likely to destroy ourselves as a species. Such a formulation moves, of course, at an extremely high level of abstraction, and will tell us nothing about what such terms as 'free' and 'self-realization' signify in any actual historical context. As far as that is concerned, the Habermasian answer is that we simply have to talk it over. Concrete ethical life, Hegel's *Sittlichkeit*, means negotiating and renegotiating, from one specific situation to another, what such an abstract injunction could possibly mean, with all the intense political conflict that this entails. It also means critically scrutinizing the whole concept of 'self-realization', based as it has historically been on a clearly inadequate productivism. The term 'self-fulfilment' suggests, perhaps, less of an incessant activism.

The fullest instance of free, reciprocal self-fulfilment is tradition-ally known as love; and there are many individuals who, as far as the personal life goes, have no doubt that this way of life represents the highest human value. It is just that they do not see the need, method or possibility of extending this value to a whole form of social life. Radical politics addresses the question of what this love would mean at the level of a whole society, as sexual morality tries to clarify what counts as love in sexual relations between individuals, and medical ethics tries to define what counts as love in the case of our treatment of bodies which are suffering. It is because love is a highly vexed, obscure and ambiguous topic that such ethical discourses are necessary in the first place. Modern ethical thought has wreaked untold damage in its false assumption that love is first of all a personal affair rather than a political one. It has failed to take Aristotle's point that ethics is a branch of politics, of the question of what it is to live well, to attain happiness and serenity, at the level of a whole society. One consequence of this blunder is that it is harder than it might otherwise have been to achieve love even at an interpersonal level. A materialist ethics holds that when we attain to this highest value, we are enacting the best possibilities of our nature. Such an ethics is aesthetic, concerned with pleasure, fulfilment, creativity; but it is not aesthetic in the sense of trading in intuition, believing as it does that the most rigorous analysis and discussion are needed if what counts as these values is to be adequately formulated. It is also not aesthetic in so far as it holds to the necessity of instrumental political action to bring such values about, and in so far as it recognizes that in this process the forgoing of pleasure and fulfilment is sometimes necessary.

The aesthetic is preoccupied among other things with the relation between particular and universal; and this is also a matter of great importance to the ethico-political. A materialist ethics is 'aesthetic' in that it begins with concrete particularity, taking its starting-point from the actual needs and desires of individual human beings. But need and desire are what render individuals non-identical with themselves, the medium in which they are opened out to a world of others and objects. The particular from which one begins is not a self-identity – a point which traditional aesthetics, in its eagerness to banish desire

413

from sensuous concretion, is unable to appreciate. This particular individual is self-transgressive; desire springs to birth through our material implication with others, and so will finally give rise to questions of reason and justice, of which and whose desires should be realized and which constrained. It also gives rise to the question of the education and transformation of what desires we have, which lies at the centre of a radical politics. The incessant process of arguing all this belongs to the public sphere, in which all individuals must have equal participatory rights whatever their distinguishing particularities of work, gender, race, interests and so on. The individual particular is thus raised to the universal. It is at this point, in effect, that bourgeois liberal thought generally halts, discovering a grave problem in the hiatus then opened up between this necessarily abstract universality, and the concrete particularity of all individuals. Radical thought, however, carries this process one stage further. For the final purpose of our universality, of our equal rights to participate in the public definition of meanings and values, is that the unique particularities of individuals may be respected and fulfilled. Particularity returns again at a 'higher' level; difference must pass through identity if it is to come into its own, a position disastrously abandoned by much contemporary theory. It is not a matter of what Raymond Williams calls a 'militant particularism' – of those currently categorized as 'other' – women, foreigners, homosexuals – simply demanding recognition for what they are. What is it to 'be' a woman, a homosexual, a native of Ireland? It is true, and important, that such excluded groups will already have developed certain styles, values, life-experiences which can be appealed to now as a form of political critique, and which urgently demand free expression; but the more fundamental political question is that of demanding an equal right with others to discover what one might become, not of assuming some already fully-fashioned identity which is merely repressed. All 'oppositional' identites are in part the function of oppression, as well as of resistance to that oppression; and in this sense what one might become cannot be simply read off from what one is now. The privilege of the oppressor is his privilege to decide what he shall be; it is this right which the oppressed must demand too, which must be universalized. The universal, then, is not some realm of abstract duty set sternly against the particular; it is just every individual's equal right to have his or her difference respected, and to participate in the

414

common process whereby that can be achieved. Identity is to this extent in the service of non-identity; but without such identity, no real non-identity can be attained. To acknowledge someone as a subject is at once to grant them the same status as oneself, and to recognize their otherness and autonomy.

In the pursuit of this political goal, there are meanings and values embedded in the tradition of the aesthetic which are of vital importance, and there are others which are directed towards the defeating of that goal, and which must therefore be challenged and overcome. The aesthetic is in this sense a markedly contradictory concept, to which only a dialectical thought can do sufficient justice. One of the most debilitating effects of much cultural theory at the present time has been the loss or rejection of that dialectical habit, which can now be safely consigned to the metaphysical ashcan. There are now, to parody the case a little, those who would appear to believe that some time around 1970 (or was it with Saussure?) we suddenly woke up to the fact that all of the old discourses of reason, truth, freedom and subjectivity were exhausted, and that we could now move excitedly into something else. This leap from history to modernity has a long history. The discourses of reason, truth, freedom and subjectivity, as we have inherited them, indeed require profound transformation; but it is unlikely that a politics which does not take these traditional topics with full seriousness will prove resourceful and resilient enough to oppose the arrogance of power.

Notes

1 The classic account of the avant garde is now surely Peter Bürger, *Theory of the Avant-Garde* (Manchester and Minneapolis, 1984).
2 Franco Moretti, *Signs Taken as Wonders* (London, 1983), chapter 7.
3 Peter Dews (ed.), *Jürgen Habermas: Autonomy and Solidarity* (London, 1986), p. 204.
4 Tony Bennett, 'Texts in history: the determinations of readings and their texts', in D. Attridge, G. Bennington and R. Young (eds), *Post-Structuralism and the Question of History* (Cambridge, 1987), p. 66.
5 See Hayden White, 'The Politics of Historical Interpretation: Discipline and De-Sublimination', in W. J. T. Mitchell (ed.), *The Politics of Interpretation* (Chicago, 1983).
6 For an excellent study of Louis Althusser, see Gregory Elliott, *Althusser:*

The Detour of Theory (London, 1987). See also Ted Benton, *The Rise and Fall of Structural Marxism* (London, 1984).

7 See Jürgen Habermas, *The Philosophical Discourse of Modernity* (Cambridge, 1987), p. 270.

8 Peter Dews, *Logics of Disintegration* (London, 1987), p. 177.

9 Quoted in Michael Walzer, 'The Politics of Michel Foucault', in D. C. Hoy (ed.), *Foucault: A Critical Reader* (Oxford, 1986), p. 61.

10 Charles Taylor, 'Foucault on freedom and truth', in *Philosophy and the Human Sciences: Philosophical Papers 2* (Cambridge, 1985).

11 See Dews, *Logics of Disintegration*, p. 181.

12 Quoted in Hoy, *Foucault*, p. 60.

13 Ian Hacking, 'Self-Improvement', in Hoy, *Foucault*.

14 See Hoy, *Foucault*, p. 22.

15 Michel Foucault, *Madness and Civilisation* (London, 1973), p. 61.

16 Quoted in Hoy, *Foucault*, p. 112.

17 Michel Foucault, *The History of Sexuality, volume 2: The Use of Pleasure* (New York, 1986), p. 27. All subsequent references to this work will be given parenthetically in the text.

18 Jean-François Lyotard and Jean-Loup Thébaud, *Just Gaming* (Minneapolis, 1985), pp. 14–15. All subsequent references to this work will be given parenthically in the text.

19 Michel Foucault, 'On the genealogy of ethics', in Paul Rabinow (ed.), *The Foucault Reader* (New York, 1984), pp. 349–50.

20 See Denys Turner's discussion of this point in his *Marxism and Christianity* (Oxford, 1983), p. 86.

21 Ibid, p. 113.

22 Ibid, p. 85.

23 See Jürgen Habermas, *Legitimation Crisis* (Boston, 1975).

24 Peter Dews (ed.), *Jürgen Habermas: Autonomy and Solidarity*, p. 711.

25 Ibid, p. 72.

26 Ibid, p. 155.

27 See Jürgen Habermas, *The Theory of Communicative Action*, volume 1: *Reason and the Rationalisation of Society* (Boston, 1984), chapter 6.

28 Jürgen Habermas, 'A Reply to my Critics', in John B. Thompson and David Held (eds), *Habermas: Critical Debates* (London, 1982), p. 239.

29 Quoted in Thomas McCarthy, *The Critical Theory of Jürgen Habermas* (London, 1978), p. 273.

30 See Fredric Jameson, *The Political Unconscious* (London, 1982), p. 291.

31 Raymond Williams, *Modern Tragedy* (London, 1966), p. 176.

32 Quoted in Dews, *Jürgen Habermas: Autonomy and Solidarity*, p. 51.

33 See ibid., p. 174.

34 Ibid., p. 127.

35 For an excellent critique of non-cognitivist ethics, see Sabina Lovibond, *Reason and Imagination in Ethics* (Oxford, 1982).

36 See Seyla Benhabib, *Critique, Norm, and Utopia* (New York, 1986), chapter 8, for a valuable summary of the critical controversy over universal pragmatics. See also the essays by R. Bubner, T. McCarthy, H. Ottmann, J. B. Thompson and S. Lukes in John B. Thompson and David Held (eds.), *Habermas: Critical Debates*.

37 See Dews, *Logics of Disintegration*, p. 20.

38 Turner, *Marxism and Christianity*, p. 119–20.

39 McCarthy, *The Critical Theory of Jürgen Habermas*, p. 308.

40 Norman Geras, *Marx and Human Nature: Refutation of a Legend* (London, 1983).

Index

absolute, *see* Idea, Absolute; reason, absolute; sublime, the
absolutism, political 14–15, 19–20, 23–4, 100, 116, 137, 190, 281–2, 388–9
Adorno, T. W.: and the aesthetic 1, 99–100, 341–64, 370–1, 379, 407; and Benjamin 323, 329–31, 332; on concept 342–7, 361; and constellation 342, 346, 356; dialectics 215, 241–2, 345, 357; and fascism 358–9; on universal and particular 345–7, 353–6, 362; *see also* body; cognition; commodity; contradiction; ego; freedom; history; materialism; objectivity; philosophy; politics; reason; society; state; style; subject; suffering
aesthetics: as bourgeois concept 8; British tradition 11, 116; current status 1–3; and dialectics 143–4, 415; feminine in 16, 55, 58–9, 112, 115–17, 144, 178–9, 257, 313; German tradition 116; and ideology 8, 10–11, 40–1, 61–3, 65, 94–5, 99–100, 136; marginalization 367–8; masculine in 54, 58, 116–17, 221, 244–5, 257; rejected by art 370–1; as social critique 118–19
aggressiveness, in Freud 270–3, 276–7, 410
alienation 92, 369; in Benjamin 327, 337–8; in Heidegger 294, 301; in Marx 206, 219, 221; in Nietzsche 267; in Schopenhauer 161, 165
allegory 326–7, 332–4, 352, 356
Althusser, Louis 24, 39, 41, 55, 384, 387, 391–2; on theory 87–8, 266
altruism 60, 97, 241, 244
Arnold, Matthew 11, 36, 60, 62, 263
Auden, W. H. 272, 410
autonomy: and aesthetics 8–9, 23–4, 27–8, 36, 41, 91–2, 99–100, 266–70,

349–52; in Foucault 392; in Hegel 123–6; in Lyotard 398
avant garde art 318, 325, 349–50, 370–3, 373, 386, 398

Bakhtin, Mikhail 10, 153, 264, 337, 343, 363–4, 376
Barthes, Roland 7, 379
base and superstructure 63, 198–9, 223–4, 242–3, 258–9, 331, 374–6
Baudelaire, Charles 318, 327, 338, 391
Baumgarten, Alexander 13, 15–17, 19, 49, 65, 116, 196, 197, 203, 410, 403
Beckett, Samuel 11, 321, 357, 360, 363
Benhabib, Seyla 21, 407
Benjamin, Walter: on aesthetics 316–39, 328–39, 363, 363–4, 374; Arcades project 332, 335–6; on constellation 328–34, 337–8, 378; on faith 184; on individuality 165; on mechanical reproduction 327–8, 338; on radical critique 8; on subjectivity 332; *see also* alienation; cognition; commodity; communism; epistemology; history; humour; materialism; meaning; objectivity; politics; time
Bennett, Tony 382
Bentham, Jeremy 62, 167
Benthamism, *see* utilitarianism
Bersani, Leo 271–2, 275
Blake, William 159, 165, 244
body 7–8, 9–10, 13, 17, 369, 407, 410; in Adorno 343–4; and concept, in Benjamin 334–8; in Foucault 7; in Freud 262–7, 277, 284–5, 335; in idealism 142–3, 196; in Kierkegaard 192; and morality 20–1, 23, 28, 33–4; in Nietzsche 234–6, 258, 263, 264; *see also* experience, bodily; materialism

Bond, Edward 284
Bourdieu, Pierre and Darbel, Alain 196
bourgeoisie: British 26–7, 31–42, 50–1,
    61–3; German 14–15, 19–26, 28, 31,
    241–3; in Marx 8, 218; neglect of 8–9;
    see also capitalism; ideology
Brecht, Berthold 8, 282–3, 334, 338, 349,
    362, 372, 375
Brown, Norman O. 272
Buddhism, influence on Schopenhauer
    162–3, 166
Burke, Edmund 26–7, 28, 61, 277, 369;
    on morality 36, 42, 43, 45, 54–7, 59, 62;
    on rights of man 57–9, 61; *see also*
    sublime, the; taste, aesthetic
Butler, Joseph 52

capitalism: and bourgeois ideology 61, 63,
    73–4, 92, 241, 297; consumer 373;
    critique 118, 168–9, 206, 211, 252, 401;
    English 31; in Freud 273; German
    308–10; in Marx 199–201, 206–7,
    210–12, 217–21, 239–40, 247, 309,
    317, 375; monopoly 316–18, 320–2,
    333, 349, 351, 358–9, 369, 374–5, 377;
    in Nietzsche 241–3
Carlyle, Thomas 63
carnival, in Bakhtin 337, 376
Cassirer, Ernst 24, 42, 95
Caygill, Howard 116
chance, and necessity 317–18, 324
civilization *see* civil society
civil society: Britain 32, 116; and coercion
    113–14, 116, 206; and culture 376–7;
    in Freud 264–5, 268, 270–1, 273,
    276–7, 283; in Hegel 146–8, 151, 209;
    in Heidegger 297; in Kant 76, 83,
    146–7, 172; in Marx 203–4, 209–10;
    and morality 19–26, 49–51, 63–4, 117;
    in Schopenhauer 168, 172; *see also* state,
    and society
class, social: and aesthetics 111; ideology
    3–4, 61–3, 75–6; in Marx 206–7, 246,
    383–4; in modern left politics 5–8, 402;
    in Williams 409
coercion 20, 27, 63, 104, 236, 255, 345; in
    Adorno 215; in Burke 55–7; in Foucault
    389–91; in Freud 272, 275–6; in Kant
    97; and law 39, 42–3; *see also* civil
    society
cognition: in Adorno 341–8, 360–1; aes-
    thetic 2, 15–17, 45, 65–6, 102, 227,
    341; in Benjamin 335; bourgeois 74–5;
    in Heidegger 85, 290–2, 299, 302, 304,
    306; and imagination 46–7, 123, 143; in
    Kant 65–6, 74–6, 85, 102, 107, 131,

304; in Marx 225–7; in Nietzsche 235,
    246; in Schelling 131, 134, 136, 143; in
    Schopenhauer 170–1; *see also* knowledge
Cohen, G. A. 216–17, 220
Cohen, Ted and Guyer, Paul 93
Coleridge, S. T. 11, 60, 62, 118, 369
colonialism 321–2
commodification 64–5, 240
commodity: in Adorno 348–9, 352; art as
    9, 368, 370; in Benjamin 92, 281,
    317–18, 320, 322–5, 326–7, 338; in
    Lukács 76–7, 324–6; in Marx 205,
    207–9, 212, 215, 220, 241, 374; in
    postmodernism 2, 374–7
communism: in Benjamin 338; in Marx
    201, 206, 215, 217, 227
concept, and reality 150, 343–6
Connolly, James 11
consciousness: in Freud 266; in Nietzsche
    238–41, 243, 254–5
consensus 17, 27, 98–9, 111–12, 137,
    192, 273, 354, 404; and coercion 55–6;
    in Hegel 145–6, 151; in Hume 46; in
    Kant 96–7, 145, 147, 405; in morality
    38–9; and Nietzsche 254–6, 259; in
    postmodernism 398; in Schiller 104
constellation, *see* Adorno, T. W.; Benjamin,
    Walter
contradiction: in Adorno 352; in capitalism
    211, 330, 384; in Freud 269, 270, 272
Croce, Benedetto 17
culture: autonomy of 9, 60; bourgeois
    373–5; commodification 64–5; expecta-
    tion of 284–5; in Freud 264–5; in
    Hegel 145, 147, 150; in Marx 219; in
    Nietzsche 238, 258; in Schiller 109–12,
    114, 117; and social unity 42, 97–8,
    111–12, 145–6, 376, 411; and state 63,
    106
'Culture and Society' tradition 2
custom: and law 20, 26, 28, 53, 58, 61, 84;
    in Nietzsche 236, 254; and reason 22,
    45, 48, 147

Dasein 290–307
Davis, Thomas 11
De Man, Paul 9–10, 311, 358–9, 379
death, in Heidegger 297
decision, in Kierkegaard 179–80
decisionism, 81, 383
Deleuze, Gilles 102, 159, 247–8
Derrida, Jacques 44–5, 75, 379, 387, 395
desire 108, 121–3, 369, 376, 382–3; in
    Freud 263, 265–7, 272–81, 284; in
    Kierkegaard 177, 192; in Marx 201,

desire (*cont.*):
207; in Nietzsche 247; in Schopenhauer 155, 158–63, 165, 167–8, 171
determination 241; freedom from 107–10, 120, 122, 127, 131
determinism 252; cultural 383
Dews, Peter 386
difference, in Kierkegaard 173, 176–7, 179
Ding-an-sich 76–7, 80, 120–1, 123, 131, 159, 161
disinterestedness 39, 97, 146, 180, 206, 378; in Freud 262, 274; in Habermas 406; in Heidegger 292, 311; in Nietzsche 246–7, 262; in Schopenhauer 163–6, 168, 171
dread, in Kierkegaard 176–9
dreams, in Freud 264
drives: death drive 270–1, 273; formal drive 103, 107, 113; in Freud 263, 265–7, 271, 273; in Marx 199, 202, 207; in Nietzsche 235, 238–9, 255, 258, 263; play drive 103, 107–9, 117, 207; sense drive 103, 104–5, 107, 113

economism 384
ego: absolute 83, 123–4, 132–4, 225, 304, 316–17; in Adorno 348; in Freud 79, 266–7, 269, 269–75, 277, 279, 281–2; in Kierkegaard 184; in Schopenhauer 164, 168–9
Eliot, T. S. 60, 318–19, 369
Elster, Jon 220, 222
empiricism: British 32–3, 39, 72; in Kant 121
Empson, William 264, 282
Engels, Friedrich 206, 309
Enlightenment: rationality 20–6; study of aesthetics 3–5, 8, 15, 99, 389
epistemology 65–6, 70, 72–100, 102, 120–3, 126–8, 131–3; in Benjamin 78, 92, 328–9; in Fichte 132–3; in Hegel 78, 122, 126–7, 136–7, 143, 148–9; in Heidegger 290; in Kant 74–5, 77, 89–100, 120–3, 131–2, 136, 143, 291–2; in post-structuralism 387–8; in Schopenhauer 161, 168
Eros 164, 270–1, 276–7, 284
ethics: and the body 7; formalist 21; in Kierkegaard 176, 178, 179–85, 188–9, 193, 243, 254; *see also* morality
evil 412
exchange-value 198, 205, 209, 322–3, 353, 363, 376
existentialism, and Nietzsche 250

experience, bodily 2–3, 13–16, 39, 64; and political right 60–1; and reason 49

fact, and value 166, 367, 397, 407, 410–11; in Hegel 148; in Heidegger 304, 306–7; in Kant 80, 82; in Marx 222–3, 225–6, 229–30; in Nietzsche 248–51
faith, in Kierkegaard 182–9, 192–3, 297
fantasy, in Freud 263
fascism 297, 303, 310–11, 333, 343–4, 357–9, 372–3, 396, 398
father, identification with 269–71, 274–6, 281
feminine: in Heidegger 313; in Nietzsche 253, 257
feminism 385, 396
Fichte, Johann Gottlieb: on imagination 131–3, 143; on irony 175; on subjectivity 122–5, 126–33, 136–7, 304; *see also* epistemology
Fish, Stanley 383
form, and content 121, 130, 151, 188, 250, 256–7, 350, 369, 371; in Benjamin 322–4; in Hegel 124, 126; in Marx 207–17
formalism 10, 33, 112, 137, 209, 224, 293, 386, 408
Formalism, Russian 89
Forster, E. M. 379
Foucault, Michel 98, 380–1, 384–95; on morality 387–8, 391–5, 397; on power 387–91; *see also* autonomy; body; coercion; hegemony; power; sexuality; society
foundationalism 102, 248, 383, 403
Frankfurt school 359, 369, 379, 387, 407
freedom: in Adorno 201, 347–9; and aesthetics 107–9, 112–14, 117, 143; in Heidegger 303–4, 307; in Kierkegaard 177–9; and law 35–6, 107, 279; in Marx 203, 207, 226; and necessity 20, 124, 132, 151, 177, 184, 207, 226, 239, 255, 303, 324, 369; and subjectivity 72–5, 79–84, 91, 98–100, 114, 123, 129–32, 134, 263; *see also* determination; Nature, and freedom
Freud, S.: and the aesthetic 1, 159, 262–85; on consent and coercion 55, 101n.; on law and desire 269–81, 284; and politics 283; on subjectivity 267, 272–3, 277, 281, 316; *see also* body; capitalism; civil society; coercion; consciousness; contradiction; culture; desire; disinterestedness; dreams; drives; ego; *Eros*; fantasy; guilt; hegemony; history; humour; idealism; instincts;

materialism; meaning; morality; politics; power; reason; repression; sexuality; subject; unconscious

Geist, in Hegel 121–4, 139, 144–6, 148–9, 160–1
gender, in modern left politics 5–6
genealogy, in Nietzsche 236
Geras, Norman 409
God, death of 258
Goethe, Johann Wolfgang von 263, 332
Golden, Sean 321
grace, in Schiller 111, 114–15
Gramsci, Antonio 62; on civil society 19–20; on culture 145–6; on hegemony 17, 58, 106
guilt, in Freud 270–1, 275

Habermas, Jürgen, 199, 225, 246, 327, 354, 357, 361, 379, 384; and aesthetics 402–3, 406–7; on capitalism 401; on ideal speech community 404–7, 412; on system and life-world 401–3, 407; on universal pragmatics 403–9; *see also* disinterestedness; morality; state; truth
Hacking, Ian 388
Hardy, Thomas 87
Hare, R. M. 383
Heaney, Seamus 11
Hegel, G. W. F.: and the aesthetic 1, 25, 33, 42, 123, 142–5, 196; dialectics 100, 121, 125–6, 138–51; on Kant 20, 120–1, 136; Kierkegaard on 180–1, 183, 192; on subjectivity 123–6, 160–1; on symbol 10, 122, 144; *see also* autonomy; civil society; culture; epistemology; hegemony; history; idealism; intuition; morality; Nature, and freedom; philosophy; reason; religion; state; subject, and object
hegemony, political 3, 17, 24, 26–8, 61, 325; and faith 184, 189; in Foucault 389–93; in Freud 272–7; in Hegel 145, 147; and morality 36–8, 41–5, 55–9, 106; in Nietzsche 236, 254, 255–6, 392; in Schiller 113–14, 117–18
Heidegger, Martin: and the aesthetic 1, 163, 288, 296, 301–4, 310–13, 369; on Being 289–94, 297–307, 310–13; on *Gelassenheit* 221, 310; on humanity 299–301, 305–6; on Kant 291–2, 304; Nazism 297, 302–3, 306, 310–11, 313; on Nietzsche 247, 251, 253–4, 292, 313; on subject 296–8, 301, 302–3, 306–7, 310–11, 313, 316; *see also* alienation; civil society; cognition; death; dis-

interestedness; epistemology; freedom; history; humanism; imagination; materialism; meaning; morality; objectivity; philosophy; poetry; reason; ruralism; subject, and object; time; truth
history: in Adorno 343, 362–3; in Althusser 266; in Benjamin 158, 213–14, 216, 281, 318, 325–7, 331–4, 339, 377; class 74; in Freud 281; in Hegel 124, 140, 149–51; in Heidegger 296, 298, 299, 306; in Kierkegaard 182–3; in Marx 199, 202–3, 213–16, 217–18, 220, 223–6, 230, 240, 247, 331–2, 376; in Nietzsche 236, 240, 245, 258; in postmodernism 377–9; in Schopenhauer 156–8, 166, 171; textuality 45, 68 n., 363
Hobbes, Thomas 39, 167, 268, 382
Horkheimer, Max 28, 357
humanism 8, 72, 90, 118, 156–7, 160–1, 325, 358, 376–7; in Heidegger 294, 298; of Marx 219, 221
Hume, David 148, 167, 382; on history 68 n.; on imagination 49–51; on reason and morality 45–9, 52, 53, 60, 65, 72, 397; *see also* taste, aesthetic
humour: in Benjamin 337–8; in Freud 264, 282; in Kierkegaard 180, 193; in Schopenhauer 154–5, 157, 171
Husserl, Edmund 17–19, 319
Hutcheson, Francis, on morality 37, 40, 45, 49, 60

id 83, 155, 269–75, 279, 282
Idea, Absolute 124–5, 138–9, 144–5, 148–50, 160, 182
idealism 2, 11, 14, 32–3, 100, 116–17, 121, 201–5; in Freud 270–1, 282–3; and Hegel 142–3; in Schelling 133
identity, ideology of 186
identity principle 345–7, 350, 354–5, 363
ideology: and reality 87, 140; ruling class 3, 61, 75, 82, 96–7, 99–100, 123, 258, 265; *see also* aesthetics; proposition
imagination: aesthetic 175, 256; in Heidegger 292, 299; and ideology 87–8, 90–2, 102, 123; and knowledge 131, 132–3, 169; and morality 39–40, 45–7, 50–1, 85, 89, 112, 117; and political right 60
imitation 53–4, 186, 256, 338, 350, 353, 356
immediacy 32, 147, 323, 332; in Kierkegaard 173–4, 176–9, 181, 184, 188; in Marx 207, 209
individualism: appetitive 32, 50, 105, 118–19, 159–60, 164, 167–8; autarchic

individualism (*cont.*):
241–2, 254; and bourgeoisie 22–3, 25, 32, 70–1, 84, 100, 218–19, 256, 259, 297; critique 36–7, 38–9, 50; in Kierkegaard 189–92; and state 114
instincts 199–200, 235–9, 253–5; in Freud 266, 269–71, 276, 280, 411
intersubjectivity 75, 96–7, 145, 147, 186, 225
intertextuality 68 n., 213, 231 n.
intuition: in Freud 269; in Hegel 133–8, 141, 143, 147, 150; intellectual 131, 304, 361; and middle-class ideology 61, 75; and morality 35–6, 38, 45, 48–9, 59, 64, 67 n., 85, 88, 132, 255; and political right 60, 62, 81; in postmodernism 397–8
irony 123, 141, 174–6, 181, 183, 186–8, 190, 192–3

Jameson, Fredric 70–1 , 266, 404
Joyce, James 11, 317, 317–22, 372, 375–6
justice, in Lyotard 395–7, 400

Kant, Immanuel 11, 15, 298, 355–6; and the aesthetic 10, 17, 33, 41, 81, 83–5, 89–100, 137, 142, 145, 196; and bourgeois philosophy 76–8; on desire 90, 272; and imagination 85–8, 90–2, 102, 123, 132, 169, 256, 292, 398; and practical reason 14, 78, 81–3, 84–7, 94, 103, 104, 121, 131, 147, 292, 406; and subjectivity 15, 21, 72–84, 87–93, 98–100, 102, 120, 124, 131, 169; *see also* civil society; cognition; consensus; epistemology; law; morality; Nature, and freedom; taste
Kemp Smith, Norman 45
Kierkegaard, S.: and the aesthetic 1, 173–93, 196; on faith 182–9, 192–3, 297; on Hegel 150; on subjectivity 173–6, 178, 180–1, 184, 186, 190, 192–3, 296–7; *see also* body; decision; desire; difference; dread; ego; faith; freedom; history; humour; immediacy; individualism; irony; morality; politics; self; sexuality; sin; subject, and object; truth
Klee, Paul 339
knowledge 35, 75, 85–8, 96, 128, 131, 366–7; in Fichte 132–3; in Hegel 22, 136–7, 143, 148–9; in Hume 45–7; in Kierkegaard 183; in Lyotard 396; in Marx 197–8, 203, 225–8; in Nietzsche 235, 246; in Schopenhauer, 165, 168, 170; *see also* cognition

Kojève, Alexandre 149
Kolakowski, Leszek 225–6
Kristeva, Julia 177, 284

labour, and coercion 56–7
labour, division of 108, 111, 146, 148, 218–19
Lacan, Jacques 87, 277
language 411; in Adorno 342–3; in Benjamin 334–5, 338; in De Man 311; in Freud 265–6; in Habermas 403–5, 408; in Heidegger 301, 313; in Marx 197, 199
Laplanche, Jean 275
law: and aesthetics 112, 114–16, 210, 248; and autonomy 19–28, 35–7, 41–3, 54–5, 58, 64, 112, 132, 147, 325; of beauty 217; in Freud 269–81, 284; and imitation 53; in Kant 20–1, 39, 64; in Lyotard 398–9; natural 116; in Nietzsche 236, 238–9, 254, 255–6; universal 16, 20–1, 78, 85, 94–5, 184, 188, 248, 319, 392; *see also* custom
Lawrence, D. H. 310, 316
Leibnitz, Gottfried Wilhelm 116, 289
Lem, Stanislav 289
Lenin, Vladimir 282
Lévi-Strauss, C. 16, 316, 319
Levin, Charles 262
Levine, Andrew & Wright, Eric Olin 222
Lewis, P. Wyndham, 316
liberalism, middle-class 76, 97, 414; *see also* humanism
libido, in Freud 263, 271–2, 276, 283
life–world: formalizing 17–18; in Habermas 401–3, 407
Lifshitz, Mikhail 208
Locke, John 60, 400
love 55, 413; in Freud 283–5; *see also* Eros
Lukács, G. 379; on aesthetics 1, 296, 323–6, 330–1, 353, 356; on subjectivity 76–7, 206, 322; *see also* commodity; realism
Lyotard, Jean-François 231 n., 384, 395–401, 406–7; on justice 395–7, 400; on morality 398–400; on politics 397–8; *see also* autonomy; truth

McCarthy, Thomas 408
MacIntyre, Alasdair 80
MacMurray, John 102
manners, and morality 41–2, 59, 336
Maoism 384
Marcuse, Herbert 118, 369, 371
Marx, Karl: and the aesthetic 1, 99, 204–13, 220–1, 226–8, 262–3, 268,

368–9; on forces and capacities 218–24; on freedom 79–80, 203, 207, on German bourgeoisie 19; and Hegel 141, 209, 224; on human nature 118, 207–8, 409, 411; and Kant 205–6, 210, 217, 228; on radical critique 8–9, 100; and Schiller 203, 206; on subjectivity 201–3, 219, 221–2, 224–5, 241, 245; on use-value 198, 202, 204–5, 207, 211, 214–15, 240; *see also* alienation; capitalism; civil society; class, social; cognition; commodity; communism; culture; desire; drives; fact, and value; form, and content; freedom; history; humanism; immediacy; materialism; morality; perception; politics; production; Romanticism; senses; socialism; state; subject, and object; sublime; the

Marxism, and aesthetics 4–5, 206

masculine, in Nietzsche 244–5, 253, 257

masochism 253–4, 271, 274–5, 279

materialism: in Adorno 1, 357; of aesthetic 5, 13, 193, 196, 413–14; in Benajmin 336; of Freud 282; of Heidegger 302; of Marx 196–8, 201–3, 206–10; of Nietzsche 234, 239–41

meaning 10, 372–3, 375–6; in Benjamin 326–7, 334–5; in Freud 265–7; in Heidegger 301–2

Merleau-Ponty, Maurice 18

Mill, John Stuart 62, 399

mimesis, *see* imitation

Mitchell, Juliet 267

Mitchell, W. T. J. 208

modernism 131, 140–1, 317–18, 320–3, 325, 348–52, 361, 369, 371; institutionalization 272–3

money, in Marx 201, 209, 212

moralism 8, 227

morality: and aesthetics 366–8, 372, 413; 'concrete ethics' 121, 146, 304, 412; and desire 159, 162, 164–5, 168; Enlightenment 20–8; in Freud 133, 269–70, 272, 283, 285, 410; in Habermas 408–9; in Hegel 20, 21–2, 28, 121, 142, 147, 412; in Heidegger 304–6; in Kant 20–1, 22, 52, 64, 78, 80–4, 86, 97, 105, 109, 115, 143, 147, 189; in Marx 223–7, 228–9, 239–41; moral sense 34–5, 37–8, 40–52, 61–4, 67 n., 116, 312; in Nietzsche 236–41, 244–5, 249–51, 253, 256–8; in post-structuralism 387–8, 391, 392–5, 397–401; relativism 60; in Schiller 36, 104, 106–10, 114–17; and sensibility 32, 40–5, 52, 76, 81, 89; and social unity 111–12; *see also* reason;

sensibility; state

Moretti, Franco 44, 376

Morris, William 11, 36, 369

music, in Schopenhauer 167

myth 16, 61, 316–19, 323, 327–8, 348

Nature: and freedom in Hegel 121–2, 124–5, in Kant 1, 79–80, 83–4, 99, 121, 123, 125, 131, 169, in Schiller 112–13; in Nietzsche 249–50; and reason, in Schiller 104–5, 113, 116–17, in Kant 84–5, 103–4

neo-pragmatism 383

Nietzsche, F.: and the aesthetic 1, 49, 117, 207, 234–59, 262, 267, 390–1; epistemology 120, 168; and Marxism 239–41, 244–7; physiological reductionism 153, 167, 234; on subjectivity 236–9, 241–4, 254, 256, 267, 389; on *übermensch* 238–9, 242–3, 245, 250, 252–5, 259; and the will to power 222, 238, 240, 243, 245–53, 256–9, 262, 375; *see also* alienation; body; capitalism; cognition; consciousness; consensus; culture; custom; desire; disinterestedness; drives; hemegony; history; materialism; morality; philosophy; politics; production; reason; sexuality; sociality; taste; truth

nominalism 240

Norris, Christopher 282

nothingness, in Heidegger 289

objectivity: in Adorno 341–6, 349, 351–2; in Benjamin 78, 326–30; in Heidegger 288–92, 310; *see also* subject, and object; *Ding-an-sich*

O'Brien, Flann 321

O'Casey, Sean 11

Oedipus complex 55, 144, 269–73, 278–80

ontology, in Heidegger 1, 290–4, 297–9, 303–4, 310, 312–13

organicism 10, 25, 311, 336, 388

Paine, Tom 61

particularism 14, 25, 94–5, 99, 146–7; and morality 21–2, 28; *see also* universalism; universality

Paton, H. J. 86

Pearse, Padraic 11

perception: in Marx 197–8, 199, 203; in Schopenhauer 155

perspectivism 248

philosophy: in Adorno 303, 360–1; and art 133–6, 137, 312; in Hegel 144–5,

philosophy (*cont.*):
148–51; in Heidegger 303–4; neglect of aesthetics 13–14; in Neitsche 48, 234, 249; role of 17, 43, 48–9, 127–31, 137–41; in Schopenhauer 166–7
pleasure principle 263, 265, 268, 284
pluralism, liberal 180, 193, 194 n., 399
poetry: in Adorno 342; in Heidegger 301, 312–13; and political right 61
politics: in Adorno 350, 354, 356–7, 359; and aesthetics 10, 114, 368–75, 385; in Benjamin 338; in Freud 283; in Kant 97; in Kierkegaard 186, 190–1; in Marx 207–8; in Nietzsche 256; in postmodernism 395, 398
positivism 298, 312; and idealism 400
post-Marxism 8, 381, 383–4
postmodernism 373–82, 395–401, 406, 409
post–structuralism 227, 354, 359, 369–70, 379, 382, 384–95
power: consent and coercion 55–6, 58; in Foucault 387–91, 394; in Freud 263, 272–3, 274; in Nietzsche 238, 240, 243, 245–53, 256–9, 262; subjectivization 19–20
pre-understanding, in Heidegger 85, 291
Price, Richard, on morality 40, 41, 44, 49
production: ideology of 92; in Marx 204, 217–23, 240, 247, 376, 384; in Nietzsche 253, 259
proletariat: in Hegel 148; in Marx 225–6
property, private 50–1, 71, 146, 199, 201
proposition, ideological 93–6, 98
psychoanalysis, role of 265, 280–1, 284–5
public sphere 19, 32, 35–6, 111, 297, 376, 401–2, 414

race, in modern left politics 5–6
rationalism: bourgeois 26, 32–3, 88–9, 102–3; communicative 361, 401–6, 408–9; radical 26–7, 61, 65
realism: of Lukács 324–5; in Schopenhauer 163, 169
reality principle 263, 265, 352
reason: absolute 133, 137–8; in Adorno 345, 347–8, 350–2, 357, 361–2; and aesthetic 14–17, 60, 91–3, 134–6, 382; dialectical 149–51; in Freud 266, 268; in Hegel 136–7, 141–5, 147, 151; in Heidegger 292; as instrumentalist 166–7; in Marx 227; and morality 20–2, 26–8, 38–49, 59–61, 64, 91, 107; in Nietzsche 239, 246–7, 255; and perception 15–19, 32–3, 45, 65; practical/pure 84–5, 94, 103, 104, 131,

185, 210, 292; in Schopenhauer 154, 171; *see also* Nature, and reason; rationalism
reductionism 4–5
relativism, cultural 385, 408
religion, in Hegel 144–5, 150
representation: in Kant 142, 188, 196; sensuous 15–16, 141–4, 150–1, 302
repression, in Freud 273–4, 277–8, 281, 283
revolution: bourgeois 210, 213–14, 218, 241; socialist 214–15, 221
Richardson, William J. 313 n.
Ricoeur, Paul 267, 268, 272, 284
Rieff, Philip 275, 279
rights, natural 57–8, 61, 111, 146
Romanticism 65, 74, 81, 102–3, 136, 143–4, 160, 170, 210, 264; of Marx 219, 221, 224
Rorty, Richard 383
Rose, Jacqueline 280
Rose, Margaret 203
Rousseau, J.-J., on law 19–21, 24–6, 210, 236
ruralism, in Heidegger 307–10
Ruskin, John 36, 62–3

sacrifice, and Marxism 228–9
sadism 271
Sartre, Jean-Paul 298, 303
Saussure, Ferdinand de 316, 318, 334, 415
Scarry, Elaine 198
Schelling, Friedrich Wilhelm: on aesthetics 133–6, 137, 141, 177, 312; on subjectivity 127, 128–31, 133–4, 141, 304; *see also* cognition; idealism; subject, and object; taste
Schiller, Friedrich 5, 19, 203, 273; on aesthetics 103–18, 143, 164–5, 196, 263, 268, 281, 369; *see also* culture; hegemony; morality; Nature; women
Schlegel, on romantic irony 123
Schoenberg, Arnold 360, 363, 372
Schopenhauer, Arthur: and the aesthetic 1, 17, 162–71, 196; on the body 153–4, 170–1; on desire 155, 158–63, 165, 167–8, 171, 251, 252; pessimism 155–8; on subjectivity 161, 163–6, 168–71; *see also* alienation; civil society; cognition; desire; ego; epistemology; history; humour; philosophy; realism; reason; sociality; sublime, the; will
self: in Adorno 348; in Kierkegaard 175–6, 178–82, 184–5, 191–2
self-determination 36, 78–9, 106–7, 111, 127, 132, 180, 182, 184, 193, 210, 296

self-realization 3, 111, 219, 221–2, 223–5, 228, 245, 250, 254, 298, 412–13
senses, in Marx 197–8, 199–203
sensibility: and law 20, 24–7, 27, 61, 277; and morality 24, 32–4, 39–45, 61, 64, 65, 147; and understanding 14, 17, 292, 304
sentiment: and bourgeoisie 23, 32, 61–2, 65; and reality 45, 132–3, 250–1
sexism: in Burke 55–6; in Freud 280; in Marx 221–2; in Nietzsche 257; in Schopenhauer 257
sexuality: in Foucault 393–4, 395; in Freud 263–4, 275, 276–7, 284–5, 411; in Kierkegaard 179; in Nietzsche 253, 257
Shaftesbury, Earl of 3, 268; on manners 41, 42; on morality 34–5, 39–40, 60, 226; and political hegemony 36
signifier 319–20, 327, 334–5, 373, 376, 387
sin, in Kierkegaard 177–9, 182
Smith, Adam: on imagination 51; on morality 37, 38–9
socialism 5–7, 323–4; in Marx 211, 215, 218–22, 224, 226, 228; Nietzsche on 244
sociality: and hierarchy 331; in Nietzsche 48, 245, 258; in Schopenhauer 156
society 410; in Adorno 359–60; aestheticization 373; in Foucault 393; see also civil society; state
Spinoza, Baruch 43, 123
state: in Adorno 347; in Habermas 401–2; in Hegel 22, 146–51; in Marx 202, 209–10; and morality 23, 27, 51, 55, 63; and religion 145; and society 20, 113–14, 116, 117, 145–7
structuralism 316
style, in Adorno 241–2, 346, 363
subject, and object 70–88, 98–9, 121–3, 127–32, 317, 369; in Adorno 301, 350; in Freud 267–8; in Hegel 78, 123–4, 126, 147; in Heidegger 290–1, 296, 298, 304; in Kant 72, 76–7, 87–8; in Kierkegaard 181–3, 186; in Marx 201–3, 205–6; in Nietzsche 243; in Schelling 133–5; in Schiller 114
subjectivity: and autonomy 9, 19, 23, 25, 27–8, 99–100, 113, 377, 415; modern 3, 316–19, 322–3, 374–5; and morality 34, 40, 44, 44; in post-structuralism 389, 395, 398; revolutionized 106; universal 96 7; of work of art 4, 9, 18
sublimation, in Freud 277
sublime, the: in Burke 53–6; in Freud

264; in Kierkegaard 189; in Marx 212–13, 217; and morality 54 7, 60, 73; in Schopenhauer 163–4; and subjectivity 89–93, 98
suffering, in Adorno 343, 362
superego 155, 269–83, 285
surrealism 332, 338
Swift, Jonathan 268
symbol 10, 61, 127, 144, 169, 319–20, 327–8, 373, 376
Synge, John 11

taste, aesthetic 55, 59–60, 64, 76, 87, 88; in Burke 52–4, 59; in Hume 39, 40, 50, 60; in Kant 15, 93, 96–103, 143, 248, 253, 405, 407; in Nietzsche 258, 267; in Schiller 110–11, 115–16
Taylor, Charles 123, 387
Taylor, Mark C. 194 n.
teleology: in Benjamin 325, 333–4; in Heidegger 311; of humanism 379; in Marx 218, 229–30; of Nietzsche 238; in Schiller 109; in Schopenhauer 161–3
Tennyson, Alfred Lord 87
Thanatos 164, 271, 277
Thébaud, Jean-Loup 384
time: in Benjamin 326, 327, 338; in Heidegger 288, 290, 292, 295–6, 313
Tone, Wolfe 11
totality 18, 109, 346, 351, 355–7, 380–1, 399; in Benjamin 326, 327, 329–31, 334; in Hegel 146–7, 149–50; in Kant 78, 81, 85
Tracy, Destutt de 98, 99
tradition 58, 61, 369, 377–8
triumphalism, left 337, 407–8
Trotsky, Leon 378
truth: and aesthetics 35, 368, 372; in Burke 59; in Habermas 404–6; in Hegel 138–9, 150; in Heidegger 290–1, 293, 300, 304, 311; in Kant 102–3; in Kierkegaard 187–8; in Lyotard 396, 400; in Nietzsche 235, 248, 256–7; in postmodernism 378–80; in Schiller 104, 105–6
Turner, Denys 400–1, 407
type, in Lukács 330

unconscious: in Adorno 348; in Freud 79, 90, 262, 264–7, 270–1, 273–6, 278
universal, concrete 319–20
universalism: and morality 21–2; and particularism 2, 9, 16, 21–2, 33, 345–7, 353–6, 362, 413–14
use-value 77, 198, 202, 204–5, 207, 211, 214–15, 240, 323, 374

utilitarianism 61–2, 65, 252
utopianism 229, 240, 369, 371, 407

value: aestheticizing 52, 59, 62–6, 382–3;
  as autotelic 40–1, 64, 81; *see also* fact
Vischer, Friedrich 208

White, Hayden 383
Whitebrook, Joel 403
Wilde, Oscar 11
will: freedom of 252, 255; in Freud 263; in
  Nietzsche 238, 240, 243, 245–53,
  256–9, 262; in Schopenhauer 153,
  155–63, 165–71

Williams, Raymond 215, 320, 404, 409,
  414
Wittgenstein, Ludwig von 64, 72, 136, 166,
  312, 319, 362, 370, 397
Wolff, Christian 116
Wollstonecraft, Mary 55–7, 61
women: in Freud 280; in Kierkegaard
  178–9; and morality 55–6, 59; in
  Schiller 115–16, 117
Woolf, Virginia 316

Yeats, W. B. 11, 318, 369

Index compiled by Meg Davies (Society of Indexers)